MW00389182

THE LIFE OF JOHN ANDRÉ

THE LIFE OF JOHN ANDRÉ

The Redcoat Who Turned Benedict Arnold

D. A. B. RONALD

CASEMATE

Philadelphia & Oxford

Published in the United States of America and Great Britain in 2019 by
CASEMATE PUBLISHERS
1950 Lawrence Road, Havertown, PA 19083, USA
and
The Old Music Hall, 106–108 Cowley Road, Oxford OX4 1JE, UK

Copyright 2019 © D. A. B. Ronald

Hardback Edition: ISBN 978-1-61200-521-8
Digital Edition: ISBN 978-1-61200-522-5 (ePub)

A CIP record for this book is available from the British Library

All rights reserved. No part of this book may be reproduced or transmitted in any form or by any means, electronic or mechanical including photocopying, recording or by any information storage and retrieval system, without permission from the publisher in writing.

Printed and bound in the United States of America

Typeset in India by Versatile PreMedia Services. www.versatilepremedia.com

For a complete list of Casemate titles, please contact:

CASEMATE PUBLISHERS (US)
Telephone (610) 853-9131
Fax (610) 853-9146
Email: casemate@casematepublishers.com
www.casematepublishers.com

CASEMATE PUBLISHERS (UK)
Telephone (01865) 241249
Email: casemate-uk@casematepublishers.co.uk
www.casematepublishers.co.uk

Front cover: Major John Andre, posthumous portrait by John Smart. Signed JS 1781. Mounted on snuff box. (By kind permission of John and Roger Andre)

In Memory

of

Colonel David Bruce Ronald CBE

Contents

Notes on Dates, Spelling, Language and Names and Titles

Dates

Until the reform of the calendar in 1752, Britain conformed to the Julian Calendar (Old Style). Dates recorded in this calendar are referred to as old style and designated (os). All other dates are new style, the Gregorian Calendar which was eleven days ahead and used in most of the rest of Europe. The convention by which English New Year began on 25 March has been ignored, and it is given as starting on 1 January.

Spelling

Unless specified otherwise, all quotations retain their original spelling and punctuation. Italics, underlining and lower/upper casing are retained as found in the original texts, and vessel names, for instance, are only italicized if printed thus in quotations cited.

Language

Being that this work is a biography, it is important to understand how its main subject, John André, and, to a lesser extent, those around him reacted to the events they were part of. How these subjects expressed themselves is crucial to that objective. Hence, this work draws frequently on the language of the times. Moreover, original quotations are used copiously in this work, but are generally kept short in the interests of accessibility. Key words and phrases from these original texts are then repeated as navigation devices, their importance as biographical signposts highlighted by retaining their position in inverted commas even after they were first cited. The integration of these subjects' language into the fabric of this work is intended as a pass-key facilitating entry into the life and times of these Britons and Americans witnessing one of the great events of modern history, the birth of a nation.

Names and Titles

The main subject, John André, takes his place informally in this work under his forename, 'John', except when being addressed otherwise by third parties. All other male subjects are addressed by their surnames. Female subjects are generally referred to by their forenames.

The length of military titles and of titles of office has dictated their shortening.

Preface

This book has as its background one of the most important periods in British and American history. It examines war, one of the most important events in human history. Nevertheless, it does so through the whole-life exploration of just one young man, John André, who was an officer in the British Army during the American Revolutionary War. Accordingly, this work is cast substantially as a biography. Events are seen primarily through this one young man's eyes, as his quest for honour dramatically unfolds into a story of heroic self-sacrifice.

To understand who John André was as a military officer, it is necessary to, first, probe how and why he became who he was. Essential to that is an investigation of his formative years, especially the influence of his family and what it meant to be a Huguenot 'refugee' in Britain. His father, Anthony, cast a lifelong shadow over who John was obliged to become. His influence figures large in this work.

Once 'fully-formed', John André went to America at the age of twenty-four, ostensibly to help quell a riot which became a rebellion which became a revolution which became a war. This book follows John's unique military career, as these successive events gathered pace and threatened to overwhelm all individual identity, but helped move him from the periphery to, fleetingly, the heart of history. There, John deservedly earned his right to be honoured by George III who commissioned a monument to his memory which has taken its permanent place in the nave of Westminster Abbey.

Reconstructing the full arc of John's all-too-brief life has proved a challenge, long, tantalizing gaps when he disappeared from view alternating with short, sharp bursts of hustle and bustle during which his every thought and action became magnified. These extremes are mirrored in the intermittent nature of the writings by him which have survived, lengthy letters appearing suddenly to interrupt interminable periods of silence. Yet, by his own claim, he was an assiduous writer—of letters, journals, newspaper articles and poems—which suggests that many, certainly, of his private writings were destroyed. If so by whom, when and why? Negative space—the perennial curse for historians and biographers—often tells its own story and, given the dramatic and controversial circumstances of John's life and death, these silences invite, in his case, the notion that whoever came by his correspondence—his friends, his family, his enemies—decided that John's life and who he was as a person should only be partly known. That has been the position until now, space left precariously vacant for John to be portrayed by successive biographers—all of them Americans seemingly interested in him only once he arrived in America—as the quintessential caricature of the British redcoat officer and perfect counterpoint for the rebel heroes in America's Continental Army.

However the attrition occurred to his personal records, the first of John's private letters to survive intact are three written in quick succession during October and November 1769 when he was nineteen. The next to survive was from 1772, followed by approximately one a year thereafter until his death in 1780. Two important military journals written by him have also survived, one from 1775, another from 1777–78. These journals have become important official source documents for the history of the American Revolutionary War, one of the most written-about conflicts. Like John, many of those active in it were, evidently, conscious that they were living/witnessing history in the making and were determined to keep their record of it.

There is also a small collection of John's official correspondence dating from 1779 and 1780. The most important of these letters, including two sent to George Washington, have long been a matter of public record, written, as they were, in anticipation of his imminent death. Given the dramatic circumstances leading up to John's premature death, previous biographers have been drawn magnetically to this period of his life, encouraged, in part, by the abundance of material from other sources close to John at what was such a turning-point moment not only in the story-arc of his short life but also in the war itself. In the process, however, John's earlier letters have largely been ignored by previous biographers.

All while drawing on the same sources addressed by these earlier biographers, this book revisits John's earlier letters in greater depth. This close reading has not only prompted a significant reappraisal of John's early life and army career both in Britain and in the first years of the war but also laid bare the tortured motivations that guided him in his later actions as a senior officer in the British army and led directly to the dramatic, albeit tragic, circumstances surrounding his untimely death. As a result, the tantalizing gaps which have so far eluded biographers have been sketched in comprehensively such that this work is more truly a whole-life, real-life biography of John and ensures a proper understanding of John the person and his actions and reactions leading up to his early death.

Acknowledgements

First a special thank you to the current generations of the André family—including Stephanie Sanders, Major John André in England and Charles, John and Roger André in Australia—who rallied round and pointed me to where I might find original material on John. This book draws, in part, on archives kindly made available by members of the André family, specifically Major John André in England and Roger André in Australia. Among these archives are letters written by John together with images of John, his father and John's tea-urn. These were made available by kind permission of Major John André. Images of John's three sisters from original miniatures by John Smart were provided by kind permission of John and Roger André, as were extracts from two books owned by John: *Geodaesia* and *Select Exercises for Young Proficients in the Mathematicks*.

I next extend a special thanks to the staff at Casemate Publishing, especially Ruth Sheppard, commissioning editor, who instantly and instinctively saw the rich potential that the life of John André offered as a dramatic point of entry into the truly fascinating story of the American Revolutionary War.

Casting the net more widely to all those who gave me access to occasional sources on John's career, may I thank those many institutions which helped me track down and harvest André nuggets from around the world. Among these institutions were the L. Tom Perry Brigham Special Collections at Brigham Young University (Provo, Utah), Buxton Museum and Art Gallery (Buxton, Derbyshire), Derbyshire Record Office (Matlock, Derbyshire), the Devonshire Collection at Chatsworth House (Derbyshire), the Library and Archives Canada (Ottawa and Toronto), the Library of Congress Digital Reference Team (Washington DC), the Library and Museum of Freemasonry (London), the National Army Museum (London), the Society for Army Historical Research, and the Special Collections and University Archives at Wichita State University Libraries (Fairmount, Kansas).

Many individual people also contributed their special research services which have made my task that much easier, and I want to thank, especially, my son, Alex, Christa Hook, Philippa Parkhouse, Andrea Schlecht, Markus Stoetzel, and, last but not least, my wife, Susan, a historian and biographer of note in her own right whose advice and support has been immense.

Thank you again, one and all.

List of Abbreviations

BHO	British History Online
BL	British Library
GM	*Gentleman's Magazine*
GEP	*General Evening Post*
LC	*London Chronicle*
LEP	*London Evening Post*
LG	*London Gazette*
LGE	*London Gazette Extraordinary*
LM	*London Magazine*
MJ	*Middlesex Journal*
MC	*Morning Chronicle*
MP	*Morning Post*
ODNB	L. Goldman (ed.) The Oxford Dictionary of National Biography (Oxford, 2011) (Online resource)
PA	*Public Advertiser*
PRO	Public Records Office (now known as the National Archives, Kew)
PV	Present Value, (being current value of sterling amounts based on the Bank of England inflation calculator).
WEP	*Whitehall Evening Post*

Prologue

PHILADELPHIA, MONDAY, 5 SEPTEMBER 1774

The diary entry by John Adams for Monday, 5 September 1774 recorded the opening moments of the proceedings in Philadelphia of America's First Continental Congress: 'At Ten, The Delegates all met at the City Tavern, and walked to the Carpenters' Hall, where they took a View of the Room, and of the Chamber where is an excellent Library. There is also a long Entry, where Gentlemen may walk, and a convenient Chamber opposite to the Library. The general Cry was, that this was a good Room...'[1]

In the forecourt outside, a throng of well-wishers, passers-by and street-sellers had formed, jostling with those only there 'out of curiosity'.[2] All kept one eye on the sky. It was the season for the devil's weather. Three nights before, there had been 'Lightning, Rain and Thunder', followed two nights ago by an almighty 'flood of rain' and 'the Wind north east stormy.' The previous day, the Sabbath, what with the damage overnight and the threat that the 'Mill-Dam' would burst, there was 'no Church to Day'[3] at Nomini Hall in nearby Virginia. Today was all sunshine and blue sky, but the damage visible all around was a reminder of the storms just passed.

Everyone watched in fascination as Adams and his fellow delegates gathered expectantly at the entrance to the Hall, shaking hands and making introductions. Mingling among the delegates was John Dunlap, self-appointed firebrand in the mounting war of words between Britain and its thirteen American colonies in their 'cry for Liberty'.[4] Claiming privilege for his *Dunlap's Pennsylvania Packet*,[5] he freely worked his way among the delegates, notebook in hand, harvesting ripened rhetoric ready to fire up the hot-press edition he had planned.

What America—and his newspaper—needed more than ever now was a headline grabber: some electric event to light '"that Spark of Liberty which shall illumine the latest Posterity"'[6] and galvanize a nation just waiting to be united. Burn an effigy of 'the infamous Lord North',[7] as the patriots did over the Schuylkill River in Richmond County back in June? Old news! Tar and feather a British spy caught snooping around Carpenters' Hall? For sure that would make good copy. But to have any chance of outdoing the *Boston Gazette* and *New York Gazette* with their colourful tales of 'Mohawks', what *Dunlap's Pennsylvania Packet* needed was for another of those

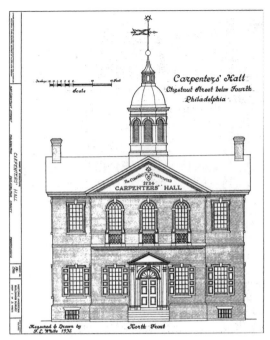

Carpenters' Company Hall, Philadelphia. (Library of Congress)

'Tea-Ships from the India Company' to show up, not 'in Maryland'[8] as happened back in August, but here, a couple of streets away, down on Carpenters' Wharf.

Tea! Everything was about tea. It was a world gone mad. In London, people could not get enough tea. Read the *Lady's Magazine*, and all the ladies of the 'bon ton' were obsessed by 'tea-time'.[9] It was such that 'a fine Lady has no leisure hours,' what with the 'hour and a half ... spent taking tea'[10] every day. 'The present East-India sale' was the talk of the town in 1769. 'Said to be one of the greatest there ever was since the establishment of the Company ... above 33,000 chests of tea' were sold, when, just 'a few years ago, 11,000 chests were thought a quantity sufficient to glut the market, from whence may easily be drawn the amazing progress of luxury in this age.'[11]

Not so among America's provincials. Not so since the Tea Act of 1773 when Britain's Parliament imposed a duty on tea and granted the East India Company a monopoly over its supply to America. The cry went up throughout the colonies that tea 'ought not to be used by any person who wishes well to the constitutional rights and liberty of British America'.[12] Instead everyone 'drank Coffee at four. They are now too patriotic to use tea.'[13]

Soon 'all America is in a flame,' wrote a British officer in New York to his friend back in London in November 1773, telling him also how 'the New Yorkers as well as the Bostonians and Philadelphians are determined ... that no tea shall be landed.'[14]

The able Doctor, or America Swallowing the Bitter Draught.

Engraving for *Royal American Magazine* of 'America Swallowing The Bitter Draught of Tea'. (Library of Congress)

Philadelphia took the lead, and, when Captain Ayres of the *Polly* arrived with his cargo of tea, he was sent back to England, 'the inhabitants' informing him 'they would not suffer him to land or enter his cargo at the custom-house.'[15]

Still the 'Tea-Ships' kept coming. So, the Bostonians decided on 'destroying the tea',[16] when they boarded 'the ship Dartmouth' and dumped its '342 chests' of tea 'into the sea'[17] in December 1773. From there, the fires of resistance spread, and towns across New England began 'burning several casks of tea ... in the presence of many thousand spectators.'[18] Four months on and it was New York's turn to take the law into its own hands with the arrival of 'the ship London', when 'the body of the people ... took out the tea ... broke the cases and started their contents in the river'.[19]

Boston and New York had pointed the way. Now, with the opening of the General Congress, surely it was Philadelphia's turn. The 'Tea-Ships' had stopped coming, but not the tea. Instead crafty owners and captains had begun disguising their cargoes. That was evident from 'the ship London' debacle in New York back in June. According to the 'New-York Gazette',[20] the jig was up for Captain Chambers and his '18 boxes of fine tea', when intelligence from 'Captain All, of Philadelphia' alerted New York's 'committee of observation' where to find the '18 boxes' disguised 'under another denomination'. Confronted with the evidence, Chambers 'confessed.'[21]

Since then, there had been nothing. No tea-ships. No tea. Not a whisper. Only an eerie silence, when what America hankered after was the sound of another '342 chests of tea' crashing into the sea … not in Boston bay, nor in New York harbour, but right here in Philadelphia and now … just as the Congress was getting underway.

The word had gone out. The hunt was on. Customs officers made a beeline for the river, where, just a stone's throw from Carpenters' Hall, dozens of vessels lay at their moorings, laden like sitting ducks. Arriving breathless at the wharf, the officers scanned their victims, eying them greedily, sensing their moment in history. Among the vessels unloading were two recently in from London: the *St. George* and *Nancy and Molly*. They had arrived on Saturday, two days ago.[22] The officers knew them well: both were registered locally, the *St. George* as a 'ship', the *Nancy and Molly* as a 'brig'.[23]

By all rights, the *St. George* should be searched first: at 200 tons, it was four times the size of the *Nancy and Molly*.[24] Indeed, it was the biggest of the vessels currently unloading. More to the point, its captain, 'John Inglis Jr',[25] was the infamous tory captain who had a brush with the officers back in June for running up the royal 'colors', then ringing the ship's bell on 'the birthday of King George III'.[26] If there were any India Company tea to be found on the waterfront that morning—and there just had to be—it would be in the hold of the *St. George*.

Yet, the instructions from on high could not have been clearer. Give the *Nancy and Molly* a good going over. Hands off the *St. George*. But why had these two vessels been singled out at all? It made no sense. The customs officers guessed it was because both vessels were owned by the mighty 'House of Willing, Morris and Company'.[27] Down on the waterfront, reputations did not come much bigger than those of Thomas Willing and Robert Morris. These two had their fingers in every pie. Importing 'dried Hides'[28] was their main line, but, across the river in Virginia Willing was known to 'trade for either Flour or Bread in any Quantity'.[29] Morris's speciality was bringing slaves from Africa and servants from the Palatines, and when George Washington was seeking advice on this matter, James Tilghman told him to ask 'Mr Robert Morris, whose Judgment in a Matter of this Nature I would rely upon sooner than that of any Man I know'.[30] To cap it all, both Willing and Morris were delegates to the General Congress, representing Pennsylvania.[31] More unimpeachable figures you could not find in the cause of American liberty, and if they had tea hidden in the hold of the *St. George*, they doubtless had their reasons. It certainly was not worth an officer's career to contradict orders. Still, at least, the customs officers would get to search the *Nancy and Molly*. It might only be a fig-leaf, but honour was salvaged.

As the delegates filed into Carpenters' Hall, Dunlap put his notepad away and took in the historic scene. Some of the well-wishers were clapping and cheering. These were the labouring 'Mechanicks'[32] from the lower orders. Others—those from Philadelphia's genteel 'Societies'—politely murmured in hushed voices. Those there 'out of curiosity' pointed, guessing who was who, especially which were the patriot heroes from Massachusetts Bay. The names of the delegates rolled along everyone's lips.

What was all this telling Philadelphians? Listen to Robert Paine, one of the delegates for Massachusetts Bay just arrived in Philadelphia, and here, surely, were welcome auguries for the '"Collision of British Flint and American Steel."'[33] Read the diary of Philip Fithian, tutor to the children of Virginia patriot "Councillor" Robert Carter,[34] and hear only the sober cry that 'Heaven only knows where these Tumults will end.'[35] For John Adams, this was surely history at a turning-point.

The last of the delegates disappeared into the sombre half-light of the hall's 'Entry'. Ushers closed the great doors, shiny but creaking from their newness. The

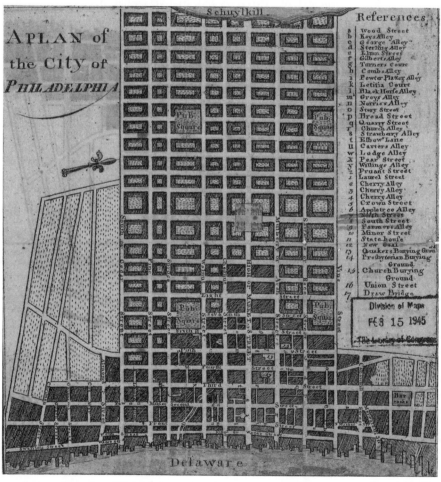

A plan of the city of Philadelphia. (Library of Congress, Geography and Map Division)

sons of Liberty tarried in the forecourt, murmuring, alive with anticipation, eager for some cathartic sign from within that, here, in this "City of Brotherly Love", all would finally be well for their troubled land. When none came, expectation gave way to patience. The crowd slowly unravelled, knots of twos and threes peeling off, blending back into the rhythm of their city.

One of the last to leave was a young gentleman, handsome and debonair in his merchant dress. He had arrived alone and quickly moved through the crowd, his dewy, dark eyes searching as if seeking a friendly face. Women saw his easy grace, men his formal merchant attire. He was still alone as people dispersed. He lingered briefly before heading onto Chestnut Street. There, he made as if to turn right, back down to where he had come from earlier, to the street dead-ending at Carpenter's Wharf, and the *St. George*. Until two days ago, that vessel had been his 'boisterous' home for the previous seven weeks, since 16 July when it had 'cleared outwards ... for Philadelphia' from the 'Port of London'.[36]

Instead, he hesitated and looked up to the sky as if to take a quick compass bearing, then crossed the street. He must hurry along. There was much to do before he made his way north. Before parting company on the quayside, Inglis had made him promise to visit him and his family, as had 'Mr Smith',[37] a fellow-passenger returning after four years in Europe on business.[38] He had also agreed to dine with 'William Thomas', another passenger on the *St. George*, planning 'to settle'[39] in America.

The young gentleman quickened his pace. Before any social calls, he had his orders to deliver. He must locate St. Tammany Street.[40] He had been given an address there. He could ask the way, but it should be easy to find.[41] It was in a district called the 'Northern Liberties'[42] he had been told by Inglis. Better he locate it for himself. Best he not be seen entering the British barracks.

He had been warned on the voyage over—first by Inglis, then, surprisingly, by Smith as well—to take precautions and to keep his own counsel. Now he understood why. He must beware, watch his every word, his every action. He had to, because, for the next few days, he must pretend he was other than who he was. To anyone he met in the streets of Philadelphia, he would be Jean André, a French Huguenot, one of the many visiting North America at this time, his commission to explore on behalf of the family's Parisian counting-house ways to open up new merchant connections in Philadelphia, America's 'most populous city'.[43]

Still, he was not comfortable going in disguise. He was proud of who he was, for, to Lord Robert Bertie, colonel of the regiment, 'one of the Gentlemen of His Majesty's Bed Chamber'[44] and his commanding officer back in England, he was Lieutenant John André of the Royal Fusiliers, sent to Philadelphia with urgent orders to conduct the Royal Irish Regiment in garrison there to New York, thence if required to Boston. The message from the king himself was: riot must not become rebellion.

Yet, John André must also remember that, to his dear mother, three sisters and little brother back home in Southampton, he would always be their 'cher Jean', his solemn vow to himself and to them: to restore the honour of the André name, delivering it from the ruin, the shame and the ignominy brought on it by his father, 'père Antoine', and his poisonous dealings with the East India Company five years earlier. Overnight made head of the family following his father's sudden death in 1769—by his own hand almost certainly—at the age of 52,[45] John had been waiting for this moment ever since. The anticipation and exhilaration had briefly overwhelmed him as he descended the gangplank from the *St. George* and first touched American soil. Finally, he could deliver on that vow he had made back in 1769 when, in his own words, a mere 'novice of eighteen'.[46]

PART I

'The Chicaneries of Bubble'

CHAPTER I

Refugees

For Americans at home in their farmsteads, the East India Company meant tea and the burdens of the Tea Act. For Britons shopping at their nearest emporium, the Company meant every luxury imaginable: diamonds, silks, spices, and yes, tea, too. You name it, the East India Company could come by it. For stockjobbers on London's 'Change-Alley, it meant the next easy-money 'bubble'. The South Sea Bubble had burst in 1720, but not the speculators' love affair with the merchant companies, the mighty leviathans that spread their tentacles out into every corner of the world, even starting wars at will, all while buying votes in Parliament back home.

For John's father, Anthony, greed, too, would come to drive his interest in the East India Company. He was not alone in this. How he embroiled his family in the fortunes of the East India Company is to probe the extent to which Britons, French, Spanish, Dutch alike became obsessed with riches and the allure of quicksilver ventures. Forget the sacred coinage consecrated to cathedrals, churches and chapels and buying eternal salvation. Forget the 'landed interest', its wealth locked in castles and mansions. Enter the easy money that came from commodities, consumption and commerce. Enter the 'ready money', the money on credit and the money on paper, all of it frenzied, fluid, free-flowing speculation which knew no boundaries. Enter the 'Monied Interest'.[1] Meet the 'moneyed men': the 'Change-Alley Broker', the 'jobbing-brokers,' the banking 'Mercuries' and counting-house alchemists, all practising 'the chicaneries of Bubble', indulging in the 'Nefarious Practice of Stock-Jobbing', and chasing one and all after the mighty merchant companies.[2]

The 1760s and 70s were their heyday. In the Caribbean, Holland had its Dutch West India Company, France its Compagnie des Indes Occidentales. Africa—with its lucrative slave trade—was awash with them, one of the oldest being the Danish Africa Company, founded in 1660. Still, it was Britain that perfected the dark arts of the merchant company. It had its very own Turkey Company,[3] Royal African Company, Muscovy Company, Russia Company and so on. But these paled into insignificance next to the maw and raw power of the British East India Company. It was so mighty that it began conducting its own wars, even drove Britain's foreign policy, as it vied with Holland's 'Dutch East India Company', France's 'Compagnie des Indes Orientales' and the 'East India Company of Sweden'[4] for control of the Indian subcontinent. Forget smoky tobacco from America's troublesome thirteen colonies, sweet sugar from the Caribbean and warming furs from Quebec. Mughal India, with its saucy spices, gorgeous gems, shiny silks and tangy teas, was the ne plus ultra of colonial ambitions. 'India Company' fever took hold of the nation as never before in the heady days following victory after victory during the Seven Years' War.

For John's father, Antoine ('Anthony'),[5] one of many Huguenots[6] arriving in Britain in the early 1740s and seeking escape from Catholic persecution, greed could not have been further from his thinking. Welcomed in Britain, he nevertheless came to his new country as a non-person, a refugee. This defined who and what he was: insecure, restless, ambitious, in a hurry, eager but anxious to put down permanent roots in wherever his new home might be. For him, Britain's merchant companies initially meant safety and security. Protected within Britain's 'Establishment' of commercial, financial and political power and influence, the Andrés could continue to trade freely in the Mediterranean, safe now not only from the French and Spanish navies, but also, according to Captain Lewis André, from the 'Corsairs' and 'Maltese Gallies' plundering all, as almost happened with 'three Xebecks which gave him Chace' on his journey 'from Alexandria'[7] in October 1752.

Starting out from Nimes in the Languedoc region of southern France, the Andrés had been on the move for too long by the time they arrived in Britain. 'Born in Genoa',[8] John's father spent his childhood in Geneva. It was not long, however, before Catholic France set its sights on Calvinist Switzerland, and, once again, the Andrés, along with other Huguenots, must pack their bags and find a new haven. Their only crime a wish to worship in the Protestant faith, many sought refuge in Holland, others in the northern German states. Anthony and his brothers, David and John-Lewis, came to Britain, arriving in the 1740s.

They chose Britain primarily because of Anthony's new bride, 'Marie-Louise'.[9] She was from 'the notoriously Huguenot Girardot family',[10] one of the 'Grand Group of Families'[11] that had fled France for Britain during the first wave of expulsions following the Revocation of the Edict of Nantes in 1685. There were a number of branches of Girardots, including Tillieux, Marigny, Vermenoux and Chancourt. The first to arrive in Britain was 'John Girardot'.[12] Naturalized by Act of Parliament in 1686, he was followed by 'Andrew Girardot alias Vermenoux'[13] in 1705. Bringing the skills, money and merchant connections vital to a new life in Britain, these early Girardot refugees quickly established themselves in the high echelons of Britain's merchant community. Their money enabled them, in turn, to marry into powerful political families.

Money unlocked the doors to power, but marriage was the bond that tied the sinews of that power. The Tillieux branch was so successful that, by 1747, 'Miss Girardot, the only Daughter and Child of John Girardot' could marry 'Capt

Hamilton, a near relation of his Grace the Duke of Hamilton'. Lest readers of the *Penny London Post* wonder why such an important personage in British society would marry a relative unknown, the bride-to-be had two irresistible qualities: 'she was a beautiful young Lady, with a Fortune of 30,000*l*'.[14]

John André's mother, Marie-Louise, was from the Chancourt branch of the Girardots. Relative latecomers to Britain, this branch originated at 'Chatel Chinon in Nivernois'[15] in the south of France, but, following confiscation of its lands, first moved to Paris where it was possible to buy immunity from persecution. There they established a timber-merchant business, centred on 'the heavily forested Morvan area'[16] north of Paris. Reprieve for the Chancourts was temporary. Further persecutions forced their emigration to Britain, where, in 1721, James Girardot was naturalized.[17]

Still, the Chancourt women must wait their turn. As with the Tillieux branch, marriage was their passport into Britain's merchant and political 'Establishment'. The alliance which achieved this was between Marie-Louise's cousin, Anne Judith Foissin,[18] and John Bristow in 1733. The Bristows were a wealthy well-connected English family, John's father described as 'a very eminent Merchant of the City', his mother deemed 'very rich'[19] on her death in 1751.

The marriage brought instant rewards to both husband and wife. The benefits to John Bristow were commercial, evident in the marriage settlement which detailed the dowry brought by Anne to the union. As the third son, he was dependent on a good marriage, and Anne's '6,000*l*' dowry gave him vital commercial firepower. The marriage settlement stipulated that the dowry 'be invested in the purchase of South sea annuities'.[20] The South Sea Company had been through its 'Bubble' thirteen years earlier, but had recovered its former pre-eminence as one of the three 'monied Companies'[21] that constituted Britain's financial 'Establishment' (the other two being the Bank of England and the East India Company).

The South Sea Company's prized plum was its continuing monopoly over trade into Spanish and Portuguese South America. As a result, elections to its board were always hotly contested,[22] and 'his Majesty'[23] made sure to remain as its governor. Hence, Anne's 6000*l*' dowry grew to '20,737*l*'[24] by 1765. Bristow could not touch this money, but the purchase of the 'South sea annuities' in 1733 enhanced his influence within the company. Already listed as one of the company's 'Directors'[25] in 1730, he was appointed a 'Deputy-Governor'[26] the same year as he purchased the annuities. He was subsequently promoted to sub-governor, only relinquishing this post in 1762.[27]

Bristow used this enhanced influence to help the Girardots join him in Britain's moneyed 'Establishment'. During the contested election which brought him to the board in 1730, 'John Girardot de Tillieux'[28] was on the rival list of nominees and missed out on election. When, however, another disputed election occurred in 1733, Bristow secured Tillieux's appointment as a director. To cement the interlocking family ties, one of Bristow's daughters, Louisa, later married into the Tillieux branch.[29]

The decision to anchor Anne's dowry on 'South sea annuities' was no accident: it was almost certainly through the South Sea Company that the Girardots had first made Bristow's acquaintance. The Girardots had long conducted significant trading operations out of Lisbon, and it was from there that Bristow, a leading 'Portugal Merchant', oversaw the South Sea Company's monopoly of British trade with South America. He had, however, endured a chequered relationship with the Portuguese crown: in 1721, he was imprisoned for smuggling when 'his firm shipped gold and money in specie in contravention of an old law'.[30]

Thirty years on and still 'known as something of a hothead', Bristow again risked imprisonment when once more caught playing fast and loose over the 'export of bullion'. This time, he talked his way out of trouble, but only after he had agreed to broker contracts for 'acquiring in Brazil, Portugal and Spain silver to supply the needs of the East India Company.'[31] These strong-arm tactics were no accident: the East India Company had long been trying to break the South Sea Company's monopoly over British trade into South America. At stake was diamonds, a commodity that the East India Company had dominated until the 'discovery of diamond fields in Brazil'[32] in the 1720s. However, Bristow stood in the way: as Deputy-Governor of the South Sea Company,[33] he had worked it so that, 'between 1753 and 1755, Messrs Bristow also held the lucrative contract for the export of Brazilian diamonds from Portugal'.[34] All of this meant that, 'by 1754, he was perhaps the foremost British merchant in Portugal'.[35]

Meantime, Bristow was also riding high back in England. So influential was he in financial and commercial circles that he headed a who's who of London merchants underwriting 'Publick Credit'[36] during the constitutional crisis of 1745 and, in 1754, led a list of 'Merchants, Traders and Liverymen.'[37] In 1752, he was made 'sheriff'[38] of Buckinghamshire, a royal appointment, but it was as a Member of Parliament from 1734 to 1768 sitting 'as a regular Government supporter ... on the interest of his brother-in-law, John, 1st Earl of Buckinghamshire'[39] that Bristow was of most value to his young bride in 1733. This political influence enabled him to secure Anne's rapid naturalization by 'Royal Assent'[40] in the same year as he entered Parliament. Soon, other relatives of Anne made the journey to Britain: two were naturalized in 1742, including Marie-Louise's older brother, John Girardot.[41]

Next, it was the turn of the Andrés to receive a helping hand. Bristow probably encountered them through their extensive interests in the Mediterranean. He had been a remittance agent for the War Office handling 'pay and subsidies'[42] since the 1730s. This work took him into the Mediterranean where, together with his partner and fellow MP, Peter Burrell, he 'held important government contracts ... for the forces at Gibraltar and Minorca.'[43] At the same time, 'Messrs André and Co of Genoa' were selling 'Corn' and 'Quarters of Wheat'[44] to the British government.

Their paths could just as well have crossed in Portugal where the Andrés also had extensive interests, in this instance, trading diamonds. John-Lewis,[45] Anthony's youngest brother, had a 'partner', Lionel Darrell, who was married to the daughter of the British vice-consul for Portugal.[46] How long the Andrés had been active in Lisbon is unclear, but John-Lewis was certainly there with Darrell in November 1755 negotiating contracts with 'Mess. Dodd and Bonifas',[47] both traders in diamonds.

It is also possible that Bristow knew the Andrés through their Girardot connection. The Andrés and Girardots were already acquainted from their time in Geneva. Anthony André and John Girardot were near-contemporaries at the Academy of Geneva in the 1730s.[48] Again, marriage was what sealed the bond between these two families. First, came the union of Anthony André and Marie-Louise Girardot in Paris. When they married is unknown, but it was before 2 May 1750—which was when John was born[49]—and after 25 March 1748 when, doubtless with Bristow's help, royal assent was received to a bill 'for naturalizing Anthony André and David André'.[50] To cement the burgeoning André–Girardot connection, in October 1751 David André married 'Miss Girardot, only daughter of Andrew Girardot Esq. of New Broad-Street'. Readers of the *General Evening Post* were duly instructed that the bride was 'a beautiful young Lady, adorned with every Qualification to render the Marriage-State happy, with a Fortune of 20000*l*'.[51]

However Bristow became acquainted with the Andrés, his influence on their early days in Britain was significant, a fact acknowledged by Anthony and Marie-Louise André, when he was named senior godfather to their firstborn son, John, for his baptism on 16 May 1750, this ahead of 'Jean André',[52] the infant's uncle and the family's benefactor, ahead even of his grandfather, 'Paul Girardot de Paris'.[53]

CHAPTER 2

'A Heap of Rubble'

On the morning of 1 November 1755, a massive earthquake struck Lisbon. John-Lewis André was there at the time, as were 'Mess. Andrew Gerardot and Stephen Gerardot [who] are saved on board a Ship'. In his letter to the *Public Advertiser*, John-Lewis made an initial estimate of casualties numbering 'not above 10000 Souls lost in this Calamity'.[1] This was wide of the mark: by the time the subsequent tsunami and conflagration had completed their work, 75,000 people had died, among them thirty-nine from 'the English Factory of Lisbon'.[2] John-Lewis also told of 'the City reduced to a Heap of Rubble'. Another eye-witness told how 'the Strangers are all ruined, but they have not suffered so much in their Persons, as in their Goods'.[3]

Bristow was not in Lisbon at the time, but he was among the 'Strangers [who] are all ruined'. At the pinnacle of his power only a year earlier, now his 'position was much impaired by the very severe losses he suffered', and 'his firm never altogether recovered.' By 1761, when Lord Bute was preparing for the upcoming elections to Parliament, Bristow was marked as a 'Government' supporter, but with a warning note: 'Hurt in circumstances'. The mistake Bristow had made was to lend to the 'Crown of Portugal' as a way to protect his trading monopolies following the earthquake, but, soon, 'sums were owing him to the amount of £120,000 and upwards.'

Bristow became so 'hurt' he had to write to the Duke of Newcastle in 1765 asking 'assistance of Government in securing his rights against the King of Portugal'. This impacted, meantime, on his ability to fulfil his British government supply contracts, and, in 1767, he wrote to the Treasury asking it 'to remit the payment of interest on his debt of £17,000'.[4] The loans had still not been repaid when Bristow died in 1768.

In these circumstances, any thoughts Anthony and Marie-Louise may have harboured following John's baptism that Bristow might continue as the family's patron were, necessarily, abandoned. What influence Bristow retained after becoming so 'hurt' was reserved for his immediate family, and only those bearing the Girardot name were invited to join him on the board of the South Sea Company.[5]

Henceforth, the Andrés must look elsewhere for the security and support they were seeking as they made Britain their new home. Fortunately, they had emerged relatively unscathed from the Lisbon disaster. Their main business traditionally was cloth, and this continued to prosper. Indeed, the emergence of high-quality English woollen textiles—so-called 'bayettes anglaises'—was another reason why they had chosen to settle in Britain. Despite having been expelled from France, the firm of 'Messieurs Antoine et David André' continued selling into the country, but they could now do so from the safety of Britain, shipping these 'bayettes anglaises' to, among others, 'Jean Abraham Poupart', and having a 'sieur Dubois'[6] finish the cloth in northern France. From there, the cloth was re-exported to, among other countries, Portugal where, by 1760, Darrell, on behalf of 'Messrs Anthony and David André,' was regularly consigning 'Superfine Cloth' and 'Yorkshire Cloths' to the 'Rio fleet' and 'Bohia fleet'[7] bound for Brazil.

Still, with the loss of Bristow's patronage, the Andrés must look elsewhere if they were to break into Britain's Establishment. With this in mind, their first priority was to integrate into their new home's social, religious and cultural fabric. They made every effort to do so. This was evident from their decision to adopt British ways in the practice of their religion. John's baptism was a statement of future intentions. The church at St. Martin Orgar' where John was baptised conducted services strictly 'according to the rights of the Church of England'.[8] This was unlike many other Huguenot places of worship in London where services were carried out in French and according to their traditional liturgy. As further evidence of the Andrés' desire to become anglicized, the baptism of John's sister, Ann Marguerite, in December 1753, was performed at another church in the City, 'St Andrew Undershaft', where, unlike John's baptism record three years earlier, which was in French, she was registered as the 'daughter of Anthony André by Mary-Louisa his wife.'[9]

The Andrés also shunned the 'mercantile clusters' which inevitably formed with the arrival of so many Huguenots in so short a time. Migrating to Britain in large numbers since the 1680s, with each successive wave the size of this refugee community had mushroomed to, it is estimated, between twenty and twenty-five thousand. The burden fell primarily on London, or more specifically, 'the City', London's merchant district, where, soon, 'Frenchmen accounted for over 10 percent of all City merchants.'[10]

All while avoiding these 'clusters', the Andrés did seek out certain Huguenot families that had lived in Geneva prior to coming to London. This was necessary if they were to find patrons to replace Bristow. These families were part of the 'Protestant International'[11] which linked Huguenot refugee communities in a commercial and financial network of trust and amity across the big commercial cities of Switzerland, Holland, Britain and the German states. Long before the arrival of the Andrés, many of these families were already pillars of London's financial, commercial and, even, political Establishment, having successfully penetrated the key bastions of Britain's 'monied Interest.'[12] These strongholds were the two principal merchant trading companies—the South Sea Company and the mighty East India Company—and the privately owned Bank of England, which bankrolled their trading activities. In addition to these three 'monied Companies',[13] there were the two insurance companies—Royal Exchange Assurance and London Assurance—which, alone since 1720, were authorized to provide the marine assurance without which the trading companies dared not dispatch their ships. These 'five Companies',[14] making up Britain's 'monied Interest', were so powerful that successive governments could not finance Britain's wars and ballooning National Debt without first 'securing' their financial backing.

Among the Huguenot families from Geneva to have successfully established themselves within these 'five Companies' were the Bosanquets. Active, like the Andrés, in cloth, specifically silk, the first Bosanquets to reach Britain arrived in the 1680s. By the time the Andrés came to Britain in the late 1740s, Samuel Bosanquet, its then scion, was ensconced as governor of the Royal Exchange Assurance.[15] Within two years of Anthony's naturalization, Bosanquet secured his election to the company's board.[16] Anthony would remain a director the Royal Exchange Assurance for the next eighteen years, his name appearing in triennial lists of those re-elected and published in newspapers and periodicals, such as the *Universal Chronicle*[17] in 1759 and, for the last time, in the *St. James's Chronicle* in 1768.[18]

Anthony was on his way: now that he had one foot inside Britain's Establishment, he wanted everyone to know who the Andrés were and where they ran their business. To this end, Anthony made sure the André name featured in *The Compleat Compting-House Companion or Young Merchant and Trader's Sure Guide*, the who's who of the business community. Published in 1763, there was a section headed 'List of merchants, factors, tradesmen, agents etc in and about London, Westminster and Southwark', and in it were 'André Anthony and David'. They gave their business location as 'Bishopsgate street' in the City of London. There was also an entry for 'Girardot, Andrew, jun. Esq', but his business address was at 'New Broad Street'.[19] The Girardots and Andrés clearly had separate business interests.

These were exciting times for Britain. During those years, the country embarked on the Seven Years' War, its most victorious conflict thus far. The Andrés wanted to be part of the success story. To that end, the Andrés joined the other 'Merchants and Traders of the City of London' who, in 1763, published a 'humble address' to 'His Majesty' expressing loyalty and thanks for the successful war just ended. All three brothers—Anthony, David and John-Lewis—featured on the list that was published in numerous newspapers, including the *St. James's Chronicle*[20] and *Gazetteer and New Daily Advertiser*. It even appeared in the *London Gazette*, the official newspaper of government.[21]

In these euphoric, harum-scarum days following victory in 1763, the Andrés, John's father especially, must have wondered at their good fortune in having chosen to come to Britain. They had not only found safety and security but could now ride the imperial wave which had come with the conquests in Canada, India and the West Indies. John's father could now turn his attention to providing a good home for his wife and five children, one that befitted his magnified status.

CHAPTER 3

'The Three Mile Stone'

Many merchants chose to live over their business premises at this time. The Andrés doubtless did the same, at least in their early years in Britain. If so, their 'yearly rent' in London's City district would have been in the order of '26l'. This according to an advertisement from 1766, was the cost for the lease on a 'dwelling house' together with watch-maker's 'complete shop and parlour', situated in 'the lightest, pleasantest and most airy part of Ball-Alley, Lombard-street'[1] and just a stone's throw from the Andrés' business premises on 'Bishopsgate street'.

However, by 1758, if not earlier, Anthony and Mary-Louisa had decided to move out of London and establish their own 'country seat'[2]—an essential accoutrement to their enhanced mercantile stature. According to the 1763 *Sure Guide*, which had a separate entry for 'André Anthony',[3] this 'seat' was in 'Walthamstow', a 'village in Essex on the river Lea'[4] located some '6 ½ miles'[5] to the north of St. Paul's Cathedral. Walthamstow was already known as a 'retreat' for Huguenots, like the Lefebure family,[6] which had big land-holdings there. Another near-neighbour was Samuel Bosanquet, Anthony's patron and fellow director on the board of Royal Exchange Assurance, who had taken the lease on Forest House, Leyton, in 1750.[7]

For a 'fare' of '1s', it was possible to commute daily into London's 'City' from Walthamstow on a 'coach', arriving at the 'Four Swans, Bishopsgate Street'[8] before 9 a.m. and leaving for home at 4 p.m. This presumes that Anthony would have travelled by public 'coach', when, of course, he was more likely to have his own 'Chariot', as 'a Lady' had, when 'returning … to Walthamstow'[9] in late March 1763. Realistically, however, Walthamstow was at the outer limit of what was practicable for a City merchant, whereas Clapton, to which the family moved in 1764, was 'at the three mile stone',[10] as measured from London's 'Shoreditch Church'.[11]

More significantly, John's mother had relatives with long-standing connections to Clapton, 'a village in Middlesex joining to Hackney'.[12] Among these was 'Ann Girardott alias d'Vermenoux',[13] listed as residing in Hackney when she married in 1690. Moreover, 'Mrs Mary Girardot'[14] was currently living in the village.

Another compelling reason for the move would have been Clapton's fine reputation for schools. Choosing the right one for young John as he reached the age of fourteen was a crucial next step for the Andrés in their plan to root themselves in Britain's Establishment. St. Paul's School, where young John had been studying since the age of nine if not younger,[15] was excellent academically. Located in the shadow of the Wren cathedral and sporting the highest pupil numbers in the country, it regularly sent its 'young gentlemen' on scholarships and 'exhibitions to various colleges in Cambridge and Oxford.' It had been an obvious choice for Anthony and Mary-Louisa given the family's professional connection to the cloth trade and that 'the Worshipful Company of Mercers' which oversaw it were also the 'Governors of the School'.[16] Still, what Anthony wanted for young John more than academic accomplishment was that he should mix with the great and the good of Britain's social, commercial and political elite, making the friends that would help him get ahead in the world. St. Paul's did not offer this: young John's contemporaries there were the sons of an 'innholder', 'distiller', 'bookseller' and 'apothecary',[17] very worthy but hardly the stuff of Britain's patrician class.

Before considering a move to Clapton, John's parents doubtless sought the opinions of relatives, including Mary Girardot, already residing there. They would have been told of nearby Hackney's 'many boarding schools for young ladies',[18] important information given that the Andrés had their three daughters to educate. This, however, remained secondary to what must be arranged for their firstborn son, and Clapton had a school that, by all accounts, perfectly met their aspirations. It was known variously as 'Dr' or 'Mr Newcome's school, at Hackney'.[19]

CHAPTER 4

'Young Gentlemen'

John's schooling was crucial to Anthony. All the trappings of commercial and social status that Anthony had been acquiring were nothing if he could not endow his firstborn son with a true blue British pedigree. For that, the starting point must be choosing the right school for young John. Anthony would settle for nothing less than the best. This would explain why Anthony removed John from St. Paul's and placed him instead at 'Dr. Newcome's school'.[1] There, both at study and at home, young John would be rubbing shoulders with Britain's upper orders.

'Dr Newcome's' was, along with Westminster School, Harrow and Eton College, one of the teaching establishments of choice mid-century for Britain's aristocratic families and political dynasties alike. Among the former were Lord John Cavendish, who went there in 1747, and the 'black Duke of Grafton', a future prime minister, who entered in 1750. Among the latter were 'four sons of Lord Chancellor Hardwicke'[2] who were 'all indeed educated at Hackney School'.[3] So popular was it among Britain's political elite that, during the period 1754 to 1790, 'there were in the House of Commons 26 members who had attended Hackney School.'[4]

Anthony and Mary-Louisa would doubtless have heard about Dr Newcome's reputation from Mary Girardot, but confirmation that it was the right school for their firstborn would surely have come from reading articles like the one in the 7 May 1761 edition of the *Public Advertiser*, which reported that 'the play of the first part of Henry the Fourth was performed three evenings last week at Mr Newcome's school, at Hackney by the young gentlemen of that School'. Reading on and imagining his son in the cast, Anthony would have noted that the performance was put on 'before very numerous and brilliant Companies'. Still, this was as nothing when compared to what came next, for, 'on Monday evening it was again performed before several of the Nobility and Gentry when their Royal Highnesses Prince William and Prince Henry honoured them with their presence'.

The theatre critic writing this feature was soon into his stride: waxing lyrical, he enthused about 'every one of the Characters very judiciously cast and most admirably performed'. When attention turned, however, to the 'Character of Falstaff', the critic bubbled over, saying how it was 'so well played, that it received universal Applause and Acclamations every Night', his effusiveness inviting the suspicion that 'Falstaff' was played by the son of one of Britain's famous families. This was entirely possible: many of Britain's patrician sons could be seen in these productions for which the school became so famed. 'On the 29th of April 1751', for instance, 'the young gentlemen at this school performed one of Terrence's plays, in which the young earl of Euston played a part.' The feature also noted that Euston's father, 'his grace the duke of Grafton honoured the performance with his presence.'[5]

Puff or not, these accounts were intended to convince parents like the ambitious and increasingly prosperous Andrés that this was the school for their young son. And if the Andrés needed any further convincing, the school routinely placed advertisements in newspapers announcing 'the Anniversary Meeting of the Gentlemen educated at Dr Newcome's'. Each read like a who's who of Britain's great and good: the one in 1768 told readers that the 'Stewards' would be 'the Right Honourable the Earl of Hardwicke and Right Honourable Lord Grey' as well as 'Lieutenant-General Honywood'.[6] Again for the 1770 reunion, the 'Stewards' included the 'Hon. J. Yorke' and 'Hon. J. Grey'.[7] This was just the social circle the Andrés' firstborn should be mixing in as a young adult if he wanted to get ahead, and who knows what doors they could open for Anthony and his brothers?

When exactly John started at his new school is unclear, as no school records have survived. It was likely between the ages of eleven to fourteen, which was when earlier pupils—for instance, Philip Yorke,[8] John Hoadley and Henry Taylor[9]—began their attendance. Much depends on when the Andrés moved to Clapton. It was certainly sometime between 1763, when, according to that year's *Sure Guide*, the Andrés were still living in Walthamstow, and '8 April 1765' which was when, according to minutes of the 'Select Vestry' at Clapton's local church, Anthony paid 'the usual fine to be excused serving the offices'.[10] Most likely, the move followed the death of Anthony's uncle, Jean, in Geneva in May 1764. As heir to one third of the estate of David André, an unmarried uncle who 'clearly possessed considerable wealth',[11] Jean died a rich man. In his will, he named Anthony as sole heir. Anthony proved his Uncle Jean's will, first in Geneva on 16 May 1764, then in London on 5 December 1764. At a stroke, Anthony became a wealthy man.[12] The time had come to send his firstborn to one of England's finest schools.

Assuming young John arrived at Dr Newcome's in late 1764, he would just have missed the school's production of the 'Siege of Damascus … performed … last Tuesday night by the young Gentlemen of Mr Newcome's school, Clapton.' As in 1761, this performance was put on 'before a great Number of the Nobility and Gentry.' The *London Chronicle* published the cast list for the nine main characters, and here was confirmation—if Anthony needed it—that Dr Newcome's was the perfect school for young John. Heading the cast was 'Lord Harrington'.[13] Fifth on the cast list was a second aristocrat, 'Ld. Rob. Cavendish'.[14] Which of the Cavendish boys this was is unclear: there were three Cavendish boys in that generation: William, born in 1748,[15] Richard born in 1752[16] and George born in 1754. This 'Rob. Cavendish' would have been either Richard or William, who, as the eldest, became Duke of Devonshire in 1755. William may have attended Dr Newcome's,[17] but Richard is known to have.[18] This was illustrious company indeed for young John arriving later that year!

The Cavendish brothers were just some of the highborn youngsters attending Dr Newcome's when John was there. The Cavendishes were stalwarts of Whig politics in Parliament and, like many political families, entrusted their offspring to Dr Newcome because he would reinforce those opinions. Others, like Crisp Molineux who was the son of a West Indies merchant and attended the school in the 1740s, came by their independence of thought through the influence of Dr Newcome, 'a Dissenting minister and a Whig of the old stamp', for whom theatre was integral to the teaching of new, independent ways of thinking.[19] Reflecting on his schooldays, Molineux later reminisced how 'Old Newcome so strongly rivetted the Whig principles in his boys, that … none of us has ever deviated from them.'[20]

As a 'Dissenting Minister', it was no coincidence that 'Old Newcome' had opened his school where he did. Clapton and Hackney were renowned as a refuge for Dissenters and the location for a number of 'Independent' and 'Presbyterian Meeting-Houses.'[21] Many Dissenters were opposed to the government's policy towards the thirteen colonies. Whether people were drawn to Clapton as a known haven for these opinions or, like Molineux, became 'rivetted' by the village's dissenting spell, a number of its residents developed close ties with like-minded 'friends' in the thirteen colonies. Joseph Sherwood, attorney-at-law and, later, 'one of his Majesty's Justices of the Peace at Clapton',[22] became 'agent at the Court of Great Britain' for the 'northern colonies' in 1764 helping them in their attempt to have the 'Sugar Act etc'[23] repealed. In 1766, the 'Assembly of the Province of New Jersey' appointed him as their agent, his task to keep it informed of reaction to 'American Complaints'.[24]

As the dispute intensified, the loyalties of these agents were compromised: some, like Dennys De Berdt, 'a Dissenter' with connections to Clapton and appointed 'special agent' for the 'Massachusetts House of Representatives'[25] in 1765, sided with America, albeit not openly. De Berdt's daughter, Esther, was not so coy and in 1770 married Joseph Reed, delegate for Pennsylvania to the Continental Congress and a leading figure in the Revolutionary War.

This begs the question what, if any, 'principles' were likewise 'rivetted' in young John through his exposure to the influence of 'old Newcome'. For this, a good starting point is in the school's reputation for creative independence, the most visible manifestation of which was the once-yearly dramatic productions. It was surely thanks to these and the school's enthusiasm for original artistic achievement that young John acquired a taste for composing verse. Integral to the performances were the poetic prologues and epilogues composed to bookend productions.

Dr Newcome's was not the only school to set a high store by these original poetic titbits. In 1762, *Lloyd's Evening Post* published a list of recommended poetry, among which an 'Epilogue' furnished by Dr Newcome's 'Hackney School' and 'a Prologue and Epilogue spoken at Merchant Taylors School'.[26] However, Dr Newcome's had more clout: it could line up well-known literary figures, including the dramatist Richard Steele and the versifier William Taylor, to supply its poetic tours de force; and, in a major coup, the 'Epilogue to the Andria acted at Hackney School' in 1763 was 'written by David Garrick,'[27] the foremost actor of his time.

For the 1764 production, Dr Newcome's reverted to Dr Hoadley, the school's resident poetaster, and he composed a 'Prologue to the Siege of Damascus'. Its influence on young John can be seen clearly. While the first line aptly went 'Your modern men of wit laugh at our schools', its last was more sombre as it imagined 'an injur'd lover frantic with despair.'[28] Whether John was in the audience that 'Tuesday night' or read the Prologue subsequently, these words stayed with him, and he would recall them in 1779 when composing a poem entitled 'The Frantick Lover' to exorcise his own 'pangs of Despair'.[29]

No such creative catharsis interrupted past pupil Crisp Molineux's chosen career path. Armed with his own take on Dr Newcome's 'principles', Molineux was soon 'blessed … with an ample fortune at home and abroad'.[30] He became a Member of Parliament from where his Whig independence of thought inclined him away from Britain's hostile policy towards the thirteen colonies, such that 'all his recorded votes were against North's Administration'.[31]

Other Dr Newcome's pupils who went on to support the American cause included young John's contemporary, Benjamin Vaughan.[32] Born in 1751, Vaughan was the son of a West Indies merchant and grandson of Benjamin Hallowell of Boston, Massachusetts. A supporter of the American Revolution, Vaughan published the works of his friend, Benjamin Franklin, in 1779 and was sent by Britain as an emissary to Paris in 1782 to open peace talks with the American colonies.

Two other pupils with American roots became more extreme in their support for the cause of freedom: Thomas Nelson Jun., born in York, Virginia in 1738, was sent to England 'at the age of fourteen years' and 'placed under the instruction of Mr Newcomb whose school was near Hackney.'[33] Arthur Middleton followed in his footsteps. Born in South Carolina, he was sent to England and, in 1754, 'at the age of twelve … was placed at the excellent seminary of Hackney'.[34] After completing their studies, both Nelson and Middleton returned to America, were signatories of the Declaration of Independence and served in the Continental Army.

Middleton spent two years at Dr Newcome's. This was not necessarily typical of the time boys spent there. The school adjusted its programme to suit the circumstances of individual families: the 'Earl of Euston' was only there for a year;[35] Lord John Cavendish was there for longer. Born in 1732, he began attendance at Dr Newcome's in 1747, spending three years there, before going on to Cambridge.[36]

However, his brother, 'the Hon. Henry Cavendish' was there even longer. Born in 1731, he 'became a pupil at Dr Newcome's school' in 1742, remaining there 'till 1749.'[37] Given these variations, it is difficult to say how long young John was at Dr Newcome's. Most likely, he left aged sixteen, since there was one more important leg of his education to complete before he joined his father in the family 'compting house'.[38] This would be at the Academy of Geneva, where his father had studied, enrolling in 1733 aged sixteen.[39]

Reflecting on the time his son spent at Dr Newcome's, Anthony could congratulate himself on his choice of school. Mixing in the company of Britain's future leaders, young John could soon imagine himself trying 'my interest in Parliament'.[40] This was not mere hubris: there were numerous examples of Huguenot refugees who had quickly made their mark high in Britain's Establishment. Having acquired fortunes as merchants, many, including Claudius Amyand, Isaac Barré and Anthony Chamier, entered Parliament.[41] Beyond these circles were other illustrious Huguenots constantly hitting the headlines, among which David Garrick, the Drury Lane theatre impresario, feted in 1763 as 'Poet, Painter and Philosopher; Musician, Manager and Mimic; Critic, Censor and Composer; and Professor of Tragedy, Comedy and Farce';[42] and Daniel Layard, appointed 'Physician Extraordinary' to 'Her Royal Highness the Princess Dowager of Wales'.[43]

No wonder young John could have such lofty ambitions. The world was, truly, his oyster, and his father was there to help him on his way. Anthony had no intention of melting invisibly into his adopted country. Mediocrity was not for him. He had high ambitions for himself as well as his firstborn son. He wanted to stand tall; cut a figure; become a leading light in Britain, and as he moved up in society, what he needed was a residence in a locale which befitted his rising status. Clapton fitted the bill perfectly.

CHAPTER 5

'Claptonians'

Clapton was closer to London than Walthamstow; there were relatives of the Andrés already living there; and it had one of the best schools in England. Compelling as these reasons were for the move from Walthamstow, more so was that Clapton was *the* place to live. Its chic reputation went back at least sixty years. In his *A Tour through the whole Island of Great Britain* published in 1706, Daniel Defoe, the novelist, noted that Hackney 'is so remarkable for the retreat of wealthy citizens that there are at this time near an hundred coaches kept in it'.[1] One source claimed that the origin of the 'Hackney horse', and by extension the 'Hackney Cab', was because 'the village of Hackney being anciently celebrated for the numerous seats of the nobility and gentry, occasioned a mighty resort thither of persons of all conditions from the City of London, whereby so great a number of horses were daily hired in the City on that account'.

Such a heavy concentration of wealth, in turn, attracted its share of villains, and 'in the early part of the eighteenth century, Hackney was much infested by robbers, which rendered travelling after dark very insecure.' Highwaymen, including Dick Turpin, worked the route across Hackney Marshes, using lowlife public houses as their hideaways. Desperate times called for desperate measures, but 'it was not until January, 1756 that lamps were erected between Shoreditch and Hackney, and patrols, armed with guns and bayonets, placed on the road.'[2] Seemingly, that put paid to the problem, and, by 1767, one correspondent writing into the *Gazetteer and New Daily Advertiser* could compliment the 'parish of Hackney' on its 'several improvements of late, as witness the care they took in lighting and watching the streets'.[3]

Indeed, the roads through Clapton and Hackney were so much safer that, by the time the Andrés had moved there, the *Lloyd's Evening Post* could report how, come 2 June 1766, 'several eminent Taylors, Haberdashers etc began to set out for their Country Seats in Islington, Mile-End, Hackney, Hummerton, Clapton etc on the Saturday and return again on the Monday following', an exodus repeated each weekend through that year's 'Summer season'.[4]

The occasional 'footpad' still worked the area, as one 'Gentleman' found to his cost in early 1769 when, 'passing the field which leads from Stoke Newington Common to Clapton, [he] was attacked.'[5] But no fears of footpads intruded on young John's thoughts as, later that same year, he made his daily strolls from Clapton to the family 'compting house in Warnford court'. According to him, the journey back from the City at 'seven o'clock' on a late October evening was 'a sweet walk home', or, if a whimsical mood caught his fancy, 'a jog to Clapton upon my own stumps, musing as I homeward plod my way', his route illuminated only by the moon or, in his heightened imagination, by 'Signora Cynthia ... in clouded majesty' and 'silvered by her beams'.

In this same mood, young John could feel inspired to describe the beauty around him as he 'returned to town' the following morning. Of course, the weather helped, 'it has been the finest day imaginable. A solemn mildness was diffused throughout the blue horizon; its light was clear and distinct rather than dazzling; the serene beams of the autumnal sun.' Thus uplifted, he conjured an Arcadian scene in which 'gilded hills, variegated woods, glittering spires, ruminating herds, bounding flocks, all combined to enchant the eyes, expand the heart, and "chace all sorrow but despair."'[6]

Even allowing for young John's moody poetic licence, it is clear Clapton was still a rural haven. Yet, being so close to the City made the area especially appealing to City merchants, with the result that its population and that of Hackney parish as a whole increased substantially at this time.[7] Demand for desirable residences in the locality exceeded supply such that advertisements began appearing in London newspapers, one in 1767 saying: 'wanted at Hackney or the beginning of Clapton a convenient house in thorough repair fit for a large family'.[8]

Clearly, Clapton was the place to live. There, Anthony could rub shoulders with those grandees who would ease his rise through Britain's Establishment. Indeed, the village was teeming with residences owned by leading City merchants, including 'Jeremiah Pratt, gent of the South-Sea-House', 'Edmund Boddicott, accountant-general to the East India Company'[9] and 'Capt. Charles Beringer, who formerly acquired a large fortune in the East-Indies.'[10] Many of the residents were the Andrés' fellow Huguenots, including 'Peter Cazalet' and 'John Le Febure Esq'.[11]

By moving to Clapton, Anthony was not only making new business connections, but also cementing existing ones, such as with 'James Fremoux Esq' whose 'fortune' was upwards of 10,000*l*'[12] and Benjamin Mee. Both were Clapton residents and fellow directors with Anthony on the board of the 'Royal Exchange Assurance'.[13] In addition to leading merchants, major civic figures made Clapton their home, among whom were: 'William Nash, Alderman of Walbrook ward and one of the present Sheriffs of this city';[14] John Patereche, sheriff of Warwickshire;[15] 'George Ann Burchett ... clerk to the Admiralty near forty years'[16] and 'Mr Small, one of the Governors of Christ's Hospital'.[17]

These were the people to whom Anthony wanted to demonstrate the newfound affluence he had come by from his uncle's will. It was no coincidence, then, the timing of the family's move to Clapton. For all the many reasons behind the decision to relocate from Walthamstow, it would have been impossible for Anthony to undertake the move if there had not been this significant improvement in his fortunes. Very simply, property in Clapton did not come cheaply. When the Andrés were living in Walthamstow, their lease would have been not far off the 'yearly rent of 8l 8s'[18] advertised for a 'dwelling house' in that location in July 1766. By contrast, 'two substantial brick-built dwelling houses' put up for sale in 1766 and located next to the André family home at Beecholme House in Clapton, had tenants, one, 'Mr Isaac Mendez Da Costa', who was paying '50*l* per annum'; the other, Mrs Ridley, who was paying '48*l* per annum'.[19]

To ensure everyone knew he was now a successful, wealthy businessman, Anthony did what all the great and the good did at this time. He became a patron and benefactor, his largesse certain to be known in all the right circles. In 1766, a 'new History of England' was published. In the advertisement carried by the *Public Advertiser*, there was a short list of the subscribers, who financed the cost of the book. It read like a roll-call of European royalty beginning with 'Her Imperial Highness of all the Russias, His Danish Majesty, His Polish Majesty'. High on the list was the name 'Anthony André'.[20] That same year, Anthony was also on a 'List of Subscribers'[21] to a *Complete Dictionary of Arts and Sciences*.

Anthony's brothers were also making themselves visible. Not only was David on the list of subscribers to the 'new History', but he and John-Lewis were also active philanthropically, adding their names to 'A list of the Subscribers for the Relief of the Palatines' published in 1765. The task of 'the Committee' behind this initiative was 'relieving the poor Germans who were brought to London and there left destitute in the month of August 1764.'[22] Anthony had his own ideas about charity, judging that Clapton was where he could have the most impact. So, this was where he sounded his biggest charitable noise, when, in his will made in 1766, he left '50*l*, S[outh] S[ea] annuities', the 'interest' of '£2 10s'[23] to be given to the poor of Hackney. It seems Anthony computed every decision based on his ambition to rise within Britain's Establishment.

Still, the move to Clapton had not just been good for Anthony. It was so for the whole family. It was just the social milieu Anthony wanted his five children to mix in so that they, too, might make the same advantageous marriages as had come the way of the Girardots. Fifteen years after his naturalization, Anthony was still living in the shadow of the mighty Girardots, but at least Mary-Louisa had inherited well from her father, Paul Girardot, when he died in Paris in 1756.[24] What still wrankled, though, was the snub Anthony had endured when John Bristow brought 'Andrew Girardot jun', but not him, onto the board of the South Sea Company in 1760.[25]

Now, five years on, Anthony must watch as his Girardot brother-in-law continued effortlessly climbing the social ladder. Newspapers were regularly peppered with court and social circulars tracking London's fashionable 'Bon Ton' as it migrated from spa to spa around the country: in August 1765, it was the turn of Southampton when 'the Earl and Countess of Clanricarde and family' decamped there with, among others, 'Sir James Gray [and] Sir Thomas Hesketh'. Among those in train was 'Mr Girardot'.[26] A year on, it was Scarborough's turn, and this time both 'Mr and Mrs Girardot'[27] accompanied London's upper orders on their annual caravanserai.

Especially galling would have been to read in the newspapers how, despite the financial travails brought on by his Lisbon misadventures, Bristow could still make favourable marriages for one after another of his 'Girardot' offspring: two daughters 'married sons of the Earl of Buckinghamshire and Lord Lovat',[28] including Anne-Margaret whose marriage in 1761 to the 'Hon, Harry Hobart, youngest brother to the Earl of Buckinghamshire'[29] was a joint ceremony with her sister, Frances, whose husband-to-be was Richard Neave, a partner in 'Messrs Truman & Douglas, Merchants in Old Broad Street.'[30]

Anthony could not compete as yet. John and the other four children were still some years away from being at a marriageable age. Nevertheless, young John was already becoming an invaluable asset to his sisters. Handsome, articulate and gregarious, he expressed an easy sociability which drew others of his age—both young gentlemen and young ladies—to the André home, eager for the radiated warmth of a close-knit family. It was surely as fellow 'Claptonians'[31] that John first got to know the Ewer family. William, the father, was cousin to Lord Shaftesbury, director of the Bank of England[32] and, since 1765, a Member of Parliament.[33] The two Ewer boys became regular visitors to the André home such that Walter—'my friend Ewer'—became as if one of the family, John describing a scene in the drawing-room of 'five virgins writing round the same table, my three sisters, Mr Ewer and myself.'[34] Acknowledging the enduring strength of their childhood bond, John later named both Ewer brothers in his will, made in 1777. As well as making them beneficiaries each to the tune of 'One Hundred Pounds', John also 'desired that Walter Ewer Jr of Dyers Court, Aldermanbury, have the inspection of my Papers, Letters, Manuscripts.' Just how personal this stipulation was, John further clarified: 'I mean that he have the first Inspection of them, with Liberty to destroy or detain whatever he thinks proper'.[35]

Armed with all the social attributes that his schooling could provide, young John was almost ready to follow his father into the family 'compting-house'. It remained only for him to spend time in Switzerland, studying at the Academy of Geneva and renewing the family's connections with the wider 'Protestant International'. His education for business would then be complete. The academy's reputation had grown since Anthony was there in the 1730s, not least in Britain. By the 1740s, one local inhabitant was noting the strong 'influence of the English, who flocked to Geneva as an orderly non-Catholic centre of the Enlightenment'.[36] Indeed, the academy came second only to Leyden University as a continental destination for Britain's young gentlemen preparing for a career in politics.[37] Among these was Thomas Conolly, 'the richest commoner in Ireland',[38] who attended the academy in 1755.

If, additionally, Anthony wanted John to continue where he had left off at Dr Newcome's, then Geneva suited as one more rung on up Britain's social ladder. There, John would get to meet many young aristocrats passing through in search of the delights of Europe's courts, all under the guise of a cultural Grand Tour. For those Grand Tourists needing more robust academic cover to explain their extended stopover in Geneva during the 1760s, Rousseau and, later, Voltaire were on hand. Oracles of the Enlightenment, these luminaries were waiting nearby, ready to dispense words of wisdom to a steady flow of eager sibylline pilgrims, among which Edward Gibbon in 1757,[39] James Boswell in 1764–5,[40] and Adam Smith in 1765.[41]

It helped that, for John's time in Geneva, he would be going among family. Anthony had a brother, James, still living there, and a sister, Louise. Her husband, the Reverend Daniel de Rochement, was 'a faithful minister of the Holy Gospel' and could administer Calvinist piety to young John if needed. Conveniently, Peter de la Rive, John's cousin from Genoa, planned to study 'humaniores litteras'[42] at the academy and would be there at the same time. Anthony's mother, Mary, also lived in Geneva, though she was sinking fast and died in late 1767.[43]

Through these many relatives, John would get to meet other Huguenot families that had decided to hold out against Catholic France's earlier failed attempts to subdue Switzerland's much-cherished freedom of thought. Surely all that was past history. Little did Anthony expect, then, that his son would arrive in Geneva just as France was about to mount yet another assault on Switzerland's liberties. In retrospect, it was clear tensions had been building for a while but, in January 1766, events gathered pace, the *London Evening Post* reporting that, according to 'letters from Basel … great differences have arisen in Geneva concerning the famous Sieur Rousseau'.[44] This should have remained an internal matter, but the French king, who had his sights on Rousseau for his republicanism, decided to meddle and, in February, agreed with 'the Cantons of Zurich and Bern to be Mediators between the Senate and the people of Geneva'.[45] Prussia promptly intervened, making an offer of sanctuary to Rousseau. In July, a letter from Geneva warned of 'the most imminent danger' and that 'France is against us'.[46] By year's end, France was issuing an ultimatum in the form of 'Imperious Terms'.[47]

As if this were not reminder enough of the earlier persecution the Andrés had endured at the hands of Catholic France, 'Genevan Bankers and Houses of Commerce' operating in Paris and 'in other cities of the kingdom' were told in January 1767 that they had nothing to fear from 'what passes at Geneva,'[48] this despite France imposing sanctions and that 'French troops were quartered along the Lake of Geneva'.[49]

London newspapers began printing letters from Geneva sent in by their readers. On 8 January, the *London Evening Post* reported how 'we hear from Geneva … that everything there wears a very gloomy aspect'.[50] On 15 January, the same newspaper had a letter to hand reporting that Geneva was arming itself. By mid-February, 'letters from Geneva' passed to the *Public Advertiser* were reporting that 'upwards of one hundred of the principal Families there, are preparing to retire to the island of Corsica'.[51]

The moment Anthony heard this news he would, surely, have instructed John to return home immediately. In any event, he urgently needed his son by his side. He was about to put into action his plan to conquer Britain's Establishment, and it would be all hands on deck. A desk in the 'compting house' at 'Warnford court' awaited John as he began his apprenticeship for a career as a 'quill-driver' working in 'the midst of books, papers, bills and other implements of gain.'[52]

CHAPTER 6

'Change Alley

Returning from Geneva in 1767 and joining the family's 'compting house'[1] firm of 'Messrs André',[2] John found himself working, not on Bishopsgate Street but in 'Warnford court'[3] on 'Throgmorton Street.'[4] All part of his father's desire to signal a step up in the world, the firm had moved premises while John was in Geneva. The previous location on Bishopsgate Street had put the firm on a main thoroughfare, which was 'large, long and spacious and generally well inhabited'. However, the Andrés' neighbours were an almshouse, meeting-house, 'Gresham College' and 'divers great Inns'.

The new premises were altogether more exclusive. A *History and Survey of London* from 1756 described how Throgmorton Street 'is very well built and inhabited; the chief Place here is the House and Gardens belonging to the Drapers Company. In this street there are these Courts',[5] nine in all,[6] each varying in quality and size: 'Red-lion court' was 'both small and ordinary', and 'St Bartholomew's court' was 'but mean'; 'Angel-court', at the upscale end and where the Andrés' early patrons, the Bosanquets, had their premises, was 'very large and handsome with good Buildings, the habitation of Merchants and People of Repute'. One notch down from 'Angel-court' was 'Warnfordcourt', where the Andrés had their 'compting house'. Described as 'a good, large Place, very well built and Inhabited',[7] the neighbours were very different from those on Bishopsgate Street, and included no fewer than five Huguenot merchant houses.[8]

For John, the move to new premises made little difference to how he felt about the family's business. Try as he might, he found it hard to 'look upon [his] future profession with partiality.' As he later owned, he had no 'wish for wealth' and dreaded the thought of looking back in his old age and seeing 'John André by a small coal fire in a gloomy compting house in Warnford court, nothing so little as what he has been making himself and in all probability never to be much more than he is at present.' For him, the only saving grace to 'all the mercantile glories' he would be working towards was so he may 'see Orphans and Widows, and Painters, Fidlers and Poets and Builders protected and encourag'd'.[9]

Study of John André in the gloomy compting house. (By Christa Hook)

For his father, however, the move was about projecting status as he sought to position the family for the final assault he had planned on Britain's financial Establishment. As a director of the Royal Exchange Assurance, Anthony was part of Britain's hallowed 'monied Interest', but still on its fringes. That was no longer enough. Ever ambitious, Anthony had set his sights on the biggest prize—the East India Company. To capture that, he needed to become a power broker in the one commodity he knew would be in short supply as Britain sought to capitalize on its stunning victories during the Seven Years' War: money.

To the victor the spoils had been the cry echoing round London in the euphoric days following peace in 1763. By the Treaty of Paris, France and Spain were forced to cede vast chunks of the world. Victorious Britain acquired Canada's 'few acres of snow',[10] Grenada and Dominica's sugar plantations, Florida's swamps and Moghul India's mighty Bengal. Everywhere Anthony looked there was land-fever, British carpetbaggers rushing in behind swords and sabres to get their hands on abandoned, confiscated and distress-sale estates in all these 'ceded territories'.

Anthony had to be in on this Klondike, but, cannily, he saw that the real profits to be made and the real influence to be had were as bankers to Britain's new empire. And good as the Huguenots were as 'Mercuries reclin'd on bales of Goods' garnering their 'mercantile glories', they were even better as magicians conjuring tricks with the new-fangled paper money taking London by storm. 'Genii playing with pens, ink and paper'[11]—as John imagined these money alchemists—they could conjure 'wealth' and 'opulence' from nowhere, all while seated at a desk in their 'compting house'.

Take Anthony Chamier, his career truly eye-catching. A successful merchant, he had mutated himself into a ''Change Alley'[12] wheeler-dealer. Using his accumulated wealth, he made himself indispensable as a government financier and advisor during the Seven Years' War,[13] able, in 1763, to remind the incoming 'Prime Minister', Lord Bute, of his power and influence as a major subscriber to government loans, having 'never paid in less than One Hundred and Fifty Thousand pounds every year during the course of the late war'.[14] Chamier had, by the end of the war, 'acquired such a fortune, as enabled him, though young, to quit business'.[15] This 'fortune' and the power it leveraged brought Chamier a career in Britain's heady post-war political firmament. Already private secretary to the Earl of Sandwich in the Foreign Office during the war, in 1764 he became secretary to Lord Barrington in the War Office before entering Parliament in 1778.

Stellar as was Chamier's rise, the most direct influence on the Andrés' decision to enter the business of banking was, surely, the arrival, in 1760, of another Huguenot, Peter Thellusson, from Geneva's Protestant International. Sent by his brother to set up a branch of the family bank, 'his most important client was the Paris firm, Thellusson and Necker.'[16] The André and Necker families were entwined through Isabella, one of Anthony's sisters, who was married to Louis Necker.[17] The family connection was so close that, in the early 1770s, 'Thellusson and Necker' changed its name to 'Germany, Girardot et Cie'.

Eager to follow in these footsteps, the house of 'Messrs André'[18] opened its doors as 'compting-house' Mercuries in 1764. The beginnings were not auspicious: the early clients and the amounts and purpose of the loans to them were a far cry from the prestigious government stock syndications that Chamier had arranged. One of the earliest loans was to the 'Honourable Topham Beauclerk Esq', a society rake whose two claims to fame were that he was the illegitimate great-grandson of 'Charles II by the beautiful and fascinating actress Mistress Nelly Gwynne'[19] and that, by virtue of this parentage, he could become a founder member of Dr Johnson's famous 'Literary Club'.

This pedigree was hardly the stuff of empire. Nor, at £5,000,[20] was the amount of the loan, nor, indeed, that it was advanced to cover debts incurred by Beauclerk following extravagancies on his Grand Tour.[21] This 'dissipated idler who died a melancholy wreck at the age of forty'[22] was an unusual person for the Andrés to have on their 'compting-house' books. Very likely, the 'debt was sold on to them',[23] which was often how banking houses built up their lending books when starting out. This was certainly how Anthony came to his next speculative venture, becoming one of the 'Proprietors' of what were known as 'Canada bills'.[24]

Among the many fast money schemes doing the rounds of London's City at this time, 'Canada bills' were the inevitable financial fallout inherited by Britain when, following defeat in 1759, 'France had left in the colony over eight million dollars of inflated paper money'.[25] Facing ruin, local French-Canadian merchants and farmers who held these worthless 'Canada bills' petitioned General Murray, the British military governor, seeking relief. As part of the pacification and appeasement of these new subjects, the British government agreed to negotiate for France to honour this 'inflated paper money'. Negotiations rumbled on beyond the Treaty of Paris, until, in 1766, 'a Convention' was 'made' whereby France agreed to 'liquidating the Canada Bills'.[26]

Following this, a 'Letter of Thanks' appeared in British newspapers congratulating the government for negotiating 'the final settlement of the Canada Bills'. The letter was signed by fifteen members of a 'Committee' for 'Proprietors of Canada Bills,'[27] formed to put pressure on the British government. Among the names on the list was Anthony André. This might suggest that the Andrés had been trading into French Canada and, like the local merchants, were caught with money still owing to them when Britain overran the French possession. If this were the case, the André name would surely have appeared on the many lists of petitioners[28] who lobbied the British military governor following the colony's occupation in 1759. However, the André name does not feature on these lists. Nor is there is any record that the Andrés traded into French Canada. More likely, then, was that, as with the Beauclerk loan, 'the debt was sold on', in this instance by one of the many distressed French-Canadian merchants, and bought up cheaply by a syndicate, including the Andrés. Supporting this is the presence of other London Huguenots on the list of fifteen signatories, including Henry Guinand and one of the Bosanquets, which might explain how Anthony came to be involved in the first place.

By August 1764, the total of 'Canada bills' accumulated by 'English subjects … is said to amount to four hundred thousand pounds sterling'.[29] Previously, the British military governor had tried to outlaw this profiteering, passing a 'Proclamation'[30] in 1759 expressly prohibiting the activity. However, by the time the convention was signed in 1766, the status of these speculators had been legitimized when they were formally recognized as 'actual proprietors who are not original proprietors having been intermediate purchasers.'[31] The Andrés could collect their profits.

When exactly the Andrés bought their share of these 'Canada bills' is lost to history, but very likely it was during 1765 or, maybe, as late as the early months of 1766. Either way, they stood to make a substantial profit over a short period. By then, a lively trade had built up in these 'Bills', as European bourses got wind of progress in the negotiations between France and Britain. In January 1765, the 'Bills' could be bought 'at public auction in the City for twelve and a half per cent.' By January 1766, 'Canada Bills had risen at Paris to thirty-five per cent'.[32] When, four months later, the final 'Convention' was signed, the 'first article ... for liquidating the Canada Bills' generously stipulated that 'the reduction of the said Paper' would be on 'the footing of fifty per cent for Bills of Exchange.'[33] The speculators had made fifteen per cent plus in next to no time. No wonder the effusiveness of the 'Letter of Thanks'!

Young John was still in Geneva when the profits from Anthony's speculation in Canada bills were realized, but he would be back home and working as a 'quill-driver' at the firm for its next venture, this time in Grenada. One of the so-called 'Ceded Islands' retained by Britain at the Treaty of Paris, Grenada quickly became a target for all the 'Mercuries' and 'Genii' scenting speculation and profit when, to pay off its accumulated war debts, the government auctioned property on the island, to include, controversially, estates confiscated from French planters who refused to swear allegiance to the British crown. The planters were given a grace period of eighteen months to decide, but many voted with their feet, selling out immediately. This gifted British carpetbaggers—mainly Scots and Huguenots—a sumptuous harvest of cheap plantations to choose from.

A new arrival to Grenada wrote in July 1765 describing the feeding-frenzy which descended on the island. First came a description of the rich pickings on offer: 'this island is certainly capable of very great improvement and its soil is allowed to be the richest in the West Indies.' Next came the vultures, and 'you'll scarce find an officer, of a Captain's rank, that has not purchased an estate.'[34] Flipping these estates for a quick profit became big business: 'three considerable sugar plantations' bought cheaply were put up for sale in December 1766 with the puff that 'the purchaser may be assured of making very great interest of his money'.[35] Typical of these early speculators was John Harvey who bought a sugar estate from the French owners, 'Lataste and Jeyfons',[36] in 1764 and quickly sold it on to George Amyand, one of the most active buyers of estates in the island. Amyand was not the only Huguenot to descend on Grenada. Among others were two 'Protestant International' families which the Andrés knew from Geneva: the Bosanquets[37] and Thellussons. Their interest was, like the Andrés, as bankers rather than owners, wisely so it seems, since 'West Indian plantation ownership was often seen as problematic by merchants in England.'[38]

The Andrés were one of the earliest of the Huguenot bankers to come into Grenada, lending to the Fournilliers, a French settler family who had owned the Bacolet estate for some years. The Fournilliers were Huguenots, which might explain why they decided to remain in Grenada after it was captured by the British. As early as 1763 the Andrés became London agents for the Fournilliers.[39] The relationship developed from there and, in 1767, the Andrés made a loan to 'Peter and Marie Fournillier'[40] secured by a mortgage. Again in 1769, they acted as London agents to the Fournilliers.[41] In 1772, however, the Thellussons replaced the Andrés as lenders to the Fournilliers.[42]

While working at Warnford Court, young John became directly involved in the Andrés' banking business in Grenada. Their most important account was with the firm of 'Campbell and Aitcheson Company',[43] one of the first of the Scottish settlers to acquire land in Grenada, when they bought the Tivoli estate in 1763. The Andrés made a loan to Tivoli in 1767. John clearly knew 'poor Aitchison and Campbell' personally and was 'afraid' for them five years on should they become victims of the financial 'storm' that, by then, 'has fallen on the Scotch houses'. John was also concerned 'if the Grenadians were subject to being Creditors'.[44]

This was in 1772, and, by then, the Andrés were no longer involved at Tivoli, their loan having been taken over 'by reconveyance'[45] earlier that year by 'Hope and Co',[46] a Scottish bank, based in Amsterdam.[47] Meantime, the Andrés' agency activities in the island had also fallen away, as a result of which their merchant-financing of various commercial counterparties was also taken over by the Thellussons.[48]

Bit by bit, the Andrés had surrendered their business interests in Grenada. This retrenchment had nothing to do with their fortunes there, and everything to do with Anthony's next speculative venture, this one having, by 1772, gone horribly wrong.

CHAPTER 7

'The Great Scheme'

The Andrés first became actively involved in the East India Company in September 1766 when David André appeared as one of thirteen 'Proprietors of East India Stock' behind a petition published in the *Gazetteer and New Daily Advertiser*. To those not following the company's fortunes, the purpose of the petition would have seemed anodyne: a request that the 'Court of Directors' change the venue for September's 'Quarterly General Court of Proprietors' from the 'Sale Room at India House', being as this was 'too small for that purpose', to 'some other capacious space'. The reason given was that attendance would be 'very numerous'.[1]

Behind this request, however, lurked a simmering battle so toxic it would eventually cost the company its independence. This battle and the proprietors' sudden interest in the company's activities can be traced back to August 1765 and the successful negotiations by Robert Clive, 'President at Bengal', for the company to assume tax-gathering powers (the so-called 'diwani') for three Indian states. That September, Clive wrote from India informing the Court of Directors in London that this would bring in annually a 'clear gain to the Company of £1,650.000 sterling'[2] (= PV £263.4m). His letter travelled slowly, and when news of the bonanza was finally made public at the September 1766 Quarterly General Court, it 'turned East India stock … into a gambling venture'.[3]

Long before the announcement, however, secret speculation in the stock was already underway. Clive was behind these shenanigans. Before writing to the Court of Directors, he had 'instructed one of his attorneys, John Walsh, to purchase as much India stock as possible'.[4] These secret instructions reached London ahead of Clive's official notice to the Court of Directors. Clive also let a close circle of thirteen 'Knowing-ones'[5] in on the imminent gold-rush.[6] Between them, Clive and these 'friends' began buying in April 1766. The price at that point was '165 1/4.'[7]

The Andrés were not among these 'Knowing-ones', but they would soon twig what was going on because, in the instructions, Clive told Walsh to buy using not only 'whatever money I may have in the public funds or anywhere else' but also 'as much money as can be borrowed in my name'.[8] Dazzled by 'the general buzz'[9] of speculation which Clive foretold, Walsh went wild and, as a result, the vast majority of the bubble fund was borrowed. It was a question of time before the Andrés got wind, which happened when Walsh approached, among others, 'several insurance offices'[10] for a loan. One of these was the Royal Exchange Assurance, which Anthony was on the board of. The request for a loan was declined, but the cat was out of the bag. Now Anthony could, finally, move in on the East India Company.

The timing could not be better from Anthony's point of view. He was riding high. His gamble on 'Canada bills' was just coming good, as were his forays into Grenada. It seemed everything he touched turned to gold. It was no coincidence, then, that Anthony made a will at this precise moment. This was not the act of someone facing his mortality, rather the scion of the André dynasty, in his own mind, reaching the peak of his power and potential and taking stock of all he owned, had achieved and had planned.

It was also a statement of how he saw himself as head of his branch of the Andrés. In the will 'dated 29 March 1766', he 'bequeathed to his wife all the residue of his estate, including the life-rents on the heads of his children in both London and Paris.' Mary-Louisa was his partner in the family's business interest. He also 'directed that £25,000 [= PV £3.99 million] should be placed in the public funds to be divided equally among their five children as they attained their respective majorities'.[11] This was curious: the indications so far—especially with the care taken over his education—were that John, the firstborn, should be the favoured child. Yet, here he was being treated as an equal. Still, this was the Protestant ethic. Each child must prove itself in its own way: the two sons following their father into the business; the three daughters receiving dowries large enough to make good marriages.

It was in this mood of euphoria mixed with self-satisfaction that Anthony decided the time was right for the family to involve itself in the affairs of the East India Company. The first step was to acquire a sizeable block of stock in the company. Anthony had to strike quickly: already 'by 27 May 1766, Clive owned a total of £74,500 India stock at a market value of £129,630'.[12] When exactly the Andrés made their move is unclear, but sometime between April and September 1766, they became significant owners of India stock, enough certainly that David, Anthony's brother, could feel emboldened to sign the petition to the Court of Directors on 18 September. It is significant that David, not Anthony, became the owner of record and made the running when the petition was lodged ahead of the September 1766 Quarterly General Court. It was clearly important to keep Anthony's name out of the public eye to avoid the imputation that he had acted on privileged knowledge come by in his position as a director of the Royal Exchange Assurance.

The purchase of India stock was intended as more than a financial investment. It was to give the family power ... a significant say in the company's future at this important juncture. This was possible because of the company's byzantine constitution which gave each proprietor owning £500 or more of stock just one vote. Big proprietors had lived with this distortion while the company was a 'sober security'. However, as the company's fortunes improved following the successes of the Seven Years' War, big proprietors sought to leverage their influence by splitting their holdings into £500 blocks and temporarily transferring them to third parties who agreed to vote according to their instructions. The splitting manoeuvres that ensued pitted rival proprietors against each other.

Among these big proprietors were Clive and 'his Knowing-ones'.[13] They should have been content to sit back and enjoy their profits, watching as the price of their India stock rose. However, they had the bit between the teeth, and greed fed on greed. Next only to 1720's South Sea Bubble, the financial shenanigan of the century was about to play out. It had all the makings of a Drury Lane drama. In an 'Act One', Robert Orme, one of the 'Knowing-ones', made the early running, his 'little scheme' being to use blocks of split stock to outvote the directors and force through an increase in the company's dividend from 6% to 8%. The objective was to ramp up the share price. The increase was rejected at the June General Court, but not before the market scented blood. By 12 July, the price was up at '194 ½'[14] and climbing.

'Act Two' saw Orme's 'little scheme' mutate into what he called 'the Great Scheme',[15] an ambitious plan he had to force through a dividend increase to, not 8%, rather 12½% and thereby engineer a further stratospheric rise in the company's stock price. Enter the 'Change-Alley Broker' and 'jobbing-brokers' ready to manipulate the market. To benefit from 'the Great Scheme', a consortium of like-minded speculators would 'in the first instance ... purchase, chiefly in Amsterdam, £30,000 East India stock'.[16] Given that over ninety-five percent[17] of India stock holdings were below £5,000, this level was considered sufficient to kick-start the 'Great Scheme', but larger amounts would be deployed should the speculation achieve lift-off.

'Act Three' saw the Great Scheme swing into action. Enter stage left Lauchlin Macleane, Undersecretary of State to Lord Shelburne, adventurer extraordinaire and 'rogue and trickster of the highest order'.[18] Enter stage right, Lord Verney, aristocrat, playboy, gambler and first-class dupe of the Burkes, William and his cousin, Edmund. Enter downstage, Isaac Panchaud, serial bankrupt, budding financial wizard, and current money manipulator par excellence, a Huguenot refugee, late of Geneva, now of London, Paris, Amsterdam and all points on the compass where paper money rotated fast and loose. A more motley collection of fellow travellers could not have come together, except that, as the greed grew, so others joined the feeding frenzy. And just like Clive and his 'Knowing-Ones', all these Great Schemers needed to borrow, borrow and borrow again. Anthony had called it right.

'Act Four'. Enter the 'Monied man',[19] banking 'Mercuries' and 'Genii', all ready to lend, lend and lend again. Step forward 'the prominent firm of dealers, Anthony and John Lewis André,'[20] armed with a battle-plan: Anthony's immediate objective, to join Clive's 'Knowing-Ones'; his ultimate goal to bend the company to his will; his weapon, money. He planned his assault meticulously. His first step was to have the Andrés noticed by Clive. Buying India stock was the start. That way, when Clive's 'friends', William Johnstone and John Motteux,[21] put together their petition to the company in September 1766, they made sure David André was on the list of petitioners.

The next step was to approach Clive with an offer of help. Again, David stepped forward: in early 1768, he wrote to Clive asking for his 'legal opinion on the legality of negotiation of Bills of Exchange with the French East India Company'.[22] David was flying a kite, knowing that what he was hinting at was sure to be of personal interest to Clive and his 'Bengal Squad'[23] of returning nabobs. These 'servants' of the British East India Company—with Clive the wealthiest of them all—had a perennial problem remitting home their vast riches accumulated in India and were dependent on money dealers ready to discount their bills of exchange and release cash to them in London. However, the company outlawed the practice. Enter the Andrés, who, as David signalled obliquely, had a 'legal' solution, having already acted for servants of the French East India Company with similar problems.

The message was not lost on Clive: the Andrés were duly invited to assist in financing the company's much-coveted trade in diamonds. When this began is unclear, but certainly by 1770 the firm of 'Anthony and John Lewis André' was routinely appearing in the Company's books holding 'bills of exchange' drawn by various of the company's merchants. Among these, the most prestigious was 'Vansittart, Darell and Holland'. George 'Vansittart' was a 'junior merchant' with the company in Bengal and brother to Henry, a previous, and soon to be reappointed, governor of Bengal. Lionel 'Darell' was the son of the Andrés' partner in Portugal. He had married the daughter of Timothy Tullie, a director of the East India Company, in 1766 and, having 'applied to the Company for a post in India', in 1767 'was appointed ... with the rank of senior merchant.'[24]

The specific company trade financed by the Andrés was 'the produce of coral imported per sundry ships'.[25] Coral was an important component to west–east trade at that time, being as 'certain commodities—especially silver and coral—were sent out in order to purchase diamonds'.[26] The Andrés' success breaking into this trade was reinforced when the partnership of 'Hananel Mendes da Costa, John Lewis André and Nathaniel Thomas'[27] also began discounting bills of exchange issued by 'Vansittart, Darell and Holland'. The Mendes da Costa family were Jewish merchants important to the international diamond trade.[28] Once again, the commodity being financed by these 'bills' was 'the produce of coral'.[29]

It was doubtless these 'mercantile glories' John was referring to when, returning from Geneva in 1767 and joining the family compting house, he conjured in his imagination 'gorgeous vessels "Launch'd on the bosom of the silver Thames" [which] are wafting to distant lands the produce of this commercial nation.' Was it this ancient and noble trade in coral and diamonds which, two years later, inspired him to think that 'instead of figuring a merchant as a middle aged man with a bob wig, a rough beard and snuff coloured clothes, grasping a guinea in his red hand', he could imagine a 'comely young man with a tolerable pig-tail wielding a pen with all the noble fierceness of the Duke of Marlborough, brandishing a truncheon upon a sign post, surrounded with types and emblems and canopied with cornucopias that disembogue their stores upon his heads'?[30]

If so, John was deluding himself. His father, as John would soon discover, had other, wilder, murkier ambitions for the family 'compting house'. Securing a position in the East India Company's coral and diamond trade was valuable business for the Andrés, but, for Anthony, it was still only a stepping stone. The breakthrough Anthony was looking for came in 1768 when Macleane became the driving-force behind the next wave of 'East India Gamblers'[31] and went looking for new sources of finance to ratchet up the Great Scheme. How the Andrés came to Macleane's notice is unclear. By then, Clive's influence was on the wane, he having sold down his India stock holdings.[32] Macleane had decided meantime to jump ship in the 'splitting' battle for control of the Court of Directors, abandoning Clive and siding instead with his arch-rival Laurence Sulivan.

Into this febrile atmosphere stepped the Andrés. Macleane may well have come across them in Grenada, where, along with his partner, John Stuart, he had interests in sugar plantations.[33] More likely they were introduced by Richard Bosanquet who became a director of the East India Company in 1768, joining the Sulivan interest.[34] However the tributaries of influence converged, it is no coincidence that, in February 1768, the Andrés were invited to take over a loan originally provided by the firm of 'Sir Joshua Vanneck & Co' to two of Macleane's Great Schemers, Lord Verney and William Burke. Security for both the Vanneck and André loans was the same: '£20,000'[35] (= PV £3.2 million) of the £30,000 stock acquired as an initial scheme fund. Macleane had 'his new agent, the broker, Elias de la Fontaine'[36] mastermind the arrangements for the André loan.

The door to the hallowed sanctum that was 'India House' on London's Leadenhall Street was ajar. Soon, the Andrés flooded through, doing business with anyone prepared to join the Great Scheme and vote the Sulivan interest. Among these was Alexander Crauford. He had stood in April 1767 for election as a director of the company but was unsuccessful. He was already a proprietor of India stock at that point and 'by September 1768' was 'possessed of £3000 of capital East-India stock'. However, he needed to increase his holdings to have any chance of securing successful election next time.

'Being desirous of possessing £14,000 more of the same stock but not having money enough for that purpose', Crauford applied to 'Elias Benjamin de la Fontaine and William Brymer, brokers [to] procure him as much money as would purchase £11,000 capital of that stock, to make up the said £14,000 stock.' With the share price standing at '£276', this made the loan he needed to raise the 'amount of £30,800' (= PV £4.9 million), which was what the Andrés lent him 'on 11th of

October 1768'. Although this loan—as with the one to Verney and Burke—was arranged through 'Elias Benjamin de la Fontaine and William Brymer, brokers'[37] and marked for Crauford's account, the Andrés would almost certainly have known him personally. Crauford was a London merchant married to the daughter of Charles Crokatt, one of the petitioners with whom the Andrés had collaborated on the 'Canada Bills' venture.[38]

In addition to lending to those prepared to vote the Sulivan interest, the Andrés also increased their own holdings in India stock. The transactions associated with these holdings passed through various stockjobbers, including John Hobson, who held an account for 'A and J L A' at De la Fontaine and Brymer, the coded acronym being the custom of the time for disguising client identity but evidently referring to 'Anthony and John Lewis André'.[39] By October 1768, the Andrés owned '19,000*l* capital stock',[40] which at the prevailing market price of 274 was worth £52,060 (= PV £8.3 million). This was the amount they sold on 11 October, but was doubtless only a fraction of their India stock holdings.

As 1768 turned into 1769, all the pieces were in place. Anthony could surely congratulate himself that his grand plan to gate-crash Britain's mighty East India Company was finally paying off: he had broken into the company's coveted trade in diamonds and, to protect that lucrative business long term, now had his partner's son, Lionel Darell, embedded within the company in Bengal; the Andrés were now an integral, if not crucial, part of the Great Scheme, the upshot of which was that their man, Sulivan, was all set—with one final push over the line—to return to the helm of the East India Company; and—as if that were not enough—political associates like Macleane, Verney, Crauford, and Edmund Burke were all clamouring to borrow from the Andrés which put Anthony, surely, only one short step away from Parliament and the epicentre of the British Establishment. Meantime, he had made some £20,000 (= PV £3.2 million) trading in and out of India stock over the past couple of years. With all these achievements, it seemed somehow rather unimportant that Anthony had also been re-elected for a further three-year term on the board of the Royal Exchange Assurance.[41]

For young John, hurrying back from the turmoil of Geneva in early 1767 and thrust headlong into the frenzy of the family's 'compting house' in Warnford Court during this dizzying annus mirabilis of 1768, his father's financial and political wizardry must have been a source of awe and amazement. Sitting at his junior merchant's bench and checking the daily quotes for India stock as it broke towards £300, he could only imagine an uninterrupted future of wealth and social distinction. It all seemed so perfect. What could possibly go wrong?

CHAPTER 8

'Lame Ducks'

Three reports would have caught Anthony's attention as he scanned the London newspapers on 4 April 1769:

The *St. James's Chronicle* announced the results of the 'Ballot' for 'the Choice of Directors of the India Company for the Year ensuing'. After a five-year absence, his man, 'Laurence Sulivan', had been re-elected to the Court of Directors with '859' votes.

The *St. James's Chronicle* also recorded, in its section headed 'Prices of Stock this Day at 1 o'clock,' that 'India Stock' was trading at '276 1 half'.[1] The company's shares were back trading at their all-time high.

The *Public Advertiser* reported 'from Paris that the French East India Company are now negociating for the Sale of their Charter and Trade with several Bankers etc, among whom are named Foley, Panchaud & Co.'[2] The troubled French company was finally going to be bailed out.

Anthony already knew all this—he had so many of his own sources of market intelligence. In his line of business it was essential to know what was happening, preferably before it happened, but certainly before anyone else knew about it. That was why he had prospered for so long. Still, it was good to read what he already knew in the newspapers. He heaved a sigh of relief mixed, of course, with some self-satisfaction. Everything was going to be just fine.

Anthony's relief and self-satisfaction were short lived. Within days, it became apparent that 'Foley, Panchaud & Co' could not bail out the French company. This set the Paris rumour machine running again. On 6 April, some 'eclaircissements' were issued by the French government 'to prevent the proprietors of India stock from being alarmed'. These promised that 'debts of the French East-India Company will be punctually paid.'[3] Too late: 'the bankruptcy of the French East-India Company'[4] became a foregone conclusion when, by 'Letters from Versailles, dated April 8, it was announced that "The King has issued an Arret of his Council of State, authorizing the Directors of the [French] East India Company to form a lottery of 11,100,000 Livres in order to enable that Company to fulfil its Engagements."'[5]

For those reasoning on the time-honoured adage that France's loss was Britain's gain, this debacle could only be good news. The *Whitehall Evening Post* even claimed that the French company's demise was the work of the English company: 'We hear that the support the French East India Company had from money advanced by English gentlemen in India, in order to its being remitted home, having been greatly diminished, partly by there being less money wanted to be remitted, partly by the measures taken by our Company, has been the principal occasion of bringing their affairs to a crisis at this period.'[6]

What the *Whitehall Evening Post* did not understand was the interlocking nature of international finance and that what happened in Paris could affect London. This was what transpired, as the *St. James's Chronicle* explained in its account, on 8 April, about 'a Military Man in the East Indies [who] has lost 75000*l* by the bankruptcy of the French East-India Company.' What made the story so compelling to readers was that the 'Military Man' was British. The mistake he had made was that 'the above sum he had remitted over to a Friend here' was sent via 'the French East-India Company'.

That, however, was as far as the report went to explain how the 'Military Man' lost 'the above sum', preferring instead to take delight in his inability to 'spend the Remainder of his Days in his native Land'[7] enjoying the fruits of his '75000*l*' Indian gains. What the *St. James's Chronicle* failed to grasp was how this 'Military Man' planned to receive his '75000*l*'. Previously, he, like all the returning nabobs of Clive's 'Bengal Squad', would have issued bills of exchange in India payable by the British company in London ninety days hence to the value of '75,000*l*'. What the newspaper did not explain was that these bills would have first been discounted with money dealers operating either in India or London. The 'Military Man' would have received his '75,000*l*' on day one, less the usual discount fee.

The British company having recently outlawed this practice, the 'Military Man' had resort to the French company instead, this despite 'the measures taken by our Company.' This meant that money dealers in Paris and London were still discounting bills issued by British nabobs, including this military man, but through the French rather than the British company. When, therefore, the French company went bankrupt, the money dealers—not the 'Military Man'—lost '75,000*l*' (= PV £12 million).

From the correspondence in 1768 between David André and Clive 'on the legality of negotiation of Bills of Exchange with the French East India Company', it is clear the Andrés were already involved in this activity or were contemplating it. Either way, it is probable that the Andrés were among the many London bankers holding this Military Man's bills and, if not his, other nabobs' bills. If so, they stood to lose heavily which would explain why, only days before, 'several Bankers etc, among whom are named Foley, Panchaud & Co' had tried to bail out the French company.

As bad as this was, worse news lay lurking in the 15 April edition of the *St. James's Chronicle*, which announced 'that the Report of great Armaments going from France to the East Indies is without any Foundation.' At that point, 'India Stock' was still trading at '274 1–4th',[8] just a tad down on its all-time high of ten days earlier. Anthony was not fooled. This 'Report' had been dismissed as 'without any Foundation', but he knew better. His sources were telling him what only became public knowledge on 25 May 1769 when reports finally appeared in London giving 'disagreeable news received from the East Indies by some ships just now arrived'.[9]

For many of the 'Unwary', this news came out of the blue. Whereas the previous inward-bound fleet which had departed Bengal on 'the 13th of October' brought positive news on 2 May that 'operations … have been successfully conducted against Hyder Ally', these latest 'Ships left the Indies at a time when the Company's affairs bore a very unfavourable Aspect.' The cause of this sudden reversal was that 'the Marattas were in arms'.[10] The *London Chronicle* went into more detail reporting 'that the Marattas … were ready to come to an engagement with the English Army'.[11] More disturbing still was that 'they are supposed to have been spirited up by the French, who, it is well known, have been privately sending over Forces to that part of the Globe, for some time Past.' Unsurprisingly, the effects on the market were crushing. The 'News affected India Stock near 20 per Cent: that Stock being done last Thursday at 267; whereas this Day it has been down as low as 248.' Gloom now overhung the market with dire predictions 'by many that it may fall 40 or 50 per Cent lower'.[12] These proved self-fulfilling, and, by 27 October, India stock was down at '214 ½'.[13]

So, Anthony was right to doubt 'the Report' in April that 'great Armaments going from France to the East Indies' was 'without any Foundation.' But what could he do back then? He could sell the family's remaining holdings of India stock, which he doubtless did, but the Andrés' main exposure was on the loans to the Great Schemers, and, in the case of Verney and Burke, Anthony could do nothing until February 1770 when these loans matured. Already 'cautious' in February 1769 when the one-year loan made to them in February 1768 came up for renewal, Anthony had stood firm as the borrowers 'pressed for better terms'. He reduced the amount of the loan but only from £42,000 (= PV £6.7 million) to £39,100. He also 'added a new proviso. A further £1,000 stock should be deposited with them if the price of stock fell to 240'. Still, he had to accept a proportionately smaller amount of India stock as collateral (£17,000 instead of £20,000). Anthony was nervous, but not overly so.

Verney and Burke accepted these terms, but this only delayed the inevitable once the price of India stock started to tumble in May. Typical of gamblers desperate for one more throw of the dice, they anted up the extra £1,000 stock when the price went below 240 in June, but defaulted when the price continued to fall, doing so at the next margin call in July. As for the Andrés, they were powerless, borrower and lender locked in an umbilical death spiral as the price of India stock continued to plunge.

Crunch time for the Great Schemers and all the other dealers, brokers, stockjobbers and bankers, who, along with the Andrés, had bankrolled them, came in the lead up to settlement day on 18 July. 'Panic set in',[14] newspapers vying for an 'account of the lame ducks [defaulters] expected to limp out of Change Alley next week.'[15] The *London Chronicle* counted 'six Lame Ducks,'[16] but the *St. James's Chronicle* finally settled on a figure of 'nine Ducks ... crippled within these eight days, and some of them very considerably; the Price to one only amounting to 80,000*l*'.[17] Among these was the Andrés' broker, De la Fontaine and Brymer, which compounded the family's problems.

As for the Andrés' loan of £30,800 to Alexander Crauford, he was made of sterner stuff than Verney, Burke and the other 'Asiatic plunderers of Leadenhall-street'.[18] When, 'about the 27th of May 1769, the price fell to £240 percent ... John Lewis André made a demand ... for £10 percent', and Crauford 'accordingly on 1st June following transferred to ... John Lewis André £500 capital East India Stock'. However, unlike Verney and Burke, Crauford paid over a further 'deposit of £10 percent' when 'on the 17th of July 1769, the price of East India Stock [fell] to £230 percent',[19] and the Andrés made a second margin call. The monies loaned to Crauford were safe for the present. Not so the loan to Verney and Burke, and, as the 'Lame Ducks' limped out of 'Change Alley, the Andrés found themselves queuing at the courtroom door with all the other creditors desperate to recover what they had lent Verney, Burke and all the other Great Schemers.

To what extent Anthony foresaw these events in early April when he first got wind of the problems in Paris and India is difficult to tell, but the way matters subsequently unfolded begs the question whether it was a coincidence that, in the same ill-omened 15 April edition of the *St. James's Chronicle*, the following notice was posted: 'Died, at his house at Clapton, Anthony André, Esq.'[20] Was it possible that Anthony's death came by his own hand, or was it a heart attack brought on by shock from the successive blows that he sensed were about to fall on the family? Either way, according to the *Lloyd's Evening Post*, his death was sudden, 'after a few days illness'.[21]

CHAPTER 9

Shakespeare's Jubilee

Anthony André was buried on 20 April 1769. The choice of a family vault in the cemetery at 'St John at Hackney'[1] symbolically completed his induction as an Englishman. From that moment, John became head of his family, but not its scion. His uncles, David and John Lewis, stepped into that role, their task being to unscramble their dead brother's disastrous foray into the affairs of the East India Company.

The full extent of the damage done to the fortunes of the Andrés was not apparent in the immediate aftermath of Anthony's sudden death. Instead, grief at the loss of a dear husband and father was the pervading sentiment in the family home through the summer. In the despond, the family retreated into itself, preferring the comfort of relatives, such as the Boissiers and Mourgues, proudly acknowledged as part of the Clapton social circle. When 'my dear Boissier is come to town',[2] he would, as John recounted, make a point of visiting the 'Claptonians'[3] and, despite bringing 'a little of the soldier with him' courtesy of his new career in the army, 'he is the same honest, warm, intelligent friend I always found him'.[4] This 'dear Boissier', born in 1748,[5] remained an anchor in John's life and the same 'friend Peter Boissier of the Eleventh Dragoons' to whom he bequeathed 'a Ring'[6] in his will.

Despite these visits, the memories of happier days were too acute, and John was soon admitting openly that 'we none of us like Clapton'. His mother and sisters preferred Putney, and again that was because, there, were 'our kind and excellent Uncle Girardot and Uncle Lewis'.[7] To alleviate the gloom, Mary-Louisa decided the family needed a change of air. The youngest daughter, Louisa, and John's younger brother, William Lewis, were sent to relatives in Paris. As for John and the two older daughters, Anna and Mary, Mary-Louisa decided they needed some fun, and where better than the up-coming Shakespeare Jubilee everyone was talking about. Arranged by David Garrick, the leading actor and theatre manager of his generation, this 'gala' was to be held in Stratford-upon-Avon between 6 and 8 September. The Andrés were not the only Claptonians planning to go: 'James-Henry Castle, Esq.' also 'went to amuse himself at the so much talked-of Jubilee.'[8]

Preparations for the Jubilee extravaganza had been underway for a while, with, in July, 'above one hundred trees … cut down near Stratford upon Avon in order to enlarge the prospect against the approaching jubilee'.[9] The centrepiece of the 'gala' was to be 'Shakespeare's Hall', a large wooden building erected as a temporary structure and 'more generally known as The Amphitheatre'.[10] As interest built up, accommodating the anticipated influx of visitors became nightmarish. By August, the warnings were so direful about 'the Difficulty getting beds at the ensuing Jubilee' that 'several Gentlemen have made Parties to pitch Tents in the common Field for their Accommodation.'[11]

With so many visitors descending on the town, unsurprisingly 'the inhabitants of Stratford made what may be called "a good thing" of this: a bed and sitting-room in any genteel house, fifty pounds or more for the time; a bed for the night three guineas or two or perhaps down so low as one; half a guinea for the privilege of sleeping in a carriage or chaise; and five shillings at least to be in a waggon or sitting by a fire-side'.[12]

James Boswell was one of those foolish enough not to book accommodation in advance, so endured a couple of uncomfortable nights, made worse by the bad weather, when, according to the 'genuine account of the Jubilee' by one visitor from London, it 'rained a deluge all night and continued to pour down when I awaked at noon'[13] which meant that the pageant planned for that day had to be cancelled. At least Boswell and this 'visitor' survived their ordeal. Not so lucky was 'James-Henry Castle', the Claptonian, who died at 'his Lodgings at Clapton' soon after returning south, 'his Death attributed' to 'having laid in damp sheets at Stratford-upon-Avon'.[14]

Sketch of amphitheatre built for the Shakespeare Jubilee, at Stratford-Upon-Avon on 6 and 7 September 1769. (*Gentleman's Magazine* Volume XXXIX September 1769)

Notwithstanding, the Jubilee became the big event of 1769: according to the genuine account, 'our company amounted, by my guess, to about 800 at breakfastings, to 1500 at the dinners, at the oratorio, ball and masquerade, to about 2000'.[15] Among this 'company' were, according to Boswell, 'almost every man of eminence in the literary world,' all eager to 'partake in this festival of genius'.

There was one notable absentee, Dr Samuel Johnson, Boswell 'very sorry'[16] that the subject of the biography he was preparing should have preferred a visit to the seaside at Brighthelmstone.[17] 'The absence of Johnson could not but be wondered at' given that Garrick had been his 'brilliant pupil'[18] while both still lived in Lichfield and that so many fellow 'Lichfieldians'[19] came to support their hometown hero.

Numbered among these 'Lichfieldians' was 'Miss Seward (authoress)',[20] a budding but, at the age of twenty-seven, already fiercely intellectual poet. It was during these three days at the Jubilee that Anna Seward and the André family first became acquainted. They may have met sharing the same cramped and expensive accommodation at one of the 'genteel' houses in Stratford. More likely it was at the masquerade ball with its company of '2000' guests, the social free-for-all where an ill-assortment of 'characters which were mistaken', including just 'one sailor out of six [who] could dance the hornpipe' and 'one Oxford scholar in five [who] could speak Greek', mingled with an authentic Shakespearean cast including 'sweet Ceres' and 'three weird sisters' who, on being unmasked, were revealed to be 'the three handsomest faces in England, Mrs Crewe, Mrs Bouverie and Mrs Payne'.[21] Boswell went unmasked but 'in the dress of an armed Corsican chief', Lord Grosvenor 'in the character of a Turk', and Captain Thomson as an 'honest tar'.[22]

John and his two sisters, it appears, went as characters in Shakespeare's *The Merry Wives of Windsor*, Anna Seward as a character from *Two Gentlemen of Verona*. The plots of these two plays were threaded through with hidden identities. Disguise fed into the cultural mores of the time which required literary soulmates to find each other through a system of coded language that, much like paramours, facilitated instinctual communication in a secret world. According to John, he and Anna easily formed their own code, 'intuitive knowledge' and 'sympathy'[23] the enabling catalysts. Thus could he invite Anna to 'recall to your memory of the fat knight's love letters to Mrs Ford and Mrs Page'. She would instantly have conjured up that first sight of him at the masquerade ball dressed as fat 'Falstaff'. Addressing Anna as 'Julia'[24] at the same time would, in turn, have been an equally playful reminder that she had come as the eponymous character in *Two Gentlemen of Verona* who disguised herself as a boy so she might get close to Proteus, the object of her love. The disguises and the sensual frisson that masquerades could excite in those who attended ignited the charged friendship that John and Anna struck up, but it was instinctual 'sympathy' born of 'intuitive knowledge' that set its mood.

The Stratford encounter was so pleasing for all concerned that whatever plans the Andrés had to return to Clapton were temporarily put to one side, John, his mother and two sisters content to follow in Anna's wake as she journeyed to 'my native Eyam',[25] a village in the Derbyshire Peak District where she was born and where her father still had duties as its rector. The Andrés were unfamiliar with the area. As their adoptive host, Anna may have suggested a visit to the nearby 'palace of Chatsworth',[26] ancestral home of the Devonshire family, which was being dressed up in preparation for the young Duke's return after 'three years absent' on his 'tour of Europe'.[27]

However, sightseeing was not why the Andrés followed Anna to Derbyshire. The excuse—if one were needed—was so Mary-Louisa could 'take the celebrated warm bath of Buxton', an up-and-coming spa resort some thirteen miles from Eyam. Mary-Louisa was still only forty-eight but, if a previous visitor's experience were any guide, she was certain to benefit from 'the efficacious qualities of the waters'. Five years her junior, Thomas Pennant had recently stopped there before embarking on his *Tour in Scotland* and had written of the 'return of spirits, the flight of pain, and re-animation of my long, long-crippled rheumatic limbs.'[28] Anna would surely have talked up these qualities to the Andrés: her father, aged sixty-one, may previously have taken the waters, and one of the reasons for her current trip to Derbyshire was to help her protégée, Honora Sneyd, recuperate from a 'threatening disease'. Though only eighteen, Honora was sickly and in need of treatment.

As for Mary-Louisa, however weary her 'limbs', she would certainly have enjoyed a much-needed 'return' of her 'spirits', and it was John's duty as new head of the family to be solicitous of his grieving mother. He must also be mindful of his future duties as matchmaker for his sisters. A further appeal of this leg of the northern excursion, then, was Buxton's growing popularity as a summer retreat for the 'Bon Ton'. As yet, it did not rival Bath, Bristol Wells, and the seaside resorts of Brighthelmstone and Southampton, but regular reports in the society columns of the newspapers were beginning to talk it up, and everyone knew that 'spa holidays'[29] were where marriage, if not love, could be kindled. Readers of the *Public Advertiser* were told in July 1766 that 'the Earl and Countess of Suffolk set out with a grand Retinue from their House in North Audley-street to Buxton in Derbyshire.'[30] In August 1767, it was the turn of the *London Evening Post* to note that 'her grace the Dutchess of Portland set out to Buxton-Wells'.[31] Doing so, she would have arrived just as 'the Right Hon. Lord Clive and his Lady came to town from Buxton-Wells'.[32] The ultimate seal of Bon Ton approval came, however, when Buxton became the locus for amorous trysts, 'the D of K' (Duke of Kent) and 'Mrs S-d-s' (Sarah Siddons) said to have had 'their first conference ... at Buxton Wells'[33] in June 1769.

Ever attentive to the needs of his mother and his two sisters, John may have already had Buxton marked on the family's itinerary when making the original plans for the Jubilee excursion. If so, he would have had a collection of *Poems* published the previous year to thank for the choice of Buxton. He would have been drawn naturally to this collection by its juvenilia, which included 'Winter

... begun at Winchester School, 1757'[34] and, from 1764, a 'Prologue to the Tragedy of Cato ... spoken by a boy'.[35] Also included in the collection was an *Ode to Health written at Buxton, Derbyshire 1765*, which roundly sang the 'praise' of 'thy healing founts.'[36]

In this poetry, John and Anna Seward found something—other than the sensual frisson of the masquerade—to make them true kindred souls. In the custom of the time, John brought his copy of the *Poems* to read excerpts to his family. Anna was invited to join the readings, as she recalled in a letter of 1799 to the collection's author, Francis Mundy: 'When I was at Buxton with my dear Honora in the summer of 1769, these elegies were first introduced to me and to her, before whose young eyes, for she was then only eighteen, no poetic grace, or defect, passed unnoticed.'[37]

The Mundy collection had originally been published anonymously, but Anna would have told John that she knew Francis personally from Lichfield. There she and Francis were part of a budding poetry circle. This explains later coded messages John shared with Anna. It may have been mere synchronicity that there was a poem in the Mundy collection entitled *Epilogue to the Merry Wives of Windsor spoken by Falstaff.*[38] However, when, later, John also referred to 'my Sisters Penserosos',[39] he was inviting Anna to recall the intimacy of their shared reading of *The Harehunter*—another poem in the Mundy collection—this one billed as 'a burlesque Imitation of ... Milton's L'Allegro and Il' Penseroso.'[40]

As part of what would become a literary 'pas de deux', Anna and John began exchanging poetic challenges, but always with her, aged twenty-seven, the teacher, him, in his own word, still 'a poor novice of eighteen'[41] endeavouring to 'carry out the poetic task you set me'.[42] Anna threw down the first gauntlet as early as the Buxton sojourn. The bad weather had followed the fellow travellers from Stratford-upon-Avon, the *Public Advertiser* describing how 'a violent Tempest began suddenly at Buxton' on 15 September. 'The Lightening broke the Windows and also descended down the Chimney of the public School.'[43] Undaunted, Anna 'composed' a sonnet 'at Buxton on a rainy season'.[44] Writing in the teeth of 'the gale' and echoing Pennant's reference to Buxton as a 'cheerless spot',[45] Anna manfully sought inspiration 'from these wild heights, where oft the mists descend' and found it ten lines later in 'wat'ry sun-beams'.[46]

Whether John took up the challenge immediately is unclear. He did, however, respond 'apropos of verses' a month later when prompted by Anna to 'recollect my random description of the engaging appearance of the charming Mrs...'. Dutifully submitting three lines of doggerel for Anna the teacher's approval, John, the pupil, declared with a flourish 'Here it is at your service':

> Then rustling and bustling the Lady comes down,
> With a flaming red face, a broad yellow gown,
> And a hobbling out-of-breath gait, and a frown.[47]

Where Anna and John had caught sight of 'the charming Mrs...' that she could be
set as a poetry test is unclear. While it is possible it was in Buxton, the more likely
spot was in Lichfield, the last leg of the family's northern excursion. This stage of
the family's journey was unplanned, and since, on its own, Lichfield offered little
that would have appealed to the Andrés, there was no reason for this detour other
than to visit the Seward family home.[48] The town's resistance to industry had given
it an 'air of sleepiness'.[49] This might explain why its most famous sons, Dr Johnson
and David Garrick, had long since left for the brighter prospects of London.

What remained behind was a tight-knit community of polite society 'chiefly
inhabited by the reverends of the cathedral and persons of independent fortunes,'[50]
though it still numbered among its current inhabitants Dr Erasmus Darwin, the
luminary and founder member of the Lunar Society.[51] The exalted ecclesiastical
status of Anna's father allowed him to reside within 'the bishop's palace',[52] where
the Seward family home became an important hive for local society life. There,
Anna held court. Whereas 'cheerless' Buxton was neutral territory, Lichfield was
her domestic and cultural world and, if John's 'charming Mrs...' were part of
this social circle, the tone he chose to describe this 'Lady' would have played well
to Anna's waspishness. It would also explain why John kept the identity of this
'Lady' hidden even within the privacy of his and Anna's shared code. He likewise
pandered to Anna's local 'Lichfieldian' grievances indulging 'her resentment against
the Canonical Dons' whose sin was to 'stumpify [cut off] the heads of those good
green people [trees].'[53]

As Anna's pupil, John did her bidding in other ways. She had made it her mission
to find a suitable suitor for her protégée, Honora. John was a good-looking young
man: easy on the eye with, at the same time, a seductive hint of dark otherness. He
was from a good family, wealthy (or so she thought), well respected and connected.
He was also intelligent, cultured, an artist, caring and gifted with words. Above all,
he was full of 'emotions' and unafraid to express them, a godsend to the language
of love at a time when female social circles were placing a premium on masculine
sensibility and would soon idolize the 'Man of Feeling'[54] made famous in Henry
Mackenzie's seminal novel of that name, first published in 1771.

John was, surely, the perfect match for Anna's beautiful, fragile Honora. Anna
could not abide that Honora should choose a man unworthy of her own admiration.
A controlling woman, who had tasted love and been disappointed, Anna 'knew what
was best' for her Honora. So, she decided that John should love 'her Honora'. For
John, Anna's platonic *ménage à trois* would become his schoolroom, her lessons his
coming of age, her approbation his reward.

Yet, he, in his own words, the 'poor novice of eighteen', was young and expectant
but also confused. Was he, then, 'Cher Jean', willing that this 'name of kindness
by which Mr André was often called by his mother and sisters'[55] be adopted by the
Sewards, so he might find among them the same comforting family love that he

knew so well from his home life? Or, was he John, the young buck, striking out on his own, exploring the persuasive power of his many gifts and allures, and trying them out on Anna and Honora? And why not? Both women were beautiful: Anna, severe and striking in her beauty; Honora, soft and gentle in hers.

Or, was he, again in his own words, 'poor Cher Jean', 'doleful' and 'ready to weep for sorrow' as he tried earnestly to escape the demanding pull, down south, of both 'Scylla', in the form of the unloved Clapton, and 'Charybdis', in the form of the 'gloomy compting house in Warnford court'? Was this 'poor Cher Jean' a vulnerable, sensitive, lost soul in search of meaning, eager to protect and care for weak, sickly Honora but, at the same time, desperate to please 'my Julia', his teacher in all things, in poetry and in love? If so, he would do what was instructed and adore Honora because, by his sacrifice on the altar of love, he could earn his teacher's admiration. He believed this because, 'though you never told me,' teacher and pupil shared 'an intuitive knowledge' evident 'from the sympathy I have constantly perceived in the taste of 'Julia' (Anna) and cher Jean'.[56]

The early contours of this essay in sacrifice emerge from three letters written by John to Anna in the autumn of 1769 shortly after the Andrés returned from their northern excursion to Clapton, and the 'gloomy compting house in Warnford court': the first letter was headed 'Clapton' and dated 'October 3, 1769';[57] the second was marked 'London' and dated 'October 19, 1769';[58] the third was, again, headed 'Clapton', and dated 'Nov. 1 1769.'[59] These three letters are the first written by him to have come down to later generations, and the only ones of, without doubt, a copious correspondence conducted over many years between Anna and John to have been made public. Anna decided it that way, these letters meant to fix for ever who John was, as articulated by her.

John set about his essay in sacrifice with gusto, the three letters an enthusiastic assault on Honora, Anna the courting couple's self-appointed interpreter and go-between. Deploying the language of courtly love to woo Honora, John even invoked his skill at drawing, alternately teasing her with 'the face of a Lamb ... but indifferently expressed in a corner of my paper'[60] and, more seriously, telling of 'my Honora's picture' which he carried close to his 'bosom'.[61]

John duly announced his love for Honora from the first moment he saw the 'fortunate spires' of the 'beloved Lichfield' on his arrival there. From the early passages of this first letter, his 'eternal reverence and love' for Honora was imagined in high sensibility, the catalyst for these emotions being 'the joy that danced in Honora's eyes when she first shewed them to me from the Needwood Forest on our return with you from Buxton to Lichfield'. Doubtless, these 'spires' deserved this adulation, but, as John expatiated on their 'lightness and elegance', and how 'every object that has pyramidical form recalls them to my recollection with a sensation that brings the tear of pleasure into my eyes',[62] he was inviting Honora to imagine her own 'form' in these 'spires'.

Should the imagery be beyond her emotional range, 'Julia' was on hand to 'plead my cause to Honora more eloquently than the inclosed letter has the power of doing.'[63] Likewise, when John said he 'lov'd them [the spires] from that instant',[64] he wished Honora to understand that he 'lov'd' her. So total was this 'eternal reverence and love' meant to appear that it could only be fully comprehended as a courtly sacrifice expressed in this primal Cri de Coeur of the lost soul: 'But oh! My dear Honora. It is for thy sake only I wish for wealth'.

By making 'eternal' sacrifice the defining element of his feelings for Honora, John was knowingly seeking to pass the ultimate test of courtly love which 'Julia' had set. The teacher's reward, in return, was that 'cher Jean' be permitted to articulate 'the tender feelings of my soul' for 'my dear Julia' also. To do this, however, John must first take heed of Mr and Mrs Seward, who, as Honora's guardians, should approve of the 'eternal reverence and love' he professed for their ward.

A subterfuge was required, which John and Anna alone conspired in, whereby these three letters were contrived as a critical examination of John, the 'young novice' writer, by 'Julia', the teacher. Uncertain whether to pursue a vocation as wordsmith of verse and prose, he had been called on to submit examples of his work in these two genres and must await judgment from 'Julia', his teacher, on their relative literary merits. If the sole purpose of these letters, then, was for John to seek guidance from his teacher concerning what vocation he should follow, 'Julia' could not but have remarked on the contrast between the shallow flippancy of his 'versifying grumbling'[65] and the persuasive thoughtfulness of his prose.

Whatever the clandestine nature of this literary examination, John took its ostensible purpose seriously. He valued Anna's critical opinion and, knowing what awaited him in the 'gloomy compting house', must soon decide whether he could afford to pursue his preferred career of writer. Hence, he agonized that 'when I would express the tender feelings of my soul, I have no language that does them any justice.' Equally, he lamented 'that whatever one communicates must go such a roundabout way, before it reaches one's correspondent; from the writer's heart through his head, arm, hand, pen, Ink, paper, over many a weary hill and dale to the eye, head and heart of the reader.' Aware of his own literary shortcomings, he complained that with 'our sensations ... passing through an imagination whose operations so often fail to second those of the heart' the risk was that 'the feelings' are lost 'of those who are truly attached' while those who are not can mislead with their 'flowers of rhetoric'.

Claiming his reward from 'Julia', the teacher, John set about expressing his 'tender feelings' for her. He must tread carefully: at first, 'Julia' would not let him speak of them as other than an extension of his 'eternal reverence and love' for Honora. Instead, he could empathize with 'Julia' that 'dear Honora was not so well as you wished', but, simultaneously, praise 'her tender care' of the sickly patient. He was licensed to make both Honora and Anna objects of his mock-jealousy.

Flirtatiously, he claimed that 'Billy', his younger brother, was 'not old enough for me to be afraid of in the rival way, else I should keep him aloof, for his heart is form'd of those affectionate materials, so dear to the ingenuous taste of Julia and her Honora.' Similarly coquettish was his response to Julia's 'absolute exclusion of the Beaus' from her recent excursion to Shrewsbury, John chiding that he 'thought when five wise virgins were watching at midnight it was in expectation of the bridegroom's coming'.

However, when asking 'Julia' to have Honora 'put in a little postscript were it only to tell me that she is my very sincere friend who will neither give me love nor comfort', he was going further and, bemoaning Honora's unresponsiveness, he was clearly inviting 'Julia' to fill the void. The invitation was coded, but, emboldened by his own honey-words, John went further still, introducing a note of physical sensuality to his feelings for 'my dear Julia'.

Initially, these advances were tentative, his first letter inviting her to write 'the least scrap of a letter' if only to 'give us the comfort of having a piece of paper which has recently passed thro' your hands.'[66] Again, in the second letter, he talked of lifting his 'drowsy head to converse a while with dear Julia.'[67] By his third letter, however, he talked openly of himself as 'your affectionate and faithful friend.' Just back from his second visit to Lichfield which took place at the end of October 1769, his senses had been galvanized, and whatever his feelings for Honora, he was now locked onto 'Julia, my dear Julia' whose 'sympathizing heart partakes all the joys and pains of your friends—never can I forget its kind offices, which were of such moment to my peace—Mine is formed for Friendship, and I am so blest in being able to place so well the purest passion of an ingenious mind.'

Recalling his earlier visit to Lichfield, John told how, once again, 'his eager eyes drank their first view of the dear spires', but this time Julia was to the fore, Honora relegated to second place when with 'what rapture did I not feel on entering your gates!—In flying up the hall steps!—In rushing into the dining room!—In meeting the gladened eyes of dear Julia and her enchanting friend! That instant convinced me of Rousseau's observation. That there are moments worth ages.' In a flourish of courtly anguish, he exclaimed 'Ah Julia! The cold hand of absence is heavy on the heart of your poor Cher Jean.'

For all the 'emotions', 'raptures' and 'musing moods' expressed in these three letters they, like the earlier northern excursion, could only offer brief respite from the reality of the 'news' crowding in on John as he put pen to paper. He felt this keenly, his third letter concluding with the admission that 'the near hopes of another excursion to Lichfield could alone disperse every gloomy vapour of my imagination.'

Believing he had, in Anna, a kindred spirit who would 'like anything better than news', he had earlier launched into another of his 'versifying grumblings', exclaiming:

What is it to you or me
If here in the City we have nothing but riot
If the Spital-Field Weavers can't be kept quiet
If the weather is fine or the streets should be dirty
Or if Mr Dick Wilson died aged of thirty.[68]

Clearly, John was well up with the latest 'news'. Yet, in all this, not a word about America, about Tea-ships and 'the agreement of non-importation'[69] nor about 'an Informer' for the Admiralty recently 'tarred' and 'feathered' by 'indignant Sailors'[70] in Philadelphia, nor, indeed, about 'Lame Ducks' and the demise of the Great Scheme.

CHAPTER 10

'A Gloomy Compting House'

The picture John painted to Anna of life in the André household when the family first returned to Clapton in early October was one of happy domesticity. There was 'the joy of seeing Louisa and ... little Brother Billy,' as well as 'our kind and excellent Uncle Girardot and Uncle Lewis André,' and charming was the image of 'my three sisters, me and my friend Ewer seated in the drawing-room and 'writing round the same table' all while 'my mother is gone to pay a visit'.

This was all pretence. The low spirits that had impelled the Andrés on their northern excursion soon returned with a vengeance. John was especially downcast. He 'was glad to see' his uncles, but 'they complain'd, not without reason, of the gloom upon my countenance'.[1] His uncles were not the only ones to notice his depression: 'I fear it hurts my mother to see my musing moods; but I can neither help nor overcome them.'[2] Confiding thus to Anna, John tried blaming his dejection on a lingering hangover from Lichfield's 'fortunate spires' and the Sewards' 'dressing room fire place', memories so cheering when compared to depressing Clapton where 'the evenings grow very long' and 'my zephyrs are wafted through cracks in the wainscot; for murmuring streams, I have dirty kennels; for bleating flocks, grunting pigs; and squalling cats for birds that incessantly warble.'[3]

John put on a braver face when comparing the social circles of Clapton and Lichfield, but visits from his cousin, 'my dear Boissier', 'my friend Ewer'[4] and 'the Claptonians with their fair guest, a Miss Mourgue'[5] evidently paled and palled into 'gloomy evening' when set against memories of 'our Lichfieldian friends'[6] and 'the idea of a clean hearth and a snug circle round it, form'd by a few sincere friends'.[7]

Desperate to escape Clapton, which 'we none of us like,' his 'mother and sisters' decided to 'go to Putney in a few days' and, pointedly, 'stay some time'.[8] There, at least they would be among family, Putney a village on the south bank of the Thames and the home of Uncle John Girardot and his son, Andrew.[9] As for John, he would try a dose of stoicism, which, when imbibed, meant 'I need not care, for I am all day long in town'. Reading this, Anna could readily put John's long face down to a resurgence of grief at the loss of a dear father, the return to Clapton reviving all-too-bittersweet memories of happier days.

Less easy for her to explain away was John's iconoclastic reaction to his return to the gloomy compting house: being 'all day long in town was avoiding Scylla' only, so he bemoaned, 'to fall into Charybdis'.[10] Eager to match-make, she knew the importance of John's 'future profession' to his prospects for marriage to her Honora. Putting aside her role as teacher in the art of courtly love, Anna must surely have heard alarm bells ringing as she read that John's primary motivation was her 'fervent wish to see' him become 'a quill-driver'.

As was the custom of the day, she should have shown John's letters to Honora, but how could she when he rambled on about 'mercantile glories' which 'croud on my fancy, emblazoned in the most refulgent colouring of an ardent imagination' and appeared to take leave of his senses when 'borne on her soaring pinions, I wing my flight to the time when Heaven shall have crowned my labours with success and opulence, and saw 'sumptuous palaces rising to receive' him?

With every new image conjured in his letter of 19 October, John damned himself out of his own mouth. Romantic and noble as a statement of courtly love was his offer to sacrifice himself for 'my dear Honora!' Nevertheless, John's deep-rooted aversion and temperamental unsuitability for his 'future profession' was clear. This became evident when, following his second visit to Lichfield in late October, he came back on the subject, this time with even more vehemence. Again in response to Anna's 'interest in my destiny,' he avowed in his letter of 1 November that 'I have now compleatly subdued my aversion to the profession of merchant, and hope in time to acquire an inclination for it,—yet God forbid I should ever love what I am to make the object of my attention!—that vile trash which I care not for but only as it may be the future means of procuring the blessing of my soul.' Next came the ritual offer of sacrifice, this time wordily amplified for full effect: 'Thus all my mercantile calculations go to the tune of Honora and when my consciousness whispers in my ear, that I am not of the right stuff for a Merchant, I draw my Honora's picture from my bosom, and the sight of that dear Talisman so inspirits my industry, that no toil appears oppressive.'[11]

Viewed from the ethereal heights of eternal love, here was courtly sacrifice made heroic. Grounded, however, in the reality of 'Warnford court' in late October 1769, here was a primal cry for help uttered by 'poor Cher Jean' who knew his world was in the process of falling apart but could not bring himself to tell his teacher, 'dear Julia', the bare truth. Instead, he must hint and hope she would read between the lines and see how the family's fortunes were changing, literally, as he wrote.

The clues were there. When John wrote that 'my dear Boissier is come to town [but] sacrifices the town diversions because I will not partake of them', did Anna see this as sacrificial faithfulness to his love for Honora, or did she recognize his banal need to make economies? Similarly, when reading that 'my mother has gone to pay a visit and has left us in possession of the old coach,' did Anna smile when he joked that 'as for nags, we can boast of only two long-tails … being no other than my friend Ewer and me'[12] or did she realize that his mother had started trimming everyday expenses?

There was no mistaking, however, the intended impact of his bald announcement that 'I am going to try my interest in Parliament'. Coming out of the blue, this statement made in the third letter was fully intended to shock Anna, hence why he promptly exclaimed 'How you stare!' On a roll by then, he left her in no doubt about the reason for this decision, declaring in crude vernacular that 'it is to procure a frank.'[13] This was, surely, the first time Anna had heard John express such raw thoughts. She may have wondered what had changed so dramatically since his recent visit to Lichfield. As the daughter of a cleric living a cloistered life in 'the bishop's palace' and with aspirations to become a poet, she would have been at a loss what to make of it all. John's talk of 'mercantile calculation', 'vile trash' and procuring 'a frank' came from a commercial scene alien to her.

Equally, the excitable 'news' unfolding since April in remote London's 'Change Alley would have meant little to her if she read about it in the newspapers. Yet, as bleak as this 'news' was when the family embarked on their northern excursion in early August, returning to Warnford court in mid-October John found that matters had only got worse. For a start, there were now daily riots by the 'Spital-field Weavers',[14] which, if John's 'versifying grumblings' were anything to go by, were clearly weighing on his mind. This was unsurprising. Not only was Spitalfields a stone's throw from Warnford court, but, with the 'Weavers' and 'the notorious gang of Cutters'[15] literally at daggers drawn, these riots directly affected the family's traditional trading activities in cloth. Moreover, three of John's near relatives—Andrew Girardot and the two Boissier brothers Peter and John Louis[16]—were in the army. The 'Hon. Capt. Andrew Girardot'[17] was in 'the third regiment of guards'.[18] The Boissier brothers were in the Dragoon Guards, Peter, since 21 June 1769[19] a humble 'Cornet' in the '11th Regiment of Dragoons',[20] John Louis a captain. Both regiments had been recalled to London, and Captain Girardot's had been sent into Spitalfields to 'quell any disturbances'.[21]

As unsettling as these events were, more serious were the mounting repercussions from the financial broils that his father had drawn the family into. In addition to the Verney and Burke loans, which were in default, and the ongoing fallout from the French East India Company's bankruptcy, the Andrés must also address a potentially damaging outcome from the Crauford loan, which was set to mature on 'the 11th of October 1769'.[22] To date, Crauford had met both margin calls from the Andrés. This suggested he was made of sterner stuff than Verney and Burke. He was also luckier: by chance, he found irregularities in the administration of the Andrés' £30,800 loan to him. As a result, he defaulted on the loan when it matured on 11 October 1769 and sued the Andrés for breach of contract, launching his case in the 'Court of Chancery' in 'the Michaelmas Term 1769.'[23]

The discovery of irregularities was made following the 18 July debacle in 'Change Alley. In the ensuing mayhem, the various 'lame ducks' were forced to open their books for scrutiny so creditors could retrieve their monies. Among the 'lame ducks' were the brokers, 'Elias Benjamin de la Fontaine and William Brymer', who had arranged the loan to Crauford and were administering it on behalf of the Andrés. What Crauford unearthed related to the East India stock he had put up as collateral. This stock had been sold contrary to the terms of the loan agreement, which stipulated that the Andrés 'not sell or transfer the said 14,000*l* capital East India stock or any part thereof prior to the 11th of October 1769 without the consent of De la Fontaine and Brymer.'[24] The Andrés' professional integrity was suddenly under public attack. This was one court case the Andrés could not afford to lose. If the court found against them, they stood to incur substantial financial loss when damages were awarded against them, this at a time when their finances were already stretched elsewhere. Far worse, though, would be the damage to their reputation. The Andrés must fight this court case to the bitter end.

Given the prevailing 'chicaneries of Bubble and Stock-jobbing',[25] such fastidiousness might have seemed misplaced. However, as the Great Scheme fell apart and the latest bout of financial high jinks was laid bare, anyone known to be associated with it, meaning, variously, the 'merchant', the 'bank director', the 'broker', and the 'assurance director', soon appeared on a 'Black List'. Published by the *Middlesex Journal* in April 1769, among names on the 'List' was 'Anthony André', there in his capacity as a 'Royal-Exchange Assurance Director'. It was small comfort that he shared his notoriety with other directors of the Royal Exchange as well as with East India and South Sea Company directors. Ominously, any known, rather than 'Undiscoverable', addresses were published, which meant that Anthony's was given as 'Clapton.'[26]

The family's reputation was important to Anthony's brothers, David and John-Lewis, but it was especially so for John. How much so he made evident in his plaint to Anna against the 'censoriousness and envy of the world.'[27] Reputation was all to him: it was a man's honour, which was why he was so upset when writing to Anna on 1 November and railing bitterly against 'that vile trash which I care not for'. It is no wonder, then, that he did not come clean to Anna. Instead, he could only hint at his personal distress, admitting that even his favourite pastime, 'the poetic task you set me, is in a sad method,' the reason being that 'my head and heart are too full of other matters to be engrossed by a draggletailed wench of the Heliconian puddle.'[28]

With John dealing only in hints about these 'other matters', it is unsurprising that Anna continued to press John's suit with Honora well into 1770, and that John remained fixed in 'Mr. and Mrs Seward attachment'. From the outset, however, all were fighting an uphill battle: Honora never had the feelings for John that Anna wished her to have. Anna acknowledged this later when accepting that Honora's 'attachment to him had never the tenderness of her friendship for me' [Anna]. Rather, 'it was a mere compound of gratitude and esteem, of which his letters show that he was always aware.'[29] What Anna was not prepared to admit publicly, however, was that, for all his blandishments, John was equally indifferent to Honora. Yet, this was already plain to see in the three letters Anna made public.

There were surely more letters between Anna and John, certainly in the year following John's first visit to Lichfield, but Anna decided to publish just these three. Her overriding imperative, when she did so in 1781,[30] was to fix John's legacy for posterity. Revealing as those were about her relationship with John, she dare not publish other letters of his, even at a later date. This, doubtless, was because they would have shown the full extent of John's attachment to Anna, a fact she must keep hidden not only from the outside world but also from Honora.

It was imperative for Anna's reputation that John and Honora remain locked in a budding romance. That way she could welcome John to 'the bishop's palace' throughout 1770, his courtship of Honora her alibi, enabling her to lead John a merry dance, dangling her beauty and poetic charms under his nose and basking in his adoration, all while deploying his courtly duty to Honora as a shield to protect her own reputation for chasteness.

Anna was what the French euphemistically call an *allumeuse*—a flirt. John was not her first victim (if 'victim' is the right word) and certainly not her last. Most famously, she allowed her budding relationship with Boswell to turn on the knife-edge separating the sensual and the sentimental, as the two negotiated over the meaning of his request for a 'lock of Seward's hair' in 1784. She initially refused when Boswell asked her to 'conspire in "a rape of the lock"', but did so in such a way as to suggest a come-on: "with pleasure shou'd I have sent you a lock of my hair if you had not ask'd for it in a style that wou'd make it a pledge of intercourse, which never … can subsist between me and *any* Man."' So far so chaste, except that, after the briefest exchange of letters, she did send him 'that lock of hair'.[31]

In her younger years, Anna was especially partial to men in uniform, and 'the loves of her youth were two young soldiers named Taylor and Vyse'.[32] The relationship with Hugh Taylor covered the years 1762 to 1764, and in a later letter to his wife, Anna admitted, tellingly, that she had 'made an experiment upon his heart'.[33] When, in 1765, she formed a brief relationship with the then Cornet Vyse, she, by her own admission, found herself on the receiving end of love's experiments, as a result of which she swore never again to be 'the victim of contemned affection'.[34]

It seems evident, then, that John and Anna's relationship, coming as it did just four years after Vyse broke her heart, was only the latest of her love 'experiments'. Anna would later deny there was anything other than friendship between her and John, but Richard Lovell Edgeworth—the wealthy inventor, educationist and member of Darwin's Lunar Society—thought otherwise. Arguably, as Honora's future husband Edgeworth was an unreliable eyewitness, and, yet, the account he included in his

Memoirs tallies with the sorry history of Anna's amours and the tenor of John's three letters to her that have survived.

Edgeworth's account was from late in 'the year 1770' when he 'spent some time at Christmas with my friend Mr Day, at Stow-hill.' He told how 'we went every day to Lichfield and most days to the palace' and that 'while I was upon this visit, Mr André ... came to Lichfield.' From their encounter, it becomes clear that John's relationship with both Honora and Anna had changed substantially from when he was in Lichfield in the autumn of 1769: 'the first time that I saw Mr André at the palace, I did not perceive from his manner, or that of the young lady [Honora], that any attachment subsisted between them. On the contrary, from the great attention which Miss Seward paid to him, and from the constant admiration that Mr André bestowed on her, I thought that, though there was a considerable disproportion in their ages, there might exist some courtship between them. Miss Seward, however, undeceived me.' With the unanswered question, if not 'courtship' then what, Edgeworth had left hanging the exact nature of Anna and John's relationship.

Concluding his account of meeting John, Edgeworth put the spotlight back on the relationship with Honora which, naturally, was what interested him most: 'I never met Mr André again; and from all that I then saw, or have since known, I believe that Miss Honora Sneyd was never much disappointed by the conclusion of this attachment. Mr André seemed pleased and dazzled by the young lady. She admired and estimated highly his talents, but he never possessed the reasoning mind, which she required.'[35]

Whatever Honora's feelings for John, she was not stupid. She would surely have seen through the artifice John and Anna had constructed round their literary intercourse and, with a woman's instinct, would have realized by Christmas 1770 that the real object of his 'attachment' was Anna not her. Not only had his relationship with Anna progressed to the point where, as Edgeworth witnessed, he only had eyes for her, but also the court case brought by Crauford had come to the boil, when, 'on the eighteenth day of December' [1770], 'a Decree in the High Court of Chancery was made and pronounced by the then Lords Commissioners for the custody of the Great Seal of Great Britain' presiding in the House of Lords wherein 'Alexander Crawfurd was Plaintiff' and 'John Lewis André and others' and 'Elias Benjamin de la Fontaine and William Brymer were Defendants'.[36] The decree went against the Andrés.

Following this humiliating news, the parents stepped in: Mary-Louisa to rescue John from an attachment he could no longer afford; Mr Sneyd to extract Honora from Anna's oppressive clutches. Edgeworth described the parents' intervention: 'this gentleman [John] had met Miss Honora Sneyd at Buxton or Matlock and had paid his addresses to her without at first meeting any discouragement from Mrs André, the young gentleman's mother, or, I believe, from Mr Sneyd. But when the parents on both sides came to consider more coolly, they saw that a match, even where each party seemed well suited to the other, should not be determined upon, till a sufficient fortune for a comfortable maintenance could be provided between them.'[37] Unsurprisingly, Anna had a more melodramatic version of events, describing how Honora's father suddenly 'recalled her [Honora] to his own family', this 'after having been fourteen years resident' in the Seward family-home.

Whatever the exact circumstances of the parting, it is clear that, by the beginning of 1771, the bizarre triangulated relationship between Anna, Honora and John was over. It would later suit Anna to pedal the notion that John was 'a fellow-sufferer'[38] with her when Honora married Edgeworth in 1773, but this was only so as to shore up her own alibi. By then, John had moved on in his life and, if he were still a 'fellow-sufferer' in 1773, it was only in lip service to his sense of courtly duty.

PART II

'A Little of the Soldier in Him'

CHAPTER II

'House of Lords'

'On 22nd March 1771', 'John Lewis André, David André, Andrew Girardot the Younger and Mary Louisa André' lodged a petition and appeal against the earlier 'Decree in the High Court of Chancery'. The following day, a notice appeared in the *Public Advertiser* announcing that 'yesterday came on to be heard in the House of Lords an Appeal from a Decree of the Lords Commissioners, wherein John Lewis André and others were Appellants and Alexander Crawfurd Esq., was Respondent, when the Decree was unanimously affirmed'.[1]

The news should have come as no surprise to the family. What John's father had not realized, but his mother and uncles were now discovering, was that Britain's Establishment had had it in for 'Change Alley ever since the South Sea Bubble. In its sights was 'the dishonest practice called stock-jobbing'.[2] Parliament had tried outlawing these 'Chicaneries', but the problem was how to define in law what, essentially, were dark arts. An Act of 1734 tried to prevent the practice, but failed. However, 'not only did the Act fail to stop speculation; it had the unfortunate consequence that, by making jobbing contracts illegal, it encouraged one of the parties to default if prices moved against him.'[3] This was what happened in the aftermath of the July 1769 bloodbath, with the result that case after case involving the Great Schemers found their way into the courts.

Britain's Establishment—here in the person of the Law Lords—was waiting in the wings, and when this next Bubble came, it pounced on any lone stragglers, meting out exemplary justice. Most of the India stock cases that came before the Court of Chancery—including those brought by the Andrés against Lord Verney and William Burke—were simple defaults by overstretched borrowers. The Craufurd case was different. In this instance, the borrower, not the lender, brought the case to court. 'Their Lordships' scented blood, and whatever defence the Andrés mounted, their case was doomed from the off, not least because the public mood favoured punishment of all ''Change-alley Financiers'.[4]

Yet, the Craufurd claim turned on the arguable interpretation of one narrow set of facts: that 'soon after' the loan was made by the Andrés 'on the 11th of October

1768,' they 'sold or disposed of the whole of the said 14,000*l* East India stock which they were to have had in trust' as collateral for their loan to Crauford, and did so 'without his consent or privity, or the consent or privity of the brokers for the transaction, De la Fontaine and Brymer.'[5]

This was the irregularity that Crauford claimed to have unearthed when examining the brokers' books. The Andrés argued, however, that they 'always had £14,000 East India stock and upwards, ready to transfer' to Crauford 'and would have transferred the same, had it been demanded ... but that the same was not demanded.'[6] They also claimed that they 'did not sell or dispose of any part of the whole or any part of the said 14,000*l* India Stock ... until after the expiration of the time mentioned in the agreement and in default of Crauford's redeeming the same.'[7]

It emerged, however, that, with the agreement of the brokers but unbeknownst to Crauford, this specific parcel of stock had, indeed, been sold by the brokers, the necessary collateral of £14,000 being substituted from a parcel of £19,000 India stock that the Andrés owned and had been planning to sell at the exact same time. It was only a technical breach, but 'their Lordships' smelt the whiff of 'Chicaneries' whereby 'lenders ... borrowed on the stock they held as collateral, transferring into the name of a second lender under a new loan agreement.' This was the latest sleight of hand in the murky arts of stock-jobbing, and, so it went, the paper chase continued on again such that 'this operation was repeated when the second lender pledged the collateral to a third one'.[8]

Whether or not the Andrés were involved in these chicaneries was irrelevant. There was certainly no evidence that they were. Nevertheless, 'their Lordships' not only found in favour of Crauford but also made an exemplary financial award against the Andrés. To ram this home, they even increased the amount that Crauford had asked for in his original 'bill', such that the final award was 'more advantageous to him than the relief prayed by the bill'. To rub salt in the wound, 'their Lordships' dismissed the case against the brokers and ordered that the Andrés 'pay ... the costs' owed by Crauford to the brokers. This was despite the Andrés' claim that the 'contract was entered into by de la Fontaine and Brymer the brokers, without the intervention of' Crauford and 'under a general unlimited authority from him for that purpose'. Under that authority, these brokers 'had given their express consent that no specific identified £14,000 East India stock should be retained by and in the names of the Andrés.'

When, 'aggrieved by this decree', the Andrés appealed, 'their Lordships' still would hear nothing of it. 'On 22nd March 1771' the appeal was dismissed and 'the decree therein complained of, affirmed.' Left to ring in the ears of the family were the words of Crauford's counsel—which became a permanent judgment in the Records of the House of Lords—that, 'having thus sold' Crauford's 'pledged stock and afterwards calling upon and receiving from him deposits upon the £14,000 stock, which had in reality no existence, and then selling such deposit, was as gross a fraud on the part of the Andrés, as ever appeared in a Court of Justice.'

For John, intelligent, sensitive, proud and bound, above all, by the prevailing precepts of gentlemanly honour, this judgment was the final straw. However, the writing had been on the wall ever since it had emerged in early 1769 the extent of his father's dealings with, not only the British East India Company but also its French counterpart. By virtue of all this skulduggery, his father had brought shame and ruin on the Andrés, and it was now John's overriding duty to recover the family's lost honour.

To achieve that, he must make whatever sacrifices were necessary. Most immediately, he would turn his back on a career in the family 'compting-house'. This, in itself, was no sacrifice. As was evident from his letters to Anna, he had already decided that 'Business' was not for him. It was all so much 'vile trash'. However, he must also give up all thoughts of becoming a writer and must end his courtship of Honora. With these decisions, he would almost certainly lose all hope of winning Anna. His life, as he imagined it, had ended. He would have to start over.

On 'April 1' 1771, the 'War Office' posted a notice appointing 'John André to be Second Lieutenant' in the '23d Regiment'[9] of Foot. According to service protocol, the appointment was then made public in the *London Gazette*, the announcement in the 9 April edition explaining that John had gained his army commission by 'purchase' from Onslow Beckwith, who became a 'First Lieutenant'.[10]

This announcement came just nine days after the final judgment had been handed down by the House of Lords. Yet, buying a commission in the British Army took months. It seems, then, that John had not been waiting around for this latest court judgment and had decided to strike out on his own. Arguably, his choice of a career in the army was a spur of the moment impulse, given that the timing coincided with 'rumours of impending war' when, 'that same January of 1771 the dispute over the Falkland Islands seemed on the point of eruption' and 'the military estimates were consequently increased'.[11]

John had certainly made no mention of this idea in his earlier letters to Anna. Instead, he had talked about trying his interest in Parliament, but, of course, this avenue was also ruled out now: not only had the Andrés been shamed by the Law Lords, but there was a suspicion that the court judgment was politically motivated. Taking stock, it must have been abundantly obvious to John that his family had made a fatal error when deciding to lock horns with the Craufords, an ancient and powerful Scottish clan lineage.[12] The 'Scotch influence'[13] was on the rise, especially at court,[14] this trend most evident with the elevation of George III's Scottish tutor, the Earl of Bute, as Prime Minister from 1762–3. Helped no doubt by the special friendship he enjoyed with the powerful Duke of Queensberry,[15] Alexander Crauford was in the vanguard of this growing 'Scotch influence'. That his relative, John Crauford, was already an MP for the Old Sarum seat in Wiltshire[16] further bolstered Alexander's sense of entitlement. This centred on the East India Company, and he was in a hurry. His younger brother, Quintin, already held a senior position in the company and was amassing a sizeable fortune for himself. The Crauford brothers were part of a cluster of 'Scotch influence' seen to be circling round the company, the *Middlesex Journal* noting in April 1771 'that if the present Chairman and Directors of the East India Company are re-elected for the ensuing year, the weight of Scotch influence will be seen in all future transactions and promotions belonging to that Company.'[17]

Given these ambitions, the Andrés were, however unwittingly, making an enemy of the Craufords when, by their bookkeeping irregularities, they deprived Alexander of his voting power among the proprietors of the company. Crauford had already tried unsuccessfully to get himself elected to the Board in 1767 and, because of the André debacle, had to wait until 1774 before trying again.[18] The Andrés may or may not have understood these political realities, but by deciding to fight the case, they showed how desperate they were to protect their reputation as bankers. Nevertheless, their decision to then appeal the December Decree was foolhardy: with the Scot, William Murray, the Lord Chief Justice,[19] presiding, it was a racing certainty in the prevailing political climate that 'the Lords Temporal and Spiritual in Parliament assembled'[20] would reject their appeal and support Crauford.

As for John, with all quill-driving ruled out by choice and politics a dead letter, the armed forces alone remained open to John as a young Huguenot gentleman seeking to make an honourable destiny for himself. Whichever of the two services—navy or army—John decided was for him, he would be following in the footsteps of previous generations of Huguenots who had chosen to make their name in battle, with Admiral James Gambier the most notable of those entering the navy[21] and Peter Garrick, the grandfather of David Garrick, a captain in the army.[22] John would also find himself serving alongside many Huguenots.

If procuring 'a frank' were still in John's thinking, then, of the two services, the obvious choice was the navy. For a start, going to sea as a so-called 'young gentleman volunteer' or 'midshipman' did not require money to pass hands (although it did help), whereas John's commission as a second lieutenant had to be by 'purchase' from his predecessor, Beckwith, and entering 'the 23d', a foot regiment, would have cost him £450.[23] Moreover, although neither service offered much more than a nominal pittance[24] by way of pay, one of the standout attractions of the navy was the opportunity for substantial prize money.

Traditionally, the British Navy had been very adept at capturing valuable enemy ships. The share of 'the Havannah prize-money' received by the successful admiral in 1762, for instance, was '£86,030 17s 6d'[25] (PV = £16.2 million). All ranks shared in prize money even down to the lower-deck men and the sea boys, and when the *Hermione* was captured in 1763, a midshipman's share was '1802*l*'[26] (PV = £328,000). Of Britain's two traditional foes, France and Spain, the latter offered the easier and juicier pickings. So, it would have been with some anticipation that naval officers joined their ships at 'Sheerness, Plymouth, Portsmouth and Spithead'[27] in September 1770 after news filtered through that Spain was disputing sovereignty of the Falklands

Islands. All autumn, reports appeared in newspapers telling of escalating tension, hot pressing of seamen and 'sixteen men of war of the line now fitting out'[28] for sea.

However, procuring 'a frank' was no longer a factor in John's current thinking. He would be twenty-one shortly, and reaching his majority meant he would inherit his one-fifth share of the £25,000 put aside by Anthony André for his five children in his will. With this legacy of £5,000 (PV = £774,000), John would be independent if not wealthy and could decide on a career based on what was most important to him, namely his quest for honour. He could certainly afford the cost of an army commission, even though there were additional costs associated with this step, including £200 (minimum) for the all-important uniform.[29]

John may still have chosen the navy if he had friends or relatives currently serving at sea. He did not, but three of his cousins—Andrew Girardot and the two Boissier brothers, Peter and John Louis—were serving as army officers. Moreover, back in 1747, another relative, 'Miss Girardot, only child of John Girardot of Tillieux' had married a 'Capt. Hamilton'.[30] Given the powerful influence Anna Seward was then exerting over John and that she had a penchant for men in uniform, most likely it was she who first gave him the idea to make a career in the army. They may already have discussed it before they started corresponding. This would explain why, in his first letter to Anna, John could casually launch into a discussion about one of his soldier cousins, Peter Boissier, as if Anna already knew of him: 'My dear Boissier is come to town' was how he began in his 3 October letter. Continuing on, John described how Peter 'has brought a little of the soldier with him'.[31]

Here, John was inviting a response, testing exactly how Anna felt about army officers, especially their uniforms. This was one of the attractions of the armed forces for both sexes. Considerable trouble was taken, especially by the army, to provide officers with eye-catching attire and regalia to suit their rank in the service and promote their exalted status within wider society. This became a hot topic, and opinions were divided. It was the time of the 'Macaroni',[32] military and otherwise, and the running intrigues surrounding 'the Real Sex'[33] of the Chevalier d'Eon, a transvestite, if not transgender, French army officer-cum-diplomat turned spy, then residing in London. 'Dressing en militaire' was especially important for affirming 'men's distinct masculine role'.[34] However, the complaint soon went out that 'young gentlemen, on entering the service, think that the whole profession they are to learn, consists in dressing en Militaire, being punctual at Parades, understanding the manual exercise and learning to be a Martinett.'[35]

Clearly, there was an element of vanity to John raising this subject, being that he was handsome and, doubtless, aware of his good looks. Nevertheless, he still needed reassurance and valued the opinion of the woman he admired the most. His interest was about more than the frivolous trappings and trimmings of military life, as became evident when he went on to note very pointedly that—despite being in the army—Peter was still 'the same honest, warm, intelligent friend I always found him.'[36]

John was probing whether Anna considered the army an honourable profession. Behind this was an acute awareness that Britons were ambivalent in their attitudes to the army. This went back to the English Civil War when the army was seen as a force for tyranny and revolution. Since then, there was an almost pathological aversion to whatever might be considered a standing army.

However John came to his decision, he certainly seems to have made initial enquiries well before the December Decree, as, according to regimental records, his commission was dated from '25th Jan., 1771'.[37] Yet, from Edgeworth's account of his one and only meeting with John in December 1770, it is evident that, if he had already begun the process by then, he certainly did not share the plans with his 'Lichfieldian friends'. John's silence suggests that he was deeply ashamed about the financial and legal crisis that had first prompted his decision and that his plans to enter the army were kept a closely guarded secret until they were fixed, and, then, only made known to the Lichfieldian circle, including Edgeworth, on 'March the 4th 1771'.[38]

Even then, the Lichfieldian circle was never made aware of the real reasons behind John's decision to go into army. Anna and Edgeworth each came up with their versions when they locked horns over Honora's early death in 1780. According to Anna, John 'purchased his commission upon hearing "tidings of Honora's marriage,"'[39] but Edgeworth retorted that 'despair, on hearing of the marriage of Honora Sneyd, could not have driven him to quit his profession and his country; he having quit both two years before that marriage'.[40]

What neither knew or understood was that shame, not despair, was the driving force behind John's decision to enter the army, a crucial step from which flowed numerous sacrifices, among them the decision to end the fledgling relationship with Honora. When Edgeworth insinuated that Honora parted with John because he did not have a 'reasoning mind', he may have been endeavouring to quash the notion put about by Anna that he had stolen Honora from John. In trying to represent himself as the better suitor for Honora, he betrayed not only his ignorance of the Andrés' financial affairs but also a misunderstanding of what truly motivated John.

The only person who would know the full truth was John's mother. He would almost certainly have discussed his plans with her. Purchasing his 'first commission' would have taken planning and organizing.[41] John could not do it alone, which is why he must have initiated the process prior to the December court decree. First and foremost, he needed to locate a patron who would ease his path and secure for him that vital 'letter of recommendation … to be signed by a field officer or higher rank'.[42] Who came forward at this crucial turning point is unknown, but most likely it was from one of the two families—the Girardots and Boissiers—who already had sons serving in the army. Both were from Mary-Louisa's side of the family. No matter how big-hearted her André brothers-in-law, instinct would have told her to turn back to her Girardot family roots in this dark hour.

Which of these two branches of the Girardot family might have helped is difficult to tell. How Jean Daniel Boissier[43] arranged for his eldest son, John Louis, to enter the Dragoon Guards is unclear, but once that hurdle was overcome, he was more easily able to secure a commission in the same regiment for his younger son, Peter. How Andrew Girardot came to be a captain in the 3rd regiment of Foot Guards on 25 March 1768[44] is also lost, but the vital patronage needed may have come from the family's business connection to Anthony Chamier.[45] Still, once in the regiment, Andrew Girardot was able, like the Boissiers, to arrange for a young relative, Henry Cerjat, to become a 'Cornet' in the same 'Royal Regiment of Dragoons'.[46]

This begs the question why Peter Boissier and Henry Cerjat were so easily able to follow their older relatives into the same regiment, whereas John ended up in a different one—the 23rd Regiment of Foot—where there were no prior family connections. This, in turn, raises the spectre that neither the Boissiers nor the Girardots helped John. In the case of the Boissiers, any suggestion that they turned their backs on Mary-Louisa in her hour of need can be quickly dismissed: Peter and John were close friends and remained so, John even mentioning Peter in his will. There is, by contrast, no evidence that the branch of the Girardots which patronized Cerjat was ever close to the Andrés. This Andrew Girardot died in 1773, and his will[47] made much of the connection to the Cerjats, naming one—John-Francis Maximilian—an executor, and granting bequests to all the Cerjat sons. The will made no mention of the Andrés, even though Andrew's wife, Jean, and Mary-Louisa, were both Foissins.[48] Arguably, then, Mary-Louisa had an equal claim to Andrew's help in arranging John's future in the army.

Still, there were many factors beyond patronage determining the choice of regiment by a young gentleman beginning his army career, not least relative cost.[49] The Boissiers and Girardots could afford the cost of a commission in the elite Dragoon Guards, whereas John, with his more limited funds, may have had to settle for the 23rd Foot, a mere regiment of the line, albeit that, as the 'Royal Welch Fusiliers', it enjoyed 'certain special privileges, including the right to wear the colours of the royal livery.'[50] Equally, having decided on a career in the army, John was in a hurry: aged twenty, he was fully three years older than was typical for subaltern officers first entering the service. A commission in the 23rd may have been all that was available at the time. That said, an overriding consideration for John was to serve overseas, where he might see active service and thereby earn fast promotion. This was more likely in a foot regiment. Time would tell if he had made the right choice.

CHAPTER 12

'The Drill Book'

On 13 December 1770, the *Public Register* carried the following notice that 'Orders are issued to augment the Land Forces; each Regiment of Dragoons to complete their several Troops the full Complement of 60 Men each Troop... The same measures are to be observed in regard to the Foot.'

The Royal Welch Fusiliers were on duty in Scotland when John completed the purchase of his commission in January 1771. The regiment received its marching orders to move south on 4 January, and John joined it in Manchester in time for the 'Muster Returns' on 7 February.[1] Soon after, John was thrown into the deep end of regimental social life when the Fusiliers celebrated St. David's Day, their sacrosanct event carried out annually 'every 1st March, being the anniversary of their tutelary Saint'. According to Robert Donkin,[2] then a newly appointed captain in the regiment, 'the officers give a splendid entertainment to all their Welch brethren' including 'the band playing the old tune of "The noble race of Shenkin," when an handsome drum-boy elegantly dressed, mounted on the goat richly caparisoned for the occasion', is led thrice round the table in procession by the drum-major'.[3]

This brief diversion aside, John's early days in uniform would have been humdrum, his routine subject to a new regulation instituted in 1767 which 'decreed that every young officer on his first joining should remain in quarters "until he shall be perfected in all regimental duty."'[4] As a young gentleman officer, he would have been expected to arrive in the regiment having already 'acquired some branches of polite and useful knowledge, particularly French, Drawing and Fortification.'[5] Of these three, 'Fortification' would have been absent from his education thus far. Still, there is no evidence that he took steps to fill the hole prior to joining the regiment. Instead, he bought a copy of *Geodaesia*. The edition he acquired was from 1771, which, being the 'ninth edition corrected and improved',[6] indicates a purchase sometime during the first year after he entered the army. Complementing the 1752 copy of *Select Exercises for Young Proficients in the Mathematicks*[7] which he had from his schooldays, this second purchase suggests what service the army initially had in mind for their latest subaltern officer, being as its subtitle was *The Art of Surveying and Measuring*

Land made Easy.[8] Not for him duty on the Continent, where understanding the art of 'Fortification' was essential; instead frontier service in Britain's new empire, where uncharted lands must be surveyed for settlement.

In addition to John's own collection, there were a number of army manuals[9] already in print that he would have borrowed from fellow officers. These set down what was expected of an army, whether on a march, in barracks or 'quartered on a town'.[10] John must learn the rules, not only as they applied to himself but also so that he could supervise and properly inspect the men in his squad. Some idea of the men he had under his supervision can be gleaned from an advertisement in the *London Evening Post* which reported that 'George Whistler, of his Majesty's seventh regiment of foot, or royal fuzileers, commanded by Lieutenant General Lord Robert Bertie,' had 'deserted from Gravesend on the 12th of August 1771' and gave a detailed description, 'the deserter' being '34 years of age, five feet nine inches and a quarter high, by trade a painter ... is of a fresh ruddy complexion, of a slender make, and has a stoop, is a little pock-marked, has brown hair, and grey eyes.'[11]

Cuthbertson's System explained the importance of 'cleanliness and neatness':[12] 'Rules' set out in minute detail how, for instance, 'the cleanliness of the Soldiers' is better assured if 'the Commanding-Officers of the Companies will order towels to be fixed on rollers;'[13] and copious 'Rules governing Neatness and Uniformity' covered 'the dress of regiment'.[14] Administration was especially important to a regiment's good running, and John must learn the necessity of 'Regularity in keeping Regimental Books, with the general use of them'.[15]

What John could not glean from these army manuals, he must learn in post under the immediate supervision of the adjutant, Frederick Mackenzie, who, although only a first lieutenant in the company—David Ferguson's—he was joining, crucially was a veteran of the Seven Years' War. One of the most demanding duties that would devolve to John by roster was as Officer of the Guard. Again, *Cuthbertson's System* explained what was required, namely that 'it is in a particular manner necessary when ... Companies are quartered in a town, that a subaltern's guard be mounted in some convenient place, to be obtained from the chief magistrate, whose interest is to provide it.' The reason for this was that 'the ease and comfort of the inhabitants depends considerably, upon having a Guard always ready, to prevent the Soldiers from engaging in riots and quarrels with them'.[16] This was a wise precaution as there were all too many reasons for 'disputes and quarrels ... between the Soldiers quartered in a town and the inhabitants'.[17]

In addition, however, the function of 'subaltern's guard' embraced a wider, more contentious duty, namely 'to suppress all kinds of disorder, particularly in the night.'[18] Here was recognition of the army's de facto role in matters of civil administration, when, albeit only at the express request of 'the Justices',[19] the military could be called on to restore public order. Arguably, this was the army's main peacetime function, the figure of 25,708 soldiers[20] dispersed around Britain in 1770 a sure sign that the House of Hanover still feared for its survival.

Given that the size of this peacetime establishment raised the dreaded spectre of a standing army, 'the propriety of calling in the Military to the aid of the civil Magistrates has of late been the cause of much altercation.'[21] With the increase in social and political unrest in the late 1760s, however, local magistrates found themselves of necessity 'ordering the Riot Act to be read'[22] more frequently. As a result, troops were increasingly called into potential hotspots to act as a deterrent. Whole regiments were moved round the kingdom as a show of force. This, naturally, excited tensions between the justices and the government, and 'Sheriffs' complained that 'military force' was being deployed 'by order of his Majesty and the Secretary of State'[23] and without their approval.

Yet, even as the government sought to project its power, so the army that was its most visible instrument must be represented as benign not oppressive. In these circumstances, news management became crucial: the *London Gazette*, supreme organ of official information and disinformation, chose what official measures for keeping the peace should be made public. Depending on whether they were pro-government or not, newspapers would decide how to interpret these measures. The army, even as a peacetime establishment, became a vital tool of government propaganda. Writing to Anna Seward in the autumn of 1769, John may have chosen to 'like anything better than news', but eighteen months on, as an army officer he was now part of the news being reported. Like it or not, he must not only keep abreast of events, but also understand them.

To read the newspapers of the day, there was no reason John could see why his regiment had been quartered in Scotland the previous year, nor for its presence in Manchester at the time he joined it in January 1771. Ostensibly, this was part of the normal rhythm of the regiment as part of the peacetime establishment going back many years. Yet, if he had been keeping his ear to the ground, he would have known that Britain was going through uncertain times and that there had been a succession of serious riots in London in 1768 when a 'very great Mob assembled and demanded'[24] the release of John Wilkes from prison. From his letters to Anna, he certainly knew about the Spitalfield riots of 1769. What he may not have known was that riots were also occurring round the kingdom: following a bad harvest, Scotland was the scene of so-called 'Meal Riots' in Edinburgh and the Borders during 1770. This might explain the Fusiliers' tour of duty in that part of the country.[25]

Early 1771 brought fresh outbreaks of violence around the kingdom, with 'riots' in February 'at the meeting of the Irish Parliament',[26] followed in March by numerous incidents, beginning with the 'Irish mob at Brentford' on the outskirts of London, but continuing into the heart of metropolis when 'the populace were very riotous yesterday in the Park'. The immediate cause of this riot was 'the Lord Mayor's being sent to the Tower'. So serious were the disturbances that 'there has been a great run upon the Bank',[27] and a Parliamentary 'Committee' had to be established 'for enquiring into the Causes of the Riots ... in St. George's Fields at Brentford and other places'.[28]

The government decided on a show of force, and 'orders were on Tuesday evening sent to the Tower for the normal evening guard to be doubled'. This was deemed insufficient, and a report was put out that the dreaded 'third regiment of guards' was 'now doing duty in the Tower'.[29] Its reputation preceded it, the *London Packet* complaining that the soldiers watching the prisoners in the Tower were from 'the very Company of the Third Regiment, which committed the Massacre in St. George's Fields'.[30] This was only the latest supposed atrocity committed by the regiment: John's relative, Andrew Girardot, had been in command, when, a year earlier, his foot guards went into Spitalfields to quell the unrest among the weavers.

Unsurprisingly, following these latest riots there was more than the usual redeployment of regiments round the country. In April, a report came in from Leeds that 'on Thursday last a party of the 37th regiment of foot, quartered in this town, set out for Kendal, in order to quell some riotous proceedings, among the weavers in that place'.[31] A letter from Portsmouth, dated 'May 5 1771', caught two further such movements, reporting that 'the 19th regiment landed at Gosport from a man of war ... and marched up the country' and that 'the 30th regiment is to land on our beach on Monday and to march to Petersfield.'[32]

Similarly, John's regiment was soon on the move: leaving their Manchester quarters in March, the Welch Fusiliers headed south towards London, its ultimate destination the barracks at Chatham on the lower reaches of the Thames. However, instead of making direct for the metropolis, the regiment took a circuitous route, first going east to Newark in April. Before turning south, it made another detour, this time to Lincoln, where 'last week several outrages were committed by some riotous persons, who assembled at Louth, Sleaford and other markets in Lincolnshire and put a stop to the carrying of all kinds of grain, cattle etc even into the neighbouring counties, either by land or water'.[33] According to the *Travelling Dictionary*, this diversion would have added some forty miles to an already long march of two hundred and twelve miles.[34] All in all, this was a far cry from the 'sweet walk home'[35] John enjoyed daily when working at Warnford Court. Especially demanding for John was that he would have been at the head of a column not less than '484'[36] men and 'possibly as many as 737'.[37]

This detour does not appear in the regimental records,[38] it deemed too inglorious that the regiment be on duty to serve as a deterrent or, if late on the scene, to put down the 'outrages'. Needless to say, this necessary but unsavoury work would have been a sharp initiation for John into the realities of army life. He had seen riots in Geneva and Spitalfields first hand, but, as a subaltern officer, he was now integral to the forces of law and order. This was not why he had chosen the army: he had joined a regiment of the line so he might serve overseas. Quelling 'riotous proceedings' in Lincoln was work for the foot-guards and other home regiments.

Finally turning south via Bedford and Hampstead, the regiment reached Chatham in time to begin preparation for the 'Great Review' to be conducted in front of the king in August. The 'royal public review'[39] was an annual event that all regiments then stationed in the London area must undergo. It involved performing a series of intricate parade-ground drills which entailed 'as many as eighteen or twenty motions', all conducted 'almost entirely by the sounds and beating of the drum.' Officers and men alike must also be perfected in the 'Manual Exercise',[40] which demonstrated agility and aptitude in the handling of a firearm while in parade-ground drill. This would take weeks of training and rehearsal.

Hence, it would have come as a shock to John when, arriving in London in the middle of June after three months on the march, the regiment was informed that the king planned an immediate review. News of this appeared in the *London Evening News*, its 18 June edition reporting that 'yesterday the 23d regiment of foot commanded by Gen. George Boscawen were reviewed by his Majesty in Hyde-Park on their march to Chatham.'[41] Two days later came a report of another impromptu review, but this time the news was given in advance, the *Middlesex Journal* announcing: 'we hear that his Majesty will this day review the 33d regiment of foot, commanded by Earl Cornwallis on Blackheath.'[42]

Being so hastily arranged, both reviews were evidently intended as propaganda exercises, the purpose being to send a clear message to the public that there was an enhanced military presence in the metropolis. That, in consequence, the two regiments were ill-prepared for what they must perform on the parade ground was soon apparent from the storm of criticism unleashed by one 'military man'. Styling himself 'Germanicus', on 11 July he launched the first in a series of satirical salvoes aimed initially at 'Lord Cornwallis' and 'your new system of military discipline but only as it consists in making buffoons of yourself and your men.'[43]

Another correspondent, 'Britannicus', came to the defence of Cornwallis, and, on 16 July, discountenanced 'that Germanicus shou'd abuse the Guards.'[44] Battle was joined and, on 15 August, 'Germanicus' turned his full fire on, this time, the Welch Fusiliers. Addressing himself to 'General Boscawen', commander of the regiment, he, again, laid into the 'adoption of a new system of discipline which seems chiefly to consist of putting a regiment into as much disorder as possible; for to see a regiment that was steady, carry their arms well, or step together, would not have the appearance of real service. All that is now aimed at, is a light pair of heels.'[45]

Waiting two months before launching this attack on the Welch Fusiliers was deliberate. As a 'military man', Germanicus knew about the Great Review coming up in August. He knew also that the Welch Fusiliers were at Chatham Barracks, preparing for the review. Unlike their impromptu review in June, this time there would be no excuse for any sloppy drills. The regiment had had ample time to prepare. There had even been a full-dress rehearsal overseen by General Monckton on 1 August.[46] Their sister regiment, the 7th Foot or Royal (English) Fusiliers, was also at Chatham Barracks drilling for the review. The Welch Fusiliers were sure to come off second-best.

As anticipated, on 5 August a report appeared in the *Public Advertiser* that 'this morning his Majesty will review the royal regiment of Welch Fuzileers on Wimbledon Common.'[47] Three days later, the *Middlesex Journal* recorded that 'this day his Majesty reviewed on Blackheath the two regiments of English and Welch Fusiliers.' However, it appended a footnote stating that 'a detachment of the guards marched early this morning to prevent obstructions etc.'[48] This begs the question what 'obstructions' were anticipated. Was it because further 'riotous proceedings' were feared, this time aimed directly at the army, or were the 'obstructions etc' the many 'spectators'[49] expected to line the route, enjoying what, at least in past years, was a showpiece event?

On previous occasions, certainly, the Welch Fusiliers had been an especial favourite with the public, given the quirky sight of 'the celebrated goat, which passed in review at the head of the regiment, groomed white as snow for the occasion, its horns gilded and garlanded with flowers.'[50] Whatever the reason for the Guards escort, the march to Blackheath passed off without incident, which was a relief as, according to the *Gazetteer and New Daily Advertiser*, this was to be 'the last royal public review this year'.[51]

Among the 'spectators' were relatives of the officers and men, in which case the Andrés—mother Mary-Louisa, sisters Anne, Mary and Louisa, and younger brother, William Lewis—would surely have been among those enjoying the spectacle of John carrying the colours of the regiment, a signal honour which he shared with fellow subaltern, Benjamin Bernard. Whereas the choice of Bernard as standard-bearer was forgone, being as he was the son of the major in the regiment, John's selection can only have been the result of merit. Intelligent, diligent and ambitious, he had already made his mark, performing to perfection the duties required of him thus far. Moreover, with his eye-catching looks, fashionably 'enormous pig-tails'[52] and 'good figure (at least a genteel one)',[53] he cut the right 'ornament'[54] that so many military manuals of the day deemed obligatory for a coming officer and that the regiment needed on display on the day of its Great Review.

Watching John as he 'dipped the proud Union with its three-feather device',[55] Mary-Louisa may have heaved a sigh of relief that, after all the turmoil of the past two and a half years, one of her children was finally on his way. She surely needed that tonic because force of economy following the Crauford debacle—or was it shame?—had obliged her to give up the family home in Clapton[56] and seek the social seclusion of 'the town of Southampton' whose only 'places of public resort are Martin's and the Polygon.'[57] Yet, she still had three daughters to marry off. Seeing John in all his scarlet finery, she must have hoped that the family might be able to hold its head up high once more, in which case there would be dashing young subalterns lining up to court her daughters. Time pressed, however: Mary, the oldest, was already nineteen.

Proud to see John in full dress uniform with the new bearskins on show as headdress for the first time, Mary-Louisa may, nevertheless, have had mixed feelings when 'the Officers and spectators' began gossiping among themselves, and 'expressed a Regret, and thought it very impolitic, to send so fine a body of men to a climate which it is very probable in a short time may kill half of them.'[58] They were alluding to reports in the newspapers that 'an Exchange of troops will certainly take place early next autumn' which would mean both fusilier regiments being sent 'to relieve the 36th ... and 66th at Jamaica'.[59]

According to the *General Evening Post*, the review went off splendidly when 'this Morning, his Majesty accompanied by the Duke of Gloucester, and Lord Ligonier in his new regimentals, and other General Officers reviewed the Royal English and Welch Fusileers on Blackheath-lawn; when they went through their different manoeuvres and firings, and received the praise of the King and every Officer present.'[60]

'Germanicus' was having nothing of it. He could smell court propaganda a mile off. Attending the impromptu reviews in June, he had already seen enough to suspect that the 1771 reviews were about propaganda, not military professionalism. Being a military man, he was a stickler for the proper drills. Hence, he mocked that 'a little gentleman, who appeared to be one of the faculty ... had seen the fusileer regiments reviewed' on the previous occasion and reported to him how 'they appeared to him to be in a very declining state... They were every now and then seized with convulsion fits, that terminated in a very rapid motion of the legs which is a very bad symptom; for when a running once breaks out there, it has a very dangerous tendency, and the only cure which he could prescribe, was to send them to some warm climate, which he made no doubt would effectually stop it.' (Obviously, 'Germanicus' had heard the same reports about 'an Exchange of troops' in Jamaica as John's mother.)

To give further authority to his volleys of vitriol, 'Germanicus' assured General Boscawen that, 'hearing that your regiment was to be reviewed with the fusileers on Saturday last, I took a ride as far as Blackheath to see them'. Armed with the authority of the eyewitness, he praised the men who, 'notwithstanding the disadvantage of ground which your regiment laboured under, their superiority, as to size and youth, was obvious. Your light company may safely be deemed the finest in the service.' By contrast, 'it was a pity you had not displayed a little more taste in the choice of their officers; for, instead of being handsome, active, and well-made young men, they were old, ugly, and lazy.'[61]

Reading this, John would, surely, have laughed to see himself described as 'old, ugly, and lazy'. Self-evidently, these were the rantings of a military old-stager consumed with professional jealousy when 'more complicated evolutions were performed, including some innovations by the Light Infantry Company not yet to be found in the Drill Book'.[62]

Obviously, 'Germanicus' was desperate to challenge the new ideology of 'open tactics'[63] adopted by the army during the Seven Years' War. Knowing how well the regiment had performed these new 'evolutions' and believing how important these 'innovations' were to the future agility and mobility of a light infantry regiment in the field, John could easily laugh off the barbs by 'Germanicus' that 'while your regiment looked on them, all those ridiculous innovations must have been received with the contempt which they deserved.'

John also knew that he had a sharper pen than 'Germanicus'. Better attuned to Grub Street's rhetoric, John could deliver the satirical putdown that 'Germanicus' deserved. Just as 'Britannicus' had taken exception to the earlier attacks by 'Germanicus' on Lord Cornwallis, so these August attacks on the Welch Fusiliers attracted the ire of 'An Unfledged Ensign'. This correspondent wrote in to the *London Evening Post*, and his letter was printed in 24 August edition. Mocking in its tone, it took delight in offsetting the author's youth and junior rank against 'Germanicus', the 'veteran', and, in pretended deference to the senior officer, accepted that 'there is no confuting such a military genius who must have seen a great *deal* of service.'[64]

There is no firm proof that John was the author of this letter but apart from the military context which places him close to its authorship, clues within the letter's style suggest that it was by him. When asking—'was ever a poor epistle so becriticised?'—the author mangled English in much the same as John did when writing to Anna Seward and inventing words like to 'stumpify' and 'unsay'[65] and playing with others such as 'draggletailed'.[66] If John were, indeed, the author behind the 'Unfledged Ensign', this would be the first of many letters by him to find their way into the public domain. Reading this letter, John's superior officers would have seen that he understood the power of words and could use it to good effect.

CHAPTER 13

'Petite Guerre'

On 24 September 1771, just six weeks after he had carried the colours for the Royal Welch Fusiliers at the annual review on Blackheath Common, John transferred into the sister regiment, the Royal (English) Fusiliers.[1] At first glance, there was nothing exceptional in this. It was common practice for subalterns to chop and change between regiments. That was often the quickest means of gaining promotion up through the junior ranks. The timing and circumstances of John's decision indicate, however, that factors other than the speed of his advancement were uppermost in John's mind. What first points to this was the lag in time between the September date when, according to regimental records,[2] John joined the English Fusiliers (also known as 7th Regiment of Foot) and the date four months later when the 'War Office' confirmed the move with his promotion to the rank of lieutenant in his new regiment. This finally came through on 25 January 1772 with the following notice published in the *London Gazette*: '7th Reg. Foot: Second Lieut. John André of 23d Reg to be Lieut, vice Rowland Mainwaring, preferred'.[3]

If quick promotion were John's sole consideration, he might have been better off remaining in the Welch Fusiliers. There, he could have jostled to be part of at least three rounds of promotions announced by that regiment in the immediate aftermath of the successful Great Review, the first on 10 September 1771 when 'Edward Evans and John Jennings Esqs'[4] were made up to captain, a second on 21 September 1771 when 'Thomas Mecan Gent is appointed a Captain Lieutenant',[5] and a third on 3 October 1771 when 'Harry Blunt Esq. was appointed a Major'.[6] These all afforded early opportunities for junior subalterns in the regiment to move up a rank. Moreover, given the signal honour accorded to John of carrying the colours at the Great Review, it was clear he had already made a success of his short time in the Welch Fusiliers, in which case he should have been in line for early preferment within that regiment.

Given that quick promotion was not uppermost in John's thinking, this raises the possibility that he had set his sights on the English Fusiliers from the outset and that the Welch Fusiliers were just a stepping stone. With the minimum age set at sixteen for aspiring officers entering the army and many starting aged eighteen, John, at twenty-one, was already 'old' when he joined. Hence, a sense of his own dignity required John to enter at a rank above ensign. That meant a lieutenancy, but irrespective of the cost, coming in at that rank necessitated substantial patronage, which John did not have. He must settle instead for a second lieutenancy, and that was a rank recognized by the Welch Fusiliers, but, significantly, not by the English Fusiliers.

Certainly, the move to the English Fusiliers was not impelled by any desire for radical change on John's part. Both regiments were light infantry fusiliers, their duties indistinguishable. Furthermore, he did not, for instance, seek to capitalize on his proficiency in mathematics and draughtsmanship and transfer into specialist branches of the Army, such as the Royal Artillery or Corps of Engineers, where these skills were held in high regard. Nor was there any significance behind John's move from a Welsh to an English regiment. From Robert Donkin's comments regarding the celebrations for St. David's Day, it seems that the 'Welshness' of John's current regiment was confined to the men, and that officers were expected to be British, as evidenced by Captain William Blakeney, an Irishman, and the Adjutant, Frederick Mackenzie, a Scot.

The Royal (English) Fusiliers was equally eclectic at officer level but with one notable difference:[7] two of its lieutenants—John Despard and Francis Le Maistre[8]— were Huguenots. It was surely no coincidence that Le Maistre[9] and Despard[10] had both chosen the English Fusiliers: the colonel of the regiment, Lord Robert Bertie, though not himself a Huguenot, had a close family relative who was. His brother, Lord Brownlow Bertie, had married Mary Ann Layard in December 1768.[11] The Layards were an influential Huguenot family.[12] Mary Ann's brother was 'Dr Layard, physician to Her Royal Highness the Princess Dowager of Wales'.[13] A Lord of the Bedchamber to George III and Member of Parliament, Lord Robert Bertie was susceptible to the call of family when deciding who to accept into the regiment, evident when he brought Mary Ann's other brother, Anthony, over from the 70th Regiment and made him a lieutenant in the regiment in April 1772.[14]

The Andrés were not immediate family but there were distant ties to Bertie through John's godfather, John Bristow.[15] The connection was too distant to have triggered formal patronage but would have smoothed John's path into the new regiment if, as seems probable, he caught the eye of Bertie's second-in-command, Richard Prescott who, as the lieutenant colonel, was in charge of the day-to-day running of the English Fusiliers. A no-nonsense career officer aged 46, Prescott had seen tough service with the 50th Regiment in the Seven Years' War, in particular during the campaign of 1760–61 in Germany,[16] before transferring into the English Fusiliers. Hard-nosed and ambitious, Prescott was looking to attract, on merit, the best up-and-coming young officers.

Prescott would have had ample opportunity to see John in action with the Welch Fusiliers. Like them, the English Fusiliers had seen recent service in Scotland, the

Public Advertiser reporting on 7 April 1768 that on 'Thursday morning the party of Lord Robert Bertie's Regiment of Foot quartered at Glasgow marched for Perth.' From there, the regiment went to Fort William before returning to Berwick-on-Tweed in 1770. En route to Chatham in the spring of 1771 they rendezvoused with the Welch Fusiliers in Lincoln, the two joining forces to quell the local riots.[17] Prescott may have first seen John on duty at that point.

The two regiments then went their separate ways, the Welch Fusiliers to Chatham, the English Fusiliers to Plymouth where 'four transports' were standing by 'to take some troops on board for Minorca'.[18] According to a report by the *Middlesex Journal* dated 18 April 1771, 'on Wednesday sailed the four transports' but only 'with the 51st regiment on board for Minorca.' The English Fusiliers had diverted, meantime, to Portsmouth from where a report dated 7 April was filed that 'on Thursday, the 7th regiment, as well as the 61st was embarked from Stokes Bay on board the transports that had waited for them some time.' According to this report, 'these troops are countermanded for some little time'.[19]

These on-off preparations were part of the fracas with Spain over the Falklands. This was resolved by 25 April 1771, when, according to the *London Evening Post*, 'Falkland Island is left on the same footing (with respect to the Spaniards right to it) as Gibraltar and Minorca.' With that, the English Fusiliers disembarked and marched to Chatham Barracks, where, as the officer responsible for preparing his regiment ahead of the August Great Review, Prescott would certainly have seen John drilling with the Welch Fusiliers on the parade ground.[20]

John clearly impressed, but more than his skill at performing 'evolutions' and 'motions' on the parade-ground, what, doubtless, brought John to Prescott's notice was his aptitude for money management, his organizational capabilities and his facility with languages, a rare and valuable combination, all the result of the intensive apprenticeship he had received at the family's compting house. This combination of skills marked John out from the other subaltern officers as a future quartermaster[21] in the regiment. It also made him an obvious candidate to learn the art of 'petite guerre' ('little war'), activities that Prescott believed would be integral to how Britain conducted any future conflicts, wherever that might be.

Broadly defined as 'all the movements that merely back up the operations of an army', 'petite guerre' was essentially irregular activities, or what, in today's conflicts, would be deemed—at least at the sharp end—commando operations. Conducted by light infantry—which the two fusilier regiments quintessentially were—these operations 'harassed the enemy, gathered intelligence and carried out deep strikes'.[22] As European armies increasingly organized themselves for ever grander trials of strength on the battlefield, so weaker adversaries must perfect the art of petite guerre, using fleetness of foot, secret intelligence and unconventional tactics to offset superior numbers and firepower. Forced to defend New France (Canada) against overwhelming odds in North America during the Seven Years' War, the

French elevated petite guerre from an occasional tactic into a formal military strategy involving sustained irregular combat.

Prior to joining the English Fusiliers, Prescott had served with the 50th Regiment in Canada during that conflict. That taught him the importance of petite guerre. Another convert was Donkin, under whom John had served in the Welch Fusiliers.[23] Donkin wrote a military manual and devoted its last—and lengthy—chapter to 'La Petite Guerre'.[24] In it, he described the scope of irregular warfare, the archetypal officer material it would need to attract and, last, but not least, the role of the 'partizan'[25] who would command these operations.

Between them, Prescott and Donkin would have seen that, of all the young officers in the two regiments, John offered the promise of what it took to be a 'petit guerrier',[26] even eventually a 'partizan', not least because, among the skills required was to be a 'master of several languages, chiefly that of the country where the war is'.[27] To a military man serving in the British army at that time, 'languages' meant principally two: French, because Catholic France was the eternal foe; German because, in amongst the 'approximately three hundred sovereign territories within the Germany Empire',[28] there were many Catholic enemies but also many Protestant friends of Britain. Listening to Prescott and Donkin describe what they had in mind for him, could it be that John was about to have his prayers answered and sent overseas, away from Warnford Court, Clapton and Lichfield? If so, what a relief that would be after the misery of the past three years.

CHAPTER 14

'A Terrible Conflagration'

'Yesterday arrived the Mail from Holland,' according to the *Public Advertiser* for 20 May 1772. Dated 'Amsterdam May 14', there were two items of note. The first was the news of 'the Emperor of Morocco having as good as declared war against the [Dutch] Republic'. The second reported at great length how 'last Monday evening a fire broke out in the playhouse … which occasioned a terrible Conflagration, the consequences of which cannot be sufficiently lamented.' In raw detail, it described how 'in two Minutes the Stage was all in a Blaze and the Chandeliers all falling down caused an inexpressible Disorder among the Spectators, everyone flying to save his life.' Panning out to a wider panorama, a scene from hell was conjured where 'in a few minutes the whole town seem'd illuminated. The Flames, driven by a violent North East wind, communicated to some houses in the Runstraat'. With foreboding, the report announced that 'we all already know a few of the most important Burghers who have been the Victims of this unhappy Accident. The number of the others cannot as yet be ascertained.'[1]

As the smoke cleared following this first report, London received a flurry of updates and news flashes including, on 23 May, the 'following printed account received in yesterday's mail,' which had 'the pleasure to inform our readers that the calamity attending the late fire at the playhouse at Amsterdam was not so bad as has been represented.'[2] Contrary to earlier reports that 'the number of unhappy persons… is generally supposed to amount to 200',[3] it appeared that 'thirty-one persons only perished.' These later accounts also named the casualties. Second on the (nonetheless) long list of those known to have 'perished' was 'Mr Jacob de Neufville van Lennep and Lady'. Doubtless, Lennep was the tragic 'gentleman' in one of the 'dismal anecdotes' taken from an 'extract of a letter from Amsterdam dated May 15.' Briefly separated from his 'wife', he 'turned back, threw himself in her arms and both fell. In this affecting position, they were dug from under the ruins the next morning.'

In no particular order of civic status after 'Lennep and Lady', the list named 'Cornelius Raus, City Architect', then, the 'director of the playhouse', followed by a 'figure dancer', a 'bricklayer' and so on, ending with 'two or three that assisted at the engines'. Ahead of them and first on the list, however, was 'Mr Louis André, merchant'.[4] In normal circumstances, seeing this name reported among a list of victims in a foreign 'Conflagration' would have excited, at best, curiosity, at worst, sadness among the London Andrés, depending on whether they knew of, or knew, the Amsterdam branch of the family. On this occasion, however, it was likely to cause anxiety, if not panic. John was known to be in Amsterdam at this precise moment. What if the newspapers had got the victim's first name wrong?

Anticipating his family's reaction, John had, however, hurried off a letter or, so he explained, a flurry of letters, to London. In the one addressed to 'mon cher oncle' (John Lewis) and dated 'Amsterdam le 14 May 1772', John described how he had seen *un monsieur André*—meaning 'a Mister André'—on the casualty list and immediately 'feared' that some 'newspaper' (*papier de nouvelle*) in London could recount the 'terrible Conflagration' and, by giving just the surname 'André', might 'frighten (*effrayé*) those who interest themselves' in his well-being. As a result, he had been writing 'to all quarters' (*dans tous les quartiers*) where he had friends to put them at ease. The first of these letters was to his friend 'Ewer'.

In the letter to his uncle, John proceeded, next, to list the casualties, beginning, as in the London newspapers, with 'Mr Louis André'. This raises the possibility that John was the main source for the later reports sent to London newspapers: not only did 'a Mister André' become, very precisely, 'Mr Louis André', but also, this 'Mr Louis André' was positioned first on the list of the 'well-regarded Citizens' ('Gens très consideré'[5]) featured as casualties in later London newspaper reports of the 'terrible Conflagration'. By contrast, a Dutch magazine only listed 'Louis André' third in its list of casualties after Lennep and a 'Margaretha Feitama'.[6] Further circumstantial evidence to support this comes from John's inclusion of an item about Morocco, which he knew would impact on the family's Mediterranean trading activities and, hence, interest his uncle.

Yet, this was the same news item featured in the *Public Advertiser* report from 20 May. If so, either John had a hand directly in the articles that appeared in the London newspapers, or, equally likely, one of the letters he sent to his friends in London was copied on to those newspapers. This was common practice at the time, in which case 'the extract of the letter from Amsterdam dated May 15' and featured in, among others, the *Gazetteer and New Daily Advertiser*, is the obvious one, especially since it also supplied items of interest to his uncles, including the 'Prices of English stocks here [in Amsterdam] this day'.[7]

Understandably, John would have wished to clarify urgently that he was not the 'André' killed in the Amsterdam fire, and one sure way to do this was via the public prints. Nevertheless, coming as it did hard on the heels of his likely authorship of the letter from the 'Unfledged Ensign' sent into the *London Evening Post* the previous year, this latest item bearing John's fingerprints suggests he was growing in literary confidence for the '*livre des chroniques*' ('book of chronicles') that he intended to write. Travel journals were a popular literary genre at that time, and crucial to them were anecdotes about the people and places encountered along the way. These were 'the memorable and remarkable curiosities' that John told his uncle he had seen. Instead of recounting them, however, he said he was logging them daily in a '*fameux journal*'[8] ready for the '*livre des chroniques*' he promised his uncle he would one day publish.

Interesting though John's letter is in the context of the crisis that had recently occurred within the family, his presence in Amsterdam begs the question what he, as a newly promoted lieutenant, was doing there when his regiment was on duty variously in Dover Castle and Plymouth Citadel. It seems he was there at the behest of his commanding officer, Colonel Prescott. As part of the arrangement to entice John over to Royal Fusiliers, Prescott had recommended that, once the hoped-for promotion had been confirmed by the War Office, his latest lieutenant should take a leave of absence and tour to the Continent. Only there could John receive the necessary training to undertake the special duties Prescott had in mind.

At last, after all the turmoil in his life, John could see he was going places—where was still anyone's guess, and to what end, who knows! For the time being, frontier service surveying uncharted lands could wait. Instead, he must trust his new commanding officer, no hardship, as what awaited John on this, his second time on the Continent, promised to be so much better, so much more challenging, so much more honourable than life in the dire and 'gloomy compting house' in Warnford Court. He was in such fine spirits he could even joke with his uncle at the end of his letter, alternately preening himself for being the best dressed '*cavalier*' in Amsterdam '*avec mes habits a l'anglaise*', only, in the next breath, to recast himself as a '*Scaramouch*' and the mocking butt of '*la canaille*' ('the riffraff')[9] for wearing so short a jacket. John could not be happier. He had been so right to choose a career in the army, and now, in Colonel Prescott he had a commanding officer who seemed to understand him and know exactly what he wanted. All this was what had convinced John to transfer from the Welch Fusiliers to the Royal Fusiliers.

Starting out from Harwich in March, he had to cross over to Helvoetsluys, at that time one of the major ports for the Dutch naval fleet but also the gateway for British travellers into Holland and beyond into northern Europe. According to the *London Magazine* from 1781, this crossing 'is often performed in twelve hours … but when the wind is foul, the time in making the passage is extended to two or three days'.[10] As March was not the best of times of year to be making a Channel crossing, unsurprisingly John would recall it as a rude reminder of the 'Seafaring Life'.[11] Another landlubber to suffer on the crossing was William Short, sent to negotiate a treaty with Holland on behalf of the new United States in 1785. Writing to Thomas Jefferson from The Hague, Short pleaded 'to do any Thing you think proper in this Matter' except 'recross from Helvoetsluys to Harwich' for 'I cannot describe to you what I suffered in a short passage of twenty-four hours.'[12]

Arriving in Holland, John had two modes of transport open to him: coach or canal barge. In 1791, Mr Thomasson, secretary to John Howard, the famous prison reformer, would make the same journey by coach. He kept a meticulous record and, when submitting his expenses for the Amsterdam to Helvoetsluys leg, claimed £2 10s for what he said was a five-day journey.[13] In her travel guide from 1815, Mariana Starke estimated, however, that the distance was 33 miles which, if John took one of the 'Treckschuyt or covered barges' (the mode of transport recommended by her in winter), the journey would, at 'four English miles an hour',[14] have only taken him a little over one day. Unlike Thomasson, John had no reason to account for his expenses, but still felt he owed it to himself to volunteer to his uncle that '*mon compte de traitteur n'est pas long*'[15] ('my schedule of expenses is not long'). This was a reminder to the wider family that, whatever mistakes his father had made, he, John, would never be a burden on his uncles.

John had reason to be proud. Being dispatched to the Continent was an exceptional vote of confidence in him by his commanding officer. Nevertheless, this was to be no 'Grand Tour', and John understood that. He might meet the many Grand Tourists passing through Amsterdam[16] on their way to the capitals, courts, cathedrals and castles of Europe as they prepared to take their place among Britain's ruling elite. Having John meet these Grand Tourists as they passed through Geneva back in 1766 may have been important to his father, but, this time, John was back on serious business, one of a very few subaltern officers selected by their commanders for special training on the Continent.

Among these junior officers to be singled out was the future Sir James Murray, who, as 'a Lieutenant in the 19th Regiment of Foot' since 'March 1770',' was sent 'travelling on the Continent' by his uncles, Lord Elibank and General James, 'in 1772 and 1773'.[17] Dispatched, initially, to French-speaking Neufchatel, Murray wrote to his sister, Bessie, in January 1773 'after eight long months … elaps'd since I left my native land,' telling her about 'the observations, remarks and improvements I have made in my travels.'

Unlike John, however, he was not quite sure, at least initially, why he had been sent and wondered aloud 'how long I shall stay here, or where I shall go this summer I cannot inform you. I expect every day a letter from my uncle which shall determine me'. As Murray's set itinerary moved on, first, to German-speaking Brunswick in June, then Holland in October, he began to see clearer that his main task was to learn foreign languages, evident when he decamped from Lausanne to Neufchatel, to escape 'the greatest ressort of strangers from all countrys', his reason being that 'Englishmen don't travel to see Englishmen.' As if to emphasise the point, he then offered to 'assist [Bessie] in learning French and German.' Murray was also charged to understand the diplomacy and politics of Europe first-hand. This would be one of John's duties, and he took it on with relish, unlike Murray who abhorred meeting 'the foreign Envoys' at the courts he visited and being 'introduced to all possible princes and princesses at Berlin, which is one of the most brilliant Courts in Europe.'[18]

Of course, there was more to the time spent on the Continent by these subaltern officers than either John or Murray would let on in letters home, but some inkling of their other duties can be gleaned from the memoirs of another junior officer, George Hanger, who was in Hanover, Prussia and Hesse-Cassel at the same time as John and Murray were on their respective Continental travels. These memoirs tell at length how Hanger was instructed in 'the discipline of the light cavalry', 'attended all the reviews in the country', including 'the Prussian reviews', and witnessed 'every manoeuvre that the great Frederick [of Prussia] could devise'.[19] Hanger could be open about what he did at that time because his memoirs were published later, in 1801, whereas John and Murray were writing about their immediate experiences.

Britain happened to be at peace when these three young officers were completing their training on the Continent, but experience had taught Murray's uncles and John's commanding officer, Colonel Prescott, that the next war was always just the 'Tricker'[20] on a flintlock away and would be somewhere on the Continent. Even as Prescott was arranging for John's transfer into the English Fusiliers in late 1771, Russia, Prussia and Austria were machinating to carve up Poland. By the time of John's visit to Amsterdam in May 1772 and Murray's sojourns in Neufchatel, Brunswick and Berlin later that year, the process of dismemberment was already well underway. Reports from Warsaw on 2 May that 'the Prussians have driven all the Confederates out of Great Poland' and that 'the Austrian troops ... have orders to enter Poland' seemed to herald some kind of legality to this smash-and-grab by 'a triple alliance on foot between the courts of Petersbourg, Berlin and Vienna.'[21] What started in Poland could quickly affect vital British interests, not least because George III was also Elector of Hanover and might call on British regiments to defend his remote territories.

Prescott's time serving alongside Britain's German and Prussian allies during the Seven Years' War had impressed on him the need to know your friends, understand your enemies and always be prepared for the next war: tough to do in a Britain that rejected all notions of a standing army. As a promising, ambitious and intelligent man who was a clear cut above the rest among the rising generation of junior army officers, John must assimilate these realities. As a refugee Huguenot, he understood the French better than any Englishman could. Moreover, he had been in Geneva when France had renewed its sabre-rattling against the Swiss. He needed no further lessons to understand that France was the old enemy.

It was now time to understand the Germans. This meant him living in Germany, learning the German language and studying what the Germans did best: how a modern army went about fighting its wars. Like Prescott, Donkin had served in Germany during the Seven Years' War. Time and again in his military manual, he referred back to episodes from that conflict that pointed up the importance of petite guerre in modern warfare.[22] Only by studying in Germany could John begin to understand what was required of a 'petit guerrier'. Cuthbertson's military manual stressed the importance of learning about 'Fortification'. Donkin made clear, too, that an understanding of 'fortification and artillery' was vital even to a 'petit guerrier', but so that he could properly reconnoitre for 'any enterprize to attempt against an enemy' and learn to 'regulate his march in such a manner as to suffer as little as possible from [enemy] cannon.'[23]

There were a number of military academies across Europe—Caen, Strasburg[24] and Turin, to name three—but, doubtless on the advice of Prescott, John had chosen Göttingen University, which was where he was headed after he left Amsterdam. Located within the territories controlled by the British crown as, simultaneously, Elector of Hanover, the university had been built up from nowhere by George II. Although the city and university had suffered badly during the Seven Years' War, by 1769, according 'to a letter from Gottingen', 'the said university begins to recover its former Grandeur, since its sufferings by the last War'. As a result, 'about fifty English Noblemen and Gentlemen are now there on their studies; and Professor Hallen who was invited to Petersbourg, still stays, we are told, at Göttingen, to bring it to its former Repute.'[25]

Göttingen was frequently featured in London newspapers, puffs telling British readers what a good university it had. On 27 April 1769, the *Middlesex Journal* sang Göttingen's praises, numbering the 'English noblemen and gentlemen students' attending at '60'.[26] Much of this was the work of the court. George III continued where the previous king had left off, playing host to academics from Göttingen, including 'in April 1770 … the brilliant young physicist and mathematician, Georg Christoph Lichtenberg,'[27] and publicizing the cultural links between Britain and Hanover. In this vein, an advertisement appeared in 1769 announcing a work by 'Mr Michaelis, Court-Counsellor to his Britannic Majesty and Director of the Royal Society at Gottingen.'[28] In 1770 came a reminder that 'Daniel Layard, Physician to Her Royal Highness the Princess Dowager of Wales,' was a 'Member … of the Royal Societies of London and Gottingen.'[29] This followed an earlier announcement that he had been made 'a fellow of the Royal Society at Gottingen'.[30]

Meantime, a steady stream of advertisements featured promotions of important works of reference written by Göttingen scholars, including 'A New System of Geography' by 'A. F. Bushing, Professor of Philosophy in the University of Gottingen'.[31] Finally, in 1771, the following advertisement appeared in the *London Evening Post*. Headed 'Gottingen University in his Majesty's Electoral Dominions', it invited 'gentlemen of fortune, desirous of sending their sons to this university' to contact 'P. Pepin, Professor of the English Language in Gottingen' if they were seeking someone to 'inform them of the several particulars they may previously wish to know, concerning the general plan of the university, and the accomplishments that may be acquired by youth who are intended for military employments.'[32]

Professor Pepin's invitation was only confirming what was already well known, in that British sons of 'gentlemen of fortune' had been passing through the university for some years past. Indeed, some were currently enrolled there. At least six of these went on to make a career in the army, and four certainly served in America during the Revolutionary War. By the time John enrolled on 'July 1 1772', William Faucitt (entry: September 1767) had already graduated, as had Alexander Lindsay (entry: July 1769) and Francis Carr-Clerke (entry: August 1769).[33]

Hanger was also there, but cut short his time. With rakish abandon, he explained why in his memoirs. Believing, like Prescott, that as 'I had resolved on being a soldier, a German education was best suited to the profession I had chosen', Hanger 'was accordingly sent into Germany, to Göttingen which is one of the most celebrated universities in the world'.[34] With his course of study in mathematics starting on 'Nov, 16 1770',[35] he could still have been at the university when John arrived in mid-1772. Charles Adams, who also studied mathematics, arrived in June 1770 and, not matriculating until the summer of 1772,[36] did overlap with John. However, Hanger was somewhat of a 'military macaroni',[37] and, disaffected by the town's 'lack of society of women of the first manners, fashion and education without which no mind can be polished', he 'quitted Gottingen for Hanover and Hesse-Cassel, at which places I spent the rest of my time in Germany', but only 'after applying myself to mathematics, fortifications and the language for about twelve months.'[38] Patronage, meantime, had facilitated his 'purchase' of a commission as an 'Ensign'[39] back home in the 1st Regiment of Foot Guards in April 1771.

If John were seeking to leverage the same connections as had so motivated his father, he could not have chosen a better place to complete his studies. Göttingen had become popular among elite British society because of 'the absence of a regular Court in Hanover', which meant that 'the university acquired a surrogate courtly role'.[40] Of the four Göttingen alumni who would serve with John in the army, Lindsay was the future Lord Balcarres, Clerke the future Sir Francis Carr-Clerke and Hanger the future Baron Coleraine. As for George Rodney, John's immediate contemporary and a fellow student of mathematics, he was the eldest son of Admiral (Lord) Rodney. Enlisting as an 'Ensign'[41] in the 3rd Regiment of Foot Guards soon after he matriculated in 1773 from Göttingen, George went on to become colonel of his regiment, all while waiting to inherit the family title.

Beyond these army connections, Göttingen's select band of British alumni opened doors into an array of wider political circles, starting with the court and Edward, Duke of York, who had matriculated there in 1765. Lower down the scale—but not that far down—was Sir Richard Sutton (enrolled 1755),[42] who went on to serve as an Undersecretary of State, Commissioner of the Privy Seal and Member of Parliament. Also among John's other immediate contemporaries were Charles and Jacob Adams (enrolled 1771), whose father was the current Lord Chief Baron of the Exchequer, and George de Munchhausen, son and nephew respectively of Philip Adolphe Münchausen, one-time Hanoverian minister in London, and Gerlach Adolph Münchausen, one-time minister in Hanover and founder of Göttingen University.[43] As at Dr Newcome's School, John could, if he wished, claim easy connection to the cream of Britain's ruling elite.

Yet, John was not like his father, and seeking social leverage was not why he had come to the Continent, nor why Prescott sent him there. The immediate priority for

John was to complete his military studies, and he had no intention of waiting until he reached Göttingen. His uncle had provided him with introductions[44] in Amsterdam, but, as John pointed out in his 14 May letter, these had produced mixed results. One unnamed 'factotum' proved a busted flush, but the introduction to Cornelis van der Oudermeulen, a director of the 'VOC' (Dutch East India Company), more than made up for this. First, Oudermeulen had put him in touch with a *'scavant de sa connaissance'* ('a scientist of his acquaintance') who agreed to give him *'Lecons de Mathématiques et de Fortifications'*. Secondly, he had been able to *'procurer une lettre pour Gottingen'*.[45] The importance of letters of introduction at that time cannot be overstated. Before embarking on his Grand Tour in 1763, Edward Gibbon—'considered as a man of letters' by his contemporaries—made sure to arm himself with multiple 'letters of recommendation to their private and literary friends' from the 'Duke de Nivernois, Lady Hervey, the Mallets, Mr Walpole etc' and, in his memoirs, took care to acknowledge the value of these 'epistles' for his subsequent 'reception and success'.[46]

For John, the letter of introduction he procured was vital: as he reminded his uncle, Göttingen was *'une place de si peu de Commerce'* ('a place with little commerce'), which meant that the Andrés had no contacts of their own there. Armed with this *'lettre pour Gottingen'*, however, John could finally set off, stopping *'peut-etre un jour ou deux'* ('maybe for a day or two')[47] in Utrecht en route. While waiting to be on his way, John, it seems, had been reading up on Göttingen and wanted to share his enthusiasm with friends back home. Göttingen was a place where weird 'curiosities' occurred, or so a report that appeared in various London newspapers led readers to believe. This report, in the form of a 'letter from Gottingen',[48] was published on 5 May and told of a 'beggar' who liked to 'swallow flints, felts and other things' and, dying of this habit, his body was dissected by the university 'faculty' which 'found several flintstones and other things in his inside.'[49]

There is no direct evidence that John was this story's author. However, he had told his uncle that he had *'curiosités memorables'* ('memorable curiosities') planned for his *'livre de chroniques'*. It is possible, then, that he sent his report directly to London newspapers to test the public's appetite for such 'curiosities' or that one of his friends passed it to the newspapers. It certainly seems more than coincidental that he was en route to Göttingen just when this 'letter from Gottingen' appeared in numerous London newspapers. More so was that the source of the 'letter' was the 'Utrecht Gazette',[50] which John could readily come by in Amsterdam or as he passed through Utrecht on his way to Göttingen. What seems to confirm John as the source was the idiosyncratic nature of the anecdote. After all the dry-as-dust puffs about 'fifty English Noblemen and Gentlemen' going 'there on their studies', here was a quirky curiosity that, at a stroke, would bring Göttingen to life. If John were the source if this anecdote, he can be forgiven: clearly, he was excited and looking forward to his time in Göttingen.

CHAPTER 15

'A Man of Nearly Womanlike Modesty and Gentleness'

If John stuck by the timetable he gave his uncle in his 14 May letter from Amsterdam, he would have arrived in Göttingen by end-May. According to the university's records, he was certainly enrolled on its mathematics course by 'July 1, 1772'.[1] However, it was only on 19 July that John replied to two letters his uncle had sent to await his arrival. John apologized for his tardiness, claiming that he 'had nothing very particular to say.' This seems strange given how full of business news the previous letter from Amsterdam was, but, then again, the relationship with his uncle was founded on the practicalities of business, and Göttingen, as a centre of learning, would not offer the same commercial intelligence.

Not wishing to offend his uncle, John instead commiserated about the latest financial 'Storm'[2] to have hit 'Change Alley. The shock from 'the terrible affair of so many Bankers and great Merchants failing for prodigious sums of money' even saw the unworldly Lady Mary Coke comment how 'the Credit of this country has received a considerable shake'.[3] John had, presumably, heard about this latest financial debacle from his friend, Walter Ewer, as he could comfort himself that 'my friends the Ewers got off so well'.[4] Although the Andrés were less affected than following the implosion of the Great Scheme three years earlier, few in the moneyed classes remained immune. The 'stagnation of public credit'[5] eventually rippled out to Amsterdam, the Caribbean and even the American colonies, where it became yet one more in the growing litany of reasons why Americans lost faith in Britain as the mother country.

Yet, Göttingen seemed eerily far removed from this financial 'Storm', as John reported on his first six weeks' studying there. Writing in English this time, he let his uncle know that 'Mr Boehmer to whom you procured me a recommendation has been very civil to me.' John had struck lucky: Boehmer was 'a professor and one of the first people here' which meant that John could make rapid progress at 'learning German.' How important this was became evident from his long description: 'I understand enough of it to explain myself on most occasions', and, to emphasise the point, he told how 'I hear a lecture from a Proffessor in it which I find means to understand.'[6] John was selling himself short. One professor later recalled that John 'spoke equally perfect English, German and French'.[7] John was modest also about his written German: 'I find a good deal of difficulty learning to write it'.[8] Yet, one of his correspondents would remember receiving letters written in fluent German long after John had left Göttingen.[9]

Overall, John was 'still very contented and happy here' but did not elaborate when describing how 'my time is a great deal taken up as I have a great variety of employments.' He, nevertheless, made these 'employments' sound formal, if not official: when regretting 'that my stay here must be so short', he volunteered that 'in a few weeks I shall write about getting my leave extended.' This prompted him to update his uncle on plans for his military career and, more significantly, to open up on the important relationship with his commanding officer, Colonel Prescott.

John's eldest sister, Louisa, had written with news that 'the R [oyal] Fusiliers were at Winchester on their March to Plymouth a little while ago'.[10] This only confirmed what newspapers were reporting, namely that, after suppressing a 'tinners' riot in Cornwall in February, the Fusiliers had returned to London in time for their annual review, this time 'on Wimbledon Common', when 'his Majesty was attended by the Duke of Gloucester, Generals Harvey and Carpenter and many more.' According to the *Lady's Magazine*, the regiment made 'a very fine appearance'.[11] The *London Evening Post* elaborated, describing how 'the seventh regiment of light infantry … was reckoned to go through their several evolutions with a quickness and regularity that astonished all present.' The King 'thanked the Colonel at the head of his regiment',[12] and, in recognition, on '22nd June 1772'[13] Prescott was elevated to the rank of brevet colonel.

Louisa went further, however, and also informed John that, while en route to Plymouth following the review, 'Col. Prescott call'd upon them at Southampton'. Convenient though this might have been in terms of the regiment's travel route, this visit from a newly promoted colonel to the family of a young lieutenant was, at the very least, unusual. According, however, to how John interpreted the visit for his uncle, its intention was entirely innocent, his commanding officer only looking to reassure the family 'that there was no chance of the Regiment being sent to a bad Climate but that New York or Philadelphia would be their destination.'[14] If that were Prescott's sole intention, it was, indeed, considerate and thoughtful. It more than likely followed on from a conversation he had with the André family during the previous year's Great Review when all the tittle-tattle among the 'spectators' was that the regiment would be sent to 'a climate which it is very probable in a short time may kill half of them.'[15]

Nevertheless, there had to be more to Prescott's visit than considerate reassurances to a worried mother. In the man's world of war, this was not how significant and sensitive strategic decisions were shared beyond the inner circle of a military hierarchy, not least because the official line being put out to the public at the same time was that, following this latest review, the Fusiliers 'are to march for Plymouth and embark for Pensacola'.[16] Why Pensacola? If the next task of the Fusiliers were to subdue the American troublemakers now in more open dissent, then Pensacola, Florida,[17] was 1,800 miles south of Boston, the epicentre of those troubles.

So, what was going on? Was the War Office seeking to confuse the American troublemakers, claiming publicly that regiments were going to one place when deciding privately they should go to another? This seems far-fetched, not least because London at that time was still underestimating the strength of growing unrest within the thirteen colonies. Moreover, if there were anything which approximated to a British military policy regarding the thirteen colonies, it was to awe troublemakers into quiescence much as they did when food riots broke out again around Britain in 1772.[18] That meant advertising, not disguising, the despatch of troops to known hotspots. Another possibility was that Pensacola was a Grub Street rumour and that 'New York or Philadelphia' was always the intended destination. If so, why did the regiment wait until March 1773[19] before finally embarking and, in the event, go, not to 'New York or Philadelphia', nor to the real trouble spot, Boston, but instead to Quebec?

All this speculation only confirms what is known about this period of Britain's phoney war with America's immanent 'rebels': events were moving at a meandering pace, and plans constantly changed on the hoof to confront new circumstances. Given the fog that often attends wars in their early stages, it is tempting to see talk of 'Pensacola', 'New York' and 'Philadelphia' as proof that, as early as July 1772, Britain was preparing for war in America. If, indeed, the Fusiliers were destined for America in July 1772, it was only to relieve, in this instance, a battalion of the 60th Regiment on garrison duty, which was due to return home. Moreover, the Fusiliers had recently 'been reduced to only 340 men compared to the war strength of 1000 and the normal peace strength of 500.'[20]

The plain fact was that the thirteen colonies were still of secondary importance in British politics in 1772: British military thinking put Europe, *not* America, as the next theatre of war. The extent to which events in Europe preoccupied English minds in 1772 was evident from Lady Mary Coke's journal entries, when, in late October, she noted that 'the present imbroiled state of the North of Europe was the conversation after dinner.' Having just returned from 'the Court of Vienna', she felt she could speak her 'opinions'[21] on the subject of the next war with authority. When that next war would come was in the hands of the politicians, but, as one of the more farsighted and innovative army officers, Prescott had a duty to plan ahead. From his experience, petite guerre—more specifically the gathering of intelligence—would be crucial to preparations for that next conflict.

These thoughts would surely have been in the back of Prescott's mind when he first decided to dispatch John to the Continent in early 1772. However, with events in Europe worsening, he now needed to bring forward his plans for John.

Before doing that he must ascertain what motivated John. He had already seen enough of John to know that he had an exceptional set of skills that marked him out for a special role in the army, but did John have what it took—the ambition, the character, the will—to win? He could only judge that by seeing John's family, hearing how important John was to his mother and sisters and finding out why John had chosen a career in the army.

The Andrés were Huguenots. They were merchants. That much Prescott would have known. Yet, this was an alien world to him. He would have done his homework before visiting the Andrés in Southampton. Whether it was through the Bertie family connection or his own contacts in moneyed circles, he would have ascertained that the Andrés had fallen on hard times and, as such, must move from Clapton to Southampton. He would also have found out about the problems with the Great Scheme, even, maybe, heard about the Crauford case. He would not have known about John's father.

Yet, John's uncles had carried on in the business. So why did John not remain at Warnford court? Why did he turn his back on the 'compting house' and decide instead on the army? Was it the eye-catching uniform? Was it for the glamour? Was it to escape? Was it boredom? Was it for want of something better? Prescott had seen too many young subalterns motivated by the feckless urge to be a 'military macaroni'. None of them had what it took to win. John, he already knew, was different. Prescott had seen that John was ambitious and, exceptionally, wanted to get ahead on merit. But that was still not enough. What really impelled John? What inner daemon would drive him to make the real sacrifices demanded of, for instance, a partizan? Again, only by visiting the Andrés could Prescott hope to begin answering these questions. He needed to get to know and understand the family. He must see with his own eyes how much John meant to his mother and sisters. Only thus could he know how important they were to John and what sacrifices he would make to shield, comfort and love them. That was why he visited the Andrés. The mention of 'Philadelphia and New York' was only so as to put John's mother and sisters at ease. That way, they might open up and tell him what he needed to know about John.

Time would tell if Prescott came by the answers he sought. Hearing of the visit, John could comfort himself that his commanding officer was still taking an interest in him. Meantime, he must get on with what he had come to the Continent to accomplish—to prove himself worthy of Prescott's trust. The studies he was making of mathematics and fortifications were, he knew, only a small part of his special duties, as was 'learning German'. All this he could freely impart to his uncle, his mother and his sisters. What he could not write about was the other, more clandestine, duties on his 'tour'.

Donkin would later explain what his 'tour' meant in practical terms. In the chapter of his military manual on petite guerre he described how 'a conductor of irregulars shou'd have leave to make a tour (under a feign'd name) round the intended scene of action, the winter preceding the campaign,' the purpose being 'to gain every possible knowledge of the country, fortified and unfortified towns' and other strategic areas. Donkin recommended that, while 'in this journey', the 'conductor' should 'insinuate himself as a traveller to the nobility or bourgeoisie; particularly with those who wish well to his sovereign, either from motives of inclination or interest; and perhaps engage them to become his correspondents by promising every suitable return for their services.'[22] This was no different to the intelligence John's uncles had him collect for commercial benefit. John hinted at this work when telling his uncle that 'my time is a great deal taken up as I have a great variety of employments'.

Among these 'employments', John had already established what Donkin signalled was a vital component to petite guerre, a network of his own 'correspondents'. It was this self-same term which John used in the letter to his uncle, when he mentioned a 'multiplicity of correspondents' who needed to be satisfied come 'my postdays'.[23] Apart from Professor Boehmer, none of these newfound 'correspondents' were named. By contrast, his earlier letter from Amsterdam had mentioned numerous of the connections he had made while there.

Yet, unsurprisingly John invested considerable time and effort in developing two partially overlapping networks of correspondents: the first was among the university's professors; the second grew out of a literary brotherhood, which went under the title 'Hainbund'.[24] Founded in a wooded glade '*unter der Mond*' ('under the moon') on '12 September [1772]',[25] this circle was one of the forerunners of German Romanticism, influencing Goethe and Bach among others.[26] Its four tenets were '*Gott, Vaterland, Jugend und Freundschaft*' ('God, Fatherland, Youth and Friendship').[27] With John's passion for poetry, it was easy for him to become a member of this brotherhood.

It was easier still for John to establish correspondence with the university's professors, the earlier advertisement placed by Professor Pepin in the *London Evening Post* exemplifying their eagerness to ingratiate themselves with the latest students arriving from Britain. In Pepin's case, the motivation was financial: Arthur and Richard Heywood were among the paying guests at his home on Weender Street in 1772/3.[28] Georg Lichtenberg had loftier motives: having visited Britain in 1770 and met with the king and queen, he befriended the British students because the royal court was the source of the university's cultural patronage.

Like Pepin, Lichtenberg took a number of the British students in as his lodgers. His diary often referred to the rhythm of his domestic life. In 1771, his house guests included 'Mr Adams [who] preferred the Spectator', 'Mr Browne [who] made an unexpected observation' and 'Mr Poyntz [who] set off from here for London'.[29] Arriving the following year, John was soon part of this same circle, and Lichtenberg remembered him well. Writing to 'his friend Schernhagen, Kloster-Registrator [Monastery-Registrar] at Hanover' in 1780, he recalled that 'he [John] and Sir Francis Clarke have certainly been ... the most distinguished Englishmen whom we have had here during the last sixteen years and André was the most sympathetic and engaging.' Lichtenberg went further, describing John 'as a man of nearly womanlike modesty and gentleness' and with 'an excellent mind'.[30] Lichtenberg recalled John again in 1782, this time adding how he was 'upright in the highest degree' and 'had a vivid feeling for beauty and thorough understanding of it'.[31]

Lichtenberg was one of the most prolific diarists and letter writers of his time, with Faraday, Goethe and Kant among his correspondents. Through him, John would have been introduced to many of Germany's academic and cultural elite. In addition to its university, Göttingen was a garrison town, a hangover from the Seven Years' War,[32] and many of Lichtenberg's social acquaintances were army officers. These were introduced to his British house guests, including John and 'Mr Adams'. One of John's contemporaries, Adams 'had a present of a dog made him by the general'[33] in 1771. In time, Lichtenberg also facilitated John's reception at other German courts, as did Boehmer, whose father had been 'privy counsellor to the king of Prussia and chancellor of the duchy of Magdebourg.'[34]

Although Lichtenberg was professor of physics at Göttingen, his diary and letters highlight his many cross-currents into literary circles. One of his close associations was with Heinrich Boie, a sometime poet, leading light of the Hainbund, but, more importantly, a founder and editor of the Göttingen 'Musenalmanach',[35] Germany's first literary magazine, which was launched in 1770. Boie first met John when he became mentor, tutor and general factotum to the 'young Britons' arriving in the 'summer of 1772'. It was through these 'young Britons' that Boie soon 'had access to all Gottingen social circles.'[36] According to John, by then 'we are now only 4 Englishmen here' and 'in a week's time shall be but three'.[37] Among these 'young Britons', Boie formed a special relationship with John, their mutual interest in poetry providing the bond. John, for his part, capitalized on Boie's search for 'Correspondenz in auswartiger Lander' ('Correspondents in foreign lands') and thirst for 'Nachrichten'[38] ('News') from these sources. The two formed a busy letter correspondence which long outlived John's return to England,[39] even carrying over into his time in America.

John was an itinerant participant in the Hainbund, but this brought him close relationships with a number of poets living in Göttingen, including Johann Voss, and, further afield, Friedrich Klopstock who then resided in Hamburg. Voss compiled a 'Stammbuch'[40]—a personal 'Album'—into which he inscribed, among other items, poems he had composed. One of these from October 1772 was addressed 'An John André'[41] ('To John André').

Voss and John found a common bond not only in their love for poetry but also in their patriotic antipathy towards 'all things French, the people and the literature', feelings evident in the tone of the Voss poem addressed to John, 'a warmly-patriotic ode ... full of national self-consciousness'[42] which extolled 'Deutschlands Genius'.[43] Whether John felt as strongly as Voss is questionable, but he certainly saw the polite need to praise his German friend's patriotism. Writing to the theologian, Ernst Bruckner, Voss recalled the moment with pride when, at a gathering on 1 November 1772: 'André especially drew me to his breast and said: "You are a good man. You love your Fatherland."' Voss described the incident so vividly—including how he, Rodney and John *champagnerten und burgunderten* ('drank champagne and burgundy') until midnight—not only for the pride John's praise stirred in him, but also because it was John's last day in Göttingen. Voss later recalled how 'as a Lieutenant', John 'had been suddenly ordered home, because his regiment was going to America. He must be on his way early on 1 November. I heard it first on Friday evening.'[44]

So, after barely four months, John was leaving Göttingen and returning to England. Was he being called home urgently because the regiment was going to America or was that a pretext? What would Prescott make of John's 'tour'? What would he say about all John's 'employments' and 'correspondents'? Importantly, too, what had Prescott made of his visit to John's mother and sisters back in July?

CHAPTER 16

'Parting'

On 13 September 1772, it was reported that 'orders are stuck up at the War-Office for all persons (commissioned and private) absent from their regiments on duty in the West-Indies and America to join them without delay.'[1] Was this the moment when London finally woke up to the reality of immanent rebellion across the Atlantic?

Yes, but not in America's thirteen colonies, instead in the little Caribbean island of St. Vincent. It seems that Britain's addiction to tea—for which Caribbean sugar was the necessary companion—once again overcame other considerations of world politics, even, this time the pending threat to the 'balance of Europe'[2] occasioned by Prussia's growing power, as evidenced by completion that same month of 'the dividing of the kingdom of Poland'.[3]

Since 1769, Britain had been trying to damp down unrest among the native 'Charibbees'[4] on St. Vincent. 'Six companies of the 68th regiment' had already been brought in 'from Antigua', together with 'two companies from the 70th regiment at Grenada',[5] but, so far, they had made no impression. Quite the contrary, the 'incursions of the Charibbees to St. Lucia and Martinico' had become 'more frequent and in greater numbers'.[6] As a result, the decision had been taken to augment forces on the island and quash rebellion once and for all. This was why the War Office posted its 13 September notice recalling all officers and men to their regiments, why, according to 'a letter from Plymouth' dated 19 October, 'the Transports with the sixth regiment of foot on board still remain in Catwater' waiting only on a 'fair wind' before sailing for 'St Vincent to reduce the Charibbees who are in arms there',[7] and why John left Göttingen so precipitately in late October. News had reached him that the regiment was due to sail, replacing 'troops from America'[8] needed in St. Vincent.

By the time John arrived back home in mid-November, events had, however, overtaken these immediate plans: more food riots had erupted, first, in 'Newburgh, Perth and Dundee',[9] then in the West Country. Quartered in Plymouth Citadel but with a 'detachment at Truro',[10] the Fusiliers were close at hand on 19 December when 'the devil and all of a riot' broke out in Padstow. Rioting quickly spread to other parts of Cornwall, the tinners again taking the lead, with 'seven or eight hundred'[11] of them going on the rampage. The civil magistrates tried containing the disturbances without the army's help, but, on 2 February 1773 a report came in from Plymouth that 'this morning a company of the 7th regiment of foot marched from this place, as did a company of Welch Fuziliers from dock, both of which are gone into Cornwall ... to prevent the rioters from doing any more mischief'.[12]

Still, matters worsened, and on 10 February 'orders were stuck up at the War-Office ... for the Officers of the Royal Welch Fuziliers, now on duty in Cornwall, to repair thither with all speed.'[13] The same orders did not include the English Fusiliers, as its officers were already in the West Country. Prescott wrote that same day from Plymouth Citadel to advise Anthony Chamier, newly appointed as 'Secretary-at-War', that 'the attacks of the rioters were directed against the corn warehouses and premises of the maltsters'. Realizing that force alone would not work, Prescott tried another tack and, 'at Penryn an agreement was come to with the rioters to let them have the corn at one third less than the prime cost'.[14] This had the desired effect, and on 27 February Donkin of the Welch Fusiliers—with whom Prescott had been liaising closely—wrote to Chamier from Penryn 'stating that everything had been quiet since his arrival on the 17th.'[15]

With order restored, the two Fusilier regiments could finally embark for America, the 7th Regiment (English Fusiliers) to relieve 'the battalion of the 60th Regiment in the Great Lakes area', the Welch Fusiliers to replace 'the other 60th battalion in New York'[16] which was 'returning from America'[17] on home leave. On 22 April came news from Plymouth confirming this, when 'Thursday last embarked on board the transports lying at Catwater, the 7th regiment and the Welch Fuzileers, the former for Quebec, and the latter for New-York'.[18] Shortly after came 'a letter from Plymouth' dated 'April 25th' which reported: 'sailed the Fox and six Transports, with the English and Welch Fuzileers, for New York and Quebec.'[19]

Aboard one of the 'Transports' was Lieutenant Frederick Mackenzie of the Welch Fusiliers. Before sailing, he had time to write one 'last letter in England [which] I think was dated the 18th of April in Catwater'.[20] Some two months at sea lay ahead, followed by 'nine years' away from home if the experience of the 'poor fellows' from the '32nd regiment of foot'[21] were anything to go by, or 'two or three years if', as Mackenzie wrote, 'nothing extraordinary happens'.[22] John was equally phlegmatic when he first heard from his mother that 'New York or Philadelphia' was his regiment's likely destination. Writing to his uncle in July 1772, he imagined that, 'barring being absent from one's friends, these places must be as good as England'. General Thomas Gage, Britain's commander-in-chief in North America, could even strike a note of optimism: with the 'Charibbees' on St. Vincent finally pacified and the thirteen colonies happily humming in harmony, he decided, in June 1773, to reduce the size of 'the army in America to 6,000 men'.[23]

Assuming then that 'nothing extraordinary happens',[24] the Welch Fusiliers faced years of tedious drills and boring garrison duty. There would be parades through the streets and markets of New York, but always with their 'red coats on'[25] just to remind 'the people here' that, 'in general very civil'[26] though it might seem, the Crown remained the ultimate legal authority in the thirteen colonies. So, too, the 7th Regiment (English Fusiliers), except that its parades would be through Canada's 'few acres of snow'. 'Bound for a different port (Quebec),' they parted company from the Welch Fusiliers when the convoy ran into its first 'gale' some '600 miles [out] from Plymouth', and it was agreed that, as 'the *Fox* sailed very ill,'[27] the ships should go their separate ways.

On board the *Fox* bound for Quebec were Colonel Prescott and his fellow officers of the 7th Regiment (English Fusiliers).[28] However, John was not among them. The previous October, Prescott had recalled him from Göttingen but not so that he should go with the regiment to America. Instead, there were more urgent duties for John on the Continent, and, before departing for Quebec, Prescott needed to give him his orders. Britain's diplomacy on the Continent was in crisis: in addition to old enemies, France and Spain, new ones had been made of Prussia, Russia, Holland, Denmark and Sweden.[29] By 1772, Britain was virtually isolated: its sole remaining friends were among the three hundred or so sovereign territories within the German Empire, and some even of these were lurching towards France.

Suddenly, John's network of German 'correspondents' had become useful: even the likes of Boie and Voss. Will-o-the-wisp poetasters they may be, but they were also passionate about their German patriotism. Britain's archenemy, Catholic France, was theirs too. John had made sure to encourage this: writing to a friend, Ernst Bruckner, in February 1773, Voss enthused how 'among the English, I am universally much loved, and I esteem this Nation more than the doltish Romans. As for the French, I, along with every German Patriot, hate them all.'[30] Moreover, the influence of these young poets was growing: through the Hainbund and as editors of an influential literary magazine, Boie and Voss helped John reach like-minded scribblers attached to other European courts.

John had positioned himself astutely during his time in Göttingen. For all that Britain's diplomatic power was in crisis, her cultural influence—as the beacon of transnational Enlightenment—was on the rise. This meant that John's connections, especially with Göttingen's university professors, could open doors. Not only was Lichtenberg an intimate of many royal courts, including Britain's, but his fellow professor, Johann Gatterer, founded the widely circulated magazine, *Historische Journal*, in 1772.

This highbrow world of the Muses was one time-honoured route into the secrets of European courts. Already these agents of gossip, tittle-tattle and intelligence were gathering ahead of the next war, a new generation of artists, writers, playwrights and sculptors ready to pedal their services and play at 'The Sentimental Spy'.[31] France was well ahead of the game: it already had in place Beaumarchais the playwright, Diderot the encyclopaedist, and Houdon the up-and-coming sculptor. Waiting for the highest bidder were Thomas Mante, the British soldier turned historian and double agent,[32] Baron Frederick Grimm, the journalist-cum-diplomat, and the Chevalier d'Eon, French soldier turned courtier-spy.

Britain's pool of cultural 'agents' in northern Europe was dry by contrast. Secret intelligences must be drawn instead from a commercial network seeded by Sir Joseph Yorke, its long-time ambassador at The Hague. This network was centred on Richard Wolters, 'His Majesty's Agent at Rotterdam,'[33] and 'Emanuel Mathias Esq., agent with the Hans towns'[34] and located in Hamburg. Across northern Europe, this 'secret service'[35] worked tirelessly for Britain, but, in the three hundred German states, the network had too many blind spots. Yet, these states were the no-man's-land where the great powers of Europe manoeuvred for wider political advantage. Britain had to be there, which was why John and his correspondents were so important. Moreover, as an aspiring writer and artist in his own right, John could speak the language of Enlightenment.

These German states were especially important to Britain because they were also the well from which it drew its supply of mercenary soldiers in time of war. Again, the military connections John had made while in Göttingen were useful: as a soldier, he could relate to the militaristic world that predominated in many of these German states. John not only mixed with generals, but, as Voss recounted in awe, he also knew 'Count Wallersdorf' well, and, through 'André's friends ... dukes and barons became my new brothers'.[36] Boie's future career illustrated how the world of war and of Enlightenment so easily merged, when, three years after mentoring John and other British students at Göttingen University in 1772, he landed 'a post with the military governor of Hanover ... as under-secretary'. He had come by this position on recommendation by 'General von Walthaussen' whom he first met 'in Gottingen.'[37]

Prescott could have ordered John back to Göttingen, but the neighbouring state of Saxe-Gotha had become a pressing problem since the deaths in 1772 of Frederick III, 'the reigning duke of Saxe-Gotha'[38] and 'Prince William of Saxe-Gotha'.[39] Historically, Yorke's commercial network had responsibility for maintaining influence in the powerful, albeit sprawling, duchy of Saxe-Gotha-Altenburg, but it had lost its grip,[40] and the new duke, Ernst II, had quickly fallen under the sway of France's cultural agent provocateur, Baron Grimm. Private chargé d'affaires for Saxe-Gotha at the French court, Grimm had built on the influence he accrued over some years when Ernst II and his mother, Duchess Louise Dorothea, were subscribers to his 'Correspondance Littéraire, a semiprivate cultural newsletter distributed ... to an exclusive circle of ruling foreign families', which had become 'a powerful tool to gain the favor of the powerful and shape their opinions.'[41]

Grimm's influence in Saxe-Gotha manifested itself in many ways: benignly when he convinced Ernst II to patronize the budding young sculptor, Houdon, in 1771;[42] malignly (for Britain) when, inheriting the duchy in a parlous financial state, Ernst made one of his first acts to 'set up a claim of 30000*l* which, he says, was due to his predecessor from England in consequence of some expenditure during the last war and his Serene Highness says he will keep St. George in pawn till the debt is discharged by the Court of London'.[43] This 'claim' doubtless related to troops which Saxe-Gotha had put at Britain's disposal during the Seven Years' War.[44] However this 'claim' arose, Saxe-Gotha's newfound aggressiveness only invited retaliation, and George III ceased the 'eight thousand pounds a year' subsidy that his sister, the Princess Dowager of Wales, had been making 'to her Brother the Duke of Saxe Gotha'[45] prior to her death in February 1772.

Given this diplomatic standoff, it was imperative from a military standpoint that Britain regain a foothold in the duchy. One of the special assignments Prescott gave to John, then, was to ingratiate himself with the Saxe-Gotha court. To this end, John was certainly there 'in the autumn' of 1773. This was not his first visit, but this time was 'for longer' and, during his time at court, 'he resumed his friendship with Duke Ernst'.[46] The earlier visit was while John was studying at Göttingen, which explains why Prescott gave him the assignment. How long the second visit lasted is difficult to tell, but according to Lichtenberg, 'when Gatterer and I were at Gotha, he [John] was also there and painted for his pleasure the duke and duchess.'[47]

Clearly, John had made a hit with Ernst II. This contributed to a normalization of relations between Saxe-Gotha and Britain, such that in October the duke sent an 'express' message to 'his Majesty at Kew'.[48] This 'express' almost certainly concerned the partition of Poland which had reached its climax: Russia, Prussia and Austria had mobilized their armies, not, however, to confront each other, rather to force 'the Polish Diet to accept the partition'. This it finally did 'on 28 September'. The 'British and French governments' were briefly united but only in their 'outrage and fear':[49] both could only look on as many of Germany's three hundred petty territories succumbed to pressure from emergent Prussia. Among them was Saxe-Gotha, evident in a letter 'from Berlin dated Aug. 3' which told how 'the military preparations making by our court are carried on with greater vigour than ever; besides the troops of the Duchy of Wirtemberg, Saxe-Gotha, and Mecklenberg Schaverin, his Majesty has taken into his service six regiments belonging to the cantons of Zurich and Bern in Switzerland'.[50]

For all his efforts, then, John had failed in Saxe-Gotha, but he did succeed in Hesse-Cassel, which was the main reason Prescott sent John back to Germany in the first place. George III had an important assignment which needed to be undertaken, and John was to be 'employed by the ministry to conduct a corps of Hessians from Hesse-Cassel'.[51] Unlike the duke of Saxe-Gotha, George III, as Elector of Hanover, was not about to let himself be pushed about by Prussia. These Hessian troops were to be sent to protect the borders of Hanover against any possible aggression by Prussia.

This assignment was a singular honour for John given that George Hanger, who had also studied at Göttingen and was in the more illustrious 1st Regiment of Foot Guards, was in Hesse-Cassel when John was there.[52] John's assignment was especially sensitive as he had to navigate complex local politics. Hesse-Cassel was the obvious ally to call on for assistance: like Saxe-Gotha, it had provided troops to Britain during the Seven Years' War. However, it, too, had not been reimbursed the subsidies promised by Britain, and these amounted to a hefty 10.1 million thaler.[53] To further complicate matters, Frederick II, the ruler of Hesse-Cassel since 1760, had—unconscionably for this strictly Calvinist state—reconverted to Catholicism. To protect the Protestant bloodline against this recidivism, his father granted the landgraviate of Hanau to his grandson, William.

In his memoirs, another Briton, John Moore, endeavoured to unscramble this complex politics. Travelling as companion and physician to the Duke of Hamilton, he arrived in Hanau in early 1773 when there was still 'snow on the ground'. This put him there at approximately the same time as John. Moore described how 'Hanau is the residence of the hereditary prince of Hesse-Cassel... Besides the troops of Hanau, two regiments of Hanoverians are here at present. The hereditary prince is not on the best terms with his father. He lives here, however, in a state of independency, possessed of the revenues of this country, which is guaranteed to him by the kings of Britain, Denmark and Prussia; but there is no intercourse between this little court and Hesse-Cassel.'[54]

Since the young Elector openly disapproved the partition of Poland, it is likely then that the 'corps of Hessians' John was ordered 'by the ministry' to escort to Hanover came from Hanau rather than Hesse-Cassel. It is no wonder, then, that Voss was sure 'there should be a welcome for him [John] there at court.' John probably arrived in late January 1773: according to a letter dated 24 February 1773 from Voss to his friend, Ernst Bruckner, 'André has written to me from Hanau where he is once more, and has again thanked me for the poem.'[55] John had, evidently, visited Hanau during his earlier sojourn at Göttingen.

Having successfully completed this assignment, John took a detour back through Göttingen, where, on '13 June 1773' he inscribed in his own hand in the 'Voss Album' an 'English poem' entitled 'Parting'.[56] John was returning the compliment for the poem that Voss had written and dedicated to him in honour of his departure for England at the end of his previous trip to Germany. At some point while at Hanau, John also took time out to make the acquaintance of a supposed relative, John Andrée, who lived in nearby Offenbach.[57] 'Mrs Mills', the daughter of John Andrée, 'remembered seeing [John] at her father's house as a visitor when she was a very small child'.[58]

Further evidence that John made this excursion comes from a report that reached the *Lloyd's Evening Post* in early October 1773. It has all the hallmarks of John's growing enthusiasm for reporting 'memorable and remarkable curiosities' he encountered on his travels. Offenbach was a small town of little consequence, which had not been mentioned in the British press since 1762.[59] Yet, coinciding with John's visit, London readers were invited to believe that 'a revolution of great importance is expected in the German empire, for which every Duke and Count of the empire is obliged to send a Deputy to Offenbach, where some matters of consequence are to be decided.'[60] In the event, the meeting proved to be a dull gathering of magistrates,[61] but the *Lloyd's Evening Post* wasn't to know this: if a local correspondent wrote in with an account of 'a revolution' somewhere in the 'German empire', this was news, and the newspaper was all too happy to publish the report verbatim.

Meantime, a real 'revolution of great importance' was about to unfold across the Atlantic: 'All America is in a flame,' wrote a British 'officer at New York to his friend in London'. Dated 'Nov.1. 1773', this letter described how 'the New Yorkers as well as the Bostonians and Philadelphians are determined ... that no tea shall be landed.'[62] In Boston Harbour, on the night of 16 December 1773, 'a number of resolute men (dressed like Mohawks) emptied every chest of tea on board the three ships ... amounting to 342 chests, into the sea'.[63]

PART III

A Subaltern at War

CHAPTER 17

'America is in a Flame'

John returned to England the moment news of the Boston 'tea affair' reached Europe in late January 1774. Arriving home, he would have read with horror accounts drawn verbatim from 'the Boston (New England) Gazette' for 'December 20' that similar riotous actions were planned all along the eastern seaboard of America, even down as far south as 'Charles Town, South Carolina'. To credit these reports, Philadelphia was the most militant: 'a ship chartered by the East India Company to bring their teas to that place' was unable to enter port because 'the pilots had refused to bring her up the river'.[1] William Eddis, recently arrived from England to take up his appointment as land surveyor to the governor of Maryland, could only watch 'with inexpressible inquietude' while 'all America is in a flame.'

John had seen enough 'riotous proceedings', first in Geneva then around England, to know how quickly riot could become rebellion. Any thoughts he may have had of becoming another Baron Grimm must be put on hold. It was time to join the regiment in North America. It seems only a show of force would work. Yet, it was still not too late for Britain to step back from the abyss. Just as with previous missteps, there was a way to navigate round 'the impending storm'.[2] Ever since the Seven Years' War, cool heads on both sides of the Atlantic had been struggling to navigate their way into a new constitutional partnership. London had made mistakes, but, following angry protests across the thirteen colonies, repeal of, first, the 1765 Stamp Act, then the 1767 Townshend Acts, had pointed the way to calmer waters. The 1773 Tea Act—the latest affront to America's emerging identity—had surely only been passed as a sop to the East India Company. Repeal that Act, and the latest 'flame' would flicker and fade, allowing time for pragmatists, among them Benjamin Franklin, to find a peaceful way forward.

Lord North's government was shackled, however, to the East India Company, fatally dependent on the £400,000 (= PV £55.3 million) subvention it received annually in return for granting a monopoly on trade into the East Indies. Repeal of the Tea Act was not an option. To douse the latest 'flame' of resistance the government decided, instead, to blockade Boston harbour. On 14 April came the news that 'four regiments are ordered to go to Boston forthwith.'[3] In addition, all officers on leave from their regiments in Boston and New York were ordered to report for duty.[4] 'Transports' began assembling in Portsmouth to 'take in troops for America',[5] the *Darlington* sailing from Spithead on 10 May.[6] A measure of the panic engulfing London was that, on 30 April, 'an order' was 'issued for the muster and return of all the forces in the garrisons of England, Scotland and Wales.'[7]

Among the regiments to be sent to Boston was the King's Own (the 4th), commanded by Earl Percy. Told of his orders while 'on his Majesty's yacht Dorset' in Dublin, Percy hurriedly cut short his holiday and 'set out for Corke' from where he would 'go with his regiment to America.'[8] Joining him was the 'Hon. Captain Cochrane', until recently a fellow lieutenant with John in the 7th Regiment (English Fusiliers). A year older than John, he had already been in the army for twelve years. Like John, he remained behind when the 7th Regiment (English Fusiliers) went to Canada. Cochrane's reason, however, was to secure what he considered long overdue promotion. This he finally achieved 'in the beginning of 1774' when, according to his testimonial, he 'purchased a company'[9] in Percy's regiment.

Back in Britain after his one-year 'leave of absence' in Germany, John may also have taken soundings on the possibilities for promotion, but that would have required him, like Cochrane, to change regiments, and Lord Robert Bertie, colonel of the regiment—and John's commanding officer in the absence of Prescott—had no intention of losing one of his best lieutenants just when he needed him. Uppermost in Bertie's thinking was the fighting fitness of the regiment, and, from the pervading panic, the government evidently had no idea what type of conflict was about to be fought. The regiments going to Boston were ill-prepared militarily and were being hurried off by way of a political gesture intended as a show of redcoat force to cow hotheads among the 'People of Boston' into submission. Percy caught the tone of this posturing in a letter of 17 April to his relative, the Reverend Thomas Percy, written while waiting to board one of the 'transports' off 'Corke'. In it, Percy reasoned that 'as I find we are to have eight Reg'ts there, I fancy severity is intended. Surely the People of Boston are not Mad enough to think of opposing us. Headiness and Temper will I hope set things in that Quarter to rights.'[10]

Bertie was less sanguine: unlike Percy,[11] he was a veteran of the Seven Years' War and knew that his regiment needed to be properly schooled for war in America. That was where John came into Bertie's thinking. There were plans to send more regiments, but this time they would have proper training first. General William Howe was given this task. A veteran also of the Seven Years' War, he 'had gained some very useful experience of light infantry work in North America'[12] and knew what to expect when the shooting started. He had 'devised a 'discipline' for the new companies', which echoed the 'light armed regiments' formed during the previous war 'to serve as lightly equipped formations capable of undertaking rapid marches and heavy raids deep into enemy territory. Once in contact with the enemy, they almost invariably went straight in with the bayonet.'[13]

Howe consolidated this new 'discipline' into a *Manual on light infantry Drill*[14] issued in 1774. Training for what, in military parlance, would become known as 'loose files and American scramble'[15] began the moment Percy left for Boston with the first wave of regiments in April. 'Although marksmanship was stressed, together with considerable practice in irregular and bush fighting, the real meat of the training was to enable them to manoeuvre—and fire—in accordance with the 1764 Regulations while dispersed in open or even extended order.'[16]

The fruits of Howe's work were put on show on 3 October when, 'this day eight companies of light infantry will be reviewed before his Majesty in Richmond Park.' These companies had 'been performing their manoeuvres for several months on Salisbury Plain under the inspection of General Howe.'[17] The location was telling: normally, training ahead of reviews was carried out on the parade ground, the decision to relocate to the rugged terrain of Salisbury Plain indicating that Howe was planning for a certain mode of warfare in America. This was confirmed when Lady Mary Coke recorded in her journal that 'Lady Greenwich will give you the account of the bush fighting Review' which was 'performed Saturday, previous to His Majesty seeing them this morning in Richmond Park.'[18]

To ensure rapid and wide dissemination of the new 'discipline', Howe decided that the 'eight companies' chosen for special training should 'belong to eight different regiments'.[19] The 7th Regiment (English Fusiliers) was not among these, since it was already on station in Canada. As its commander, Bertie was determined, however, that, being one of the army's elite light infantry units, his regiment should, nevertheless, be up with the new 'discipline' Howe was bringing to America. The next best solution, then, was that one of his officers due to join the regiment in Canada should observe first-hand the new 'discipline'. John was the obvious choice: not only was he recently back from Germany and at a loose end, but his command of drilling 'evolutions' during the Annual Review in 1771 had been exemplary. Moreover, as the 7th Regiment (English Fusiliers) was not included in the War Office's April orders[20] requiring officers on leave to join their regiments in America, Bertie had a free hand. Almost certainly, then, he had John attend Howe's manoeuvres on Salisbury Plain, the intention being that, after the general review, John would go directly to Canada.

Doubtless, this was Bertie's original plan, except that John did not stay until October and the formal review in front of his Majesty. Instead, he left for America on 18 July when the *St. George*, the ship he sailed on, 'cleared outwards ... for Philadelphia' from the 'Port of London'.[21] Two days later, it was spotted off Deal, on the south coast of England, travelling with the 'Nancy and Molly',[22] also out of London.

Why the change of plan? It may have been that John had seen enough of the new 'discipline' and was being hurried on by Bertie to rejoin the regiment. If so, then why was John entering America via Philadelphia? Why not make for Canada directly? After all, there were numerous vessels routinely going direct to Quebec at that time, including a 'man of war in readiness' on 30 June to 'set out with all convenient speed for that province' taking the new 'Governor of Canada, His Excellency Major-General Carleton'.[23]

The answer was that Canada remained quiet, but, by July, events in the thirteen colonies were fast running out of control. As viewed from London, Boston and New York were the two epicentres of unrest. Smother both with a show of redcoat force, and any opposition would quickly melt away. Implementing this policy was already underway in Boston with the dispatch of Lord Percy's four regiments in April and the naval blockade of its harbour. Attention, however, switched to New York when news arrived from there in June that, on 21 April, 'the body of the people … entered the tea ship Nancy … took out the tea that was at hand, broke the cases' and scattered 'their contents in the river.'[24] This 'Tea Party' was reported in the 25 April edition of the *New-York Gazette* but only appeared in London's *Public Advertiser* on 7 June. Then came news from Philadelphia that effigies of two British officials were burnt, the local account from 4 May reprinted in London on 11 June.[25]

Still, no tea ships had been boarded in the port of Philadelphia and no tea had been dumped into the Delaware. On a relative scale, Philadelphia seemed a haven of tranquillity by comparison with Boston and New York. If tea were the litmus test of unrest in the thirteen colonies, then the government could safely contemplate stripping Philadelphia of its military presence, removing the Royal Irish Regiment that had been on station there since 1767 and transferring it to where it was required for this much-needed show of redcoat force in New York and Boston.

Briefly, the government's cavalier complacency was challenged when news arrived on 28 June that 'the cities of New York and Philadelphia … had resolved to adopt the non-importation scheme and had formed committees of correspondence to act in conjunction with the people of Boston.'[26] Yet, on 2 July, a letter from Philadelphia indicated the contrary and that support for 'the Patriots' in Boston was, at best, lukewarm for they would 'find themselves deceived in the general support of the other provinces,' many of whom are too busy fighting Indians 'on our frontiers.'[27] Other letters cautioning moderation quickly followed from Philadelphia, culminating with an announcement on 6 June from a meeting of 'respectable inhabitants' in the city agreeing ambivalently that 'a Committee be appointed to correspond with our sister colonies,' but that instead of defiant action, there should be convened 'a general congress of deputies from the different colonies'.[28]

Based on these latest accounts, the government felt it could safely proceed with its plans to withdraw the Royal Irish Regiment from Philadelphia and remove it to New York and Boston. Given the deteriorating situation, however, these instructions needed to be conveyed urgently to Major Hamilton, commander of the garrison in Philadelphia.[29] John, it seems, was assigned this duty, which explains why he travelled to America via Philadelphia. Given the reports of unrest spreading to Philadelphia, it is possible John was also told to locate loyal 'correspondents' and gather intelligence. By then, the government was thirsty for any reliable information it could come by.

A measure of its desperation at this time can be gauged from a reminder sent to General Gage by Lord Dartmouth, Secretary of State for North America in October 1774 that, 'in the present moment, every circumstance of intelligence respecting what passes in America is of importance; and information which at another time would be thought of no consequence, deserves attention.'[30]

It is unlikely that John knew that a 'general congress' was planned or that it would be held in Philadelphia: the news of it only reached England on 16 July, two days before he sailed on the *St. George*. The first inkling John would have had was when the pilots came aboard the *St. George* as it was coming up the Delaware after its 'boisterous' crossing from England. The pilots would have been full of the events that had been unfolding while John was at sea. Hearing the news, Samuel Smith, John's kindly fellow passenger, would have cautioned him to watch every word he said from now on, and be sure to change his attire. In these troubled times, it would not pay to be seen dressed as a redcoat on the streets of the city.

There were, indeed, watchful eyes everywhere: Loyalists and Patriots alike had begun seeing 'foul Play'[31] everywhere. In nearby Annapolis, loyal Eddis caught the mood of suspicion, noting in a letter home that, with the Post Office thoroughly penetrated by Patriots, 'the hour is approaching when the intercourse of letters will be greatly interrupted if not totally prohibited.'[32] Among Patriots, the fear was that the Congress delegates converging on Philadelphia would be prevented from reaching the city.

Many of the delegates—'fifty-three in number'[33]—had come by land, including Colonel Henry Lee from nearby Virginia. Washington also came by land. According to the *Virginia Gazette*, he was one of six delegates appointed by the colony's convention held in Williamsburg on 1 August. The delegates were voted 'a Sum of Money, amounting to nearly 1000*l*'[34] to cover expenses. Washington kept a diary, and his entry for 30 August read: 'Colo. Pendleton, Mr Henry, Colo. Mason & Mr Thos Triplet came in the evening.' The next day's entry read: 'All the above Gentlemen dind here, after which with Colo. Pendleton & Mr Lee I set out for Phila.'[35] Washington arrived in the city on the morning of 4 September, 'crossing the Schuylkill at Lower Ferry and went to the City Tavern for supper; after which he lodged with Dr William Shippen.'[36]

With the port of Boston blockaded, the Adams brothers also travelled by land. According to John Adams, they had set out on 10 August and, on 29 August, 'stopped at Frankford, about five miles from town whereupon a number of Carriages and Gentlemen came out of Philadelphia to meet us… We then rode into town, and dirty, dusty and fatigued as we were, we could not resist the Importunity to go to the Tavern'.[37] En route, Adams had written from Princeton, New Jersey, warning his wife, Abigail, that she would not receive letters until he 'could find a Private hand by which I can convey it', as he was in 'fear of foul Play' if he entrusted the letter to 'the Post'.[38]

Abigail had different apprehensions: writing on 15 August and not knowing 'where this will find you, whether on the road or at Phylidelphia,'[39] she worried that 'Hostile Movements' might 'impeade' or 'interrupt'[40] her husband's journey. Her fears were groundless: in the vastness of the thirteen colonies, Britain was powerless to stop her husband. Back in London, however, one important delegate, Dr Benjamin Franklin, was interrupted in his journey, 'when he was on the point of departure' for Philadelphia, and 'a noble Earl sent for him and after a long conference convinced him of the necessity of his deferring his Embarkation until after the next session of Parliament.'[41]

Other delegates had come by sea, and, given the 'boisterous' conditions expected at that time of year, made sure to arrive well in advance. On 9 August, 'in the Charleston Packet, Captain Wright, came passengers the Hon. Henry Middleton and Edward Rutledge Esq's … who are nominated to attend the Congress from the Colony of South Carolina.' Two further South Carolina delegates arrived on 22 August by the 'brig Sea Nymph'.[42] Their decision to come early was wise: one local diarist noted on 25 August: 'Still stormy. The Gentlemen who are sailing up the bay to the Congress are having a disagreeable time.'[43]

Taking a special interest in these delegates arriving by sea was the Patriot, Christopher Marshall. In the increasingly febrile atmosphere leading up to the General Congress, reliable intelligence from within Philadelphia was imperative, and Marshall was ideally placed, being as he already resided in the city and was well in with customs officers at the port. From his *Diary*, it is clear he was trading the intelligence he came by with a like-minded 'friend' in Britain. From this 'friend', Marshall had heard in March that 'our tea ship sent back arrived at Dover the 25th same month'. In return, he received the news that the 'account of destruction of tea in Boston reached London about 20th of January.' His next entry, from 25 April, was even more telling: 'received by ship Concord, Captain Volans, Bristol, eighty-four pamphlets, from my friend, George Stonehouse.'[44] Marshall was a pharmacist by profession. Hence, it is a reasonable assumption that these 'pamphlets' were promotional material for some miracle remedy, for instance, 'Keyser's Genuine Pills',[45] except that the same day entry referred cryptically to 'the great debates in the House of Commons'[46] which points to the 'pamphlets' being political tracts.

From May onwards, Marshall began taking a keen interest in the number of vessels bringing 'emigrants' to America. This was a hot topic at the time, the *London Evening Post* reporting from Belfast on 23 April that 'no less than three ships sailed from thence last week with emigrants for America' and lamenting that 'nothing but a speedy revival to the linen trade can save this country.'[47] This was a constant refrain, the *Public Advertiser* ruing the loss of 'Spitalfield Weavers' who, 'for Want of Employment here, have within these few weeks engaged themselves for Boston, New York and Philadelphia'.[48]

Marshall was interested in these ship arrivals because the immigrants were from his native Ireland. He meticulously logged the number of immigrants on board: between 21 July and 31 August no fewer than seven immigrant ships arrived carrying, in aggregate, over two thousand passengers.[49] Apart from those vessels bringing delegates to the General Congress, Marshall showed no interest in the numerous other arrivals into Philadelphia at that time. He made no mention of the 'Brig Recovery' which, according to the 3 August edition of the *Pennsylvania Journal*, had just arrived from Liverpool. Nor did he mention the 'Brig Venus',[50] which had recently arrived from

London according to the 26 October edition of the *Pennsylvania Journal*. He, as a pharmacist, should have been especially interested in this vessel, if only because of the goods it, doubtless, was carrying. According to an advertisement in the same edition, the firm of William Drewet Smith could now offer for sale 'a great variety of capital Druggs, genuine Patent Medicines and Surgeons Instruments'. Yet, not a word in Marshall's *Diary* about this ship's arrival or its cargo. Nor did he record the *Bella* which arrived on 11 July.[51] These ships were of no interest, because they were not bringing ready-made rebels from Ireland.

It is no surprise, then, that Marshall did not record the safe arrival 'at Philadelphia' of the 'St. George, Inglis,' or the 'Nancy and Polly, Burrell'[52] on 2 September. With berths for six passengers at most, neither ship was carrying emigrants. Moreover, both vessels were owned by the 'House of Willing, Morris and Company'. Like the customs officers, Marshall knew better than to interest himself in the affairs of Thomas Willing or Robert Morris. Then again, maybe he had his mind on weightier matters, as the General Congress was about to get into full swing, and America was on the march to independence, Marshall recording in his dairy on 5 September that 'the gentlemen that arrived in town as delegates ... met at the Carpenters' Hall'. Howsoever it happened, John arrived on American soil quite unnoticed by Marshall and other Sons of Liberty.

What Marshall did record, however, was that, on 12 September, 'the eight companies of the Royal Regiment of Ireland marched from hence, in two divisions, for Amboy and Elizabethtown, to be shipped for Boston.'[53] Leaving Philadelphia with them was John. He had been there precisely eleven days, time enough to see that riot was about to become rebellion.

The British Army military barracks in Philadelphia, *c*.1768.

CHAPTER 18

'Five Feet of Snow'

In the early hours of 19 April 1775, the first shots sounded across the small township of Lexington, Massachusetts signalling the bloody beginning of America's Revolutionary War. Events moved quickly thereafter. On 17 June came the battle of Bunker Hill, following which the British Redcoats found themselves 'cooped up' in Boston and 'so surrounded with lines and works as not to be able to advance into the country without hazarding too much'.[1] The days of British rule in New England were numbered.

These momentous events passed John by at the time. The previous September, he had, as ordered, accompanied the Royal Irish Regiment to Boston. Arriving at British Headquarters in early October he found General Gage struggling to keep up with events which were unfolding rapidly in the wake of the wide-ranging resolutions passed by the General Congress. John reported to Prescott, there on temporary attachment to Gage's staff, having, that same month, 'come a volunteer to offer his services'.[2] John's report certainly included an account of what he heard and saw during his brief time in Philadelphia. He doubtless made clear, from his conversations with Samuel Smith and other Patriots he met there, that the Congress meant business and that tea and tea parties were no longer the best gauge of America's mood.

What influence John's report had on Gage's thinking can only be guessed at, but it certainly confirmed the daily evidence in Boston where the local Patriots—more hot-headed than in Philadelphia—had taken the resolutions passed by the General Congress as a licence to prepare for war. Gage decided to request further reinforcements from London, including 'more ships of war, that he might be enabled to effectually stop the smuggling carried on by the French and Dutch.'

Prescott was charged with this mission. Leaving Boston in mid-December, he arrived in London on 13 January 1775, the journey made 'in twenty-five days from General Gage'.[3] A few days later, he 'had the honour of a conference with his Majesty' which was 'attended by the Earl of Dartmouth'.[4] Following this conference, a vessel bringing Prescott with the news of 'a large reinforcement of Ships and Troops'[5] left England on 25 February, arriving back in Boston on 2 April. Gage got more than he bargained for, however. Prescott also brought news that a triumvirate of generals—William Howe, John Burgoyne and Sir Henry Clinton—were arriving shortly to assume command of war operations.

Before departing for London, Prescott ordered John to take ship to Quebec, where the regiment was on post. When exactly John journeyed north is hidden from view, but certainly he was still 'in America' at the tail-end of the year, confirmation of this coming from his old friend in Göttingen, Heinrich Boie, whose letter to his brother, Reinhold, on 12 December, spoke of having just heard from John 'in America'.[6] However, with regiments in Boston going 'into winter quarters'[7] on 15 November that year, John must surely have aimed to reach Quebec while weather conditions permitted. Moreover, with hostilities imminent in Boston, it was only a question of time before war came north of the border. All was peaceful there for the moment hence why Prescott could undertake the mission to London, but the regiment must be prepared, and he would have given John orders to instruct the regiment in Howe's new 'discipline' while he was away.

As it turned out, the regiment had ample time to prepare and, on his return from London, Prescott remained in Boston and was present at the battle of Bunker Hill in June 1775, being among those listed as wounded.[8] All, meantime, seemed quiet across the border in Canada. John could attest to this, the letter 'dated Sunday 5th March 1775' to his sister, Mary, seemingly preoccupied only with 'giving her some notion of the appearance of the country'. He invited her to 'imagine a heaven of the purest blue and an Earth of the purest white' and, in the same winsome vein, recounted his frequent 'partys into the Country', all so she might understand that 'such dear Mary is the life of Quebec to-day.'

Not a ripple of rebellion invaded the idyll John conjured up for Mary. What he had heard in Philadelphia, sensed in New York, seen in Boston—not a word was said about all this. It was as if none of it mattered now he was in Canada's 'few acres of snow'. Emerging, nevertheless, through his description of the 'spirit of Society' he encountered there, it is clear he and the regiment were preparing for hard, uncertain service ahead. When he told Mary that 'my acquaintances thicken and I begin to sort them and select those whom I chuse to be connected with', he was adopting the same methodical approach to the formation of acquaintances and friendships as he had done in Göttingen, Gotha and Hanau. Whether socializing among 'the English' or 'the French', his reason to meet them was for their professional utility as immediate and future correspondents.

Whereas, in Göttingen, his friendships were made through military and poetic brotherhoods, in Quebec he sought the company of women, especially among 'the French' with whom 'I every now and then make partys into the Country in which I with my Equipage join in the string and drive out a Lady'. That way, under cover of 'dine, dance rondes, toss pancakes', he could gauge the political mood of the French-speaking inhabitants and, at the same time, reconnoitre the area around Quebec. When he was in Amsterdam, he had made out that his contact with the locals was as background material for a 'fameux journal' he was planning. So too, now, 'the figures' he was 'busy collecting of Canadians and Indians in their dresses' were 'to serve as cuts to the journal of notorious Memory'[9] which was in the making.

How private this 'journal' was intended to be is unclear, and these 'cuts' (silhouettes) accompanying it were certainly made, in part, for his own amusement. In part, however, they were a signal to his commanding officer that he was adept at draughtsmanship, a skill evident when the regiment moved from Quebec City to Fort St. John's, and one of the officers, almost certainly John, was called on to sketch a detailed plan of its fortifications.

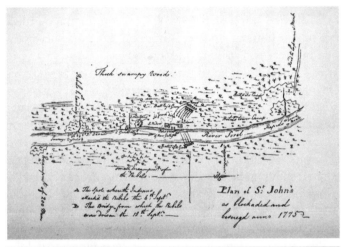

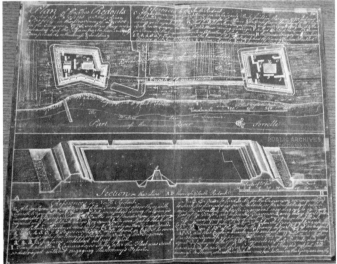

Hand-drawn map, possibly by John André, showing Fort St. John's during the siege in November 1775. (By permission of the author)

This was an important skill in the art of petite guerre, a point brought home to British forces encamped in Boston when it became evident that Gage needed to adjust the focus of his information-gathering from political to military intelligence. Hence a request went out in January 1775 that 'if any Officers of the different Regiments are capable of taking sketches of a Country, they are to send their names to the Deputy Adjutant General'. The urgency of the request brought home to Lieutenant Mackenzie how ill-prepared Gage was for the type of conflict that lay ahead. Mackenzie was from John's old regiment, the Royal Welch Fusiliers, and, holed up in Boston since shipping from New York in August the previous year, he could only lament that 'I am afraid not many Officers in this Army will be found qualified for this Service. It is a branch of Military education too little attended to, or sought after by our Officers, and yet is not only extremely necessary and useful in time of War, but very entertaining and instructive.'

That said it all. John's skill as a draughtsman would stand out, as would his knowledge of fortifications, Mackenzie going on to explain that 'we only have one professed Engineer here' in Boston 'and altho it is natural to suppose that he has taken every opportunity of making himself thoroughly acquainted with, not only the ground within a certain distance of this town (in case by any change in circumstances there should be a necessity for minute knowledge of it) but that of the surrounding country, I am apprehensive he has at this moment a very imperfect knowledge of either the one or the other.' Just giving officers the title of 'Assistant Engineer' was not a solution according to Mackenzie, since, despite the fancy title, they persisted in their 'ignorance'.[10]

John had these skills and more besides. He understood Howe's new discipline of loose warfare. Prescott had ordered him to instruct the regiment in it. John decided to hone it to local conditions. Bringing to bear what he had witnessed on Salisbury Plain the previous year, John took a special interest in 'the Indians'[11]. When Major-General Guy Carleton, the new British 'Governor', travelled to 'a village about nine miles' outside Quebec City and watched the Indians 'dance and perform some of their ceremonys',[12] the reason was for diplomacy. When John accompanied the governor on this same excursion, it was so as to employ the Indians to teach him and his men the art of bush fighting Indian-style.[13] This was unheard-of: to his fellow officers, the Indians were savages. For John, it was about survival: he explained to his sister how 'we are in a few days to go out into the woods to encamp in the snow after the Indian fashion and are to have Indians to guide us in the building our huts for this purpose'. John did not pull his punches, stressing to Mary that this was survival training, since he must 'hut in a stile little above brute creation' and 'be hunting upon snow shoes' some '30 miles out of town.' The regiment had already been through two Canadian winters without learning these skills. No wonder Prescott saw the need for John to re-join the regiment urgently!

From the letter, it is apparent John had already been in Quebec City close on three months when he wrote to his sister. It being Mary's 'turn to receive the monthly account I send of myself,'[14] which followed on 'my preceding one and from what I wrote to Mr Ewer', these previous two communications enabled her 'to frame some idea of this place and my manner of living'. As to the future, he indicated that 'we shall probably, if we do not go to Boston, move to Montreal next spring and the year after to the back posts on the 5 lakes [Great Lakes].'

This was almost exactly what happened, except that the movements were driven, not by routine rotations as his letter suggested, instead by the rapid collapse of British authority in Boston, beginning with the skirmish at Lexington just six weeks later and culminating in the battle of Bunker Hill that June. In the wake of these calamitous events, the regiment hurriedly fanned out to defend the two main overland entry points from the American colonies into Canada. One 'detachment of the 7th Regiment'[15] manned a fort at 'Shettican'[16] on the upper reaches of the Chaudière River, its duty being to halt any American invasion launched from Boston. This detachment remained on post until September 1775, when it was withdrawn to reinforce Quebec City. This left the route open for a sizeable force of Americans under Colonel Benedict Arnold to enter Canada leaving Cambridge on 11 September and reaching the walls of Quebec City virtually unopposed on 14 November.

Engraving of Benedict Arnold, 1776. (Yale University Art Gallery)

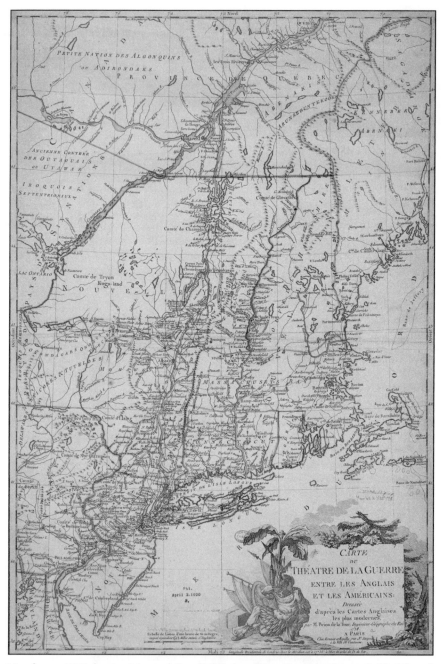

Map from *c.* 1777 showing Montreal, Fort St. John's and Fort Chambly. (Boston Public Library)

Another detachment went with units of the 26th Regiment to Montreal and thence south to two forts at Chambly and St. John's on the Richelieu River.[17] The second of these two was considered of vital strategic importance: commanding 'the entrance into Canada',[18] it barred the way against any invading force coming up the Hudson River from New York intent on seizing Montreal. John was posted there under the command of Charles Preston, a major in the 26th Regiment of Foot, and was certainly on station by 17 September 1775, the date of his first entry in a so-called 'Narrative of the Seige of St. John's Canada'[19] which he began compiling from there.

What knowledge John's mother, Mary-Louisa, had of these movements is difficult to tell, but she would surely have known of his final whereabouts, assuming, of course, that the 'monthly account' he said he had been sending home could still 'reach Southampton'[20] in a timely fashion. The first inkling Mary-Louisa would have had, then, that John's new posting had brought him to the front line of the now full-scale war between Britain and its American colonies came on 15 July when a London newspaper reprinted a 'letter from Ticonderoga dated May 23 1775' which told how 'Col. Arnold with thirty men, took the boat and proceeded on for St. John's' determined 'to take the place and the King's sloop by surprize at break of day'. Reading on, worse was to come when the report told how 'we took 14 prisoners'. Relief came, however, when the report ended with Arnold's decision to return to Ticonderoga and wait 'till men, provision and ammunition are furnished to carry on the war.'[21]

Respite for Mary-Louisa was only temporary, as more bad news filtered in from the front. Having fought off this initial raid, St. John's came under sustained siege beginning on 6 September, the American forces led, this time, by Generals Philip Schuyler and Richard Montgomery. First reports of this latest incursion reached London in mid-November when excerpts from the *New-York Gazette* dated 16 September were reproduced in, among other newspapers, the *London Chronicle* and, according to a 'letter from Isle de Nois', told of plans to 'strike a decisive blow at St. John's.'[22] Reading on in the same edition, Mary-Louisa would have seen chilling news from 29 September that the Americans 'have taken 15 prisoners' and hold 'St John's besieged'.[23]

A month later came news from 'Camp before St. John's dated 20th October 1775' that 'Fort Chamblee surrendered on the 18th instant.' Reading the report, Mary-Louisa could at least comfort herself that there were no casualties. There would have been mixed feelings, however, when, on 'the list of prisoners', there was no mention of John among the officers. This meant he was at Fort St. John's which, according to the same report, was almost certain to fall given 'the quantity of powder and ammunition of every kind'[24] already seized.

Well-stocked with ammunition but short of food, Fort St. John's held out until 3 November, capitulation hastened by the arrival of American reinforcements and the failure of a British relief column under the command of Colonel Allan Maclean and 'including sixty members of the Royal Fusiliers'[25] to break through from Quebec. John was among the 536 British officers and men who surrendered, along with 87, mainly Canadian, volunteers.

News of the debacle at Fort St. John's reached General Howe in Boston on 20 November[26] and 'Lord George Germain's office'[27] in London on 23 December. Mary-Louisa would have anxiously read a 'letter from an officer of the New York Forces' which described him 'marching into, and taking possession of this fortress, at the head of my company'. Scanning the letter for information about John's fate, again she could find no mention of casualties, only that prisoners were to be 'sent under guard as speedily as possible for Ticonderoga, Connecticut or any other place which the Continental Congress may direct.'[28]

It was a whole month before news about casualties appeared in the British press. Finally, on 22 January 1776 a letter written by 'one of the officers of the 26th regiment of foot to his friend in London' was published in the *Chester Chronicle*. 'Dated Amboy in New Jersey, 5th Dec. 1775,' it told of 'a short letter' he had just received 'from Major Preston' which described the circumstances of the Fort St. John's siege, including that 'there is only one officer of the 7th killed, two of the 26th wounded, fourteen privates killed, and sixteen wounded.'[29]

This report would surely have had Mary-Louisa fretting that the 'one officer ... killed' might be her 'cher Jean'.[30] In the event, she had no cause for concern: the 'one officer' was not her son but 'Mr Freeman, Lieut in the Royal Fusiliers'.[31] When Mary-Louisa learnt that John was alive is not known, but, with luck, her worst fears had been allayed before Major Preston's alarming account appeared in the *Chester Chronicle*. John certainly tried letting her know as soon as possible that he 'was safe and well'. He had arranged for her to receive 'a letter from Capt. Hesketh', who had also been captured at Fort St. John's. Knowing that Hesketh was being paroled compassionately to New York 'after the surrender of St. John's',[32] John had asked him to write to his mother on his behalf.

Mary-Louisa could also have heard the news from John's commanding officer, the ever-solicitous 'brigadier-general Prescott', who had arrived in Montreal 'together with two officers of inferior rank' in July 1775. Hastily dispatched there from Boston following news of 'the reduction of Crown Point, Ticonderoga and the king's ship on the Lake Champlain,'[33] Prescott had assumed overall command of both forts at Chambly and St. John's.

Prescott was soon ordering the petite guerre activities that this border campaign dictated. On 5 August, he wrote to Preston with instructions not to 'attempt anything beyond the line of the Province' but ordered that 'the Motions of all the Partisans of the Rebels must be closely watched.' A further letter on 31 August concerned a suspected double-agent informant whom Prescott wanted flushed out. Accordingly, he instructed Preston 'to send a Party and take this Fellow up, confine him at St. John's and examine him strictly, that we may see if he is equally inclined to inform us of what he knows respecting the Rebels. You must frighten this Rascal and inform me of what you can get out of him.'[34]

Prescott remained in command in Montreal[35] throughout the St. John's siege. He wrote a desperate letter on a 'Tuesday Evening 5 o'clock' ordering Preston to 'send frequent Parties for Intelligence', but, above all, 'defend St. John's to the last extremity' if only to buy 'a few days or hours respite'.[36] This letter from mid-September was the last to reach the fort before the American noose tightened and St. John's 'was now compleatly invested'.[37]

It was at precisely this moment that John began his so-called 'Narrative of the Seige of St. John's'.[38] The first entry was on 17 September. The decision to undertake it was prompted by the realization that the fort was surrounded and completely cut off. In these circumstances, it was imperative to have a formal record of events. To emphasise the official nature of the document, John noted in the conclusion to the 'Narrative', how 'it is remarkable that from the first day of the blockade we had not a Syllable of Intelligence from Genl Carleton, altho' we sent repeated Messages to Montreal.'[39]

The title of this document is misleading: it suggests a literary work composed as a personal record for the benefit of his family and much in the same vein as the 'fameux journal' that John had mentioned to his uncle while in Amsterdam or the 'journal of notorious Memory' he had promised to his sister Mary back in March. This was not the case: the title came later and by another person's hand. By its content, it is clear that this document, as originally composed, was part of a series of official formal military records of the fort's operations that John wrote up.

One of these records was a register setting out 'A State of the Troops under Command of Major Charles Preston on 17th of September last',[40] and listing the formal information—officers' names and rank, troop numbers, casualties etc—that would be published in the London Gazette following a military engagement. In addition, there was a regular inventory of (dwindling) supplies and report on the (deteriorating) state of the fortifications. Evidently, John—with his secretarial skills—had been dispatched to the fort by Prescott as a much-needed quartermaster to provide Preston with the organizational backup he would need in the event of an extended siege. As Cuthbertson had explained in his military manual, 'the Quarter-master' of a regiment was responsible for 'all March Routes and ... Arms, Accoutrements, Ammunition, Camp-equipage, cloathing and forage'[41] in addition to quartering. With these responsibilities, John had the best perspective on the operations of the fort and the regiment.

When John arrived at the fort is unclear but he may have brought Prescott's last letter, which ordered Preston to 'defend St. John's to the last extremity'. This would also explain why John only started his 'Narrative' on 17 September—'the first day of the blockade'—when, if this were simply a military journal, logic would suggest he should have started his entries from 6 September when the Americans first appeared

Plan of Fort St. John.

before St. John's or earlier still from the moment Prescott started peppering Preston with orders in early August.

Anticipating, certainly, a long siege if not total blockade, Prescott had also instructed John to record 'the Occurrences which since happened'[42] while he was on station at the fort. After the disaster at Fort Chambly, Prescott needed a formal record of events at St. John's. As a result, John wrote up a daily account of military operations between 17 September, when the fort was cut off, and 3 November, when 'the Troops march'd out of the redouts and embark'd for an Encampment of the Rebels two miles above St. John's'.[43]

However, John was also instructed by Prescott to make the journal an emphatic statement about British heroism in the midst of certain military defeat. This theme would recur and resonate throughout this war, Prescott all too aware that this still young war would be fought just as much on paper as on battlefields. The subject was especially topical at the time John was writing up the Narrative's conclusion: the prevailing opinion among British officers was that '*Timidity* and *Folly*'[44] had caused the garrison at Fort Chambly to surrender without a fight the previous month.

Prescott did not want a repeat of Fort Chambly, and not only for strategic reasons. The honour of the regiment—*his* regiment—was at stake, and he knew John was good at making words work. Honour in defeat was a point made clearly by John in the Narrative's conclusion. After describing how 'the Men shew'd a cheerfullness under their Fatigues which spite of Events can but reflect upon them, as few cou'd be devoid of Reflexion as not to see how slender our hopes of relief were, and of course to apprehend the most unfavorable Issue,' John summarized by stressing that, 'upon the whole it may be said that the Garrison at St. John's suffer'd in their Misfortunes, dangers and hardships which have often been the price of honor to more fortunate troops.'[45]

Written after the event, this conclusion could well be dismissed as a vain attempt by John to excuse defeat, except that he was acting under instructions from Prescott who would have briefed him ahead of his departure for the fort, telling him that capitulation was a near-certainty but that, militarily, time was of the essence. With winter closing in and reinforcements expected any day soon from England, the garrison's duty was to delay the American advance to 'the last extremity', giving Montreal and Quebec City time to mount a better defence of Canada. The American general Montgomery certainly understood this, refusing to grant Preston the four days' grace he requested before capitulating.

Given that this important 'Narrative' has survived through the turmoil of the siege, it is, surely, no coincidence that 'Lieutenant Andrie' was the officer 'gone to Montreal as Quarter-master'[46] following the surrender. Provision had been made for this under the terms of 'Article III' of the 'Articles of capitulation' which allowed for 'an Officer or Quarter-Master from each corps … to pass to Montreal on parole of honour there to transact and settle the business of his respective corps, and to bring up their baggage, cloathing and pay etc; for which purpose they will be furnished with carts and batteaus'.[47] In this capacity, John might have been able to bring out the 'Narrative' revealing the full extent of British heroism in defeat. It also afforded him his first close perspective on 'the enemy' when he witnessed a series of protracted brouhahas that erupted among the senior American officers concerning 'the superabundance of clothing'[48] allowed to the British prisoners under the terms of the articles of capitulation.

John's parole of honour only allowed him to remain in Montreal briefly. Under normal circumstances, this would have given him or Prescott ample time to dispatch a letter to England telling the Andrés back home in Southampton that he was safe.[49] The Americans were advancing so rapidly, however, that Montreal was soon under siege also, and, on 11 November, the governor, Carleton, gave orders to retreat to Quebec City, 'committing the defence of Montreal to Gen. Prescott.'[50] Carleton just managed to escape on 'a dark night, in a boat with muffled paddles'[51] and embarked with 'about 70 to 80 Regulars … on board some armed Vessels in the River and went to Quebec, where he arrived on the 19th of November.'[52] Prescott was not so lucky: he and '11 other officers and 120 soldiers were compelled to surrender prisoners'[53] after the city was invested by the Americans on 12 November. Prescott's capture, especially, was a feather in the cap for the Americans, not only because he was so senior an officer but also because, according to stories beginning to circulate, he had treated a captured American officer, Ethan Allen, without the due respect that his rank commanded. The incident related back to 25 September, when, according to 'a letter from Quebec dated the 2d of October ... a detached party of regulars and militia attacked a detached party of Provincials [and] about fifteen or sixteen were killed or wounded and thirty taken prisoner,' among which 'Col. Allen who it is said commanded the Provincial army.'[54] On the same day of his capture, Allen wrote a letter to Prescott complaining that he was being kept 'in irons'. He challenged whether there was like mistreatment of 'any Officers of the Crown by the Americans' and demanded for himself 'an honourable and treatment, as an Officer of my rank and merit should have'.[55]

The affair of the 'irons' quickly mushroomed into a propaganda coup for the Americans. That Allen was an 'adventurer' acting 'without any commission from the Congress'[56] was quickly lost in the rhetoric of war, as 'both parties' in the expanding conflict sought 'recourse to the powers of invention' in their struggle for strategic advantage both on and off the battlefield. In the melée of warring 'fictions',[57] Prescott's name became a watchword for British cruelty and barbarism, Allen's the epitome of the Patriot hero.[58]

With the surrender at Montreal, the way was open to Quebec City. John's 'Narrative' of British sacrifice at Fort St. John's was soon eclipsed by even greater heroics from Americans and Britons alike, as the final titanic struggle for Canada unfolded in late December at the gateway to the mighty St. Lawrence River. 'The assailants' were determined to 'assault the walls' of the great City, the defenders equally intent on resistance. Both sides battled 'in snow not less than six feet deep' as 'a tremendous storm'[59] raged around them. Canada would not be lost or won without a fight.

John, meantime, was on his way to Pennsylvania and a year in captivity.

CHAPTER 19

'Adverse Winds and Hard Frosts'

1776 was a momentous year in the history of the American Revolutionary War, with fortunes ebbing and flowing wildly for both sides in this increasingly angry conflict. January brought the beginnings of victory for the British in Canada, only for them to endure humiliating retreat from New England in March. Triumphant in Boston, the Americans in turn found themselves chased out of New York then across New Jersey, only for General Washington to mount a morale-restoring action across the Delaware in the dead of December. Away from the battlefields, on 4 July 1776 the thirteen colonies formally declared their independence. With compromise no longer an option, the end to this dispute would henceforth only come by force of arms.

John was a mute bystander throughout all these events, unhappy to be passive but unable to be active. Made a prisoner on 3 November 1775 following the capitulation at St. John's, he was 'at length restored to [his] liberty' over a year later. Writing to his mother on 17 December 1776 after his release 'a week ago', the sigh of impatient relief was audible as he explained how, 'after haggling a long time about exchanging prisoners, the Congress have at length thought it politic to consent to this measure and have dispatched the greatest part of their prisoners of war back to the British Army.'

Understandably for John writing to his mother after so long an enforced interval without contact, a major preoccupation in this letter was the absence of family news during his one year's confinement. As he explained, 'the only letter I have received since my being a prisoner is one from Uncle D. Andre dated December 1775. I should have said during my captivity for I received yours from Spa by Capt. Donkin before my arrival at N. York, and one since my arrival at N. York, and one from W. Ewer.' To emphasise his sense of isolation, he complained that 'Ewers letter is so concise that I can learn nothing of yourself or my sisters and brother by it, and your own is of so old a date that it is very unsatisfactory.' As if to reassure himself and his mother that life had returned to normal again, he instructed her: 'be so good for the future to direct to me at N. York.'

As upsetting as it had been not hearing from the family, more worrisome was the thought that his mother may have had no news of him over the past year. This prompted him to ask: 'Did you ever receive a letter from Capt. Hesketh after the surrender of St. Johns informing you I was safe and well?' Still, this came very much as an afterthought, the enquiry added as a footnote only after he had signed off as 'your dutifull and Affectionate Son.'

What preoccupied him more was how the events at St. John's had been represented to his mother and, more importantly, to the British public at large. The intention of his 'Narrative of the Seige of St. John's' was for extracts from it to be published in British newspapers. For all he knew, however, the document had disappeared for good. He had brought it to Montreal, otherwise it would have been stolen when he 'was taken prisoner by the Americans and'—so he told Anna Seward—'stript of every thing' … everything, that is, 'except the portrait of Honora which I concealed in my mouth'.

Just as there must be some doubt whether this portrait was of Honora or Anna, so the idea that John was 'stript of every thing' is equally open to question, not least because, in the letter to his mother, he said that 'the Garrison's effects' were saved 'from plunder.'[1] Readers of the *Lady's Monthly Museum* in 1811 only had Anna's word for it what John had written to her back in 1776, and the whole anecdote has the ring of sentimental hyperbole, confirmed when John was also purported to have concluded his account to Anna with the gushing sentiment that 'preserving [the portrait] I yet think myself fortunate.'[2]

Closer to the truth was that the Americans generally respected the British prisoners' personal effects in these early encounters, but that, doubtless, some items were stolen or destroyed. As quartermaster, John would have witnessed this. He had planned to give the 'Narrative' to Prescott when he was in Montreal on parole, but with that city's subsequent surrender and Prescott's capture, he had to assume that this was when his document disappeared. He had no way of knowing one way or another, not least because he had not seen a British newspaper during his captivity, and any American newspapers[3] he did see were only ever full of 'Rebel' victories and 'Rebel' heroics. The Americans would surely have shown him a one-page broadside entitled 'Carleton's defeat and Arnold's Success'. Rushed out on 3 November 1775, it announced with great fanfare that 'yesterday evening the fortress at St. John surrendered to our army'.

As far as John knew, the British public—his mother included—were quite unaware of the full circumstances of the siege. One purpose of his December 1776 letter to his mother, then, was to record the British version of events. Moreover, after a year spent in captivity alongside British officers taken at Fort Chambly, he had seen the simmering tensions between the heroes of St. John's and the curs of Chambly and was more than ever determined that he should represent the St. John's siege as a heroic defeat.

From past experience, John knew that his relatives and friends often sent private letters to newspapers for publication. He hoped his mother would do this now. A major drawback was that the events he was recounting were from fully a year earlier. To overcome this, he cast himself as a wartime correspondent who had witnessed the original events first-hand but, as a prisoner, had, dramatically, been gagged ever since. Unable to communicate with the outside world because his captors had 'at … times broken open our letters and withheld them', he could finally speak out, though, with a melodramatic tug on the emotional heartstrings, 'my situation is so new to me, that free as I am, I scarcely dare trust my pen to its former license, but ever imagine suspicious Committees may intercept my letter and make me suffer for my indiscretion.'

Unlike the 'Narrative', which, as an official military account of the siege, was laden with weighty information, John kept this version punchy, sufficient, he hoped, as the basis for a short newspaper article. Hence, he promised that, 'with respect to our siege I shall not enter into any detail, but be contented with telling you…' whereupon he recounted '…that after two or three little skirmishes, we were pent up in small redoubts where we were annoyed with pitiful Cannonading and bombardments for seven weeks'. Here, he was addressing a military audience eager to hear how, with the right resources, the rebels could be easily defeated. Quickly switching his attention to an imagined female readership—represented by his mother—he told graphically how 'our provision of rusty bacon (whereof for three weeks we had been allowed but a scanty allowance) was entirely exhausted, our cannon likewise devoured their food and our habitations were in ruins.'

Having caught the attention of his two very distinctive audiences, John set the scene for his core message of British heroism in defeat, explaining how, after 'seven weeks' under siege, 'we learnt that an attempt of General Carleton to relieve us had been unsuccessfull. The rebels were entrenched up to their teeth in every direction round us, and had beset the road to Montreal and had secured the beats on the River St. Lawrence.' Faced, then, with certain defeat, he could conclude that 'thus situated we delivered ourselves up upon honorous terms'. As if to downplay his core message—and thereby magnify it—John concluded his account of the siege with the observation that British fortitude and endurance in securing these 'honorous terms' 'had this good effect that they saved the Garrison's effects from plunder.'

The reference to 'effects' enabled John also to introduce his own, supposedly modest, role in the ongoing events when he went on to explain how 'I remained behind at Montreal to bring up the baggage and after crossing unhospitable lakes, often retarded by adverse winds and harsh frost, I at length reached Lancaster in February.'[4] In one sentence, Mary-Louisa's son had transported himself from the gates of Fort St. John's on the banks of the Richelieu River in Canada on the night of 2 November 1775 to Lancaster, Pennsylvania in mid-February 1776.[5] In the process, he had completed a journey of five hundred miles across frozen wastes through hostile country in wartime and in the dead of winter. Surely, this was a saga that deserved more than one sentence. Once having revealed himself in the drama of unfolding events, was not this the moment for John to become expansive, if only for his mother's benefit? Was this John's 'almost womanlike modesty' carried to excess?

If John's overarching message were, indeed, British heroism in defeat, was not this long trek the time when such personal qualities as sangfroid, perseverance and fortitude in adversity could be highlighted to the wider audiences he had in mind for this crucial letter? At the very least, he had saved the garrison's effects from 'plunder'. This, alone, was no mean feat, guaranteed to earn him the lasting gratitude of the officers and men in the garrison: 'effects' were what made them other than soldiers, made them human, made them people, made them individuals. So, why the brevity? Why the silence? Why the modesty? Was there something that John was not saying about the trek?

There are a number of possible explanations for the lack of detail in John's letter of 17 December 1776, among which that, during the journey south, John took advantage of his privileged freedom as an officer on parole of honour to pursue the petite guerre activities he had first trained for during his tours in Germany. As quartermaster, he had wide-ranging responsibilities requiring him to have contact with many Americans, civilians and military alike. These 'correspondents' and the strategic knowledge he acquired as he escorted the baggage down the Hudson River and into the heartland of Pennsylvania could be valuable should he be released from captivity and return to the war. If he were, indeed, pursuing these clandestine activities, it would certainly explain his silence: versed in the demands of petite guerre, he knew it was imperative not to boast about what really happened during those crucial three months from November 1775 to February 1776, even to his mother.

Another explanation is that to have recounted in detail the events of his long trek south would have been to reveal, maybe, that the officers John encountered in the Continental Army were not unruly 'Rebels' as he previously thought and as was portrayed by Britain's commanders, most especially Howe and Prescott.[6] Rather, they were professional soldiers, many of whom were veterans of the French and Indian War and, hence, had been trained in the British military tradition and understood the British military code of honour, not least in the matters of 'plunder' and the treatment of prisoners of war.

What if his experience had revealed the Americans to be as honourable as the British, possibly even more so? What if John had encountered the same 'utmost attention and politeness' on his trek south to Lancaster as the American general Schuyler had promised the officers of the Royal Fusiliers captured at Fort Chambly? What if, like them, John had been 'entertained at the publick expense … in all places' along the way and allowed 'to take the band of musick with him'?[7] To admit to all this 'politeness' in the propaganda war John was committed to fighting was to dilute the letter's central message that the British were the heroes (even in defeat), the Rebels the villains. For the British prisoners to remain heroes after the capitulation, they needed to become victims. What happened during those crucial three months that John was not writing about? John chose to stay silent but not Congress, nor, indeed, the American officers escorting the prisoners and their baggage into captivity. Detailed records were kept of the two main journeys south: the first by Major Preston with the main body of prisoners, which set off immediately following the capitulation on 3 November; the second by John, which departed from Montreal a few weeks later with 'carts and batteaus'[8] full of 'women, children and baggage'.[9] The Americans' conduct during these two journeys was broadly governed by the terms of the Articles of Capitulation. For John, two key points had been agreed by the Americans: first, 'that the garrison shall march out with the honours of war; this is due to their fortitude and perseverance'; and, secondly, that, as 'our prisoners' held by the British 'have been constantly treated with brotherly affection, the effects of the garrison shall not be withheld from them.'[10] In the event, how the British were treated en route to Pennsylvania degenerated into a tug-of-war between the Continental Army and Congress, each intent on dictating the terms by which this new conflict should be fought.

As it had been agreed in the Articles of Capitulation that 'the Garrison must go to Connecticut Government or such other province as the Hon.ble the Continental Congress shall direct',[11] the route chosen went south via Fort Ticonderoga on Lake Champlain. At first, all went well, the British prisoners seen as both trophies and bargaining chips for prisoner exchanges.[12] The public often lined the route taken by this large column of prisoners.[13]

The prisoners were also seen as propaganda tools, their worth as such less tangible but far more significant in the struggle to achieve what combatants on both sides sought: a just war. American accounts went out of their way to show the Continental Army abiding by the proper rules of war.[14] Convinced in these early days of the conflict that the 'King's Troops' were ready to desert en masse to the revolutionary cause, the Americans were especially solicitous towards the St. John's prisoners, hoping thereby to win them over. This explains General Schuyler's early 'attention and politeness' towards the officers when they arrived at Fort Ticonderoga, their first stop. Reporting to Congress on 11 November, Schuyler noted the sorry state of the 'King's Troops' and that 'the officers' had 'applied to me for blankets and shoes for their men, who are almost barefooted.'

To further acquit himself of direct responsibility, Schuyler recorded that the British officers 'then asked money and I ventured to give Major Preston one hundred and seventy-two pounds six shillings New-York currency and as much to Captain Kinnear who commanded the Seventh'. As Schuyler explained, 'I thought it best they should supply themselves, especially as they consider themselves accountable to me for the money.' With that and an ominous note warning 'we already have snow here', Schuyler sent 'the Seventh and Twenty-Sixth … on their march to Connecticut'.[15] The prisoners' next stop was Albany, New York, where they arrived by 'the 20th Nov.' This was according to 'a short letter' written by

Preston from there to 'one of the officers in the 26th regiment of foot' located in 'Amboy in New Jersey.' Despite the problems which had arisen at Fort Ticonderoga, Preston seemed well pleased, noting how the British prisoners 'were treated with great kindness.'[16]

So far, so good, but then Congress decided to take a hand and passed a resolution on 17 November that, instead of going to Connecticut, 'the prisoners taken at Chambly and St. John's be sent and kept in the towns of Reading, Lancaster and York, in the colony of Pennsylvania'.[17] It seems 'Governour Trumbull' had made known he 'was not desirous of their company.'[18] He reasoned that the British were still occupying Boston and that the New England coast was under constant threat from the Royal Navy, which might mount a rescue mission.

For Congress, however, the worry was that the British prisoners might, themselves, try to escape. Endeavouring to forestall this eventuality, the 'President of Congress', John Hancock, wrote to Captain Edward Mott, the 'Officer commanding the Guard' escorting the prisoners on their journey, ordering him to 'march the prisoners under your guard by the nearest way to Reading.'[19] Apprehensive as Congress was that the prisoners would try to escape, it was paranoid that American officers might collude with them. The prisoners were trophies to be proud of, but, at 'upwards of six hundred',[20] their numbers made them a Trojan horse entering the heart of America's still fragile revolution.

The real impulse behind the change of destination, then, was elemental: this conflict was rapidly taking on the aspects of a 'civil war' in which 'Britons fight against Britons'.[21] No-one could be trusted, least of all the Continental Army's officers, many of whom might be tempted to return to the British fold if they came into direct contact with the prisoners from St. John's. Indeed, many of these American officers were openly fraternizing with their captured British counterparts. Following the capitulation of St. John's, Schuyler wrote to Trumbull recalling fondly how, 'from Major Preston and the officers of the Twenty-Sixth Regiment I have experienced the most polite and friendly attentions when I was a stranger and a traveller in Ireland many years earlier.'[22]

As injudicious as this admission was, Schuyler and Montgomery—the officers who negotiated the terms of capitulation at Forts Chambly and St. John's—were found to have agreed that the British could maintain their military command structure even as prisoners. For Congress, this would not do. Hence, at the same time as ordering the prisoners (meaning the men) to Pennsylvania, Congress directed that only 'the officers taken at St. John's be sent to Windham and Lebanon in the colony of Connecticut.'[23] This was contrary to what had been expressly agreed with the British. Mott knew this and was having nothing of it. He, too, had become, in his own words, socially 'intimate' with the British officers during the journey, deeming two of them 'gentlemen of honour', and describing 'Mr Smith,' as a 'gentleman officer of the Artillery.'

Stopping at Kingston with his 'guard of one hundred men' en route down the Hudson River to 'New Windsor', Mott dispatched a letter to Trumbull. Dated 26 November, it explained that he had received orders while 'at Hoffman's landing from Continental Congress, to march the men to Lancaster, in the Province of Pennsylvania and the officers to Lebanon and Windham in Connecticut' but decided to ignore these instructions as 'by a previous engagement of General Schuyler's to the gentlemen officers that they should see their men quartered, I am now marching them all, officers and privates, to Lancaster.'[24] This was exactly what Congress did not want to have happen. Mott would have questions to answer when he arrived in Pennsylvania.

First, Mott had to get the prisoners to their final destinations. The next reported sighting of the prisoners was on 4 December in Nazareth, Pennsylvania, when 'the diary of a minister of that town' carried the entry: 'a strong column of Regulars ... made prisoners at the taking of Fort St. John passed through on their way to Bethlehem.[25] Another diarist watched their arrival a day later in Bethlehem. According to his 'Diary of the Moravian Congregation', 'some English officers and soldiers taken prisoner by General Montgomery at St. John's arrived and are quartered here'. The following day, a further entry recorded that 'about 200 royal prisoners of war arrived.' They had just marched a hundred and ten miles from New Windsor on the Hudson River, but, as the Moravian eyewitness noted, 'all those here will leave tomorrow.'[26] The prisoners still had to march a further seventy-five miles before reaching Lancaster, but they were evidently being hurried along, and the first group arrived there on 9 December.[27]

A small contingent of British women and children from Fort St. John's had, meantime, arrived separately on 7 December. So proud was Congress that the delegates interrupted 'their deliberation ... on advice being received that the Women and Children taken at St. John's were arrived with their baggage.'[28] Congress had first put its mind to the thorny issue of 'women, children and baggage'[29] in its letter of 17 November to Walter Livingston, Deputy Commissary at Albany where this group had stopped briefly. The letter directed that, 'if the prisoners agree,' he was to 'send the women, children and baggage, by water to Amboy'. From there, they were 'to be sent across to Bordentown, and from thence by water to Philadelphia; from which last place they will be sent to join the garrison in the Towns allotted to them; this being judged the safest, cheapest and most commodious way of conveying them.'[30] Understandably, the risk of escape was a lesser consideration. Casting off his 'apprehensions' about any British men-of-war lurking down the Hudson River, Livingston arranged that 'the women, children and baggage' be sent down river 'to Amboy and from thence to Bordentown and Philadelphia', proudly announcing that this 'will save at least three hundred Pounds'.[31] No wonder Congress could congratulate itself when this group arrived safely on 7 December. Together with those arriving on 9 December, it had taken a little over a month for 'upwards of six hundred' prisoners, women and children to make the journey safely from St. John's to their final destinations around Pennsylvania.

Congress was less happy, however, when the British officers began arriving in Pennsylvania. For a start, not all the officers arrived in Lancaster at the same time: 'Captain Livingston of the Twenty-Sixth Regiment and Lieutenant Anstruther of the 7th Regiment came to 'this town on the evening of the 1st inst. (January), under the conduct of Mr Michael Connolly'.[32] Preston, meantime, had made directly for Philadelphia, 'information being given to Congress' on 'Monday, December 4' that he 'is now in town.' This caused consternation in Congress, which was at a loss to understand how a captured British officer could roam free in Philadelphia, especially as it coincided with 'information being given to Congress, that Major Stopford, notwithstanding his parole, is endeavouring to debauch the minds of the people.'

Here was further proof that the Continental Army operated by its own gentleman's rules, ignoring Congress resolutions. Matters had come to a head: at issue was who—the Army or Congress—had the final say on what terms could be agreed for surrenders, capitulations, paroles of honour and subsequent prisoner conditions. Before making a final determination, James Duane, a delegate representing the Continental Congress, was 'ordered to call on him [Preston] and obtain a representation of facts, how he came here, and whether he and any other officers have any liberty granted him, with regard to the place of his confinement.'[33] Following the interview, Preston was told to remain in Philadelphia.

Congress next called Mott forward and, on 'Friday, December 15 1775, information being given to Congress, that captain Motte, who had the charge of conducting the prisoners to Reading, and other towns in Pennsylvania, having performed that service, has returned to this city,' it was resolved that 'the committee appointed to distribute the prisoners confer with captain Motte.'[34] The following day, after 'taking into consideration the report of the Committee', Congress passed various resolutions which appeared to endorse the army's authority, namely: that 'the distribution of the Prisoners, made by Captain Motte, is approved'; that 'the Privates who are prisoners and have been left by Captain Motte at Lancaster, be allowed to remain in that place till the further orders of Congress' and that 'the Officers be distributed in such places as are most agreeable to themselves observing always the former resolutions of Congress on this subject.'[35]

Crucially, however, in a direct slap-down to the army, Congress also stipulated that 'the Officers and Privates be not stationed in the same places.'[36] Congress had gone back on one of the key articles of capitulation agreed between General Montgomery and Major Preston at St. John's. The officers and men captured at Forts Chambly and St. John's were about to learn what it meant to be political rather than military prisoners of war.

John, naturally, was oblivious of these machinations. Charged with bringing the bulk of the garrison's baggage, together with the main contingent of British women and children, from Montreal, he was still stuck in 'adverse winds and hard frosts,' having set out on his trek south only in mid-November. Moreover—so he told his mother—the journey took him three months, not the one month enjoyed by the first group of prisoners. This raises the spectre that John deliberately 'retarded' his journey so as to more effectually pursue his clandestine operations. He certainly spent the best part of a month in Albany where he dined frequently with the Continental Army general Schuyler and, separately, with the 'tory' mayor, Abraham Cuyler[37] and his wife. As in Germany, he endeared himself to his hosts by making 'cuts' of them, which he left as gifts. When the sloop ferrying him and his charges down from Albany was 'caught in the ice' opposite 'Fort Constitution',[38] he had an early sight of the impressive new fort being built which commanded 'the passage up and down the river and scours West-Point.'[39] At nearby Haverstraw Landing, he met, among others, a local lawyer of, alternately, 'tory' and 'whig' inclinations by the name of Joshua Hett Smith. All these were useful correspondents should John ever return to the area.

It is inconceivable, however, that John deliberately delayed his journey: he knew how desperate—especially given the onset of harsh weather—the officers and men in the regiment would be for their 'effects'. More likely were a number of very real factors that certainly 'retarded' his journey. The first one was that, as he said: 'I remained behind at Montreal' to sort out 'the baggage'. This work was further complicated when that city came under siege and finally capitulated on 12 November. The Americans drew up a list of officers captured along with General Prescott. As John was already on his parole of honour, he was not on this list.[40] Complicating John's already difficult logistics, the list also included 'fifty women and ninety odd children'[41] for whom he now became responsible.

John set off in company with a second group of prisoners, leaving Montreal in mid-November and arriving at Fort Ticonderoga by 27 November. From there, Schuyler reported that 'the schooner and row-galley taken at St. John's are just arrived here, together with our sloop and schooner, full of prisoners and their baggage.' Prescott and the other officers captured in Montreal caught up with this convoy a day later, Schuyler writing on 28 November that 'at four this afternoon I was agreeably surprised with the sight of Brigadier-General Prescott and the officers taken with him on the vessels.'

As with the first prisoners passing through Fort Ticonderoga on 11 November, Schuyler hurried this group along, noting that 'I am much distressed to get them on, my cattle fairly worn out and only six horses which I sent for from my own stables.'[42] Meantime, the weather had deteriorated, significantly delaying progress. By mid-December, this group could only reach Albany, from where Schuyler wrote on 21 December telling Congress that 'the frost here is so intense, that the river is frozen over, and I expect will be passable with horses in a day or two.'

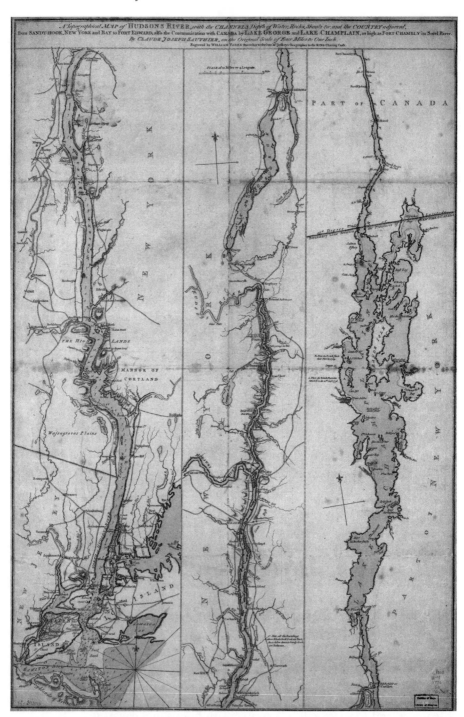

Map showing the route taken by John from Fort St. John to the Hudson River in December 1775. (Library of Congress, Geography and Map Division)

He further explained that 'baggage belonging to the prisoners and which was embarked on a sloop, is caught in the ice, about five miles below this.' The reference to 'sloop' signals this as the same group of prisoners which Schuyler had alluded to in his 27–28 November letter. That 'the greatest part of it belongs to those who are now in Pennsylvania,' and that Schuyler fretted 'how to get it to them'[43] suggests this was the 'baggage' that John had brought south and explains why, as he said to his mother, he was 'retarded by adverse winds and harsh frosts.'

On 26 December, Schuyler again drew attention to the prisoners' plight, alerting Congress that 'the officers, prisoners are making daily application to me for money to subsist themselves with'.[44] It was 2 January 1776 before this second group could move on, Schuyler writing to Colonel Wynkoop from Albany alerting him that 'Captain Billings will deliver you the officers that were made prisoners in Canada'. Confirmation that John was part of this convoy came when Schuyler instructed Billings 'to forward the officers and their baggage to Trenton, together with the baggage of the St. John's garrison, the officers' servants, and four or five men to take care of the baggage'.

Aware that weather was now a major factor, Schuyler counselled Billings: 'should the snow fall when you arrive at Delaware, and the river not be navigable, and no possibility of going down on the ice, you will leave the baggage and proceed with the officers and their servants to Trenton, from whence you will please repair to Congress, and report what you have done.' As a final point, he remarked that 'the expenses run as high that the greatest economy is to be used in conveying these troops.'[45] Still, John and the other British officers and men in this second group could hardly complain that they had been poorly treated.

Poor weather continued to dog the convoy. It took until 22 January for the officers escorted by Wynkoop to reach Trenton in New Jersey. That same day, Congress sent 'orders … to the Committee of Trenton to send General Prescott and Captain Chace under Guard to Philadelphia.'[46] Prescott was living up to his reputation: according to the 'New-Jersey Committee of Safety' he 'absolutely refuses to give his parole; we have, therefore, confined him to his room … The other gentlemen of his suite have very readily complied with the requisition.'[47] Unlike Mott, Wynkoop, on his arrival in Philadelphia, was not called before Congress: happy with his conduct, it simply reimbursed him 'the sum of 765.7 dollars … for expenses in bringing a party of prisoners from St. John's.'[48]

As with Mott's earlier group, the women, children and baggage being escorted by John had, in the meantime, been routed separately via Bethlehem arriving there on 30 January, when a Moravian inhabitant's journal recorded that 'four sleigh loads of the wives and children of the royal prisoners from Canada arrived. We assisted the poor wives and children.' The following day 'toward evening there arrived some twenty wagons filled with soldiers and their baggage, belonging to the Canadian prisoners. We found much trouble to provide for and lodge them.'[49]

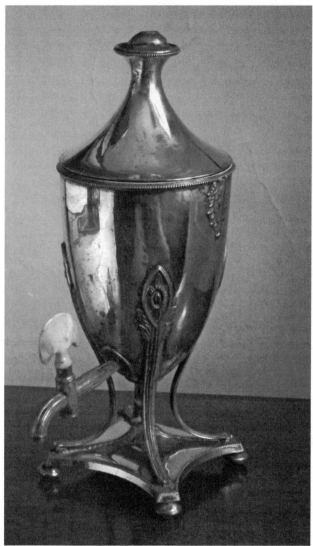

John André's tea urn. (By kind permission of Major J. E. A. André)

From there, the women, children and baggage were distributed to the towns where the officers and men were cantoned. The logistics were enormous: Connolly was again involved, on this occasion bringing the 'women and children belonging to the 26th and 7th regiments from Esopus to Reading.' On 'Thursday February 15, 1776', he was reimbursed 'the sum of 1082.8 dollars.' On the same day, 'colonel Simmes' brought 'the baggage of the 26th and 7th regiments from Walpack to Lancaster' and was reimbursed 'the sum of 569 dollars'. Finally, on 'February 20, 1776' Connolly was reimbursed 'the sum of 160 dollars' for 'expenses for Wagon-hire, carrying the Prisoners' baggage from Bethlehem to Reading, and his own expenses four days.'[50] The women, children and baggage had arrived safely, and John had completed his latest important assignment.

No wonder, then, that, in his December 1776 letter to his mother, John said little about his trek south from Montreal: he had no complaint about his treatment by the officers and men of the Continental Army. So, why, further on in this same letter, did he vituperate against 'the perfidious dastards who have worked the ruin and spilt the blood of so many credulous wretches'? Who were these 'perfidious dastards? Obviously not Schuyler, Mott and the other Continental Army officers whom he, and, before him, Preston, had encountered on their respective journeys to Lancaster. He, like Preston, had only enjoyed 'great kindness' while in their hands.

Still, John pulled no punches as he railed against the 'perfidious dastards', thundering 'that they merited the first appellation a single instance of their Conduct towards us will shew; which is that after receiving 500 of their own men out of the hands of the Indians on condition of delivering up the Garrison of St. Johns they treacherously withheld us, inventing a falsehood for a pretence not to fulfill their agreement.'[51] Here John was referring to the so-called Battle of the Cedars, fought in Canada in May 1776, and ending in an American surrender.[52] As with Schuyler and Montgomery following the British surrenders at Forts Chambly and St. John's, the American commander at Cedars agreed terms with the local British commander, and these included the prisoner exchange which John was referring to. Crucially, it would have meant his earlier release.

However, Congress refused 'to fulfill their agreement'. This, of course, was not the first time Congress had gone back on an agreement made by officers of the Continental Army in the field: when separating the British officers from their men the previous December, Congress had set aside specific terms of capitulation agreed by Schuyler and Montgomery with the British at Forts Chambly and St. John's. Clearly, then, for John the 'perfidious dastards' were 'the Congress', who, as he vented to his mother, 'have at length thought it politic to consent' to his release, 'and have dispatched the greatest part of their prisoners of war back to the British Army, but 'only after haggling a long time about Exchanging prisoners.'[53]

Unwittingly, John and his fellow prisoners from Forts Chambly and St. John's had become caught up in a battle of wills between Congress and the Continental Army over how this war was to be fought. The resulting perfidy would have come as a shock for John arriving in wintry Lancaster, Pennsylvania in February 1776, especially after the solicitude shown to him by the officers of the Continental Army during his trek south. Joining his fellow officers from St. John's, he, too, was about to discover what it was to be a political prisoner of war.

CHAPTER 20

'No Political Correspondence'

Arriving in Lancaster in mid-February, John expected to find his fellow officers settled into 'private lodgings'[1] and the men quartered in the town, awaiting only their 'effects'. Instead, both regiments, the 7th (English Fusiliers) and the 26th, were close to mutiny. The trouble had started in early January, the Lancaster Committee of Safety complaining to Congress that it was 'absolutely impossible to preserve peace and good order of this Borough, unless some regulations were made for the soldiers who are prisoners here… We have been under the necessity of appointing a Sergeant and 12 privates to mount guard at our publick Magazine every evening. They patrole the street every two hours in the night, to prevent disorder.'[2]

Matters deteriorated further, the Pennsylvania Committee of Safety summing up the mood in its 20 February letter: 'the kind treatment given … meets with very improper and indecent return.' In addition, 'they often express themselves in most disrespectful and offensive terms and openly threaten revenge.'[3] The main bone of contention was the decision by Congress that the officers and men should be separated. This prompted a letter from the Lancaster Committee on 21 December 1775, reporting that 'the officers … complain greatly of a separation from their soldiers, as a breach of General Schuyler's solemn engagement, and that they cannot remove from hence, until their baggage, with the men's clothing, and the pay of the troops comes up.' Adding weight to the argument, 'Edward Shippen, Chairman' of the Committee, explained that 'the soldiers also express great uneasiness about their clothing and pay, if their officers are removed from them.'[4]

Congress responded only on 18 January. The initial tone of the letter was conciliary: 'your civility to the officers who are prisoners, in giving them time to make choice of the places of residence and permitting them to remain with you till their baggage shall arrive, is approved.' On the main principle, however, Congress was unmoved: 'their complaint that a separation from the soldiers is a breach of General Schuyler's Solemn engagement, we apprehend not to be well-founded. All the stipulations of a capitulation ought, undoubtedly, to be held sacred … but no such stipulation is to be found in the capitulations … nor had General Schuyler a right to make fresh terms with his prisoners after they were in his power, without the consent of the Congress.' Having secured the legal high ground, Congress sought to defuse the immediate trouble, conceding that 'nevertheless, we should have paid a respect to his opinion and advice in the matter' and agreeing that 'we have no objection to your permitting two or more of the officers to come, at proper times, from their places of residence to Lancaster, for the purpose of settling with and paying their soldiers.'[5]

Before this letter could be transmitted to Lancaster, another petition arrived signed by all sixteen British officers residing there, among which nine from John's regiment, the 'Royal Fusileers',[6] six from the 26th Regiment and one from the 'Royal Highland Emigrants.' Dated 20 January and addressed directly to the 'President of Congress', it raised again the thorny issue about 'the officers being separated from their men'. Invoking 'the promise' made by Schuyler, it cited 'confirmation of it under the hands of the Congress in their orders to Captain Nott.'

Gone now were the polite pleas. Instead, Captain Kinnear, as the most senior officer, threatened that 'if the decision is to carry through the separation, the officers will be extremely sorry to be reduced to the necessity of cancelling that promise'.[8] This 'promise' related to 'the paroles of the Officers'[7] given when they first arrived in Lancaster. In the promise was an obligation to 'not go into or near any sea-port town nor farther than six miles distance from the respective places of their residence without the leave of the Continental Congress' and that 'they will carry on no political correspondence whatever on the subject of the dispute between Great Britain and these colonies, so long as they remain prisoners.'[9]

Given the present fragility of the Revolution, it was unwise these officers threatening to cancel their paroles. Congress was bound to take the matter seriously, not least the implied threat to engage in 'political correspondence'. The officers were not to know it, but their threat coincided with an investigation underway into similar activities by another group of officers from John's regiment who had been captured at Fort Chambly and sent to Trenton, New Jersey.

Major Stopford, as the most senior officer among them, stood accused of 'endeavouring to debauch the minds of the people' in breach of a collective parole signed by him and six other officers residing there. When the Trenton Committee investigated the supposed breach, its report to Congress on 9 December 1775 exonerated Stopford but recorded that 'Dr Huddleston', the regiment's surgeon, 'has been unguarded and imprudent in his discourse'. The Committee tried to assure Congress that 'there is not the least danger the people of this place being debauched by them' as 'the people in and about Trenton early fixed their principles.' The Committee also noted that 'the other gentlemen … have never failed to reprove him' and 'express great uneasiness at the apprehension of being removed as well on account of the satisfaction they have in their present situation as that it must appear to the world as punishment for breach of honour.'[10]

Nevertheless, Congress was now on full alert, not least because Stopford and the other officers of John's regiment quartered in Trenton seemed to be enjoying an especially pampered existence: Samuel Tucker, president of the New Jersey Congress, wrote to the Continental Congress on 2 April saying 'we shall have considerable difficulty getting entertainment for the officers and soldiers now prisoners in this town. Two of the officers viz Mr Cleaveland and Mr Shuttleworth have been there and complain of the quarters and are very desirous that they may be moved to Burlington.'[11] Stopford's abiding concerns were the cost of the 'clothing, Necessaries etc that was lost belonging to the Prisoners of His Majesty's Seventh Regiment of Royal Fusileers at Trenton' and that 'there is likewise a whole year's clothing lost.' He also argued that the officers should not pay for 'their lodgings' in Trenton, as the choice of 'tavern' had been provided 'by General Schuyler's instructions' on the understanding that it was 'at the Continent's expense.'[12]

These complaints were trivial, however, compared to those made by the officers quartered in Lancaster where 'the men are in great want of their clothing, not, now, having sufficient to cover them from the inclemency of the weather.' The officers there were little better off: in support of their petition to remain 'at least until the baggage arrives which is daily expected, in order to make a proper distribution of it' to the men, they begged 'leave to represent their own situation, which is such as will not admit of their changing quarters at this inclement season of the year; many of them lying in a bad state of health, and without the greatest part of their baggage, some, indeed, without any part of it.'[13]

At first, the officers were supported in these complaints by the Lancaster Committee: Edward Shippen, its chairman, reminded Congress on 21 December that 'the want of warm clothing for the soldiers, (of which they are in great need)' was 'still one of the objects of their complaints'. Lacking a senior officer to plead their case, the plight of John's regiment was especially acute: the Committee 'referred them to Major Preston' but 'the gentlemen of the Seventh Regiment tell us, they have reason to believe that the Major is to furnish clothing for the Twenty-Sixth regiment alone.'

Unsurprisingly, Congress was ill-prepared for the numbers of prisoners arriving in Lancaster, evident when Shippen pleaded that 'we are at a loss to know to what fund our barrackmaster must apply for the payment of the articles of wood, candles, bedding and blankets, and the implements of the cooking, absolutely necessary for the prisoners here.'[14] When no response came from Congress, 'J. Yeates', Shippen's replacement, took matters in hand, writing on 10 January that 'the Committee have been under the necessity of taking up a number of blankets for the prisoners, at the publick expense.'

The added problem was the significant number of 'Women and children belonging to the privates of the Seventh and Twenty-Sixth Regiments who are prisoners here'.[15] No provision had been made by Congress to feed and clothe them, meaning 'they are denied further provisions by Mr Franks, [army] agent in this place, and they must inevitably perish, unless relieved from the present distresses by your munificence.' As with the men, the Lancaster Committee could not simply do nothing when the women 'have this day implored us, in a body, that we would interest in their behalf.' Instead, as the Committee explained, 'being mindful that humanity ought ever distinguish the sons of America, and that cruelty should find no admission amongst a free people, we could not avoid considering the situation of their women and children as pitiable.' Taking the bull by the horns, 'the Committee have, accordingly, requested of Colonel Mathias Hough to supply them with necessary provisions at the publick expense.'[16]

This was the situation when John arrived in Lancaster in mid-February. Relations were at breaking point: the townspeople had generously offered a helping hand, only for the officers and men to spurn the kindness, offering only rudeness and threats in return. That must change. A new arrival in the town, John was well placed to act as peacemaker. He moved quickly to rebuild bridges, and it soon became 'a matter of remark that Major André did not, like the majority of his brother officers, indulge in vituperation against the colonists.'[17] However, time was running out: John had picked up signals that the town was militating to be rid of the prisoners.

First, he must sign the requisite 'Parole of Honour' allowing him to move around within a 'six miles' radius of 'the said borough of Lancaster'. That duly done on 23 February,[18] he mounted a diplomatic offensive to court the political worthies of the town, a melting pot of Patriots and Tories, 'Zealots'[19] and pacifists. Those most willing to accommodate the British officers on their arrival had come from the large community of 'Swiss and German settlers.' Many of these were Huguenot refugees and more readily lent an ear to John's quest for conciliation. It helped also that John spoke and wrote their language: historically, 'the Germans adhered to each other and used their own language exclusively.'[20]

How John broke into this community is difficult to ascertain, but one of the most important connections he made was with 'the Rev. Mr Hellemuth'.[21] Pastor of the Trinity Lutheran Church in the town since 1769, Hellemuth was ambivalent about the revolutionary cause and 'the rude boom of war',[22] and, in his position, was someone John could turn to in the search for conciliation between the town and its unwelcome visitors. Another early connection among the 'German settlers' was with Michael Bartgis,[23] who was already providing lodgings to John's friend and fellow Huguenot, John Despard, also a lieutenant in the 7th Regiment (English Fusiliers). Joining Despard there, John quickly ascertained that Bartgis was a key figure in Lancaster's revolutionary councils, who, with his son, Matthias, had a printing business publishing German-language tracts and almanacs.[24] Whether through Hellemuth or Bartgis, John established cordial relations with numerous town officials,[25] many of them also of German extraction, including Christian Wirtz, Matthias Slough, Hans Graff, and, most importantly, 'Mr Hillegas'.[26] As treasurer to the Continental Congress, Hillegas settled all claims relating to prisoner expenses.

The most enduring of the connections made by John was with Eberhart Michael, who was landlord to another officer, 'Lieutenant Thomas of the Twenty-Sixth'.[27] It was with Michael that John corresponded after leaving Lancaster, and it was through him that John sought to maintain contact with 'Mr. Wirtz ... and H. Graff', asking him to 'please give my respects to them' and that 'if you should see Mr Slough, have the kindness to request him to write to me'.[28] Michael it was who responded most openly to John's overtures and offered to 'faithfully comply with ... what you further command me to do'. Like John, his dearest wish was that the 'inhabitants and soldiers will again enjoy brotherly association.'[29] Michael was an important official: appointed clerk of the town's Committee of Correspondence when it was formed in June 1774, he became 'Pay-master to the German battalion' in October 1776, being nominated to this post by the 'Board of War'.[30]

Other founders of the town's Committee of Correspondence included 'Edward Shippen' and 'Matthias Slough'.[31] The committee was then expanded to include Adam Reigart and Sebastian Graff. Many of these town officials with whom John sought 'brotherly association' were, coincidentally, also important suppliers to the Continental Army. 'Powder' was an essential commodity for the war effort and, as early as May 1775, Slough, Wirtz and Graff each agreed that 'the county shall have his powder ... and his lead'.[32] The Reigart family, for its part, made muskets.[33] Slough, an innkeeper, manoeuvred himself into a position of growing influence, the result being his appointment by the Pennsylvania Assembly in April 1776 as 'agent ... to provide necessary clothing and Accoutrements for the Troops ... of this Province.'[34]

These same officials also had responsibility for managing the British prisoners: Wirtz, the town mayor, and Adam Reigart oversaw the guard for the British prisoners; Slough was employed between February and March 1776 'supplying provisions for the 7th and 26th regiment of British troops';[35] and back in November 1775, the Pennsylvania Assembly had resolved that 'Mr Slough ... be requested to have such repairs made at the Lancaster Barracks as appear to be immediately necessary'[36] in readiness for the arrival of British prisoners. This would explain why 'the officers when brought to this town by Captain Mott were placed by him in the houses of Messrs Matthias Slough and Adam Reigart.'[37]

For all John's efforts, however, in the event they proved to be in vain. He was too late: the die was cast even before he arrived in the town: on 20 February—three days before he signed his parole—the Lancaster Committee began militating officially for an 'alteration in the condition of the prisoners at Lancaster.' The stated reason was that 'Lancaster being but a day's march from navigable waters, there may be danger'[38] of escape or rescue. The Committee knew this would strike a nerve with Congress: British officers quartered elsewhere had no qualms about breaking their parole and making a run for it, 'the infamous Capt McKay'[39] being the most persistent violator.

The real reason was that the townspeople had run out of patience with some of their more unwilling guests. It seems the troublemakers were from among the officers of the 26th and that John's regiment, the 7th, was blameless. Certainly the Lancaster Committee thought so: when submitting an account for expenses left unpaid by the officers following their hasty departure, it expressly singled out John's regiment, prefacing the itemized list with the preamble: 'we must do that justice to the officers of the Seventh Regiment, to mention that none of these demands relate to that corps, except the trifling sum of six pounds ten shillings due to Michael Bartgis and part of the demand of Weitzell and Moore for Captain Newmarch and Lieutenant Hughes'. By contrast, the lion's share of unpaid expenses meaning 'the residue is entirely for the lodging of the Twenty-Sixth Regiment.'[40]

The Congress moved quickly in response to the complaints from Lancaster, resolving on 26 February—three days after John signed his parole—that 'the Committee of Safety for Pennsylvania … be authorized to distribute the officers (prisoners in Lancaster) in such places within the province of Pennsylvania, as that Committee shall deem most proper.'[41] This would set in stone the 'perfidious' decision by Congress to separate the British officers from their men. Back in December 1775, Congress had passed a resolution 'that Carlisle be assigned as well as the three Towns of Lancaster, Reading and York for the reception of the Prisoners taken at St. John's.'[42] In these circumstances, it was a formality for the Pennsylvania Committee to resolve on 14 March that 'one half of the Officers, prisoners of war … stationed in the Borough of Lancaster be removed to the Town of Carlisle, the other half removed to the Town of York.'[43] Thus it was that just six weeks after John arrived in Lancaster, he found himself among the 'officers of the Seventh and Twenty-Sixth Regiments lately removed from hence by order of the Committee of Safety … to the towns of York and Carlisle'.[44]

John's December 1776 letter to his mother said nothing about the regiment's tribulations in Lancaster. Given what awaited him next, this is understandable, but John was also silent about his social circle while in Lancaster, which, from other sources, appears to have been busy, pleasant and extended well beyond the narrow circle of his fellow officers with whom he was 'much engaged in playing duetts'.[45] Surely, he knew his mother would be captivated to read of his visits to nearby York and the home of the clergyman, John Andrews, with whom he 'formed a very agreeable acquaintance'. Andrews had founded a 'classical school',[46] and John accompanied him to meetings of the local literary club.

More beguiling still for his mother would have been John's intimacy with the Quaker family of Caleb Cope, another of the Lancaster townspeople to open his home to a British prisoner, providing 'a room, fire, candles etc for Captain Livingston of the Twenty-Sixth.'[47] One source has claimed that John also resided with the Cope family.[48] If so, it was for a short time until he moved to the home of Michael Bartgis, who, according to his official 'demand' to Congress, provided 'a room, fire, candles etc for Lieutenants Despard of the Seventh and—André of the Seventh'.[49] Since the source was from within the Cope household, it should be unimpeachable, except that it was Thomas, the oldest son, and from when he "was a small boy." More likely is that John did not lodge there, but, rather, visited so frequently as to make it seem he were living there.

Either way, those times inspired Thomas to 'well remember André's bland manner, sporting with us children as one of us, more particularly attached to John. We often played marbles and other boyish games with him.' Ostensibly, the reason for John's frequent visits to the Cope family home was to give Thomas's brother 'every encouragement and instruction … in the art of painting.'[50] For the same reason, John visited the home of Thomas Barton, the long-time 'rector of the church there',[51] whose son, Benjamin, 'became a famous draughtsman' and 'got his first inspiration'[52] from John.

Mary-Louisa would, surely, have had mixed emotions hearing of 'a crayon sketch' John drew for the Copes 'of a roadside scene composed of broad leaf trees, cottages and church spire set behind a low wooden fence'. Aspects of it suggest an American scene, but recalling the time when John made a gift of it to the family, Thomas Cope admitted that 'I cannot remember what he said the drawing represented but think it the place of the author's birth or some place at which he had resided.' If so, Mary-Louisa would, doubtless, have recognized the scene, and, if not, the sentimental treatment may still have resonated to some part of her son's childhood.

Sketch by John André of a cottage in Lancaster, Pennsylvania. (Library of Congress)

Either way, Mary-Louisa would have been pleased that Cope 'carefully preserved the relic, in memory of the Artist, and of my affection for that gifted, deceived, that noble minded, generous man.'[53]

Yet, Mary-Louisa knew none of this. Instead, much as with his three-month trek from Montreal to Pennsylvania, John glossed over his time in Lancaster noting only that, 'not long after' arriving, 'we were moved to Carlisle 150 miles west of Philadelphia.' He had been there six weeks, living in an American home for the first time. Earlier, he had told his sister Mary he was planning 'a journal of notorious memory'. Still, he said not one word about his sojourn in Lancaster or the kind people he met there.

There had to be a reason for this total silence, and it came back to the central message he wished to convey to his mother in his December 1776 letter: that the 'perfidious dastards'—not the officers of the Continental Army, not the well-meaning citizens of Lancaster, Pennsylvania, instead, as always, the politicians of 'the Congress'—had dishonourably broken their word to him and the other British prisoners, not once but twice, and for him that was unpardonable. For wars to be good, they had to be fought according to rules of gentlemanly honour. Break those rules and there would only be mayhem, hatred, evil and 'the ruin and ... the blood of so many credulous wretches.'[54] However nice the people of Lancaster were to him during his time there, however mutinous his fellow officers were during their time in Lancaster, for John nothing excused the decision by Congress to remove the officers from Lancaster and thereby separate them from the men.

It was imperative, therefore, that he remain silent about his time in Lancaster, not least because he wished to focus his mother's attention on 'the ill-treatment'[55] he endured at the place he had been sent to next—Carlisle, a town '150 miles west of Philadelphia'—which he described acidly as 'a region inhabited by a stubborn illiberal crew call'd the Scotchirish, sticklers for the Covenant and utter enemies to the abomination of curled hair, regal Government, minced pyes and other heathenish Societys.'

John treated his mother to chapter and verse on the official regime that oversaw him and his fellow officers during their eight months in Carlisle: 'a greasy Committee of worsted stocking knaves had us here under their ferule and pestered us with resolves and ordinances meant to humiliate us and exalt themselves. Sometimes they enacted penal statutes binding us to be at home at such and such Hours on pain of imprisonment, at other times broken open our letters and withheld them, or finding us guilty of some misdemeanour, attempted to extort concessions before their tribunal.'[56]

From what John wrote to Eberhart Michael in his letter of 11 April, the British officers encountered this hostility from the day they arrived, in which case Carlisle's 'greasy Committee' was acting under direct orders from Congress. Warning Michael that 'suspicious Committees may intercept my letter and make me suffer for my indiscretion,' John launched into a false panegyric, waxing how 'this is a fine country and the inhabitants show considerable respect towards me.' With sledgehammer irony, he elaborated on this 'respect', describing how 'we very seldom have conversation with them, because, generally, no good results from it; nothing but uncivil and hostile answers.' Faced with such animosity, he and his friend Despard 'pass our time in making music, reading books and await humbly our liberation.'[57]

No such circumspection was necessary once John was 'at length restored to ... liberty', the letter to his mother in December 1776 recounting how 'the Gaol was constantly threatened, and we had examples enough to judge how well disposed they were put these threats into execution. I was lucky enough never to see the inside of this kind of edifice, but in visiting my friends.'[58] At this point, Mary-Louisa doubtless heaved a sigh of relief: ever since the report in the *Lady's Magazine* back in May that 'Col. Prescot having put Col. Allen in irons, the Congress, by way of reprisal, put Prescot in gaol,' she would have feared for her son. It had been no comfort that kindly Colonel Prescott had been released into house arrest, but only 'because of some old wounds'.[59]

Any relief for Mary-Louisa was temporary. Reading on, her imagination surely ran wild as John recounted how 'we were everyday pelted and reviled in the streets and have been oftentimes invited to smell a brandished hatchet, and reminded of its agreeable effects on the skull, receiving sometime promises that we should be murdered before the next day; several of us have been fired at and we have more than once been waylaid by men determined to assassinate us, and escaped by being warn'd to take different roads.'[60] John, nevertheless, spared his mother the most extreme instance of this violence which came when the local militia surrounded the house where he was lodging intent on lynching him and was only stopped by the intervention of his landlady, Mrs Ramsay.[61]

In these extreme actions, Carlisle's local militia was, surely, going beyond the official sanction of Congress, and, instead, acting on the prevailing mood of anger among Americans in response to reports circulating about Britain's treatment of its prisoners of war.[62] So concerned was one group of British prisoners threatened with retaliation by 'the mob' in Hartford, Connecticut that they wrote to the Continental Congress on 21 March enclosing 'the last Hartford paper' and citing the public reports on Ethan Allen's treatment as 'another method made use of to inflame the minds of the people against them.'[63] The 'prisoners in Carlisle' also wrote to Congress in late August 1776. Signed by 'a number of Officers', the 'Letter' complained of 'some ill-treatment they received and of their baggage having been plundered.'[64]

Whether John was among this 'number' is not known, but, writing to his mother, the 'ill-treatment' he received in Carlisle was further proof of the Rebels' perfidy. It all came down to honour and what was 'promised' at 'our capitulation'. Back in the snowy wastes of Canada, he had believed he was fighting a war on 'fine honorous terms'. Now, after Carlisle, he knew differently, for, if 'such is the brotherly love they in our capitulation promised us,' then, he concluded, it was his duty to save the 'credulous wretches' of America from 'the clutches of the perfidious dastards' running 'the Congress'.

No maternal sympathy sought here, only a mother's respect for a son's steely resolve which went to the essence of who John was as a British officer and who he had become by dint of his father's disastrous foray into the affairs of the East India Company, with all that meant for lasting damage to the family's wealth and good name. Seven years on and little had changed: he was <u>still</u> a humble lieutenant; the family was <u>still</u> in social exile, albeit in Bath 'Spa', not Southampton; and his three sisters were <u>still</u> unable to marry. No wonder then, that, the only 'family intelligence' he sought from home at this time was regarding his younger brother, William-Lewis, who 'is employed en grand garcon and emancipated from Mr Nantz's School', John saying that 'I am exceedingly anxious to hear what he is now about.' All hope for the family <u>still</u> rested on John, but, now, he was certain that his fortunes must, indeed were about to, change for the better.

The end objective, then, of John's December letter to his mother was to signal that, through the yearlong hardship and punishment he had endured as a prisoner, he had finally found a clear path to family honour. He spelt out the way forward: 'I am now putting irons in the fire to obtain a plea for remaining in America in case the regiment should be sent home... My wishes are, to be attached as aide de camp to the person of some one of our Commanders, for which post, my understanding German qualifies me (if I were equal in other respects) in preference to most others. I believe my name has 'ere this hour been mentioned to Gen.l Howe whom we expect here every day.'[65]

Reading this, Mary-Louisa would have understood why Colonel (now General) Prescott had insisted on John taking a 'leave of absence' in Germany, not once but twice. A veteran of the previous war, Prescott understood the politics of the House of Hanover. From the moment the Hanoverians ascended the throne in 1714, Britain's land wars were fought hand-in-hand with German allies, be they Prussia, Hesse, Brunswick or Saxe-Gotha. This latest conflict was no different. The instant that hostilities erupted in Boston, Britain began negotiations with German states for troops to serve 'as well in Europe as in America'.[66] In August 1775, Hesse-Cassel offered George III troops.[67] That same month, Sir Joseph Yorke, British minister at The Hague, wrote saying that 'Sachsen-Gotha', among others, 'might furnish the numbers of soldiers wanted.'[68]

The first treaty to be signed was 'on the 9th of January 1776' with the 'Most Serene Duke of Brunswick' and provided for 'Three thousand Nine hundred and sixty-four Men'. A second treaty was signed with the 'Landgrave of Hesse Cassell' on 'the 15th of January', followed by a third with the 'Hereditary Prince of Hesse Cassell', this one 'signed at Hanau the 5th of February'.[69] By December 1776, when John 'had the satisfaction of leaving them [his captors] about a week ago, and of joining our troops at Brunswick in New Jersey,'[70] Hessians had been serving in North America since June of that year.[71]

Hearing this news, John could congratulate himself that his earlier work in Göttingen, Gotha and Hanau had borne fruit. This was no mere hubris on his part: 'Colonel William Faucitt, Captain of the Guards',[72] and the 'Minister Plenipotentiary' appointed to negotiate these treaties on behalf of 'His Britannick Majesty'[73] had also studied at Göttingen University. Nor were John's immediate plans for advancement wishful thinking: also because of their 'understanding German', other recent Göttingen alumni[74] had secured staff positions under Howe, among them Francis Carr-Clerke[75] and the Count of Balcarres.

Digesting these 'irons', Mary-Louisa could relax: John was on his way and, with a post as aide-de-camp, his 'carcase' would, he assured her, 'be very safe for this winter'[76] and beyond. What John did not tell his mother but was the real reason why he believed Howe would place him 'as aide de camp to ... one of our Commanders' was that, as important as was his 'understanding German', more valuable still at this crucial moment of the war was the network of 'acquaintances' he had made in Pennsylvania during his captivity there. Busy in Lancaster, he had been busier still in Carlisle, a town closer to the western frontiers, where Tory loyalists under Captain Rankin were marshalling for the counter-revolution.

John and Despard were prevented by their parole of honour from venturing more than six miles beyond the town, but regularly broke their word ostensibly so as to go shooting duck. One day, however, Mrs Ramsay, their landlady, 'detected two tories in conversation with these officers and immediately made known the circumstance to William Brown' of the town's Committee of Safety. 'The two tories were imprisoned'. Tellingly, however, 'upon their persons were discovered letters written in French, but no one could be found to interpret them, and their contents were never known.' No matter: the committee had sufficient evidence that the two were spying and 'after this, André and Despard were not allowed to leave the town.'[77]

Still, as John explained when writing to his sister, Mary, from Canada in March 1775, it was about sorting and selecting 'those whom I chuse to be connected with.' He had been in North America for two years. He had watched John Adams, George Washington and the other delegates gathered on the steps of Carpenters' Hall making ready to break with Britain. He had fought a frontier war in the snowy wastes of Canada. He had trekked through 'hard frosts' from Montreal, but it was only on reaching Pennsylvania that he saw the way forward ... knew how he must go about regaining the family's honour. He had endured 'ill-treatment', the 'brandished hatchet' and 'the mob' in Carlisle, but he had also experienced kindness and sympathy in Lancaster. What he now understood was that not all Americans were friends of Congress and its revolution. The king, too, had friends: these were the connections John had sorted and selected in Pennsylvania and would now present to Howe.

CHAPTER 21

'The Crooked Hill Tavern'

1777 was the year when the American Revolutionary War took a decisive turn pointing the way to ultimate success for the cause of independence. Washington's coup de main on the Delaware proved more than a tactical flourish, halting and reversing, as it did, General Howe's occupation of New Jersey and onward march south into Pennsylvania. Forced to retreat to New York, Howe changed tack, instead leading a seaborne invasion in August that, by year's end, brought the symbolic capture and occupation of Philadelphia, but little else.

To the north, a plan to retake Boston fizzled out, the British getting no farther than Rhode Island. Further north still and with Canada secured, General Burgoyne led a force of British and Hessians down the chain of waterways running south from Montreal, his first objective Albany, thence on down the Hudson River to New York. However, as lines of communication and supply became dangerously extended, his army was cut off from the north and the south and forced to surrender at Saratoga in October. This victory for the Continental Army was the cue for France, which had been sitting on the side-lines thus far, to launch headlong into the war, putting troops and ships at America's disposal at the same time as attacking British interests wherever they were around the globe. When Spain also joined the war, Britain was suddenly in an existential struggle for survival.

The reality of Britain's mounting predicament would only close in on John and his fellow officers as each wave of news unfolded through the year. For John, however, there was, at first, only devil-may-care relief that he was finally back in the war and, maybe, able to make a difference. Having sounded off against the 'perfidious dastards' who had forced him to muteness over the past twelve months, John concluded his 17 December letter to his mother on a note of blithe spirit, promising that 'you and my sisters shall certainly receive constant accounts from me and be minutely informed of my Situation, my hopes and fears, and my good fortune,' sure, as he was, in the belief that 'nothing can befall me for some time having had in this past year and a half a considerable dose of evil in Advance.'

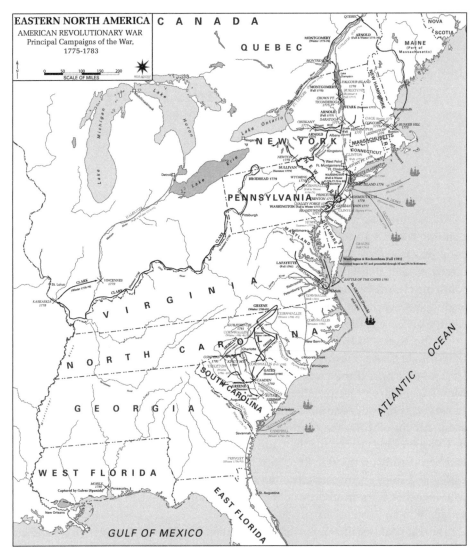

Map of the military campaigns during the American Revolutionary War. (USMA, West Point)

As to his immediate circumstances, John reassured his mother that 'the Campaign is over and our Regiment as I told you is not as yet put on duty; so that you may conclude my carcase to be very safe for this winter, and as I have some regard for myself you may depend it I shall do my utmost to make myself as happy and as comfortable as I can.'[1] To warm her further, he explained that 'I am in perfect health, am in a good house by a good fire and in company with Cpt. and Mrs Hesketh, who I may have mentioned to you, and a Mr. Despard.'

Whether or not the Heskeths had been mentioned previously, Mary-Louisa could see from John's postscript that he knew them from Fort St. John's. She would have immediately recognized the name from society columns, 'Sir Thomas Hesketh'[2] a regular among London's fashionable 'Bon Ton'. What she did not know—but would doubtless have made her mildly envious for her son—was that the Captain Hesketh with whom John was sharing 'a good fire' had been granted a special parole after the capitulation at St. John's. This allowed him to join his wife, Jacintha, and two daughters in Montreal and, from there, travel to Philadelphia where the family spent the next twelve months in the relative lap of luxury. Described by Richard Peters, secretary to the American Board of War, as 'very good' but a 'very helpless man', Hesketh had been treated with great consideration while in Philadelphia especially in the matter of his baggage which he 'wants … much at Philadelphia', but was stored 'at Lancaster under the care of his servant and Sergeant Cooper, prisoner of war.'[3]

Washington intervened personally to arrange Hesketh's early release when it became known that his wife was expecting a third child, writing to the Board of War that 'I met Captain Hesketh on the road and as the situation of the family did not admit of delay, I permitted him to go immediately to New-York, not having the least doubt General Howe will make a return of any officer of equal rank who shall be required.'[4] To formalize this arrangement, Washington wrote to Howe from Brunswick on 1 December explaining that 'besides the persons included in the enclosed list'—among which were John and Lieutenant Despard, his companion in Carlisle—'Captain Hesketh of the Seventh Regiment, his lady, three children, and two servant maids were permitted to go in a few days ago.'[5]

There was another reason why Washington 'met' the Heskeths 'on the road'. A worried mother, Rachel Graydon, had asked him to forward a letter to her son, Alexander, a captain captured by the British during the recent assault on Fort Washington. Rachel was a widow and ran a Philadelphia boarding-house where Washington stayed on visits to the city in the years before the war. Given this personal connection, Washington agreed to help Rachel, using Hesketh as a go-between to ensure that her letter reached the son.

On 30 November, Washington wrote telling Rachel that 'your letter to your son (enclosed to me) went in the day after it came to my hands, by a flag which happened to be going to New York.' Graydon took up the story from there recounting that 'I received a letter from my mother. It was brought by a Captain Hesketh of the British army … I waited upon Captain Hesketh, found him at home and was very politely treated both by him and his lady to whose notice I had been particularly recommended by Miss Amiel of Philadelphia, a mutual acquaintance. Among other things, Mrs Hesketh, who was the most communicative, informed me that they had met General Washington on their road at the head of his army.'

To emphasise how 'politely treated' Graydon was by the Heskeths, Washington arranged for two letters to be sent by his mother. He forwarded both, but suspecting that letters travelling between the lines would be intercepted, read and possibly destroyed by the British, he arranged for the two letters to go by separate channels: one was delivered privately via the Heskeths; another went officially 'by a flag', but 'wandered out of its road into the hands of a British officer, of the same Christian and surname as well as rank' and did not reach Graydon 'until some time after that by Captain Hesketh'.[6] The date of Graydon's visit to the Heskeths was not given, but it would, doubtless, have been when John was already 'by a good fire and in company with Cpt. and Mrs Hesketh', waiting for news on his 'irons in the fire'.

John had good reason to be confident about these 'irons': the treasure trove of connections he brought from his year in captivity in Pennsylvania had, fortuitously, acquired immediate strategic value to Howe. John had the Delaware River to thank for the sudden importance of his 'correspondents'. Major Stephen Kemble, the deputy adjutant general to the British Army in America, heralded the moment in his journal-entry for 10 December: 'from what I hear of General Howe's Situation, he will not be able to pass the Delaware; in that case he must return'. This was exactly what happened.

Stymied in his grand strategy to roll up Washington's army and take New Jersey and Pennsylvania by storm, Howe must now find another, more ponderous, way of seizing and holding these two strategically vital middle colonies. In preparation for this, Howe would need reliable partizan reconnaissance and intelligence from loyal friends in these two provinces, and this was exactly what John had been nurturing and garnering for the best part of the year past. His facility with German might eventually get him a plum post as aide-de-camp to one of the senior commanders, but what Howe immediately needed on John's 'return to New York'[7] in early December was reliable intelligence fresh from within Pennsylvania giving 'knowledge of the country'[8] and telling him that the king had many loyal friends there ready and willing to rally to the royal standard following a second assault.

Howe's desperation for any local intelligence was evident when, in May 1777, he tried to recruit Nicholas Cresswell, a Briton who had emigrated to America in 1774 but, by August 1776, was trying to return home. Trapped behind rebel lines for the next nine months, he finally made good his escape, reaching New York in May 1777. He had put those months to good use, travelling widely within Virginia, Pennsylvania and New Jersey and reconnoitring Rebel 'preparations for war', including 'the Fort, Gondolas and Chevaux-de-Frise … at the conflux of the Schuylkill with the Dellawar'. He also visited many places—'Hannover town', 'York town' and 'Leesburg'—which were known to John from his time as a prisoner. Cresswell also visited Lancaster in August 1776 but, unlike John, 'lodged at *The Sign of the Duke of Cumberland*' just across 'the Conistogo River'. As a result, Cresswell had 'a Scotch-Irish Rebel-Colonial' as his 'Landlord' and endured 'his house … dirty as a Hog's stye.' All while 'making his observations', Cresswell accumulated vital local intelligence: following his stay at 'The Spread Eagle, a clean Dutchman's house' on the road between Lancaster and

Philadelphia, he noted in his journal 'that I have seen only 3 signs hanging, the rest pulled down by soldiers'.[9]

Arriving in New York on 'May 15th 1777', together with Mr Keir, a fellow loyalist, Cresswell received 'orders to wait upon the General Howe, tomorrow morning at nine o'clock'.[10] At the meeting, he was 'asked ... about the affairs in Virginia and whether I thought there was a great many friends to Government there.' When he replied 'with truth to the best of my knowledge', Howe went further and asked if he would 'enter into the Army'. What Howe had in mind was that Cresswell and Keir should join 'Major Holland's Guides', the plan being that they should return to Virginia and contact those 'friends of Government'. Cresswell declined, but 'Mr Keir' agreed and was 'referred to Sir Wm Erskine, his Countryman' and 'therefore he needs not fear, for the Scotch will hang together.'[11]

What John had come armed with in the previous December when, as he told his mother, 'my name has 'ere this hour been mentioned to Gen.l Howe,'[12] was not only a network of 'friends of Government' across Pennsylvania, but also, like Keir, if not Cresswell, a brave willingness to engage with those correspondents. From his experiences in Carlisle, he knew this was dangerous work, but he had been commended to Howe by General Prescott, who was also at liberty having been part of the recently agreed prisoner exchange. John was under no illusions: for his 'friends' to be useful to Howe, he would be expected to go into rebel-occupied territory. In that event, if caught he must expect 'to hang'.[13] No wonder he had not been entirely honest with his mother about why he was so confident of his prospects for advancement.

John's range of connections in Pennsylvania was impressive. He may have drawn a blank in Carlisle where, seemingly, he met only hostility. Yet, he kept trying, and there were 'two or three families [who] shewd me very great Civilities.' Among these was 'particularly a family of very staunch rebels, who setting the mob at defiance insisted upon my visiting them very frequently'.[14] It was the same when, earlier, John had visited York: as a guest at the literary soirées of the clergyman, John Andrews, he had 'sometimes met ... some of the warmest friends of the American cause', yet 'always seemed happy in their society, as they did in his.'[15] Again, John was probing: through Thomas Barton, rector of Lancaster, whose son he taught draughtsmanship, and Andrews in York, his objective was to gain introductions to a wider network of loyalist Anglican clergy across rural Pennsylvania.[16]

As quartermaster for the regiment, John had also visited Philadelphia, and this would have brought him into contact with David Franks. Lately agent for the British Army in North America, Franks was, since December 1775, contracted to the Continental Army as its Commissary of Prisoners and charged with victualling, among others, the British prisoners from the 7th and 26th Regiments.[17] Despite this change of roles, Franks 'attempted to remain neutral',[18] but his daughter, Rebecca, so John founded out, was determinedly loyalist.

John was especially successful in maintaining the connections he had established in Lancaster. These friendships were of considerable value given the town's political importance within the province of Pennsylvania. Through the Cope family, he could gain access to a wider fraternity of Quakers, but his most extensive connections were among the influential German-speaking community. Unsurprisingly, some of these had gone dead once John left Lancaster for Carlisle: in April 1776, John was already complaining to Eberhart Michael that Matthias Slough's 'silence makes me at a loss about him'.[19] By the end of the year, however, John and Slough were back in contact, and Slough was carrying letters from him to the Copes in Lancaster.[20]

John was more immediately lucky with 'H. Graff', whom he had asked to provide maps of the area. Writing to Michael soon after arriving in Carlisle, John asked him to let Graff know that 'I have received the maps' and to please 'thank him'.[21] It is strange that Michael and Graff were willing to hand over maps of the area, but John had an unerring capacity to disarm and engage friend and enemy alike, such that they would go out of their way for him. Owning to 'my true sincerity and high esteem towards you', Michael proved especially solicitous of John even after his departure: acting as go-between, he relayed messages from John in Carlisle to Lieutenant Thomas of the 26th Regiment on parole in York.[22] Likewise the Cope family continued to correspond with John long after he left Lancaster, the bonds, especially with the children, too strong and heartfelt to be dismissed as transient.[23]

Men and children were not the only ones to engage with John. Women were especially susceptible. Whatever the fictions pedalled by Anna Seward concerning the lovelorn torch John had been carrying for Honora Sneyd over the previous seven years, sure it is that the ties between Anna and John were reciprocal and extended beyond friendship. John's 'almost womanlike modesty and gentleness' certainly captivated the women he met during his time in captivity in Pennsylvania. Briefly entering John's life, they seemed all too eager to rally to his defence. First came 'Mrs Ramsay', his landlady in Carlisle. Next came 'the mother and sisters of Mr Smith who had been a fellow passenger on board the St. George, and who had retired from Baltimore to Carlisle for fear of bombardments.' As John recounted to his mother: 'To them I am highly obliged for their attention, and the more so, as it drew great odium and much invective upon themselves.'[24]

Last to acknowledge John before he reached New York was Anna Marie Krause, whose brother-in-law, Henry Dering, ran the Crooked Hill tavern situated partway between Reading and Pottstown. Leaving Carlisle in late November and 'on our road (as we believe, to be exchang'd),' John was in Reading on 2 December, from where he wrote to Caleb Cope in Lancaster to 'take leave of yourself and Family'.[25] John and his fellow officers were making for the British lines at Brunswick, New Jersey and overnighted at the Crooked Hill tavern. Anna recalled John, describing him "as rather under the average stature, of a light agile frame, active in his movements and sprightly in his conversation. He was a fine performer on the flute, with which he

Portrait painting of an ancestor of John André, possibly his grandfather, Guillaume André (1685–1746). (By kind permission of Major J. E. A. André)

Miniature of Mary-Louisa André, *née* Girardot (1713–1821). (By kind permission of John and Roger André)

Miniature of Anthony André (1717–1769). (By kind permission of John and Roger André)

Miniature of David André (1721–91), John's uncle. Painted in Paris in 1753. (By kind permission of John and Roger André)

Miniature of unknown subject, maybe John André as a boy. (By kind permission of John and Roger André)

Miniature from 1755 of a Girardot ancestor of John André. (By kind permission of John and Roger André)

Miniature of Andrew Girardot. (By kind permission of John and Roger André)

Miniatures said to be of Louisa André and Mary Hannah André. (By kind permission of John and Roger André)

Miniature of a young girl, maybe Anne André. (By kind permission of John and Roger André)

Miniature of William André (1760–1802) by John André. (By kind permission of John and Roger André)

Miniature of Isabelle Necker (1731–52). (By kind permission of John and Roger André)

Portrait of Anna Seward. (New York Public Library)

Portrait of Honora Sneyd. (New York Public Library)

David Garrick as Benedick in Shakespeare's *Much Ado About Nothing*, 1770. Artist: Jean-Louis Fesch.

Portrait painting of an ancestor of John André, said to be his father, Anthony André (1717–1769). (By kind permission of Major J. E. A. André)

Miniature in pearl-surround of John André in 1768, said to be a self-portrait. (By kind permission of John and Roger André)

Self-portrait of John André as a compting-house clerk in 1768. (By kind permission of John and Roger André)

Miniature of John André as a subaltern officer in 1772. (By kind permission of John and Roger André)

Army officers undergoing military training in Göttingen in 1773, as illustrated in *Stammbuch Rupstein.*

Army officers relaxing after military training in Göttingen in 1773, as illustrated in *Stammbuch Rupstein.*

Caricature, 'The Upper Clapton Macaroni'. (Courtesy of the Lewis Walpole Library, Yale University)

A south-west view of St. John, Quebec by James Peachey, 1790. (Courtesy of Toronto Public Library)

beguiled the hours of twilight, and was an excellent vocalist.' According to a relative of Anna's, 'she bore full testimony of his polished manners, and the easy grace and charm of his conversation. His engaging deportment rendered him popular with his fellow-officers.' Allowing for the misty licence of memory, John evidently made a strong impression on Anna who 'always spoke feelingly of Major André, and, in after years, often sung his remembrance, as addressed by him to his "Delia"'.

Yet, Anna also noted that, 'whilst at Mr Dering's house, Major André occupied the most of his time in examining and drawing maps and charts of the country.'[26] These 'maps and charts' were the physical proof—the 'irons'—John needed at his debrief with General Howe to demonstrate his valuable network of loyalist connections across Pennsylvania.[27] They, together with his understanding of German, had the desired effect: the result was his promotion to the rank of captain. Coming on 18 January 1777,[28] this rapid advancement contrasted with the experience of John's friend, Lieutenant Despard, who had to wait until 7 October 1777 for his promotion and then only rose to 'Captain-Lieutenant'.[29]

To secure this promotion required John moving to the 26th Regiment of foot where an opening occurred with the promotion of Andrew Gordon to the rank of major.[30] For John, there was little disruption. He had reported to Charles Preston of the 26th Regiment during the siege of Fort St. John's and, arriving back in New York following the prisoner exchange, he found the two regiments routinely assigned to joint duties, Kemble recording on 'Thursday Jan. 9th' that he 'went with Major Stopford to those Posts ordered to be occupied by Detachments of 7th and 26th Regiments (the two Blazing Stars), saw them fixed and returned that Evening to New York.'[31]

Moving to the 26th did, however, necessitate John parting company with his longstanding patron, General Richard Prescott. This seems strange, coming, as it did, when Prescott had just replaced Lord Robert Bertie as colonel of the 7th Regiment[32] and, hence, was even better placed to dispense the patronage John might need to proceed further. However, Prescott was busy elsewhere when John reached New York in early December. Captured at Montreal, he had been held close-confined in Philadelphia for much of 1776. Finally exchanged in November 1776 when the capture of General Sullivan gave the British a prisoner of equal value,[33] Prescott was 'given ... General Robertson's brigade' even before his release. 'An explanation' for this snub 'being required by General Robertson, he was told' by Howe that 'the Command of a Brigade in Town and the consequence of it, was considered as of much more honor than if he acted [in the field] with his Brigade.'[34] 'Honor' aside, the truth of it was that Howe needed Prescott's brand of boldness for the imminent descent on Rhode Island he had planned, an operation that was set in motion the moment the general arrived in New York. Living up to his reputation, Prescott successfully accomplished his mission by 17 December when 'Colonel Clerk this day arrived from Rhode Island' with the news that 'we took possession without opposition.'[35]

Before departing Rhode Island, Prescott had, however, made certain to recommend John to Howe, not only for his partizan skills, but also for his facility with German, so necessary with further Hessian corps expected daily. Following the debacle at Trenton, Howe was especially conscious of the need to integrate the Hessians, evident in his later *Narrative* to the House of Commons where he talked of the risks of creating 'jealousies between the Hessian and British troops.'[36]

However exactly John was of service at this time, Howe was maturing plans that would ensure the next stage of his new captain's advancement. He did not need a German-speaker on his immediate staff, as Captain Friedrich von Muenchausen was serving as his aide-de-camp.[37] Nevertheless, further senior commanders were promised to Howe as London sought a decisive turn in the struggle to restore the king's authority in the thirteen colonies. Among these was Sir Charles Grey, a no-nonsense colonel in the mould of Prescott and, like him, a veteran of the Seven Years' War. Granted the colonelcy of the 28th Regiment on, coincidentally, the same day in March[38] that John's promotion to captain was confirmed in London, this step was a prelude to Grey's departure for America with the rank of acting major general. He arrived in New York on 3 June, assuming command of 'the 2nd and 4th Brigade' on 12 June.

John had already been assigned to Grey as his aide-de-camp, and one of his first tasks was to commence an official journal of immediate military events. This he began on 11 June, the first entry reading grandly: 'The Commander in Chief came from Amboy to Brunswick joining on the road the escort of the provision train, consisting of the 7th, 26th and part of the 71st Regiments.'[39] Howe was mustering his forces for the descent on Pennsylvania, and Grey was pivotal to the upcoming campaign. Finally, John was 'going to enter upon an active scene'[40] in the war, the road ahead visible for him, at least for the foreseeable future. Now John had the opportunity to prove his mettle, he must not squander it.

CHAPTER 22

'No Firelock'

July 1777:

'17th

Sir William Howe embarked on board the *Eagle*, Lord Cornwallis and General Grant on board the *Isis*, General Grey on board the *Somerset*. The fleet lay off the narrows.'

19th

A signal was made to prepare for sailing.

20th

The fleet weighed anchor and the transports moved down to Sandy Hook Bay. The Men-of-War came to an anchor again near the narrows.

22nd

In the morning the fleet sailed from Sandy Hook'[1]

So it was that John recorded in his *Journal* the departure from New York of an armada of '266 sail'[2] carrying 'nearly 14,000'[3] British and Hessian troops: Philadelphia the secret destination for this mighty 'King's army';[4] its objective to bring Washington's 'Rebel Army'[5] to a decisive battle; its mission the reoccupation of the province of Pennsylvania abandoned since September 1774 when the Royal Irish Regiment was ordered away.

August 1777:

'23rd

Off Sassafras river. A pilot came on board the *Somerset*.

24th

The fleet proceeded to Turkey Point. The *Augusta*, *Isis*, *Nonsuch* lay off Sassafras river with the *Somerset*. Orders for disembarking received. The *Somerset* lay at this same place. A white man and three negroes came off. This long boat and pinnace came ashore. The people were inclined to traffick for fresh provisions, but wanted salt and other articles in preference to money.

25th

The transports, frigates and the *Roebuck* sailed up Elk river and lay opposite Cecil court house, excepting the *Roebuck* which could not come so far. The Troops landed on the West side of the Elk River in five disembarkations.'[6]

Thus, John began his day-by-day account of the advance by the 'King's army' from its unopposed landing at the head of the Elk River through to 30 December, the last entry in his *Journal* for 1777, which noted that 'the Army came into winter quarters in Philadelphia'. Along the way, John recorded the two major battles of Brandywine, on the '10th and 11th' of September, and Germantown, on 4 October, and the lesser skirmishes and engagements at Aiken's Tavern, Trudusfrin (Paoli), White Marsh and Red Bank.

John's *Journal* was one of the two main eyewitness accounts of this campaign compiled by British army officers. The other one was, again, a journal, its author Captain John Montrésor. Although the two journals substantially covered the same events, their treatment was different. Montrésor's was a personal account intended for posterity and compiled self-importantly to position its author within these events. John's was an official regimental report written for and under the immediate gaze of his new commander, General Grey. Montrésor made sure he was visible; John made equally sure he was invisible. It did not need to be otherwise, for John had his sights set on a bigger prize, his *Journal* intended as an aide-memoire for the literary masterpiece—the 'journal of notorious memory'—he long had in mind. Writing to his mother partway through the campaign, he reminded her of this goal, telling her that 'my time is very much taken up so that I cannot keep all the draughts and memorandums I would wish. I hope however to retain pretty satisfactory memoirs of our campaign' that is 'unless some unlucky ball stumbles against me.'[7]

Montrésor, for his part, had good reason to feel his immediate self-importance. Born in 1736 and already a veteran of the Seven Years' War campaign in North America, he was, as 'Chief of Engineers',[8] a senior officer in Howe's army, and his 'Engineers Department'[9] had five vessels at its disposal. Self-conscious of his expertise and status but well aware that other officers would also be recording their experiences, Montrésor was zealous for detail, thereby seeking to ensure that his became the definitive account of the campaign.

At the end of his pen, readers were made to feel every motion of the armada at sea, every footstep of the troops once on terra firma. On 22 July—the day John recorded only that 'the fleet sailed from Sandy Hook'—Montrésor instead logged: 'Rainy morning and S. E. Winds. Sphynx returned down to the fleet here. Weather close and sultry. The heavy ships still remained off the Narrows, for want of wind, what little being foul. A few more of the transports fell down with the tide to the Fleet.'[10] From there, the entries became progressively more minute in their detail, Montrésor even recording on the '6th': 'dead calm all this night.'[11]

Montrésor relished his return to the sea, his occasional 'Remark' a sharp reminder that he had conducted surveys for the army along this coast during the Seven Years' War: he finished his formal entry for 24 July with the 'Remark' that 'I have observed for many years both in coming on this part of the American coast and in sailing along it, that whenever the Soundings were in 15 fathoms the land in general was to be seen.'[12] As a result of this familiarity with nautical life, Montrésor used his journal to show off his verbal sea-legs, his entry for 26 July starting routinely enough with a reference to 'light southerly winds all this morning' but livening up when 'at 3 p.m came up a gale of wind at south with a high sea, close reefed topsails, a tumbling sea all night.'[13] These detailed entries continued through the voyage.

By contrast, and maybe as a throwback to bad memories of his boisterous 'Seafaring Life' when crossing the Channel back in 1772, John kept his renewed acquaintance with life on the ocean waves to the barest minimum, making no reference to weather or sailing conditions in his three short seagoing entries and instead recording simply that on 30 July: 'Made Cape Henlopen. Stood off the whole night'; and on 14 August: 'Made Cape Charles and came to an anchor at 11 at night.'[14] Certainly, any training he may have received in navigational surveying while studying at Göttingen was kept under wraps: no mention of 'Fathoms', 'Soundings', 'Observation of the daily latitude', or coastal features along the 'Jersey Shore'. Arriving at their destination 'after a six weeks voyage', John was doubtless glad, like James Murray sailing with the 57th Regiment, to no longer be 'confined within a circle of a few hundred yards'.[15]

It could reasonably be expected that, once the 'King's army' landed, John's account would start matching Montrésor's for detailed information. However, as Chief Engineer, Montrésor had wider duties, which took him to many parts of the advancing army. John, as aide-de-camp to General Grey, must necessarily see events from the narrower perspective of his commander, as when 'a regulation was made by General Grey for the method of hutting for the 3rd Brigade'[16] or, more intriguingly, when 'General Grey thought it material that the troops move immediately into the country', which meant that 'they did not wait for the artillery.'[17]

The difference in the two eye-witnesses' seniority was immediately evident at the point of landing: Montrésor flexed his muscles describing how 'this morning I attended Sir Wm Howe and Lord Howe with my armed Schooner, an armed Sloop and a Galley to the mouths of the rivers Rappahannock, Elks and Turkey Point ... sounding the channel. The whole returned in the afternoon to the fleet.'[18] By contrast, John must record more modestly that 'this long boat and pinnace went ashore',[19] readers left to surmise that these two vessels were from his ship, the *Somerset*. Moreover, unlike Montrésor, who, here and when later accompanying the 'Commander-in-Chief' on his entry into Philadelphia, could not resist saying that 'I attended him',[20] John consistently eschewed all personal identity: Grey did not need reminding who he had sent to talk to 'the people' ashore and ascertain from them that they 'were inclined to traffick for fresh provisions, but wanted salt and other articles in preference to money.'

Provisioning was familiar work for John: as quartermaster at Fort St. John's, 'provisions' had been one of his important logistic duties, simultaneously giving him easy access to local intelligence. The subject became a recurring preoccupation as the *Journal* progressed, and, either speaking for himself or more likely voicing the misgivings of his commander, Grey, John frequently criticised the lack of forward planning noting that 'no method was yet fixed upon for supplying the troops with fresh provisions in a regular manner'. The upshot 'was a good deal of plunder committed by the troops'. John frequently recurred to this problem, it becoming evident that the chief culprits were the Hessians. As a result, Howe issued two proclamations, one addressed to Lieutenant General Wilhelm von Knyphausen, commander of the Hessian forces, promising 'most exemplary punishment'[21] on those who plundered. Montrésor made no mention of these proclamations but John cited them, the reason being that they were directly relevant to his duties as interpreter between Grey and Knyphausen.

This was not the first time John intervened with the Hessians in the matter of plunder. While he was still in New York, an incident occurred when 'the soldiers of the 5th regiment' were 'confined for plundering a house' and faced a 'regimental court martial' instigated by Grey. Skulduggery was afoot, however, because, as John revealed, 'it is worth notice that the Hessian officer who exclaimed against the depredation confessed that the Hessians had been concerned, yet confined none, but complained of the British to General De Heister.'[22] It seems this 'Hessian officer' had given himself away, still unaware that John—who was in ear-shot—understood German.

Advancing inland, John's duties multiplied rapidly: when 'Lord Cornwallis, General Grey and Sir William Erskine reconnoitred towards the head of Elk', John was, evidently, part of the scouting party. He was deputized under Erskine to locate great quantities of 'orchard fruit and Indian corn',[23] while the senior commanders were busy establishing 'the best idea of the country that information can afford'.[24] Erskine was a pivotal figure in this: as Quartermaster General, he supervised the campaign's scouting activities,[25] and it was his prior local intelligence behind the choice of the 'head of Elk' as a landing for Howe's army. As John revealed, 'the situation of the enemy being known to Sir William Erskine'[26] from the moment the King's army landed, it was evident there was a network of local 'correspondents' already in place, including the local 'pilot'[27] whom John referred to guiding the *Somerset* to a safe mooring.[28] Scouting alongside Erskine, John was in his element.

Washington's forces were said to be 'at a place called Wilmington about 23 miles'[29] away, and once Howe's army began advancing to meet them, John found himself pulled hither and thither, alternately part of reconnaissance, foraging and scouting detachments. Away from the stiff formality of his official *Journal*, he confided to his mother how 'all my works being on horseback ... 3 horses hardly suffice me'.[30] As aide-de-camp, he was expected to be Grey's eyes and ears both at the front and rear of the advancing column. This required constant bulletins, for instance, when the vanguard perilously outpaced the following baggage train, with the result that 'the line of baggage was produced, by the badness of the road and the insufficiency of horses, to a very great length.' This made it vulnerable to attack but fortunately 'we had not an enterprising, well-informed enemy near us'.

As the 'King's army' moved towards its first major clash with Washington's forces, Montrésor's assiduity to detail told against the value of his *Journal*, the overarching

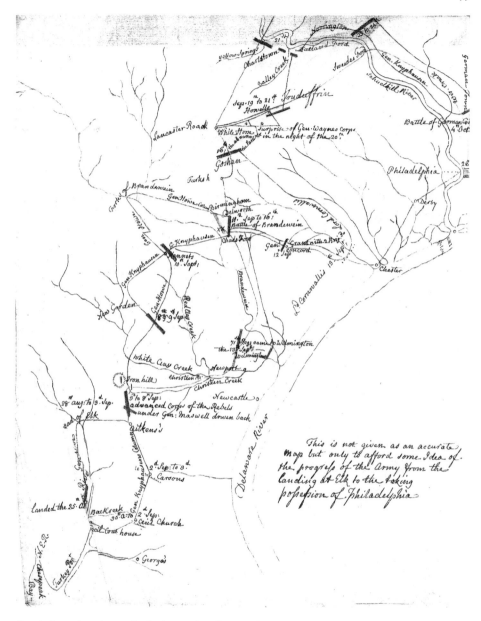

Sketch drawn by John André for his mother showing the campaign to recapture Philadelphia in 1777.
(By kind permission of Major J. E. A. André)

plan of campaign leading up to the battle of Brandywine lost in his minute description
of every movement, march, skirmish and reconnaissance. Significant was that he also
abandoned the knowing remarks that had peppered his sea-going entries. John, by

contrast, stood away from the detail at this crucial point in the campaign, describing with succinct clarity how 'the Army marched in two columns under Lord Cornwallis and General Knyphausen. Sir William Howe was with the former and proceeded to the forks of Brandywine, crossed the ford there and by a circuit of about fifteen miles came upon the enemy's right flank, near Birmingham Meeting House. The latter took the straight road to Chad's Ford opposite to which the Rebel Army lay.'[31]

For this clarity, John had his daily proximity to Grey to thank, access to his commander's mastery of strategic thinking enabling him to explain how 'the design, it seemed, was that General Knyphausen, taking post at Chad's Ford, should begin early to cannonade the Enemy on the opposite side and thereby to take up his attention and make him presume an attack was intended with the whole army, whilst the other column would be performing a detour. Lord Cornwallis's wing being engaged was the signal for the troops under General Knyphausen to cross the ford when they were to push their advantage.' As to the outcome of the battle, he concluded that 'the event fell little short of the project,'[32] with the result that victory was assured.

These journals compiled by Montrésor and John were not the only first-hand accounts of the Philadelphia campaign. John also wrote home as did James Murray. Within the intimacy of their letters, these two expressed private thoughts that should not appear in official journals. Murray's were unremittingly gloomy: writing to his sister partway through the campaign and by then a captain in the 57th Regiment

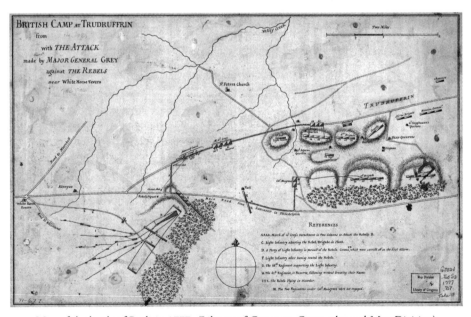

Map of the battle of Paoli in 1777. (Library of Congress, Geography and Map Division)

of foot,[33] he admitted in his letter dated 'Philadelphia Novr 29, 1777' that 'as to our operations civil and military, I am so extremely tired of the subject that I must leave you to the information of the Gazette, which will probably be about as good as mine; and I have been so very unfortunate in my conjectures, that I shall hardly be prevailed upon to give my opinion again of what is to happen.'[34]

Gone was the optimism expressed when, in August the previous year, he imagined that, with New York about to fall into British hands and the conflict promising to be over by Christmas, 'I am not altogether without hopes of waging war next campaign against my old enemies the ducks in the confines of Metheen.'[35] Even as the successes mounted up following the landing at the head of the Elk River, Murray's misgivings accumulated. Finally, he confided that 'I cannot help being still of opinion that the Cause of Liberty is in a very delicate situation: and I sincerely wish that it was over. It is a barbarous business in a barbarous country. The novelty is worn off and I see no advantages to be reaped from it.'[36]

Unspoken in this 'opinion' was the realization that the bad news filtering through from 'the Northward' risked cancelling out all that was being achieved in the march on Philadelphia. So devastating was this news that John even allowed it to infiltrate the day-by-day events of his *Journal*, when, on 13 October, he recorded that 'there was a feu-de-joie in the Rebel Camp, on account of successes to the Northward'[37] followed by the hammer-blow news of 'the Convention' made by General Burgoyne 'with the Rebels'[38] at Saratoga.

John became progressively gloomier in the run-on letter to his mother, which began on 'Sept. the 28, 1777' and was written in 'German Town', but only ended on '20th November' by which time he was at 'Philadelphia Camp'. The immediate impulse for John's letter was to reassure his mother that he was alive. He had heard that 'a Mr William Andrews of the 5th Regiment has been wounded'[39] and, remembering back to 'un monsieur André' on the list of victims following the 'Conflagration' in the Amsterdam 'playhouse' back in 1772, he wished to reassure her that 'I am safe and ungrazed', his letter by way of being 'a Certificate of Life and Health'.

Knowing his mother did not need the chapter and verse that his *Journal*, as an official document, demanded, John opened his narrative of the campaign with a short summary: 'after a passage of five weeks, the Army landed at Elk River at the head of Chesopeak Bay the 25 of August, and after a few days refreshment marched to feel for Mr Washington who had taken post at Wilmington.' To further simplify his account of events, 'the little draught enclosed will both clear and shorten my story.' One of the many 'draughts' he prepared for inclusion in his *Journal*, this sketch map would best explain—hence why he 'enclosed' it—the progress of the campaign so far. With it to hand, his mother would easily understand what he meant when he recounted that 'we first drew blood not far from Elk, this was an advanced Corps sent to watch, oppose and annoy. They were driven back on the rest with considerable loss: the next meeting was at Brandiwein on the 11th September'.[40]

For this major battle, John went into more detail, but, instead of the dry tone in his *Journal*, he adopted the robust rhetoric that permeated the December 1776 letter to his mother. Whereas Murray had nothing to say about 'the Rebels', other than that they missed opportunities to take 'every advantage of their situation'[41] to outmanoeuvre the advancing army, John was fired with polemical hyperbole, describing how Washington 'had in an involved Rhapsody spirited up his men to a belief they were to exterminate the British Army … I believe they never had been wound up to such a pitch of confidence. They credited the most preposterous accounts of our weakness and dispirited state etc.'

It is tempting to dismiss this as invention inspired by a release of hyperbolic tension, John imagining himself on the front line of the mounting war of words battling single-handed with 'Congress' and Washington's army of propagandists for the souls of a nation immersed in a civil war. Yet, behind the scornful words of derision, it seems he had first-hand information from the American camp telling him what he relayed to his mother. It is possible that the source for this was the 'great numbers' of deserters who 'came into us the succeeding days'. More likely, given John's energy on the battlefield, the information came from the 'few prisoners'[42] captured, evident when, happening on Lieutenant Whitman, an American prisoner wounded during the battle of Germantown, 'André … procured him a release.'[43] However John came by the information, it was simply too precise to have been made up, John even recounting that 'when Washington mistook, as was wished, Knyphausen's Corps for the whole Army and the sight of the baggage which was purposely shewn and had marched that road confirmed him in his error, he harangued his men, pointed to the baggage, gave up his own share and invited them to the most strenuous exertions.'

Occasionally, John borrowed verbatim from his *Journal*. At the moment when, according to his letter, 'our success was complete', he explained in both the letter and *Journal* that 'night and the fatigue our troops had undergone prevent immediate pursuit', but for hyperbolic effect, added 'which would have finished them'[44] to the letter version. Conscious that his letter might be shown around a wider reading public back home and might even reach the newspapers, John played up the fact that the French were supplying arms and materiel to the Rebels. That, he knew, would be sure to fire public opinion in favour of the war. In both versions, he alluded to the arms captured, but in the *Journal* he wrote of 'eleven pieces of ordnance: five French brass guns, three Hessian, three American.'[45] Shifting the focus markedly in the letter, he recorded that '11 pieces of Artillery fell in our hands, 5 of which were French' but, to ram home this point, added that 'their arms are almost all French and many of their stores we have since seen are evidently so,'[46] facts that were omitted entirely from the *Journal*. As for Montrésor, he noted only that 'ten pieces of Cannon and one Howitzer'[47] were taken.

Map of Philadelphia at the time of its re-occupation by the British in 1778. (Library of Congress, Geography and Map Division)

The high point for John in both his *Journal* and the letter to his mother was his account of events 'on the night of the 20th'[48] September. According to John, 'intelligence having been received of the situation of General Wayne and his design of attacking our rear, a plan was concerted for surprising him, and the execution entrusted to Major General Grey'.[49] Licensed by this 'intelligence' brought in, unsurprisingly, by Erskine from his 'reconnoitering' expedition the previous day, the 'plan' and its 'execution' proceeded with no holds barred. Surprise being deemed the key to the success of a night-time attack, orders were issued that 'no firelock was to be loaded and express orders were given to rely solely on the bayonet'. In the *Journal*, John prefaced his account of the events that night with a lengthy exposé explaining the sound military logic to these petite guerre tactics. The attack itself was described as an operation of matter-of-fact precision, intended by its careful planning to do 'great credit' to its 'principal',[50] General Grey. The tactics employed were further justified by the discovery that the prior intelligence had proved correct: 'it was about one o'clock in the morning when the attack was made, and the rebels were then assembling to move towards us, with the design of taking our baggage.'[51]

For all his military reserve, John did, at one point in his account, allow his guard to slip when describing graphically how 'the light infantry ... rushed along the line putting to the bayonet all they came up with, and, overtaking the main herd of fugitives, stabbed great numbers.'[52] When this field report reached the War Office in London, the 'Gazette' account edited out the cut-and-thrust, one reference to 'by the bayonet only'[53] the sole hint as to the attack's ruthless efficiency.

In his letter, John dispensed with military protocols, instead moving quickly to the outcome of the attack as he described how 'we ferreted out their pickets and advanced guards, surprised and put most of them to death and coming in upon the camp rushed on them as they were collecting together and pursued them with a prodigious slaughter. About 200 killed and wounded remained on the field.' Upping the raw rhetoric, John concluded with 'we brought away near 80 prisoners and of those who escaped a very great number were stabbed with bayonet or cut with broad swords.'[54] What must his mother have thought!

No wonder that, in the mounting war of words, this event became known by Americans as the 'Paoli Massacre', but for John the operation had achieved its immediate purpose in that 'we ... marched the next day with the army quite unmolested by Genl. Wayne (a Tanner)' and could 'believe our success to be decisive in its consequences, but it is not immediately so.'

The road to Philadelphia was open and 'the day before yesterday (the 26th) the Grenadiers of the Army took possession of Philadelphia',[55] John coming to the city four days later when, as he recorded in his *Journal*, 'General Grey visited Philadelphia'[56] on 30 September. John could further congratulate himself when the *London Gazette Extraordinary* published its account in London on 2 December and acknowledged that 'the gallantry in the troops and good conduct in the General were fully manifested upon this critical service'.[57] In the immediate satisfaction of reaching Philadelphia, John could briefly forget the gloom of Saratoga.

PART IV

At Secret War

CHAPTER 23

'The Fair Quakers'

1778 was the year when reality came home to Britain in its efforts to regain control of the thirteen colonies. The surrender at Saratoga hollowed out Howe's grand plan for a sweep of victories intended to put paid to Washington's fledgling forces of rebellion. The Pennsylvania campaign should have been compensation enough for Saratoga if it succeeded in its objective to bring Washington to a definitive engagement, instead of which the indecisive battle at Germantown left only questions not answers. The capture of Philadelphia helpfully provided winter quarters for Howe's Army, but the eight-month occupation proved pyrrhic leaving Britain's military planning comatose, all while France cemented its support for the rebellion and Washington set about forming a hardened standing army during the totemic winter months at Valley Forge, ready to match Britain's redcoats man for man in the new campaigning season.

The order from London to abandon Philadelphia in May 1778 was a watershed, the recall of Howe and arrival of Peace Commissioners that same month symbolizing the end of Britain's political will for the fight. Henceforth, the army was on its own, the military strategy under the new commander, Sir Henry Clinton, characterized by an increasingly desperate search for some rear-guard masterstroke which, at worst, would drive Congress to the negotiating table, at best, would keep some, at least, of the colonies loyal to Britain. Marked by a succession of increasingly desperate coups de main intended to probe for weakness in Washington's armour, petty tactics became grand strategy, Clinton forced, in the process, to put growing emphasis on petite guerre as the weapon that would decide the war.

In retrospect, it was only a question of time before Britain was ground down and capitulated. At the time, however, every plan, every stroke, every plot, every scheme was greeted as the ultimate win-all, spies, agents, partizans, and secret 'friends' enlisted to land one last herculean blow in the desperate search for some miracle of victory. Abandoned by London, junior officers either despaired of the war and, like James Murray, sought a more promising post in the West Indies, or steeled themselves and, like John, kept rolling the dice in a final death-defying quest for personal honour.

The last major engagement of 1777 occurred between 4 and 7 December. As John explained to his mother in his 20 November letter, intelligence had come in that 'Mr. Washington has been also fixed at a place called Whitemarsh, 14 miles from us.'[1] Further intelligence revealed that Washington's need to protect 'the great magazines of military stores and magazines here [Northampton], at Bethlehem and Easton'[2] and remove them to Carlisle had 'compelled' him 'to leave his favourable post at Whitemarsh ... and secure the road to Lancaster and Carlisle.'[3] Howe's plan was to surprise Washington's forces while they were on the move.

John described the events of those four days in his *Journal* but, as in the earlier engagements in the campaign, he remained invisible. Nevertheless, he was active on behalf of Grey, on one occasion rescuing Simcoe's 'Queen's Rangers' from a certain 'ambuscade' when he 'came with orders to retreat, the column being already in motion'.[4]

As with his Brandywine account, John provided a strategic overview, describing how Grey would mount a diversionary manoeuvre and 'whilst from this demonstration they [the enemy] presumed an attack impended from that quarter, Sir William Howe with the Elite and the main Army was to have made the real attack.'[5] In the event, the rebel forces were well dug-in, and the attack fizzled out, whereupon, as John explained, 'the fullest information being procured of the enemy's position, most people thought an attack upon ground of such difficult access would be a very arduous undertaking; nor was it judged that any decisive advantage could be gained, as the enemy had reserved the most easy and obvious retreat.'

Concluding this strategic assessment in his 7 December entry, John wrote: 'probably for these reasons, the Commander-in-Chief determined to return to Philadelphia.'[6] This was a curious remark to make in an official military journal: something had gone terribly wrong. John knew it but was being circumspect; so, too, Montrésor, though in his case, the caution in his *Journal* was for personal reasons: he was smarting from his recent failure to secure promotion. As a result, he feigned more interest in the gloomy weather conditions and barely mentioned the Whitemarsh expedition. He no longer cared: he had decided to 'resign my command'.[7] Chastened by the failure of his previous 'conjectures' as to the outcome of 'this unfortunate and unnatural Rebellion',[8] Murray had also decided to give up and would soon begin musing on 'a prospect of beeng sent home'.[9] John had no such luxury: too much of his future was bound up in the success of this war, hence the importance to him of the Whitemarsh expedition. His fear, as he explained to his mother just days before the attack was launched, was that, if it failed just as the campaign season was drawing to a close and winter quarters beckoned, 'Washington will quit the field with a more respectable Army than last year.' This, in turn, begged the questions: 'will he appear again in the Spring reinsured in the same proportion?' and 'Will they receive further assistance from France?'

How keyed up John was ahead of the Whitemarsh expedition is evident from his crescendo of despairing iconoclasm. Grasping for ways out of the impending military impasse should the attack fail, he implored rhetorically: 'Will not cloathing fail them, will they [the rebels] continue unanimous etc., does not famine threaten? Have we not fire as well as the sword, a horried means yet untried!' Faced with imponderables beyond his control, John concluded abjectly: 'I commit this to your consideration and beg pardon for entering upon matters I do not understand'.

Reading this, Mary-Louisa must surely have noticed how quickly John's optimism had soured. Just two months earlier he had written buoyantly how 'I am most satisfactorily situated. I have the pleasure to find myself possessed of some share of the General's good will and confidence and to live I may really say upon the most friendly footing with him. He is high in the esteem of the army and with reason so that improvement is not the only advantage I enjoy in this family'.

Why, then, so dramatic a change? Was it simply down to the bad news which had come in from Saratoga, or was it more personal? Had something gone wrong with John's plans for his 'improvement'? Mary-Louisa could surely be forgiven for thinking it was the latter and that it was the burden of his professional duties—especially the task of provisioning—when he warned that 'we have reason to fear great scarcity of provision in Philadelphia this winter unless by driving off Mr Washington, the country people can be emboldened to bring in their produce'.[10]

Mary-Louisa was not to know, however, that, if, indeed, provisioning were John's main concern, he need only wait four days and the fleet from England would have broken through the defences on the Delaware at Mud Island, and all would be well as the army headed into winter quarters. Murray's mood certainly improved briefly when he heard of 'the arrival of the fleet' on 24 November. Buoyed by this news, Murray was sure that 'every thing is now or will be soon in tolerable plenty,' and that, 'as the greatest number of the inhabitants ... have remained in town, it will be an agreeable winter quarter.' Key to this anticipated agreeability was that 'particularly the fair Quakers'[11] were among 'the inhabitants' remaining.

John had no time for 'fair Quakers' just yet. There were immediate events that might affect his chances for 'improvement'. The depression that had pervaded the late November letter to his mother had been replaced by a mood of nervous anticipation evident in his journal entry on 7 December. The Whitemarsh expedition was over, and it had gone badly: Washington had escaped. Now would come the inevitable post mortem—hence the mysterious 'probably' in his *Journal* on that day. Someone must pay. If so, here was an opportunity for his own 'improvement': he had the 'confidence' of his commander, General Grey and, if, as was the talk of the 'Philadelphia Camp', the expedition had been scuppered through mistakes of intelligence, surely he could prevail where others in Howe's inner circle had failed. Did he not have all his connections ready and waiting across Pennsylvania? Had not General Prescott and, now, General Grey, taught him all he needed to know about the art of partizan warfare? He was ready, but could he catch Howe's eye?

Breaking into Howe's inner circle would be a tall order: the Commander-in-Chief had six aides-de-camp at his beck and call, and Joseph Galloway, the new 'Superintendant General of the Police in the City'[12] of Philadelphia, had his ear on all local intelligence matters, having successfully mobilized "upwards of 80 different Spies"[13] among his Pennsylvania connections to assist the British advance through the province.

Hinging these as a loyalist courier was Andrew Fürstner, a farmer of German extraction who, according to one of Washington's agents, had settled in 'Lankister' (Lancaster) and was 'brother-in-law to a certain Captain Rankin of Browne Coar [Corps] who formerly Kept a Ferry at that Place'. Rankin was a 'colonel of the local militia' who headed 'a group of loyalists in York County',[14] and Fürstner was recommended by 'James Rankin Esq to Mr Galloway, Superintending General.' According to Fürstner's memorial of service, one of his first missions came when Galloway 'sent him out to reconnoitre the Enemy Posts at Valeyfords [Valley Forge] and brought in his report and delivered it to Mr Galloway and Major Balfour.'[15] It is possible, then, that Fürstner was the 'spy who was in our [rebel] Camp'[16] and first alerted Howe that Washington was on the move at Whitemarsh.

As good, however, as were Howe's secret sources, Washington's were better. As the Hessian officer Captain Baurmeister explained: 'we had made all the necessary preparations but, unfortunately, the enemy is informed of everything as soon as our generals get their orders'.[17] Baurmeister was not to know it, but Washington's source, so it later emerged, was Lydia Darrach, a 'fair', albeit aging, 'Quaker' whose Philadelphia home was opposite where Howe had 'established his headquarters in Second Street.' So her story went, 'a superior officer of the British Army, believed to be the adjutant-general … fixed upon one of their chambers … for private conference, and two officers frequently met there. About the 2d of December, the adjutant-general told Lydia that they would be in the room at 7 o'clock and remain late.' Being suspicious, Lydia listened in and 'overheard an order read for the British troops to march out late on the evening of the 4th and attack General Washington, then encamped at Whitemarsh… Soon after the officer knocked at her door, but she rose only at the third summons, having feigned herself asleep'.

Using as an excuse for leaving Philadelphia that 'she was in want of flour', Lydia 'determined to make her way to the American outposts.' Reaching American lines, Lydia 'disclosed her secret' and 'returned home with her flour'. That, however, was not the end of the matter for her. Realizing that Washington had somehow got wind of his plans for a surprise attack, Howe launched an investigation, searching for a spy within. Suspicion fell on the Darrach household, and, 'the next evening the adjutant-general came in … and inquired earnestly whether any of her family were up the last night when he and the officer met. She told him they all were retired at eight o'clock. He observed "I know *you* were asleep for I knocked at your door three times before you heard me. I am entirely at a loss to imagine who gave General Washington information of our intended attack… When we arrived near

Whitemarsh, we found all their cannon mounted and their troops prepared to receive us; *and we have marched back like a parcel of fools.*'[18]

That was as far as 'the anecdote of the heroine Lydia Darrah'[19] went, save only that the 'superior officer' was 'believed to be the adjutant-general (Major André)'.[20] This was patently incorrect. At this point in the war, John was still a captain, still attached to Grey's staff as his aide-de-camp, and certainly not, as yet, the 'adjutant-general'. Colonel Paterson held that post,[21] and, although briefly in England in July 1777, was back with Howe by September when, according to Montrésor, 'the Quartermaster and Adjutant-General'[22] accompanied Howe as he entered the city.

If 'Major André' were the adjutant general when Lydia pulled off her heroics, he would surely have been blamed for the lapse in security. Howe certainly needed to hold someone to account. It, doubtless, was unconnected that Paterson resigned six months later when 'Lord Rawdon' was 'to be appointed Adjutant General if Colonel Paterson should decline.'[23] Howe did, however, directly blame Galloway. As Howe explained in his later testimony before Parliament: at about this time, 'I found that my confidence' in Galloway 'was misplaced'. The specific circumstances were that, 'having relied on him to procure me secret intelligence … but having once detected him in sending me a piece of intelligence from a person, who afterwards, upon examination, gave me a different account of the matter, I immediately changed the channel of secret communication and in future considered Mr Galloway as a nugatory informer.'[24]

It is tempting therefore to dismiss Lydia's account as a fiction of Revolutionary lore, not least because her journey through the lines was no easy feat. Yet, according to one local source, this early in the city's occupation 'women are [still] suffered to come out of Philad'a without enquiry'.[25] By the following February, however, that had changed when 'orders came out for Officers to take up Women that come out from Philadelphia what comed into Camp, if Suspected and bring them to a trial'.[26] Moreover, Elias Boudinot, 'Commissary Genl of Prisoners,' who, in this function, 'managed the Intelligence of the Army', substantially corroborated Lydia's account in his *Journal*, albeit describing her 'as a little poor looking insignificant Old Woman.'[27]

Given the authenticity of Lydia's anecdote, it is possible that, as she claimed, John was at her house but as one of the other 'officers', in which case he was already active in secret intelligence activities. This was entirely consistent with the reconnaissance work John had already undertaken for Grey as the king's army advanced towards Philadelphia, and consistent also with the expanded 'partizan' duties he was given as Galloway's star waned. John's facility with languages was, once again, the proximate catalyst for his elevation, evident when he assumed responsibility for Galloway's connections among Britain's German-speaking friends in Pennsylvania. Fürstner was a case in point: originally introduced to Howe by Galloway, Fürstner increasingly reported to John as 1778 progressed. Fürstner's subsequent testimonial of service described how, following a courier run to New York, he 'was immediately dispatched to Captain André and Mr Galloway with Letters to Philadelphia.' Galloway was nowhere in evidence however, when, some months on, Fürstner 'returned and was entered upon the List with Colonel Robinson and recommended by Major André to Sir Henry Clinton...'[28] Through Fürstner, John also formed an intelligence relationship with Captain Rankin, who, according to one of Washington's spies, 'was often out with André as he Informs me.'[29] John would have known Rankin from his time in Carlisle.

John's facility with French may also have come into its own, enabling him to travel freely within Rebel lines at a time when French officers—Lafayette, among others—were everywhere to be seen.[30] When exactly John assumed these expanded functions is difficult to ascertain. This is unsurprising given the shadowy nature of John's work at that time. Still, it seems more than coincidental that an important part of John's official duties for Grey ceased on 30 December 1777 when—so soon after the Whitemarsh fiasco—he abruptly stopped making any entries in his *Journal*. Moreover, he did not resume entries until 1 June 1778—a gap of five months—when the army was again on the move, this time 'in consequence of the determination taken to evacuate Philadelphia.'[31]

In his letters home, John was also silent about his activities during those five months: his last letter from 'Philadelphia Camp' was dated 20 November 1777, and his family had to wait until 12 September 1778 for his next letter. When this arrived, it was marked from 'N. York' and said nothing of his life or duties in Philadelphia during the first five months of 1778, but instead focused on the time since the evacuation when 'very great rigour is exercised at Philadelphia against all persons who have befriended us, amongst others the Country people who frequented the market of whom they whip, fine or imprison without remorse.'[32]

John had an ostensible reason for interrupting the *Journal* when he did, being that 30 December was when 'the Army came into winter quarters in Philadelphia'.[33] Yet, this was not how others recording the events of those five months chose to see them. Montrésor briefly interrupted his *Journal* on 30 December, when 'this day is looked upon as entering Winter Quarters', but resumed his entries on '1st March 1778'—three months earlier than John—when noting that 'returned from Salem ... the 2 Battalions Light Infantry and the two Established Engineers in flat boats...'[34] From then on, Montrésor's day-by-day entries focused, much as in 1777, almost exclusively on military operations beyond the city, namely foraging expeditions, skirmishes and attacks by the Rebels on the 'market people'[35] bringing in provisions. Nor was Baurmeister's flow of war news interrupted by the advent of winter quarters: his three letters in early 1778[36] gave the fullest account of military activities during these five months. American diarists also remained active, Marshall recording local events of the war which impacted on 'poor Pennsylvania'[37] during those five months.

John could not, plausibly, have ceased making entries over that five-month period—part only of which coincided with winter quarters—without his commander's approval: the *Journal* was, quite clearly, being compiled on his commander's instructions, which explains why, on completion, it went into the Grey family papers.[38] Nor could John undertake other duties during those five months without Grey's approval. It is, of course, possible that Grey was inactive during that time, in which case, arguably, John had nothing to report. This is to suggest, however, that the *Journal* was a homage by John to his commander, which it was not: as a general record of events in the Pennsylvania campaign, Grey was sometimes central, other times peripheral. Moreover, during John's five months' silence, Simcoe's Rangers, one of the regiments under Grey's command, was especially active in marauding expeditions.[39] These should have been recorded if John were still fulfilling his secretarial duties.

There is another possible explanation for John's silence: that Grey's time in Philadelphia during those five months was marked by leisure living—hardly the stuff of a military journal. This was certainly how contemporary American commentators sought to portray the British occupation of Philadelphia, Marshall leading the moral charge from his self-imposed exile in nearby Lancaster. Writing in January 1778, he became 'anxiously concerned on account of our distressed friends'. Among these were 'our poor friends in town, many of them in want of fuel and necessaries while our internal enemies under the protection of that savage monster Howe are revelling in luxury, dissipation and drunkenness.'[40]

There is no evidence, however, that Grey indulged in 'luxury, dissipation and drunkenness' during those five months. That said, according to some commentators, these were generalized conditions in both camps, Marshall donning a hair-shirt as he lambasted Lancaster's recurrent bouts of frivolity which began on 31 January 1778 with 'a grand ball or entertainment … at which (it's said) one hundred men and women assembled dressed in all their gaiety … music, dancing, gaiety etc held till four this morning'[41] and culminated with another 'grand ball' on 21 February, 'this being the third held in town lately, notwithstanding the grievous sufferings that this state lies under.' Attended by 'fops, fools etc of both sexes, young and old', these events drew the lofty conclusion that 'without a speedy return to the course … of virtues and heroic actions, we shall soon fall into irretrievable ruin and desolation.'[42]

Whatever the efforts of Congress to purify America through revolution, it seems that the 'true Macharoni style' became as much part of the Patriot soldierly manner as it was Redcoat attire. According to Philip Freneau, the Patriot poet, it was all the fault of Redcoat foppery, and it was the duty of the colonial soldier to lead the moral crusade, 'the manly warrior' renouncing 'glittering toys' and the 'feather on his head'.[43]

To judge by the storm of protests from American commentators, this generalized descent into moral 'ruin and desolation' reached its climax when British officers clubbed together and staged a grand military pageant in Philadelphia. Held on 18 May 1778, this 'Meschianza'[44] was an 'eighteen-hour extravaganza'.[45] As a medley of what the *London Evening Post* called 'various amusements',[46] its title was apt, Montrésor describing it as 'an entertainment … consisting of a Regatta, Fete

Champetre, Tilts and Tournaments, Carosal, Procession through Triumphal Arches, Dancing, Exhibition of Fire works, musik and Feast.'[47]

Apart from the obvious extravagance, there was nothing apparent in this programme of events to explain the high pitch of protests which it subsequently excited in both America and England. Certainly, there were no voices of opposition within the Army or the Navy. Indeed, the expenses of '3,312 guineas, were borne by twenty-two field officers',[48] and among these were four relatively senior officers who were appointed as 'managers', namely, 'Sir John Wrottesley, Colonel O'Hara, Majors Gardiner and Montrésor.'[49]

With the event being arranged at 'such Shortness of the time',[50] many junior officers—John included—rallied round and helped with the entertainment's organization. This was nothing new. Among British forces serving in America, there was a tradition of staging plays. This predated the Revolution but, in recent years, officers had put on entertainments in Boston and New York, and, through this latest winter, there had been a programme of productions at the Southwark Theatre in Philadelphia. John was in his element, joining Captain Stephen Delancey, a loyalist officer, who, earlier, had overseen productions at the John Street Theatre in New York. Between them, 'these two painted, themselves, the chief of the decorations' for the Meschianza. 'The Sienna marble, for instance, on the apparent side walls was painted on canvas in the stage scene painting. André also painted the scenes used at the theatre, at which the British officers performed.'[51] Other officers known to have been involved in preparations for the event included Montrésor, who, as chief engineer, supervised the fireworks display, and Captain Stanley who, as the 'infant muse'[52] of record for some prologues to plays performed earlier in New York and Philadelphia,[53] took charge of this aspect of the event.

Hannah Griffitts, a local poet, was one of the first to condemn the Meschianza, describing it 'as a "shameful scene of Dissipation/The death of sense and Reputation."'[54] Elizabeth Drinker, a loyalist Quaker, was equally outraged at 'ye scenes of Folly and Vanity promoted by ye officers of the army under the pretence of showing respect to Gen. Howe, now about leaving us', complaining loudly 'how insensible does these people appear, while our Land is so greatly desolated and Death and sore destruction has so overtaken.'[55]

Permeating these cries of outrage, however, were strong sexual undercurrents, the sense being that, with the city vacated by young able-bodied Patriots who were off fighting for the cause of independence, it was 'mainly women and children'[56] left in the city, and the 'fair Quakers' of Philadelphia were set to fall prey to the Redcoat hordes numbering some '10,000 men'.[57] Throughout the occupation, there had been 'very bad accounts of the licentiousness of the English officers deluding young girls',[58] this according to Sarah Logan Fisher writing in her diary on 15 March 1778.

If American commentators were looking for proof of this 'licentiousness', it was in 'a very remarkable trial now depending before a courtmartial', involving Mary Figis, 'a girl of 16'. James Murray saw this trial differently, however, as he explained to his sister in his 'March 5, 1778' letter. The case related to 'a Capt. Campbell who had distinguished himself by his spirit, activity and an appearance of zeal for the cause, and had been raised from nothing to places of considerable trust and profit under Sir Will. Erskine.' So the account went, Campbell stood 'accused by a girl of 16 … of sending letters by her to the enemy.' Reflecting the climate of suspicion which lingered in the British camp some three months after the Whitemarsh debacle, Murray mulled the lesson how 'it seems difficult to account for such a crime by any degree of absurdity and villainy … and it seems almost equally difficult to conceive that the girl should frame and support such a story without any apparent motive, and though the evidence, as far as I have heard it, is such as seems fully to acquit him, charges of that kind are of too delicate a nature to be ever totally got the better of, and the unhappy man must fall a sacrifice, at least in his character and fortune, to the malice and depravity of an abandoned little wretch.'[59] Murray's foreboding proved all too accurate: 'Capt. Alexander Campbell', was acquitted of 'holding a correspondence with and giving intelligence to the Enemy' but only because 'there is not a sufficiency of evidence'.[60]

Nevertheless, whether these accounts were about Fisher's 'young girls' or Murray's 'girl of 16', the perception was that these were victims from the lower classes. What set off the local howls of protest surrounding the Meschianza was the attendance of up to fifty 'Ladies' from the City's upper social circles.[61] According to Elizabeth Drinker, 'great numbers of ye officers and some women embarked in three Galleys'.[62] Some came as guests and were among the 'one hundred and seventy-two persons' who had 'supper'[63] aboard the *Roebuck*. This was reprehensible enough, but others came 'dressed as Turkish maidens'[64] for their parts performing either as 'Ladies of the Blended Rose' or 'Ladies of the Burning Mountain'[65] in company with their chosen 'Knights'.

There were fourteen of these 'maidens', and that these '"Ladies joined the frantic show"' was especially deplored by Hannah Griffitts. Worst of all was that, unlike the nameless 'one hundred men and women assembled' for one of the grand balls of Lancaster which Marshall took exception to in his private journal, the names of these 'Ladies' were published, appearing, first, in the local *Philadelphia Gazette* before reappearing in various London newspapers, beginning with the *St. James's Chronicle* before finally receiving full coverage in the *Gentleman's Magazine*. As a result, everyone knew that 'among the principal young Ladies of the Country' performing were, for instance, 'Miss White', 'Miss N. Redman', 'Miss Franks', and 'Miss Bond'. That Judge Edward Shippen may, at the last minute, have obliged his daughters, Peggy and Susan, to withdraw from the event made no difference. It was too late: their names remained on the programme and went into the subsequent press write-up, Susan going as the 'Lady' of the 'Lieut. Underwood' and Peggy as the 'Lady' of 'Lieut. Winyard.'

That 'Ladies' were part of 'the frantic show' may have been frowned on, but their participation without seeking the veil of secrecy confirms their ongoing rebellion against, and defiance of, the moral austerity imposed on the city ever since the high priests of Congress imposed their revolutionary strictures on society.[66] Equally, American commentators might deplore 'how insensible does these people appear,' but John, for one, had long blamed 'the perfidious dastards' of Congress, for, in his mind, it was they 'who have worked the ruin and spilt the blood of so many credulous wretches.' Accordingly, if these 'fair Quakers' wished to rebel against the moral strictures of the Whiggish Congress, that was their prerogative.

With so many 'Ladies' drawn from the ranks of 'Philadelphia's leading belles',[67] it was inevitable that 'Whig suspicions of romantic or perhaps more threatening alliances between Philadelphia's ladies and British soldiers were further confirmed by the Meschianza.'[68] Whether any 'threatening alliances' did eventuate is not known. Nevertheless, American commentators had a field day, 'Josiah Bartlett, delegate from New Hampshire,' likening these 'Tory Ladies' to 'the Mistresses and Wh [ores] of the British Officers.'[69]

What is certain is that, according to 'the queen of the Meschianza', John 'was the charm of the company'.[70] He seemed especially close to Rebecca Redman, one of the 'Ladies', not only composing a love poem for her entitled 'A German Air'[71] but also cutting numerous silhouettes, including one of 'Phineas Bond Esq ... for Rebecca Redman,'[72] another of 'Major Edward Stanly'[73] and one of himself. He also took charge of the Ladies ahead of the production, designing their costumes so that they were 'in Turkish habits',[74] even 'circulating a sketch of how he wanted the women to appear.'[75]

John was not only active behind the scenes. He also took the part of the '3d knight' who, 'mounted on a managed Horse', attended 'in honour of Miss P. Chew.' This was a family affair: the 'Squire bearing his Lance and Shield'[76] was John's younger brother, William-Lewis, who, as 'Lieut André' since September 1777,[77] had arrived in America only recently.[78] Given John's responsibilities as head of the family, it is unlikely he would have been conducting any 'threatening alliances' in front of his younger brother, and if he were, it seems inconceivable he would have used the Meschianza to advertise them.

Moreover, John had his sights set firmly on 'improvement' and, for him the Meschianza was the next step on this road, the event conceived by him and the other junior officers as, first and foremost, a political statement. Dressed up 'as a compliment to Sir William Howe and by way of taking leave of him before his departure for England,'[79] its real intention was to attack British government policy regarding America. These junior officers had fought their way up from the 'Head of Elk' and captured America's City of brotherly Love. They had done all that was asked of them and brought victory only to be told on arrival that they must abandon Philadelphia and retreat, humiliated and defeated. They were not attacking their commanding officers: these generals—Howe, Grey, Erskine among others—had led them brilliantly, fought alongside them and even, in the case of Brigadier-general

James Agnew' and 'Lieutenant-colonel John Bird'[80], given up their lives. Their target, rather, was the political denizens of London who had recalled Howe, sent out Peace Commissioners and called time on the war.

Lord Carlisle, one of these Peace Commissioners, was clear who was behind the Meschianza and its political subversiveness. Writing to his wife on 21 June 1778, he ridiculed the event as 'a very foolish business though I believe it owed its birth to our relative Sir John Wrotsley.'[81] It is no surprise Carlisle seeking to mock Wrottesley. From their recent conversations, it was evident to Carlisle that the two were about to become political foes. As a lieutenant-colonel, Wrottesley was a senior army officer, but it was as a Member of Parliament since 1768[82] that he represented the more significant threat to Carlisle's political masters, the North administration.

Wrottesley had evidently warned Carlisle that he intended to give maximum publicity to the Meschianza, the objective being to embarrass the government. For this reason, Carlisle alerted his wife that Wrottesley 'gave me a long description of it, but I understand there is one sent to England which is to appear in the papers.'[83] Carlisle was right to anticipate a political storm. When news of the 'superb entertainment called the MESCHIANZA' first reached England, opponents of the government immediately rallied to Howe's side. Leading the charge was the *London Evening Post* which, in its 2 July edition, crowed that 'all ranks of people exerted themselves in shewing the greatest respect for General Howe'. Taking aim at the hated Scottish cabal of Lord Bute, which was long deemed to hold pernicious sway over the royal court, the newspaper fulminated how 'the little dirty Scotch faction in the army concealed their recreant heads, but their hearts were ready to burst with envy.'[84]

That was only the beginning. True to his word, Wrottesley followed up with the 'long description' he had promised, and, to ensure maximum publicity, two versions were sent, tripping over themselves in their rush to 'appear in the papers'. First came an 'official' version: dated 'Philadelphia May 23', this one appeared in the opposition *Morning Post* on 13 July and was headed 'a full description of the Grand Meschianza...' Opening with 'the army anxious to give Sir William Howe the most public and splendid testimony of the high esteem they entertain of him...'[85] it gave a matter-of-fact account of the order of entertainments and, apart from the two Howe brothers and Sir Henry Clinton, no officers were mentioned by name.

Composed in the style of a society column about 'Ladies of distinction' at a 'Bon Ton' event in Bath's 'Pump-Room',[86] it made sure 'the young ladies' and 'damsels' were fully in evidence, but, again, no names were given. 'In delicacy to the General', however, 'the following lines ... intended to be delivered by the herald' were 'suppressed.' These described how 'Mars conquest plum'd, the Cyprian Queen disarms/ and victors vanquished yield to beauty's charms'. A strong undercurrent of sexuality lingered on in descriptions of this 'feast of military love', but the predominant message of the verse lines was that 'old British courage glows unconquer'd' among the 'brave crowd' of young officers, who, with 'revenge and glory sparkling in every eye … their country they'll avenge, her fame restore'.

Seeking to whet appetites further, the article concluded that 'the above is the most perfect account of this elegant entertainment that the Editor had been able to collect, but hopes in a few days to give them one that is more worthy of their attention.'[87] As it happens, this 'more worthy' one had already appeared in the *St. James's Chronicle* on 7 July. Presented as the 'copy of a letter from an officer at Philadelphia to his correspondent in London,' it, too, was dated 'Philadelphia May 23, 1778', but its author could be sure of its speedy and safe arrival, as 'the ship that carries Home Sir William Howe will convey this Letter to you.'

Longer than the official version, this article was cast as a personal epistle: beginning 'for the first time in my life I write to you with Unwillingness', it launched into a panegyric on Howe. In a significant departure from the official version, the account of the 'variety of entertainment' was filled with the names of its managers, headed by 'Sir John Wrottesley', its guests, among which 'General Knyphausen', and its actors, including 'Lord Cathcart'[88] leading an array of up-and-coming British nobility. This was the version that revealed the identities of the Philadelphia belles who had acted each as 'Lady' to their chosen 'Knight.'

Although presented as a personal letter to a 'correspondent' in London, this version was obviously intended for publication. This raises the question who wrote it. Neither it nor the 'official' version was claimed by an author of record, but that was the custom of the time, especially when, as was the case here, the contents were so politically charged. It has been suggested that it was 'written, it is said, by Major André for an English Lady's Magazine'.[89] Another source was more emphatic that there was an 'account of the Mischianza from the Lady's Magazine' and that it was 'Major André's.'[90] Yet, at the time no article on the Meschianza appeared in the *Lady's Magazine*, nor did this periodical refer to the event at the time.[91]

The most likely scenario is that both versions were drafted by a junior officer acting in a secretarial capacity on behalf of Wrottesley and that the final texts went out only after amendment and approval by senior officers, including Howe. These two documents were too important to be left to a junior officer, which explains why Lord Carlisle took news of the 'long description' so seriously and why reactions from friends of government were so strident when the two articles appeared in various London publications.

The pro-government *Morning Chronicle* led the counter-punches, mocking both the 'flattering account of this Mischianza … published in the General's own Philadelphia Gazette and copied into the Morning Post the 13th July' and the 'larger one by a more flattering panegyrist … printed in the Gentleman's Magazine for August last'.[92] Hard on the heels of the *Morning Chronicle* came *Strictures on the Philadelphia Mischianza…*[93] a pamphlet that sought to destroy Howe's reputation.

That John drafted both the 'flattering account' and the 'larger one' is perfectly possible. With his *Journal*, he had earned Grey's confidence in such matters, and,

Profile cut of John André by John André. (New York Public Library)

clearly, Wrottesley knew John well and trusted his eye for detail, hence the profile cut he asked John to undertake of him.[94] Stepping into the shoes of Galloway and Paterson on matters of 'secret intelligence', John had also earned Howe's trust on such delicate matters. At a practical level, he was most intimately involved in organization of many aspects of the event, which meant he could compose the descriptions which embellished these accounts of the Meschianza. An accomplished wordsmith, he was also closest to the 'Ladies' who performed, and having earned their confidence, he was best-placed to seek and receive their permission to publish their names.

There were powerful reasons why John would want to have a hand in these articles: here was a golden opportunity to further earn his right to 'improvement'. Looking beyond the immediate future, he could begin planning for his return home at the end of the war. Hitching his political wagon to powerful friends of the opposition—as Wrottesley and the two Howe brothers most surely were[95]—he could look to fulfil the ambition alluded to nine years earlier when he wrote to Anna Seward of 'trying my interest in Parliament'. Even in the depths of the collective despair felt by the junior officers as their commander-in-chief departed, John could hope for this future success, having himself 'just returned from conducting our beloved General to the Water Side.'[96]

CHAPTER 24

'Implicit Confidence'

In the four months following the evacuation from Philadelphia, which began on 17 June 1778, John's whereabouts were relatively easy to trace: wherever General Grey was, there he was close at hand, back as his aide-de-camp recording in his *Journal* the events that impacted most directly on his commanding officer. When, on 26 August, recording in the *Journal* that 'General Grey in person went to Flushing where he met Sir Henry Clinton',[1] this was John expressly placing himself at his commanding officer's right hand.

Events moved quickly during those four months. First came the hazardous 'March' to New York, which—interrupted by the battle at 'Monmouth Court house' between 26 and 28 June—was accomplished by early July. 'Thus', as John recorded in his *Journal*, 'was completed a March of many mile thro' Enemy's country in defiance of every object they threatened or attempted to throw in our way…'[2] Next came the expedition to Rhode Island. The British fleet arrived at 'Rhode Island Harbor'[3] on 1 September, following which Grey made a series of reports to Clinton, his new commander-in-chief. Among these was one on 6 September from 'on board the Carysfort frigate off Bedford harbour.' As was the convention, an 'extract' of this 'letter' was printed in the *London Gazette*, and, signing off, Grey noted: 'I write in haste and not a little tired, therefore must beg leave to refer you for the Late Plan of Operations and Particulars to Captain André'.[4]

Mentioning John's name in a 'Gazette Letter' was intentional: though John did not know it, Grey may have decided to return home to England and was seeking to be of service to his hard-working aide-de-camp. Bringing John's name to the attention of the new commander-in-chief was only the start. Implicit in the wording of this letter was that John was hand-delivering the report to Clinton, in which case drawing Clinton's attention to the 'Late Plan of Operations and Particulars' would give John an opportunity to show off his pièce de résistance the *Journal* with its 'forty-four maps and plans, wonderfully drawn and many coloured … many with textual explanations.'[5] This proved the case when, on 9 September, Kemble, the deputy adjutant general, recorded in his *Journal* that 'General Grey's Aid-de-Camp

Captain André arrived' at Headquarters 'this day, having left the General at Block Island and informs that the Troops, those Embarked for Rhode Island with Sir Henry Clinton and left under General Grey's Command, had landed at Bedford…'[6]

There is no knowing whether this was the first time John's name came to Clinton's attention. It is possible that Grey—if not him, then surely Howe—may already have mentioned John's important role in organizing the Meschianza. Dismissed as so much decadent flimflam by its critics, this extravaganza had a serious purpose other than as a political stunt by Wrottesley. Part of a general strategic plan adopted for the hazardous evacuation from Philadelphia, the objective of the Meschianza was tactical, so that 'throughout the whole march' to New York the Americans should, as John explained, be 'perplexed in their conjectures by the secrecy observed respecting our route and by false movements meant to deceive them.'[7] Montrésor, as chief engineer, was especially busy arranging these 'false movements' in the lead-up to the evacuation, and on 10 May 'by order of his Excellency Sir William Howe, I laid out several works in the front of the lines, Picketted and Lock Spitted in order to make appearance only to the Enemy to answer certain Purposes'.[8]

These and other 'movements' had the desired effect: through his network of spies in Philadelphia, Washington knew well in advance that the British Army was on the move but could not be certain of the when, where and how or, indeed, whether the rumoured evacuation was a bluff to draw him into the general engagement he wished to avoid.[9] The exaggerated scale of the Meschianza was deliberately throwing dust in Washington's eyes with the result that he refused to commit the full extent of the forces needed to destroy the British Army when it was in 'Enemy's country' and most vulnerable as 'a column of 8 or 10 miles in length.'[10]

Although the Meschianza was sanctioned by Howe, as was his 'order' to Montrésor, Clinton was the beneficiary of these 'false movements'. Taking over from Howe only on 24 May, he commanded the 'March' to New York. Clinton can only have been impressed by all these 'movements'—including the Meschianza—which enabled him to get well clear of the city before Washington could begin harassing the military column.

An astute military strategist, Clinton was also a fragile, brittle man who needed to surround himself with those whom he could trust. Arriving safely in New York, he could reflect with satisfaction on his first engagement as commander-in-chief: his army had survived intact, ready to fight another day … but only so long as his political masters in London willed it. Now that the goal of total victory had almost certainly gone for ever, the politics of the war had changed, and it was more than ever necessary, he believed, to have on his general staff those who understood how this war must now be fought. He must begin clearing out the old guard.

Whether Grey knew it, then, sending John to New York on 6 September with news of the Light Infantry's recent exploits in Rhode Island was perfect timing. For

John, ambitious as ever, this was a golden opportunity to push himself forward with the new commander-in-chief. Certainly, to judge by the letter to his uncle from New York, which began on '12th Sept' and ended on 'September 17th', John was all optimism: writing 'as a messenger of good news from General Grey', he summarized the current military events, beginning with the expedition for 'the relief of Rhode Island' and ending with: 'I know not our views at all but I believe we are to remain at or about New York this winter.'

Aware that his uncle, ever the businessman, needed a current sense of the war for commercial purposes, John also volunteered 'the Data' on events but little more, being as 'I am tired of forming erroneous opinions'. Amongst 'the Data' was that 'the Rebels stand fast for Independence but profess a great desire to come to an accommodation with us on those terms. The cry of the people is for it.' Revealing something of the routine work he was engaged on as Grey's aide-de-camp, he told how the people 'cannot, in their conversation with Prisoners, Flags of Truce or other communications we may have with them, conceal their aversion to the French'.

Meantime, not a word from Grey about John's prospects for promotion. Instead, John fretted that 'my General is not yet returned' from New England to New York 'which keeps me on the figits and not without anxiety.'[11] Waiting in the cauldron of Headquarters, John must bide his time: gauging the military mood of the new commander-in-chief required caution and patience. Kemble was also on tenterhooks. He was one of the 'old Officers',[12] and in this febrile atmosphere of change and uncertainty, he risked falling casualty to the new broom, or what he termed Clinton's 'wavering, strange, mad Behavior.'[13] Indeed, the writing had been on the wall for Kemble as early as 'May 1st & 2d' when 'Sir Henry Clinton sailed this day to Philadelphia to take upon him the Command. Lord Rawdon and Capt. Sutherland' accompanied him and had been granted the privilege of 'raising provincial Battalions'. As a result, 'both have their views'. In Rawdon's case, however, this meant that if 'his Company in the Guards does not succeed, the temporary rank of Colonel may give him a plea to be appointed Adjutant General if Colonel Paterson should decline, which I think will be the case.'

Signing off in his journal for that day, Kemble wailed in anguish: 'what am I to do?—why wretch, Grin and bear it for you are not in a position to kick poor devil.'[14] He was under no illusions: Rawdon was a long-time protégé of Clinton's, his appointment as 'Supernumerary Aid-de-Camp to Maj-Gen Clinton' dating back to '15th Jan. 1776'.[15] Hence, it came as no surprise when news arrived from Philadelphia that one of Clinton's first orders on taking over from Howe was, on '25th May 1778 … to appoint Capt. Lord Rawdon … to the Command of a Provincial Corps to be raised and styled the Provincials of Ireland with the Rank of Colonel'.

Hard on the heels of this 'favor' came the announcement on '30th May 1778' that 'the Commander in Chief has been pleased to appoint the following officers to

be his Aids-de-Camp: Major Duncan Drummond of the Royal Artillery; Colonel
Lord Rawdon of the Volunteers of Ireland…'[16] Finally came proof of Kemble's worst
fears when, on 'Saturday June 27th … General Robertson this day arrived from
Philadelphia' and 'likewise says that Lord Rawdon is appointed Adjutant General,
Sir Henry Clinton his author; this most like true and whatever I have thought.'[17]

This was too much for Kemble to 'grin and bear', and on 9 January 1779 he
wrote to Lord Barrington, the Minister of War, complaining that, 'on Sir Henry
Clinton succeeding to the Command, I was again set aside and what I think I had
pretentions to conferred by him on a Junior Officer in every respect; this was a grating
Circumstance and could not but give me pain, and tho' I have all imaginable reason
to be pleased with the present Adjutant General, I cannot but feel myself Injured.'[18]

This was only the half of it. To compensate for this 'grating Circumstance', Kemble
requested that Clinton 'remove me to an old Regiment under his Command'. That
way, with his pension secure, he could remain as deputy adjutant general. However,
even this was not an option: according to Kemble's entry on 'Jan 3d', which laid
out 'the tenor of our Conversation', Clinton 'replied he did not know how it could
be done' and 'would promise nothing.' It seems he 'saw many Objections' but the
main one was that 'by putting me into an old Regiment while I continued in the
Adjutant General's Department, he should lose a field officer, and probably an Active
one, which in the present situation of Affairs would not be agreeable'. There was
only one conclusion Kemble could draw: 'I've reason to think he wishes me, from
the foregoing, to give up my Appointment of Deputy Adjutant General. Kemble
explained all this to Barrington and asked him to intercede. To no avail: Clinton
had set his sights on patronizing this 'field officer' and had no wish to 'lose' him
just to placate an old officer.

So, who was this 'field officer', this 'Active one' who, by 3 January 1779, had
caught Clinton's eye? If Kemble believed it was John, he certainly made no mention
of his suspicions in his *Journal*. Like many such military diaries, his *Journal* was
a day-by-day record of events. For him, these events included promotions and
appointments touching on him at Headquarters. Inevitably, there were days when
there was 'Nothing extraordinary': one such in 1778 was 'Thursday 24th December' as
were 'Sunday, Dec. 27th to Thursday, 31st'.[19] So why was there 'nothing extraordinary'
in Kemble's *Journal* on 'December 28, 1778' when, that same day, Major Clayton
of the 17th Regiment recorded in his 'Orderly Book' that 'Capt. André of the 26th
Regiment is appointed Aid de Camp to the Commander in Chief'?[20]

It may be that Kemble had other thoughts preoccupying him. Headquarters was
a hive of ill-feeling at this time: one of his damning observations on 9 November
was that 'General Officers and Commander in Chief in general upon bad terms',
the reason being 'want of steadiness in Commander in Chief.' Clearly, Kemble's
opinions should be taken with a pinch of caution: much of the ill-feeling stemmed
from professional jealousies as Clinton put a personal stamp on his command. Among

these 'Senior Officers', the 'great Complaint' was actuated by the burning desire for honour and glory in a war with ever-diminishing prospects for either. At first, each new 'Command' was sought after, as when Major Sutherland, 'late Aid-de-Camp' to Clinton, 'sailed about the 25th [of October 1778] for Bermuda' on an expedition. Again, when, on 7 November, 'Lieut. Col. Campbell' was appointed to lead an expedition to 'St Augustine … thence to Georgia or South Carolina', Kemble made an 'Observation' that 'this Command to Lieut. Col. Campbell gives cause of great Complaint to Brigadier Leslie, Col. O'Hara of the Guards, etc. Senior Officers.'[21]

With the war going badly, however, enthusiasm for honour and glory soon waned, and, a year on, these same 'Senior Officers' found any excuse not to serve. In September 1779, Leslie was tipped 'to take the Command in Georgia'. This was on 3 September, but on 'Monday Sept 6th', Leslie was suddenly 'so ill that he cannot go to Georgia.' Similarly, 'Lord Rawdon's Corps' had joined an expedition to the Chesapeake in May 1779, but by September of that year Rawdon was seeking to return home, claiming he was incapacitated and that 'it will be entirely impossible for him to reassume the office of Adjutant General to the Army.'[22] The real reason, however, was that, as Rawdon told Clinton, he had 'no longer the honour of being upon those terms of mutual confidence with your Excellency which alone could prevail upon me to continue in a station whose duties are most irksome to me.'[23] In May, Clinton had already parted company with his other trusted confidant, Major Drummond, over a dispute with London concerning promotions for provincial officers.[24] Worse was to come, however, when Clinton lost the support of 'his newest confidant, Lieutenant Colonel Charles Stuart,' who, as 'Rawdon's brother-in-law,'[25] felt bound to stand by family ties. Clinton was becoming increasingly isolated and beset by enemies.[26]

Kemble, of course, had his own grounds for 'Complaint', but these now revolved round his despairing search for security in retirement rather than any quest for honour and glory. Nevertheless, Rawdon's decision to return home presented Kemble with an irresistible opportunity to, again, press his case for promotion. Yet, John's appointment as aide-de-camp in December 1778 and Clinton's rebuff in January 1779 should have alerted Kemble to this latest threat to his prospects for promotion. If not, Clinton's decision to send John to Amboy in April 1779 as one of the 'Commissioners … to treat with the Rebel Deputies on an Exchange of Prisoners'[27] should surely have signalled that here was a rising star to watch out for.

As if that were not forewarning enough, John was also making a name for himself in battle: on 31 May 1779, Clinton led an attack on two forts, Stony Point and Fort Fayette, overlooking the Hudson just south of West Point. The two forts were captured and, on 1 June 'John André, Aid-de-Camp', was given the honour by Clinton of receiving the surrender. Doubtless keen—after Congress's 'perfidious' behaviour following the capitulation at Fort St. John's back in 1775—to show how agreements among gentlemen officers should be honoured, John took the formal surrender 'on the Glacis of Fort Fayette', declaring from there that 'His Excellency Sir Henry Clinton and Commodore Sir George Collier grant to the garrison of Fort la Fayette terms of safety to the persons and property (contained in the fort) of the garrison, they surrendering themselves prisoners of war. The officers shall be permitted to wear their side-arms.'[28]

If there were a message for the Rebels, it fell on deaf ears. Fatally, John had, meantime, caught the eye of American propagandists with his political squib published in Rivington's *Royal Gazette* back in January. Entitled 'Captain André's Dream', this polemical treatise lashed various Rebel grandees, including 'Chief-justice McKean … Mr Deane … Gen. Lee [and] the President of the Congress, Mr Jay',[29] charging them with crimes against their own people. Not one to miss the opportunity to join the mounting war of words, the *New Jersey Gazette* counterpunched, roundly debunking the symbolism of John's capitulation ceremony at Fort Fayette and mocking that 'Mr André signed a capitulation in all the pomp of a vain-glorious solemnity on the very edge of the glacis, which he had gained under cover of a flag.'[30]

All the while Kemble sat festering at Headquarters. His frustrations with the repeated 'favor' shown John finally came out in the open in July 1779 when, in a 'Letter to Lord Rawdon' dated 'July 14th', he wrote how 'I mentioned to your Lordship some time ago that I had received General Gage's directions to give in his Son's for the Purchase of a Company; allow me to remind you of it; to assure you that Mr Gage is in the nineteenth Year of Age and was an older Lieut in the 7th Regiment than Captain André when he was allowed to purchase it in the 44th.'[31]

These jealousies came to a head in September 1779 when 'Lord Rawdon having this day assured me that it will be entirely impossible for him to reassume the office of Adjutant General to the Army under your Command, and having given me free leave to make use of the pretentions which the Number of Years I have served in the department may entitle me to,' Kemble wrote to Clinton on 'Sept. 6th 1779' that 'I therefore take the liberty of submitting myself as a Candidate for that appointment.' The upshot was that 'the next Morning his Excellency told me he had received my letter but could give no answer to it, nor did he know he should appoint an Adjutant General.'

Unwilling to let the matter lie, Kemble pressed his case: 'I replied if he should find it necessary to appoint one, might I hope for his Countenance.' Put on the spot, Clinton came clean, saying 'that every General Officer had those about him that he wished to promote; that General Gage promoted me, he my Lord Rawdon etc. I then said, I observed from his language, I had little to expect; he repeated he had those about him he wished to Serve, and that I should think it hard to have a Junior Officer put over my head, adding that the Office was of such a Nature that everyone wished to fill it with a person of their own, in whom they could place an implicit Confidence. I then said I see, Sir. I have nothing to Expect and thanked him for being so Explicit.'

Kemble had anticipated this: he promptly spoke to 'Captain Ross, Lord Cornwallis's Aid-de-Camp' and 'desired [him] to repeat the above to his Lordship, with Proposals I had made to Captain André, as I thought it proper he should know what I had done.' On 16 September, Kemble again wrote to Clinton saying: 'Captain André informed me a few days ago that he had mentioned to your Excellency my desire of quitting the appointment of Deputy Adjutant General (which carries the rank of Major with it) upon conditions he is already acquainted with, either to himself or such other Officer as you may approve.'[32] This invited some form of response, but, hearing nothing, Kemble sent a chaser on 15 October, chivvying that 'Your Excellency some time ago desired me to defer troubling on the subject of my Negotiation with Captain André till the Packet had sailed … may I now take the liberty of putting you in mind of it.'

While awaiting a response, Kemble gloated as the misfortunes of war rained down on Clinton: 'How must our Commander in Chief feel with all these blows', he wrote with heavy irony, before listing with undisguised contempt how these 'blows' came 'added to his own Conduct, despised and detested by the Army, his unheard-of Promotion to the first Department of Boys not three years in the service, his neglect of old Officers, and his wavering, strange, mad Behavior.' Kemble's damning conclusion was that 'if Government does not remove him soon, our Affairs in this Country will be totally undone.'

Finally on 23 October 1779 came the news that 'this day my resignation was accepted by the Commander in Chief and Captain André, 54th, declared in orders as my Successor.'[33] The formal announcement in Clinton's 'Order Book' read: 'the Commander in Chief is pleased to appoint Captain André, of 54th Regiment, Deputy Adjutant General with the rank of Major in the Army, until his Majesty's pleasure is known, in the room of Lieut. Col. Kemble who resigns that employment; therefore all Reports and Returns heretofore made to Lieut. Col. Kemble are in future to be made to Major André.'[34]

First, Lord Rawdon, now John: these were the 'Boys not three years in the service' whom, Kemble complained, Clinton had promoted to the 'neglect of old Officers' like him. Yet, this was a war that, by its changing nature, demanded that merit be rewarded, if not ahead of, certainly as much as, long service. If so, did John deserve this promotion on merit or was he merely the beneficiary of the time-honoured desire by leaders to fill key posts 'with a person of their own'? In his trek from St. John's to Pennsylvania and subsequent imprisonment in Lancaster then Carlisle, John had shown a willingness to endure hardship and danger in the midst of a hostile enemy. His hard service in combat at St. John's, on the Philadelphia campaign, along the New England coast and more recently in New Jersey all spoke volumes for his willingness to take up arms, if necessary at the point of a bayonet.

There seems no doubt, then, that, based on this war record alone, John merited Clinton's patronage. Nevertheless, the British Army abounded with swashbuckling officers eager to earn honour and glory in battle. What Clinton was looking for, however, was a junior officer after his own heart: someone who was also industrious, intelligent, imaginative, compassionate, honourable. John was all these. Above all though, Clinton sought an officer in whom he could place 'implicit Confidence'. The quality he was looking for was loyalty beyond the call of duty. John came highly recommended by Grey, but if Clinton were looking for loyalty above all else in an officer, he was unlikely to take another general's word for it.

John must have done something to make Clinton realize that here was the loyal officer he was looking for. The one occasion when Clinton witnessed at close quarters John's capacity for extreme loyalty would have been in the aftermath of the controversial events which occurred at 'Tapaan' on the night of 27–28 September 1778. Recording these events in his *Journal*, John made them seem matter-of-fact as he told how 'General Grey on advancing received certain Intelligence of the situation of the Dragoons, a whole Regiment of which lay at Tapaan, ten miles from Newbridge'. In echoes of the night-attack on General Wayne's detachment at Paoli a year earlier, Grey 'was successful enough to come unperceived within one mile of the place so as to enable him to detach six Companies of Light Infantry by 3 in the morning to spread round the houses and barns.'

Loyal to the last word, John stuck to the bare facts as he recorded how 'the whole Corps within six or eight men were killed or taken prisoners… Amongst the prisoners were the Colonel, Major, a Captain and three or four subalterns. The rest were killed.[35]' There, John's report ended. As with the Paoli attack, these facts became substantially the basis of the official *Gazette* letter[36] published in London. John's facts also appeared as the common currency of the British camp, repeated in, among other contemporary military journals, the *Diary*[37] of Brigadier General James Pattison, commandant of New York at the time.

Kemble was having nothing of it. Initially matter-of-fact like John, his *Journal* entry for 27 September told how 'General Grey was more lucky by getting notice of a party of Dragoons lying on his Route, called Lady Washington's, which he effectually surprised and without one Shot being fired; out of 120, killed 50, and took as many prisoners—the colonel by name Baylor, and Major, with one Captain and six subalterns; of the latter number the colonel like to recover, the Major dead'.

As John had done, Kemble could have stopped there. Instead he continued, singling out 'the 2d Battalion Light Infantry', but not to praise them, rather to damn them because they 'were thought to be active and bloody on this Service.' He knew, of course, that John was serving in the '2d Battalion Light Infantry'. This begs the question whether, given the rivalry building up between the two of them, Kemble was looking to sully John's reputation. If so, Kemble's 'bloody' version of events can be taken with yet another pinch of caution.

Yet, in his version of events, Kemble also said that 'it's acknowledged on all hands they might have spared some who made no resistance, the whole being compleatly surprized and all their Officers in bed.'[38] This was damning, but it seems Kemble was not the only one making these claims. When the Americans amplified it into 'Baylor's Massacre', their protests could be dismissed as warring words, but then arch-loyalists—among them New York Judge Thomas Jones—also lamented that 'a merciful mind must shudder at the bare mention of so barbarous, so inhuman, so unchristian an act.'[39] Assuming, then, that the 'bloody' version was closer to the truth than the account in John's *Journal* and the subsequent *Gazette* letter, this begs the question whether the British camp attempted to cover up this 'bloody ... Service'. If so, was John implicated by virtue of his official report? His sense of loyalty was on trial and would have been tested in full view of the new commander-in-chief.

The Tapaan controversy could not have come at a worse time for Clinton. British military policy had reached a crucial crossroads regarding the proper and necessary conduct of hostilities. The entry into the war by Britain's sworn enemy, France, had changed the moral dynamic, as the Peace Commissioners tried to warn in their 'Manifesto and Proclamation' appeal to the Americans published in October.[40] Thus far 'the extremes of war' had been avoided, but now 'the whole contest is changed' which meant 'the laws of self-preservation must direct the conduct of Great Britain', and military strategy must, henceforth, have as its purpose to 'desolate'[41] America.

This explains why, just two weeks before the Tapaan expedition, John was writing to his uncle, and, among 'the Data' he submitted, was the observation that the Americans 'cannot be without fears that we may begin devastation'. A number of the 'General Officers' were in favour of implementing this new policy whole-heartedly, among them General Grey. Clinton was against: for him, the risk was that 'devastation' of property could get out of hand and lead to wanton violence against persons.

John thought like Clinton. In the letter to his uncle, he had relished the raids on property along the New England coast, describing the attacks at 'New London ... Buzzard Bay ... Bedford a great Privateer harbour' and, in great detail, how 'a very considerable quantity of stores and 60 sixty sail of vessels [were] burnt ... a fort' [was] 'demolished' [and] 'a few houses of committee and Colonels of Militia etc accidentally took fire to our great mortification, as our orders were only to destroy store houses.'[42]

As John reported it to his uncle, Grey followed Clinton's 'orders' on this occasion and eschewed contact with enemy forces on at least two occasions during these raids. That way, casualties could be avoided. In his *Journal*, John admitted that there were casualties, but just the once, when the rebels 'fired at the advanced party and were not quick enough getting off.' In a foretaste of things to come, however, he noted the result which, chillingly, was that 'three or four men of the Enemy were found bayonetted, one an officer.'[43] Grey's men were getting to like the bayonet.

For John, wanton violence was outside the honourable rules of war that should be applied by both sides. When, during the Philadelphia campaign, he had heard reports that 'immediate death' was the punishment meted out by Congress's 'Committee of Safety' to 'Country people' found trading with the British Army, he joked wryly whether Britain should follow suit such that 'were men reduced to the agreeable alternative of choosing by whom they would be hanged, principle alone must turn the scale, so that by threatening at the same rate as the enemy, we should render a whole Continent conscientious.'[44]

Clinton was right to apprehend how quickly a policy of 'devastation' could get out of hand. Just two weeks after the scorched-earth raids along the New England coast, Grey was leading the 'Tapaan' expedition, but, left to his own devices, he now presided over the 'bloody ... Service' on American officers and men. According to Kemble, there were noisy ructions at headquarters in the aftermath of the expedition. If, as was the case, Grey were responsible for the 'bloody' events, this put him on a collision course with Clinton which would explain why, according to Kemble, the 'General Officers and Commander in Chief' were 'upon bad terms' at this time. It suited Kemble to blame this on a 'want of steadiness' in his personal nemesis, the 'Commander in Chief', but this was wide of the truth: Clinton had decided that a senior officer must take responsibility for the 'bloody ... Service' at Tapaan. The upshot was that Grey resigned and went home. Cornwallis, the senior general on the New Jersey expedition from which Grey was detached to Tapaan, also resigned, but, arriving in London, he was ordered to return to America.[45]

Self-evidently, it was not in either Grey's or Clinton's interests to have these matters come into the open, hence why there was no court-martial and no official enquiry. This left John in an awkward, if not impossible, situation: loyalty to Grey, his patron, dictated that he should keep silent, but by doing so he risked being complicit in the wanton violence at Tapaan, and he had joined the army to restore his family's honour not tarnish it. Unsurprisingly, the quandary hit John hard, and it certainly seems more than coincidental that, having enjoyed good health thus far, he suddenly became 'ill with what he described as a "treacherous complaint"'[46] in the months following the expedition. The 'complaint' became so serious that, in early 1779, Clinton sent him to recuperate at Oyster Bay, one of the quieter military outposts on Long Island. There, John joined his friend, Lieutenant Colonel Simcoe, who had been in 'winter quarters' there since 'the 19th of November'[47] and was amusing himself courting the sisters of John Townsend, one of Washington's most active spies.

In these circumstances, it seems inconceivable—given Clinton's express wish to surround himself with a person 'of his own' in whom he could place an 'implicit Confidence'—that he would have appointed John as his aide-de-camp in December 1778 on Grey's recommendation alone. Clinton and John had to have reached some private understanding concerning how the events at Tapaan should be represented officially. John would have been given to understand by Clinton—explicitly or implicitly—that his loyal duty was to remain silent … not for the good of Grey but for the wider good of the war.

Laid out thus, John had no option but to defer to his commander-in-chief. This meant drawing a veil over the whole episode, which explains why his treatment of the Tapaan expedition was so perfunctory and why he did not include the expedition among the 'forty-four maps and plans' in his *Journal*. It explains why, in the six weeks following the events on the night of 27–28 September, John's *Journal* never once mentioned Grey, and why the *Journal* ended so abruptly on 15 November 1778 when 'the Troops were put into winter quarters'.[48] It also explains why the *Gazette* letter went out under Earl Cornwallis's name not Grey's and why John's *Journal* disappeared for generations into the Grey family archives.

Last but not least, it explains why, so soon after the events at Tapaan, John began his meteoric rise into Clinton's 'Family'.[49] Once inside that 'Family', John moved quickly to earn his rapid promotion with the promise of a 'fortunate or able stroke'[50] that he had brought from Philadelphia in June 1778 and first revealed to Clinton on 10 May 1779. Clinton quickly convinced himself that this 'stroke' would launch the secret war he now sought to wage in earnest. This growing emphasis on secret war as a major strategy led to John's increased favour in Clinton's 'Family', but caused, first, Rawdon, then Kemble, to resign from the adjutant general's department that September and led to John's appointment to the post of deputy adjutant general that October.

CHAPTER 25

'These Double Faces'

As John was preparing to join the evacuation from Philadelphia on 17 June 1778, one American officer was watching events unfold with undisguised glee. General Benedict Arnold, 'Hero of Saratoga' and the failed invasion of Quebec, had been appointed military commander of the soon-to-be liberated city. Finally, after all his military toils, tribulations and torments, he was getting the civic recognition he so richly deserved. With that status would surely come all the trappings that should justly accrue to him as one of the great warriors of the Revolution: the power, the wealth, and, last but not least, the pick of the Philadelphia Belles, those fourteen 'Maidens' whom the British had so wantonly paraded as their trophies at the Meschianza. Now the British were going, and any day soon it would be Arnold's turn. For him as a soldier, the war was, surely, over: a widower aged thirty-seven and, more to the point, 'a cripple in the service of my country',[1] he doubtless told himself he thoroughly deserved all the sweets of victory, including the comforts of a beautiful young wife, especially if she were from a Tory family desperate to turn its back on its suspect past, cleanse its political image and embrace the future that was the Revolution.

Arriving in the city within days of the British departure, Arnold quickly set about accumulating those spoils. First came the shady commercial connections which his newfound power gave him access to. So brazen was he that he was 'almost at once suspected of corruptly profiting from the disorder in Philadelphia'. Next came the move into the John Penn house in Market Street, an 'establishment quite out of keeping'[2] with his humble status as a working officer in an army at war. All this attracted ill-favour from the patriot zealots—President of Congress, Joseph Reed especially—who were looking to maintain the purity and integrity of the Revolution.

Finally came Arnold's open fraternization with the Philadelphia Belles. Initially placed 'under a patriotic ban'[3] by the forces of revolutionary fervour, 'the Mischianza ladies' were progressively rehabilitated at Arnold's behest. There was naked self-interest in this act of reconciliation: he had set his sights on the belle of all Belles, Margaret ('Peggy'), the youngest of Judge Shippen's three daughters. As early as September of that year, Arnold began courting Peggy, his age, his status, his power, his swarthiness, all suggesting he was the hunter, she—young, pretty, and available—the prey. She was all these things, but she was also steely, single-minded and scheming: nobody stole all she had been brought up to believe in and could be allowed to get away with it, certainly not if those nobodies were all so many hypocrites from Congress merely replacing one so-called tyranny with another. The British had been forced to abandon Philadelphia. So be it: she would fight on alone. Call her 'spoiled' in her wish to get her own way, but that was to miss what energized her: 'never fond of gadding'[4] according to a friend of the Shippen family, she knew what she wanted, and she had set her mind on getting it. Her heart would have to follow. Meantime, she must dissemble and deceive, fake and flatter.

The evidence was in the drawing John made of her ahead of the Meschianza. Even before the evacuation, the loyalist ladies of Philadelphia must learn to put on 'ye Mask' and, as Grace Galloway wrote in her diary, assume 'these Double faces' in anticipation of the 'Congress folks'[5] arriving to reclaim the city. Like the extravaganza itself, the dress and the head-dress John had Peggy don were 'ye Mask' drawing attention away from the portrait's underlying purpose, which was fixed in her eyes, their position central to the portrait clearly signalling that here was the work's focal point.

Sketch portrait of Miss Margaret (Peggy) Shippen by John André. (Yale University Art Gallery)

Sketch drawing by John André of one of the Meschianza Belles, possibly Rebecca Redman. (Library Company of Philadelphia)

John understood who Peggy was, as he focused on the look in her eyes. The portrait was a partnership between artist and sitter: it is inconceivable Peggy would have allowed this portrait as a permanent statement of her, aged just eighteen, unless she first approved the character whom John made appear from within those 'direct, determined eyes'.[6] Compare this to John's treatment of another Meschianza lady— very probably Rebecca Redman—who was reduced to a likeness, no feeling in her to give the sense of a living portrait. Significantly, her face was shown at half-profile, not full frontal as with Peggy. This angle emphasised this lady's chin and nose. It could also have made something of her eyes except that John reduced them to dark empty vessels staring into nothingness. Whoever this lady was, her sole purpose was to illustrate the head-dress that John imagined for the extravaganza.

By contrast, through Peggy's eyes sitter and artist were communicating intently. Looking at each other, they were fixing themselves as working partners. That Peggy was the sitter and not either of her two sisters, Polly (Mary) or Sally (Sarah), was significant in this regard. More so was that, just as Arnold would find when he began courting her, Peggy very likely made the decision that she should be the sitter. Time and again as their partnership unfolded, she made the running, not John. This was the case when the notice went out publicizing the Meschianza. John included Peggy and her two sisters in the first report that was published but then removed their names from the later publicity. The assumption subsequently was that their father 'had forbidden his daughter to appear,'[7] but, given how little control Judge Shippen had over, certainly, Peggy's future conduct, more likely she made the decision to withdraw at the last minute, obliging her two sisters to follow suit. Again, it was she who insisted John remove her name from the publicity: that way she could make it appear to the incoming 'Congress folks' that she had snubbed the British.

John let Peggy make the running in these early encounters. Certain by then that the British were leaving Philadelphia, he was not prepared to acknowledge the war was over. He was already formulating its next phase: America's revolution was, clearly, still vulnerable, its Congress politicians and Continental Army officers at loggerheads over power, money, land, the spoils of war. Greed, he believed, was the Rebels' eternal weakness, secret war the weapon to expose the fault lines, he the best person to exploit them. To put his plan into action, John must catch the eye of the new commander-in-chief. To do this he must arrive in New York armed with a readymade arsenal of agents primed for that secret war. He had inherited and nurtured Galloway's connections in Pennsylvania, but Philadelphia was the real prize, and, therein, women held the keys.

Thus far in this conflict, women were an untapped resource for the British. John changed that: for him, then, the Meschianza was a scouting mission to test which of the 'Maidens' were up for the challenge, ready to join him in his very secret war. Given her ultra-loyalist pretensions, Rebecca Franks was a likely choice, but she had a noisy mouth and was indiscreet. John courted assiduously Rebecca Redman, but, with love on her mind, she only had ears for the poet in John. Peggy Chew hankered after frippery and London lace, but not much else. Peggy Shippen, on the other hand, came at John head-on, literally, as was evident by the portrait. Moreover, she had the wherewithal to help him search out and deliver the coup-de-théâtre that would launch his secret war: beautiful, bold, intelligent, determined, resourceful, ruthless, nerveless. Above all, she was willing and able to wear the 'double faces' needed to fight his secret war.

There seems no doubt that there was an agreement between the two of them: what Peggy had in mind could not be accomplished without a friend at British Headquarters, and it needed to be someone she knew and could trust, not the likes of Galloway or Colonel Patterson. The only question was when she and John made their agreement, and, given how quickly their plans fell into place in the wake of the British evacuation, more than likely it was when John was still in the city.

Top of Peggy's action list had to be for her to snare a pliable Continental Army officer. Not for her the lowly Major Edward Burd who married Peggy's sister, Elizabeth, in the December following the evacuation. For her and John's plan to work, Peggy knew that nothing short of a general would suffice. When Peggy let John in on her decision to marry as part of the plan is unclear, but instinct would have told her to keep this to herself until it was a fait accompli. Arnold was the obvious choice: for all his status and power as the military commander of Philadelphia, his political blundering made him easy prey. So controversial was Arnold that, by February 1779, Christopher Marshall was hearing rumours in Lancaster that 'Gen. Arnold has left Philada. and gone over to the English'. That was on 8 February. A week later, news came to Marshall of 'disputes between Gen. Arnold and proceedings of Council'.[8] So loud were these ructions they even reached New York, from where Clinton wrote to London with reports that 'Arnold was said to have resigned.'[9] This was premature, but through all this, Arnold continued his pursuit of Peggy and, after a few coy rebuffs as befitted a lady of demure style, she finally allowed herself to be 'Burgoyned' by 'her adoring general.'[10]

The marriage took place on 8 April 1779, and, again, someone made sure London was kept abreast, the *Public Advertiser* carrying the news, 'Married, Major-General Arnold to Miss Peggy Shippen' in its 26 July edition. By then, Arnold was not the political catch he was nine months earlier. Matters between him and Congress had continued to deteriorate: on 19 March, Arnold resigned his command in Philadelphia, and his commercial peculations were 'turned over to Washington for trial by court martial'.[11] No matter: Arnold might no longer be military commander of Philadelphia, but he was still a general and a war hero. That sufficed for what Peggy had in view: whatever discussions Arnold and Peggy had had prior to the wedding, she knew he was ripe for the plan she and John had in mind. Again, she moved decisively: on 5 May 1779, she had her husband compose a letter to Washington, which, appealing one general to another, cast Arnold as 'a cripple in the service of my country' and made Congress the enemy of all—Washington included—in the Continental Army. That she had a hand in this letter, or, more likely, prompted it, seems certain, not only from its unctuous tone of abasement—a style quite alien to Arnold's character—but also from the entreaty being made that the 'Court Martial may be ordered to sit as soon as possible'.[12] Why the hurry for Arnold, unless, that is, his new wife was, for her own reasons, prodding him mercilessly?

At the same time, Peggy had her new husband contact British Headquarters in New York, a process which began 'about the month of June 1779' when, according to later testimony by Joseph Stansbury, an agent of the British, 'Arnold then communicated to me, under a solemn obligation of secrecy, his intention of opening his services to the commander-in-chief of the British forces in any way that would most effectually restore the former government and destroy the usurped authority of Congress, either by immediately joining the British army or cooperating on some concealed plan with Sir Henry Clinton.'[13]

That Arnold chose Stansbury for this communication under 'solemn obligation of secrecy', and that Stansbury responded without hesitation was not happenstance: it can only have meant that each of them was fully acquainted with the other's treasonous affiliations. This prior knowledge was essential: Philadelphia was a hive of suspicion, with Congress rounding up anyone suspected of treasonous association with the British Army during the occupation. So feverish were the Patriots that, to set an example, two of these traitors, Abraham Carlisle and John Roberts, had been 'actually put to Death, Hang'd on the Commons'[14] the previous November.

Since Arnold was new to the city, it is unlikely he would have known of Stansbury prior to taking over as military commander. Nor, since Stansbury was a small-time merchant who 'kept a glass and china shop in Front Street', is it plausible that their paths should have crossed naturally once Arnold arrived in the city. Peggy, on the other hand, was an obvious point of contact, but even she would only have known of Stansbury's secret affiliations if someone she could trust told her about them. Most likely this source was John, a supposition made more certain given that Stansbury expressly sought John out when he made hurried arrangements to travel 'secretly to New York'.[15] Moreover, Stansbury initiated the contact with British Headquarters at the behest of a 'Lady'[16] whom John identified as 'the other Peggy now Mrs Arnold.'[17]

Stansbury arrived in New York on 10 May (not June as he mistakenly recalled) and met with John the same day. In the letter to Stansbury immediately following the meeting, John issued a series of instructions, including that 'the other Channel you mention'd to me this morning thro' which a communication was formerly held must be kept unacquainted with this'.[18] Here was acknowledgment that Stansbury had had prior contact with the British in intelligence matters, but that this previous 'other Channel' was not with John. The identities of the two parties to this 'other Channel' were not made clear at the time, but, it subsequently transpired that, at the Philadelphia end was Samuel Wallis,[19] who, 'with his friend was,' according to

Stansbury, 'extremely useful to General Howe.'[20] At the British Headquarters end would have been Lord Rawdon, who, then the adjutant general, had responsibility under Clinton for British intelligence activities.

Arguably, it made sound sense that this 'other Channel … must be kept unacquainted': Clinton understood, especially after the previous unexplained leaks at Headquarters, that the fewer people who knew about such a high-value new 'Channel' the better. He would, moreover, have been left in no doubt that Arnold's approach came through the Philadelphia network established by John prior to the evacuation. The letter sent to Stansbury was passed to Clinton for his prior approval and, in it John made no secret of these existing connections, explaining that 'the Lady might write to me at the Same time with one of her intimates. She will guess who I mean, the latter remaining ignorant of interlining & sending the letter. I will write myself to the friend to give occasion for a reply.'[21]

John would also have run past Clinton the draft of 'the letter' he proposed sending simultaneously to this 'friend', Margaret (Peggy) Chew, his partner for the Meschianza, as part of this new 'Channel'. The way John portrayed the future modalities of this new 'Channel', it was as if his sole activity in Philadelphia during the five-month silence in his *Journal* had been the cultivation of what he called 'the little Society of third & fourth Street' where resided the 'fair philadelphians',[22] and that the Meschianza was the culmination of this work, put on solely for its value as a plausible cover in future communications along this new 'Channel'. John instructed Stansbury that 'letters may talk of the Meschianza and other nonsense'[23] and explained in his letter to Peggy Chew that he 'wou'd with pleasure have sent you drawings of head dresses had I been as much of a millener here as I was at Philadelphia in meschianza times, but from occupation as well as ill health I have been obliged to abandon the pleasing Study of what relates to the Ladies'.[24]

John went further still, using the letter to Stansbury to showcase to Clinton his command of intelligence techniques. Promoting himself as a spymaster-in-the-making already proficient in the necessary intelligence tradecraft, John reeled off a series of technical instructions, ordering Stansbury to 'leave me a long book similar to yours', setting up a secret code in which Three Numbers make a word' with 'the number representing the word' and explaining that 'in writings to be discover'd by a process, F is fire A acid.' However impressed or not Clinton was, it is clear that, by May 1779, John was already fully familiar with the technical skills of spycraft. This contrasted with Kemble who, if his private *Journal* were an indication of his working life, was ignorant of all technical matters regarding intelligence, despite being John's immediate predecessor as deputy adjutant general.

John had his sights set on more than Kemble's post. As was evident from the letter he wrote to one his 'nearest friends' in late 1779, he was already eying Rawdon's position as adjutant general, conceiving, as he did, 'the discharge of its functions … to be within my reach.'[25] To do this, it was imperative he reserve the new 'Channel' he had opened with Stansbury and Arnold (alias 'Monk'[26]) exclusively for himself. It was not enough to have told Stansbury that 'the other Channel … be kept unacquainted.' He must also exclude Rawdon from the new 'Channel'. To achieve this, John needed Clinton's approval. This would be difficult to come by explicitly.

Instead, John sought Clinton's formal approval for the letter to Stansbury. If given, the approval to also keep Rawdon 'unacquainted' could, thereby, be taken as implicit. John did not need to run the letter past Clinton, as he had already 'this morning' briefed Clinton on what he intended to write. However, 'in his opinion'—so John reasoned plausibly to Clinton—'the Matter … may be so important that I have thought on it afresh and written the enclosed, as I felt much more forcibly than you could do the kind of Confusion such Sudden proposals created when one must deliberate and determine at once.'[27]

Superficially, this punctiliousness had the ring of a dutiful junior officer. By committing these 'Sudden proposals' to paper and enclosing the draft letter to Stansbury, John was merely seeking tacit approval from Clinton to keep 'the other Channel … unacquainted with this' new one, but, by also 'requesting you to transmit' the draft letter to Stansbury 'if it meets with your Excellencys approbation', he was claiming Clinton's formal approval. To ensure Clinton sent the letter in his stead, John made the excuse that 'not finding myself very Well I in consequence of your indulgence on these occasions came into the Country.'

John was brimming with electric energy as he wrote of these 'Sudden Proposals'. In the space of one day, 10 May 1779, he had met with Stansbury, briefed Clinton on that meeting, arranged for Stansbury to have 'a Sloop and Whale boat at his orders'[28] for his return to Philadelphia, written to Clinton from 'York Island', and now gone to 'the Country' to recuperate. No wonder the excitement: for John, so much was at stake: with 'Monk' on the hook, the search could begin for the 'fortunate or able stroke'[29] that would change the course of the war. By his—and Peggy's—endeavours, he had landed the most valuable source of enemy intelligence so far in this unhappy conflict. Once the letter was dispatched to Stansbury, the die was cast. The deadliest plot to undo America's revolution was underway and John's alone to mastermind.

CHAPTER 26

'Mutual Confidence'

With the search now on in earnest for this one 'fortunate or able stroke', John was impatient to move forward, and his letter of 10 May to Stansbury also set out a long list of 'the following hints' meant to goad Arnold's ego. Some were modest in their reach and included coming by the 'contents of dispatches from foreign abettors' or 'original dispatches and papers which might be seized and sent to us'. Equally mundane was information sought on 'Number and position of troops' and the location of 'Magazines' especially 'where any new are forming'. Other 'hints' were quite fantastical in their impracticality and required 'influencing persons of rank with the same favourable disposition in their Several commands in different Quarters'.

Sandwiched between these extremes was a plan for 'concerting the means of a blow of importance',[1] which, given time, would surely be within the reach of a lone general, certainly one of Arnold's experience, seniority and ingenuity. This 'blow of importance' became a recurring—indeed increasingly obsessive—objective for John and Clinton, variously projected to Arnold as 'a grand Stroke'[2] and 'one Shining Stroke'.[3]

Arnold quickly took these early 'hints' on board, and his first letter to John in reply was dated 23 May. Much of the 'Intelligence' in this letter was of only a general political complexion relating to 'the French minister' and 'no Encouragement from Spain.' Setting limits on 'the risk' he was prepared to take, Arnold also explained that 'seizing papers is impossible' the reason being that 'their contents can be known from a member of Congress.' The next seven months brought an intermittent flow of letters with 'Intelligence', but, with the warning that 'life and everything is at stake', Arnold made financial reward for 'the risk and service' an immediate and, thereafter, persistent demand in his negotiations with John.

Although Arnold provided the content that went into his letters, he did not see the final text that arrived on John's desk in New York. There was a long chain between Arnold and John which certainly included Stansbury—'our friend S'[4]—who enciphered the messages in Philadelphia, and Dr Jonathan Odell, a loyalist clergyman from Burlington, New Jersey who had fled to New York[5] and, there, sometimes decoded the messages before passing them to British Headquarters. There were also couriers, among whom John Rattoon of South Amboy, 'whose fidelity' was 'fully assured', and 'Mrs Gordon, who accompanies Mrs Chamier to Philadelphia,'[6] but was unaware what she was carrying.

As was evident from a letter Odell sent to John on 18 July, Peggy was also part of this chain, especially since she could, more plausibly than her husband, visit Stansbury in his 'glass and china shop' and, under this subterfuge, drop off messages and receive them 'immediately delivered' to her as 'Mrs Moore'.[7] It is notable, then, that Arnold's first letter concluded with the well-wishes: 'Madam Ar presents you her particular Compliments'.[8] Given the earlier content of this letter, it is possible Peggy rather than her husband added these 'particular' well-wishes, maybe as she was passing her husband's draft text to Stansbury for enciphering. The sentiments certainly stand apart in their familiarity.

This discordance invites the possibility that there was more to John and Peggy's relationship than a working partnership and that, indeed, they were, at some level, lovers. Opinions differ. According to one historian, 'there is only the slightest foundation for the romantic story that André had been in love with Peggy Shippen, or she with him'. Yet, according to another source: 'poor André was in love with her'—as one of her grandsons wrote more than a century later—'but she refused him for Arnold, keeping a lock of his hair, which we still have.'[9]

Certainly, any suggestion they were lovers before John left Philadelphia seems fanciful: if they were that close, Peggy would surely have joined 'Miss Auchmuty',[10] one of the Meschianza 'maidens', who, following the evacuation from Philadelphia, went with her fiancé, Montrésor, to New York and from there to England. That Peggy expressly 'refused' John for Arnold seems even more counterintuitive: Arnold represented risk, insecurity and unhappiness, whereas John signified the social future she not only yearned for, but also began working towards from the moment John left Philadelphia. Most likely was that, as already outlined, John and Peggy became working partners in the hatching and development of the conspiracy as it unfolded, but with the pursuit of a common goal being enough, at least in the early days, to satisfy a mutual desire for emotional attachment.

If, then, Peggy were behind the well-wishes in the 23 May letter, she was simply telling John that her decision to marry Arnold changed nothing between them and that she and he remained the masterminds behind this conspiracy, Arnold their tool. Recalling the look in Peggy's eyes as she posed for the Meschianza portrait, these well-wishes would have chimed exactly with the reciprocal conviction sealed between the two of them prior to John's departure from Philadelphia. Love, if it were mutual, would only come as a reward following success of their plan.

It is possible, nonetheless, that Arnold was, indeed, behind the 'particular Compliments'. If so, their discordance invites the question why ever Arnold would proffer them, unless, that is, he saw himself as master of the conspiracy. This was entirely within character, Arnold, a venal, egotistical, self-made hero of his own war, for whom money and wealth was the obsessive driver. Given this impulse, Peggy became bait in this conspiracy, her task as his subservient wife being to secure for him the best financial settlement. It seems no coincidence, then, that the well-wishes came immediately after Arnold had set his financial terms in the letter, the price for defection being 'my property here secure and a revenue equivalent to the risk and service done.'[11] Placed so strategically, the well-wishes no longer seem discordant.

Time would tell who—John, Arnold or Peggy—was master of the conspiracy. The immediate test for Arnold would be if John willingly took the bait. In the first letter, John had kept his 'hints' vague how Arnold could deliver 'a general project against the whole Army'. However, Arnold had become impatient. The time had come for British Headquarters to be more precise. Yet, for his second letter John still intended to reply only in vague terms, giving the 'W Side of the North River'[12] as the locus for this 'general project'. Although John was already thinking of West Point as the strategic focus of a 'grand stroke' he wanted Arnold to deliver, to spell it out this early on would be to give the game away prematurely especially since 'mutual confidence'[13] was not yet established. Arnold could be a plant by Washington.

Clinton was even more cautious than John. Deciding that John's draft response was too specific, he amended it, and the final version sent by John in mid-June referred only obliquely to the 'North River'.[14] However, Clinton also vetoed John's plan to make a loosely worded offer of 'Generous Terms ... ample Rewards and Honors'.[15] Instead, he had John apply a strict monetary calculator to 'Rewards' such that 'the delivery of a Corps of 5 or 6000 Men would be rewarded with twice as many thousand Guineas.'[16] This was not a wise first move in the negotiations. Better to be vague in the first instance was the lesson John had learned from his father and uncles. Still only a mere aide-de-camp, John must, nevertheless, defer to his superior officer, the commander-in-chief.

Unsurprisingly, then, these terms were immediately rejected by Arnold as 'not equal to his expectations,'[17] Stansbury deputised to give the bad news in a letter dated 11 July. To make matters worse, Arnold decided to take out his pent-up frustration on John, Peggy ('Mrs Moore') once again set as the bait. On 18 July, he had Odell deliver 'a packet' to John. In it, as Odell explained, was 'one letter for you which I inclose' together with an 'inclosed List of Articles for her own use' that 'Mrs Moore requests' be 'procured for her, and the account for them and the former sent, and She will pay for the whole with thanks.'[18] The list, in Arnold's handwriting, referred only to items 'in the millinary way',[19] including 'Pink Mantua ... Pale Pink Ribbon ... Diaper for Napkins ... Neat Spurs [and] Clouting Diaper.'[20] The message was clear: Peggy was pregnant with her first child, and, if John wanted negotiations for the 'grand stroke' back on track, he must first procure these 'Articles'.

The fate of America now hinged, it seems, on John procuring 'Clouting Diaper' for 'Mrs Moore', but, to Arnold, this was about humiliation: first, 'a set of artful, unprincipled men' from Congress had shredded his 'reputation';[21] now a lowly British captain known only for his macaroni Meschianza had made him beg for a proper reward for all his risk. For the past month, this captain—a mere aide-de-camp—had patronized him with 'hints' about what grand strokes to pull. Arnold had swallowed the humiliation but only because his wife had convinced him this captain could deliver on the financial settlement he deserved, only to find that he could not. This was more than Arnold's impatient ego could stand. Ever the bullyboy, Arnold was determined to make dandy John his lackey.

To ensure John took the bait this time, Arnold included in 'the packet' a letter 'for a Major Giles at Flat-bush which I also inclose.' Giles was an American officer held prisoner by the British and about to be released. It was normal Arnold should want a letter passed to him, but, in the circumstances, it became one more way for Arnold to make John his errand boy. He had Odell spell out to John that he was 'leaving it to yourself to determine whether it is intended for you—though I confess from what my Friend says of it I suspect it is really intended for the person to whom it is addressed.' Moreover, this letter had 'contents to me unknown'.[22]

Left to his own devices, John would surely have responded promptly offering to procure the 'Articles' for Peggy, but, with Clinton now at his elbow and as impatient as Arnold for progress, John had to stand pat. His end-July letter totally ignored the matter of the 'Articles' and focused solely on the financial terms. Lecturing Arnold that 'such sums as are held forth must be in some degree accounted for [and] real Advantage must appear to have arisen from the Expenditure', the letter exhorted in a barely disguised tone of patronizing impertinence, 'permit me to prescribe a little Exertion.' This was Clinton speaking, not John, evident when the letter continued: 'it is the procuring an accurate plan of West Point, with the new roads, New Windsor Constitution, etc An Account of what Vessels, gun boats or Gallies are in the North River or may be shortly built there & the Weight of metal they carry.'[23] Finally, Arnold knew exactly what Clinton wanted and how desperate he was. He could now sit back and bide his time.

He did not have long to wait. Increasingly desperate for progress, Clinton had a change of heart about the 'Articles' and had John write to Peggy on 16 August offering his 'services'. John began the letter addressed to 'Madame' with the explanation that 'Major Giles is so good as to take charge of this letter, which is meant to solicit your remembrance, and to assure you that my respect for you and the fair circle in which I had the honour of becoming acquainted with you, remains unimpaired by distance or political broils.' Unashamed to humble himself, he then offered that 'it would make me very happy to become useful to you here. You know the Meschianza made me a complete milliner. Should you not have received supplies for your fullest equipment from that department, I shall be glad to enter into the whole detail of cap-wire, needles, gauze' and other millinery 'trifles'.

Further abasing himself, John signalled a desire to put negotiations with Peggy's husband back on track, asking her to 'infer' from his willingness to help with 'these trifles ... a zeal to be further employed.'[24] 'Trifles'! As if Arnold's ego were not bruised enough, this upstart captain who addressed his wife as he would a friend and claimed some prior 'remembrance' with her, was referring to the 'Articles' needed for his unborn child as 'trifles'. Was there no limit to this young dandy's hubris! This was more than any man's honour could bear. Arnold would have his revenge.

Two months later came the Arnolds' reply. The letter of 13 October started well enough: 'Mrs Arnold presents her best respects to Capt. André, is very much obliged to him for his very polite and friendly offer of being serviceable to her.'[25] Then came the humiliating putdown: 'Major Giles was so obliging as to promise to procure what trifles Mrs Arnold wanted in the millinary way, or she would with pleasure have accepted it.'

If, as is one possibility, Arnold was standing over his wife as she and John conducted this personal correspondence concerning 'Articles', then there is no mistaking the menace of the message: Arnold and Peggy were united as one, John on the outside looking in, his sole task to deliver the financial 'Rewards' demanded. To ensure John did this, Arnold was only resetting the bait when, in the same letter, he had Peggy write: 'Mrs Arnold begs leave to assure Captain André that her friendship and esteem for him is not impaired by time or accident.'[26]

If, on the other hand, this letter was composed by Peggy's hand alone and sent without Arnold's knowledge, every word becomes pregnant with meaning. However this brief flurry of direct correspondence between Peggy and John is to be interpreted, it was exactly that: brief. Odell made a despairing effort to keep the personal channel open, his letter to John on 21 December noting that 'a parcel long since requested by S [Stansbury] to be sent for Mrs Moore, is now made up, and I hope to be able to send it. Shall I charge it to S or is it, as one before, to be accounted between yourself and your humble Servt?'[27] There is no record of a response from John, nor of one from Peggy. By the time she received this 'parcel', she was busy preparing for the birth of her first child in January 1780.

In the meantime, Peggy must trust that whatever John felt for her was 'unimpaired by distance or political broils'. He, in turn, must trust that whatever she felt for him was 'not impaired by time or accident'. There is no record of Peggy's feelings for John at this point—except her letter of 13 October and, maybe, 'a lock of his hair'—but what of John's feelings? Was Peggy yet another of the illusions of love that had actuated his earlier attachment to Honora Sneyd? Is it possible that his burning desire to recover the family's honour and fortune had, indeed, sealed off all thoughts of true love? If so, John was not the first warrior to wait patiently until returning home armed with the laurels of war before seeking out the sweets of love.

Until then, John must make do with romantic musings on 'Delia', the chosen object of unattainable love for British officers serving in America during this conflict. When serenading Mary Krause as his 'Delia' during a brief stay at her uncle's 'Crooked Hill tavern' before being exchanged in December 1776, doubtless this was no more than John's passing gallantry intended to disarm an impressionable young girl. 'Delia' was again invoked when John's friend, Colonel Simcoe, pledged to Sally Townsend 'My happier days no more to range/O'er hill, o'er dale, in sweet Employ/Of singing Delia, Nature's joy.' But as he serenaded her on Valentine's Day 1779 with the lines 'Thou saw'st me once on every plain/To Delia pour the heartless strain,' Simcoe found himself competing playfully with John for Sally's attention. Arriving in Oyster Bay for much-needed convalescence, John's 'skill as an artist and silhouette cutter' gave him an edge over Simcoe, a drawing of Sally entitled 'A Beautiful girl in a riding habit'[28] left with the family as a lasting memento of his flying stay.

Yet, for John 'Delia' held a special significance. Superficially, she represented all womankind or, rather—if different sources are to be credited—all muse-worthy women who crossed his path. First, there was Honora Sneyd, who had him exhorting 'Return enraptured hours When Delia's heart was mine'[29] in the poem 'To Delia'[30] which he composed during his time in Philadelphia. This neatly complemented the romantic story he had pedalled to the Cope family of 'the portrait of Honora which I concealed in my mouth' when captured at Fort St. John's. Yet, according to another source, the self-same poem was 'entitled "A German Air" which André wrote in January 1778 for Peggy Chew'.[31] More authoritatively, a further source claimed that these same lines were addressed to Rebecca Redman, when 'for her, too, he wrote, on the 2nd of January, 1778 these pretty *vers de société*, to a German air that he had perhaps composed or picked up in his wanderings.'

Nevertheless, there are hints that 'Delia' stirred stronger emotions which lay below the surface of John's outward nonchalance towards womankind. The 'Delia' he represented in this 'German Air' was different to Simcoe's playful flirt. So long as 'Delia' was by John's side, 'jealousy nor care corroded in my breast' but when 'far from these sad plains/My lovely Delia flies', then, 'rack'd with jealous pains/Her wretched lover dies.'[32] Although the story-arc invoked tragedy, the sentiments expressed in poetic form were bland and matter-of-fact, as befitted his casual courtship of Rebecca Redman and Peggy Chew. They could only be flattered, not frightened by the 'jealous pains'.

A year on from Philadelphia and the Meschianza, John still harped on the theme of 'jealousy' but now the intensity had upped with the deployment of graphic visual imagery and introduction of betrayal and sacrifice as further themes. 'Delia' was no longer some remote classical muse, instead an awful spectre in the form of 'Sally' haunting him personally. Sinister now was the agonized love John imagined for his 'Sally'[33] in 'An Effusion' he composed while simultaneously navigating through the ups and downs of his negotiations with Arnold. Entitled *The Frantick Lover*, it anguished from the outset: 'And shall then another embrace thee my Fair!' Thereafter, the agonies only redoubled as he exhorted 'Must Envy still add to the pangs of Despair!' To the hortatory question 'Shall I live to behold the reciprocal Bliss?' John's answer was 'Death, death is Refuge, Elysium to this'. Night-time was worst for this 'Frantick Lover', for, 'when the Star of the Evening bids you retire,' then 'it shews me my Rival, prepared to invade/Those Charms which at once I admired and obey'd'.

So far, John could convince himself that 'my Fair' abhorred the touch of this 'Rival' and that, at the moment of reluctant surrender, she would sacrifice herself as a saint: 'Far off each Incumbrance is thrown/And Sally, thy beauties no more are thy own/Thy Coyness, too, flies, as love brings to thy View/A frame more ecstatic than Saint ever knew.' Then came the moment of supreme betrayal for John when 'yet I behold thee,'tho longing to die/Approach the new Heaven with a Tear and a Sigh/For oh! The fond sigh amidst Enjoyment will stray/And a Tear is the Tribute which Rapture must pay.'[34]

Was this 'Effusion' John's response to the news that Peggy was with child and the revelation by her that it was by 'accident'?

CHAPTER 27

Southern Interlude

By December 1779, then, the Arnold negotiations had ground to a halt, but, for all John's disappointment, the Philadelphia connection had served a useful purpose, helping him secure the prize—in October 1779—of his appointment as deputy adjutant general. In his pursuit of secret war, Clinton had, meantime, opened up other 'channels'. Again, John was pivotal to these plans, and the connections John brought from the back country of Pennsylvania came into their own.

Anchoring this network was the family-team of William Rankin and Andrew Fürstner, with Christopher Sower, Rankin's agent in New York, acting as their go-between. In its early days, the focal point of plans was to blow up 'the rebels' principal magazine at Carlisle',[1] but, as the plot to '"destroy the magazine clandestinely"'[2] rumbled on into late 1779, it became subsumed into an ambitious—in time overambitious—plan to attack the rebels along the length of the western frontier. With each message coming into New York from Rankin's camp, the numbers of border loyalists ready to take up arms multiplied from '600 men'[3] in 1778 to '1800 men'[4] in August 1779, finally topping out at '6000 men'[5] in May 1780. As the numbers swelled, so the flaws in Clinton's strategy for a 'grand stroke' in concert with the loyalists were exposed: like Gage and Howe before him, he desperately needed loyalists to rally in numbers to the royal standard, but did not trust them as a military force when they did: Rankin and his '6000 men' were left to moulder in the western back country. John had learned that there were limits to the reach of secret warfare.

Dogged by his own vacillations and faced with Washington's cussed unwillingness to come to battle in the middle colonies, Clinton's answer was to strike out in a new direction. Believing there was yet another way to win the war, Clinton briefly abandoned his strategy for secret warfare and launched a grand expedition in December 1779 to recover the southern colonies. 'By transferring the focus of the war to the south', however, 'he was tacitly admitting that he could not win in the north.'[6]

'At noon on Christmas Day, Clinton took ship to join the fleet at Sandy Hook',[7] his first destination 'Charlestown', South Carolina. For John, standing at his commander-in-chief's side, one door had closed but another had opened. Writing to one of his 'nearest friends' in England as the fleet prepared to head south, John reflected with wide-eyed wonderment on the steps which had brought his rapid rise in the Commander-in-Chief's 'Family'. Assuming an air of detachment, John promised that 'this epistle which I intend should contain all that one talks of by the fireside, entre amis, must enter further into what concerns my fortunes. I am now going to the subject of my present condition, occupations, hopes etc'. Whimsical wonderment gave way to philosophical contemplation as John mused how 'as our schemes and wishes are crossed by one unexpected incident, so another furnishes you with resource you could not have derived from yourself.'

So it was that, 'whilst I bent all my views towards the rank of Major and was offering sums of money then in my power to attain it, it pleased Monsieur d'Estaing to interfere, and my golden dreams vanished. Whilst I lamented my disappointment, the post of Adjutant General became vacant by the resignation of Lord Rawdon, and the Deputy Adj Gen Col. Kemble became desirous for private reasons to withdraw himself likewise. The Rank of Lt. Col. is inherent in the former and that of Major in the latter.'

Seemingly oblivious of the murky politics that brought this opening, John described how, 'there, then was the first office in a large Army vacant. The discharge of its functions (tho' not the office itself) I conceived to be within my reach and I saw the opportunity of getting the wished for Rank at a small expense.'[8] Miracle compounded on miracle when, seemingly out of the blue, 'my wishes were gratified. I saw myself selected by the Commander in Chief to fill the station of Dy Adj Gen in the room of Col. Kemble and with all the duties[9] of the principal of the department.'

This was the moment in John's narrative, when, just ten days earlier, Peggy's letter of 13 October had reached Headquarters telling him that his services in matters of the 'Articles' were no longer needed. This may have been coincidence in a process that Clinton had been cogitating for months but, maybe, Peggy's letter provided the final impetus that brought John's promotion, Clinton realizing that John's softly-softly approach with the Arnolds had been right all along and that he should have trusted him from the outset.

Either way, John said not a word about his secret war work to his friend in England. Instead, he made the final stages of his elevation seem as an arm's length commercial transaction which required that 'I sacrificed the pay to engage Col Kemble to retire and gave him besides £300'; except that, at the crucial moment, Clinton stepped in and 'to indemnify me for which the General is so good as to keep me on pay as Aid de Camp and in his Family.'

Yet, even as John was writing, it dawned on him how unusual this intervention must sound. Pausing, he invited his friend to wonder at the mystery of his good fortune: 'you may well conceive how much I am flattered at being called in the space of three years from a Subaltern in the Fusiliers to the employment I hold and the favour in

Self-portrait of John André as a senior officer. (New York Public Library)

which I live with the Commander in Chief.' Checking his wonderment, he came back down to earth, explaining to his friend that 'it makes no small difference in my arrangements to have gained my rank [by] £300 instead of £2100 or more...' He was especially concerned about money matters because he was still digesting the news of the 'capture of Grenada'[10] which he understood 'affects us all' and has required him to write 'to my Uncle David to ascribe my pay of Aid de Camp to my Mother's use.'

Turning to his 'future prospects', John became coy 'since it would be idle and silly to impart my hopes to any but nearest friends and such as will view them with the same estimation of their distance so as not to suppose one arrogant for entertaining them, and not to betray symptoms of expectation which I have not claims to justify.' That said, 'as I am sure that I am depositing them properly I will let you into my future prospects'. With that preamble, John launched in, declaring that 'should I continue to deserve the General's favour and he continue many months more in Command, should success attend the present Expedition and chearfulness prevail, perhaps it is not unreasonable to hope to be vested with the honour of the office I shall virtually have discharged and to be appointed Adjutant General.'[11]

It was on these hopes that John headed south with Clinton. The southern expedition proved every bit the 'success' John had hoped for, not only bringing the capitulation of Charlestown on 12 May but also cementing John's status as adjutant general in all but title. He it was who, as 'Deputy Adjutant-General', had the honour of signing the 'return of prisoners'[12] following the surrender.[13] With 'fifty-five hundred men' laying down their arms, it was Britain's greatest victory of the war'. Clinton 'stood at the pinnacle of his career', and by his side was 'Major André … appointed to confer with Lieut. Col. Ternant on the Matters you desire to have explained and to agree upon the Place to which your troops shall be conducted.'[14]

The secretarial functions that John had so confidently assumed in the relative comfort of Headquarters in New York were severely tested in the more dynamic and testing environment of a moving campaign. When he was not urging General Prevost's aide-de-camp in Savannah, Georgia to 'be so good, Sir, as to omit no opportunity of sending convalescents here' and promising that 'a vessel may possibly be sent round to receive them',[15] he was writing with regard to 'money … advanced Maj Patrick Ferguson, on account of the detachment under his command'.[16] With campaigning in full swing, injuries soon mounted up and, when a complaint came into Headquarters from Cornwallis on 18 July 1780 about 'an alarming deficiency of medicines, of medical assistance and stores for the hospital' in Charlestown, 'Dr Hayes' was directed 'to write to André relative to the things being sent'.[17]

So busy was John with these 'functions' that he occasionally made mistakes, for instance, when he 'brought together a mixed force of Hessians and British regulars' for a special task force. This was contrary to Clinton's policy that 'duties were "in general better performed by soldiers under their own officers."' The order was hastily rescinded, and John was obliged to apologize to Clinton, claiming that he 'had been "unacquainted with or insensible to" the strong feelings of the men'.[18]

When John was not at his desk juggling these routine duties, he was briefly on duty behind American lines. This, by now, was familiar work for John. He had gathered intelligence on West Point as he escorted the garrison baggage train down the Hudson from Fort St. John's in late 1775. Again, while a prisoner of war in Carlisle, Pennsylvania in 1776, he had been 'detected … in conversation' with 'two tories'.[19] Yet again in late 1777, John went on reconnaissance missions in the back country south of Philadelphia as Howe advanced from the 'Head of the Elk'.

It is no surprise, then, that reports emerged from Charlestown following its surrender that John 'had been present in its lines during the siege as a spy.' So the 'Rumors' went, he was 'clad in Homespun claiming to be a Virginian belonging to the troops then in the City',[20] his task to glean important intelligence on fortifications and troop dispositions as Clinton endeavoured to close the net round Charlestown and force its surrender. Being that he was operating under cover, these reports could not be substantiated officially, but the sources, being both British and American, give them some credibility.

There were compensations for all this hard work. Anyone seeking 'favor' from the commander-in-chief must first get past John, evident in his letter to General Prevost's aide-de-camp on 17 April. The subject of 'convalescents' was a footnote to the main topic, which, in response to 'your several letters', regarded the disposition of various commissions resigned or vacated. John promised to 'inform the General [Clinton] of the resignation you make of pretensions to purchase Major van Braam's commission' but hoped, in the case of 'Mr De Crousac', that 'this young gentleman' who 'had been wronged' in believing he could 'succeed a vacant Lieutenancy' would be 'redressed by filling the vacancy of Lieut Maltey, resigned'.[21] John was now in a powerful position if not to dispense patronage, certainly to orchestrate its disposition.

However, the main benefit John drew from the southern expedition was that he became ensconced as the commander-in-chief's trusted confidant on even the most sensitive of matters, including the ever more fractious relationship with the expedition's second-in-command, Cornwallis. The background circumstances guaranteed friction: Clinton had written to London asking permission to resign and return home. Fatally, this became common knowledge around the British camp, and authority soon ebbed away from Clinton, flowing instead to Cornwallis as his natural successor. Confessing himself 'hurt'[22] by the defections, Clinton poured his heart out to John just as the siege of Charlestown was getting underway.

Brushing aside the 'hurt', John—now growing in confidence—told his commander-in-chief bluntly that the predicament he found himself in was of his own making. The inference was that Clinton should have consulted John <u>before</u> making any decision. John would have told him then what he was telling him now: namely, that Clinton had had two clear choices at the outset: on the one hand, 'were there reason to expect this service to be prosecuted by L C [Cornwallis] it would behoove your Excellency to make every preparatory operation his Lordship's, lest you might be afterward criminated for his ill success;' on the other hand, 'were there no reason to expect you were to quit command before this service was completed, it was essential that yourself should be the sole judge of every preparatory operation, as yourself were to be responsible for the consequence'.[23]

Instead, Clinton had done neither and decided that he and Cornwallis should collaborate at all stages. Unsurprisingly, both were caught out when a letter arrived from London on 19 March informing them that Clinton was to remain in command. Cornwallis's answer was to distance himself from all 'preparatory operation' and 'request a separate command away from the main army'.[24] Clinton's answer was to turn to John for advice. Sensing danger for his commander-in-chief, John gave clear and unequivocal advice: 'his Lordship may be very useful to your Excellency on his own terms ... until he can be detached to a greater distance.'[25] Learning from the mistake he had made in the Arnold negotiations, Clinton took John's advice: he sent Cornwallis away on detachment in April, then left him in command in the Carolinas, while he returned to New York. Leaving Charlestown on 8 June, he arrived back at Headquarters on 18 June.

John had, meantime, gone ahead. So firmly was he registered in Clinton's trust that he had been sent with instructions to General Knyphausen to make preparations for a surprise move into New Jersey. Arriving at Headquarters, John found that Knyphausen had jumped the gun and launched his own expedition into New Jersey. John was less than happy, his private letter of 5 July to a friend, Richard Symes, chastising that the expedition 'exposed the troops in the march of day to a loss of more than Carolina cost us'. Revealing his growing disillusionment with prospects for the war, John reflected that 'as we went to demolish an army we could not get at, so we went to receive the submission of a country we could not protect, and of course a country locally inimical.'[26] The search for the one 'grand stroke' that would turn the course of war had become more vital than ever.

PART V

'The Grand Stroke'

CHAPTER 28

'False Friends'

John returned to New York in late May 1780 and not a moment too soon. Stung by the reprimand handed down by Washington on 6 April—following what, for all involved, seemed an interminable process of court-martial—Arnold had already set about reopening the lines of communication with British Headquarters. This time, however, Arnold believed he could deliver what, among the many grand strokes floated the year before, the British wanted most: the keys to West Point. As early as 25 May, he had begun lobbying Washington to have himself appointed commandant of the fort.

Confident these machinations would bear fruit, Arnold had already dispatched Stansbury to New York carrying 'Mr Moore's offers' to reopen negotiations regarding a 'Capital Stroke' he would initiate on behalf of the king's army. In John's absence, Stansbury met with Captain Beckwith, General Knyphausen's aide-de-camp. Speaking for Arnold, Stansbury dwelt at length on 'the channell of communication' which was now to include a provision for 'two Rings' to improve secure links along the chain. Financial proposals were also discussed, but no mention was made of what 'Capital Stroke' Mr Moore had in mind. Following the meeting, Beckwith wrote a holding letter to Arnold which excused that 'the affair in agitation is of so important a nature that General Knyphausen does not think himself authorized to give an answer to it … the more so, as the matter is already known to the Commander in Chief.'[1]

Arnold was having nothing of it and began blitzing British Headquarters with letters. Among these was one dated 15 June, which confidently predicted that 'Mr M expects to have the command of West Point offered him on his return.'[2] En route to Connecticut to sell a property there, Arnold had met with Washington. Sure now that he had within his grasp the very 'Capital Stroke' he knew Clinton yearned after, he wrote again on 16 June teasing Headquarters with a tempting account of his first visit to West Point. In detail, he described the 'greatly neglected' state of 'the works & garrison', the vulnerability of 'the Point' relative to 'the chain of Hills which lie back of it' and the dubious strength of 'the Boom or chain thrown across the River to stop the Shipping'.[3] Conscious of his strong negotiating position, Arnold pressed home his demand for 'certain indemnifications'. However, in a personal appeal aimed at John, he pleaded that the need for a financial settlement was not only 'for himself' but also for his 'Family', and that 'were it not for his Family, he would without ceremony have thrown himself into the protection of the Kings Army.'[4]

Other letters soon followed but still no reply came from British Headquarters. For good reason: John was back in New York and had picked up the threads of Beckwith's earlier contact with Stansbury, but, cut off from Peggy since October of the previous year, he had lost his trusted 'inside' source on Arnold's movements and motivations. He must now look elsewhere for confirmation that Arnold was acting in good faith and that the intelligence he was supplying was reliable. Clinton was expected back from Charlestown any day soon and would demand nothing less.

Anticipating Clinton's imminent return, John put out feelers in various directions. Beckwith was already in the know, so could be readily consulted: on 20 June he wrote to John from the Hessian command in New Jersey, reporting that 'our friend is certainly travelling to Connecticut'.[5] At the same time, John had the loyalist, Joseph Chew, enquire as to Arnold's whereabouts. Responding on this request, Chew wrote to John on 20 June: 'I have received your note at half after two yesterday and before five put two persons out in order to obtain an account of Mr. Arnold's intelligence movements.' To disguise his specific interest in Arnold, John also commissioned Chew to find out 'what other intelligence they can get from that part of the country.'[6]

John also planned to contact Peggy, but given disagreements between him and Clinton the previous year regarding the use of a woman for so sensitive intelligence work, he decided to wait for his commander-in-chief to return from the south. Back in New York, on 18 June, Clinton gave the go-ahead. Evidence for this comes from the manuscript of a 'Memo' written by Knyphausen summarizing the May meeting he and Beckwith had had with Stansbury. Following Knyphausen's concluding comments that Arnold 'relies upon a particular Token, place of meeting, Cypher & Channel of Communication,' Clinton added a short postscript of his own which read 'permission for a few Articles'.[7]

This cryptic wording could be interpreted in different ways, but, in amongst all the shifting cloak-and-dagger language of the correspondence with Arnold back in 1779, 'Articles' remained a constant: as the 'millinary' items which John had competed with Major Giles to supply to Peggy, they were John's plausible excuse to have direct contact with her. Any uncertainty surrounding Clinton's postscript hangs, then, on the meaning of 'permission' and, specifically, who gave it: was Arnold giving 'permission' for John to contact Peggy? If so, why would Clinton know this? He had not attended the meeting with Stansbury. More likely, Clinton was giving John permission to contact Peggy, the postscript a written record of that consent. John had demanded this formality, because of his disagreement with Clinton the previous year over the use of Peggy for this secret intelligence work. That Clinton now gave his 'permission' confirmed his growing trust in his junior officer's judgment.

Whether John succeeded in contacting Peggy and whether she responded has remained hidden from view, but that Clinton would wish to verify Arnold's trustworthiness by whatever means available certainly accords with the other checks John made at the time. In any event, they all took time, and once back in Philadelphia and faced with a deafening silence, Arnold chased again, first on 7 July, then on 11 July, finally on 12 July. He began fretting that 'the persons we have employed have deceived us' and that John 'may be deceived by False Friends'. As if to stress his sense of jeopardy, he further instructed: 'Mention no names. Write me in cipher and through some medium.' Having 'received no answer to my Letter or any verbal Message', Arnold now 'most seriously' wished for 'an interview with some intelligent officer in whom a mutual confidence could be placed. The necessity is evident to arrange and to cooperate'.

This followed on his request for 'a personal Conference with Captain P or some one of the Co-Partnership'.[8] In this, Arnold was responding to earlier requests made by John 'for my meeting You',[9] but these had been made during the first round of negotiations when, over a year before, John had asserted that 'the only method of compleating conviction on both sides of the generous Intentions of each and making arrangements for important Operations is by a meeting'.[10] Yet, back then Arnold had ignored John's pleas. So, why now was Arnold proposing a 'personal Conference' and why so eagerly?

Clearly, there had been a significant change in Arnold's thinking. Arguably, there was nothing more nefarious in this than a growing impatience on his part to bank the settlement he was sure would come his way now he had the 'Stroke' he knew the British wanted. What, possibly, betrayed darker motives was his insistence that the best 'method' for effecting this 'personal Conference' would be that 'an officer might be taken prisoner near that Post and permitted to return on parole, or some officer on Parole sent out to effect an exchange'.[11] By this 'method', the British 'officer' would be obliged to go within American lines, in which case, if caught in treasonable activities, he would be treated as a spy and executed according to the rules of war.

John would have nothing of it: he had enough experience operating within American lines to understand the risks for a 'partizan', which was why, during the earlier negotiations he had insisted to Arnold that any 'personal Conference' must be 'by my meeting You as Flag of Truce or otherwise as soon as you come near us.'[12] That way, John would be in uniform attending an official military meeting at an agreed 'Post' on the American lines. He could not be treated as a spy. When John finally responded to Arnold on 13 July, he repeated his insistence that the necessary 'interview' should be under a 'flag of Truce.' Moreover, John went into some detail on how this 'absolutely necessary … interview' should be arranged: 'Your visiting Elizh Town or Some place near us, which a flag of Truce could reach and where you might be supposed to be detained by Sickness is the expedient which strikes Sr H C [Clinton] as a practicable one.'

This was not the only stumbling block to plans for 'an interview'. John had completed his enquiries on Arnold and could say with confidence that 'the usefull Intelligence you have transmitted ... corresponds with other Information and gives him full conviction of your desire to him.'[13] Nevertheless, while agreeing that capture of West Point was the best 'project' for 'cooperating' with Arnold, John still refused to give 'an absolute promise of indemnification to the Amount of 10000 pounds and annuity of 500 pounds whether Services are performed or not.' The 'whether ... or not' was the issue, and John made clear that, on that basis, 'It [the promise] can never be made.'

The terms for a financial settlement recurred as a bone of contention in the ongoing correspondence, but to put Arnold's mind to rest albeit temporarily, it was agreed that '200£ shall be lodged in your Agents hands' as 'recompense' for 'Your Intelligence'[14] so far. At this point, John was working closely with Beckwith, who, though 'very unwell,' arranged to pay over the 'Two hundred guineas'[15] to Arnold's agent and kept John abreast of Arnold's movement, including, on 27 August, that he 'Commands at West Point'.[16]

As to who the British officer at the interview should be, various people had been proposed, including 'Major General Philips'[17] who was about to be freed in a prisoner exchange. However, Arnold kept insisting that the 'personal interview' be 'with an officer that you can confide in'.[18] To allay his concerns, John finally agreed that he, as 'Mr Anderson, is willing himself to effect the meeting', but repeated his absolute stipulation that it be 'by Flag of truce'.[19] These key points were all set out in a letter to Arnold dated 24 July, by which time he would have been ensconced at West Point, having 'set off' for there on 'the 20th'.[20] Once at the fort, communication with British Headquarters became even more cumbersome, requiring Arnold to address letters to Peggy in Philadelphia, from where Stansbury—on their receipt from Peggy—forwarded them to Odell who, in turn, passed them to John. Stansbury complained about the new arrangement, muttering that 'things are so poorly arranged that your last important Dispatches are yet in *her* hands. No unquestionable Carrier being yet to be met with.'[21]

Odell was more outspoken. In his note to John on 24 August, he apologized 'that the above extracts are from Letters written to Mrs Moore, but with a view of communicating information to you.' For some reason Odell felt compelled to, also, excuse the language in the 'Letters', when adding a further note that 'this remark explains the reason of the Stile which would appear extraordinary in letters directly addressed to Mr Anderson'.[22] This explanation was gratuitous: on any reading, the 'Stile' of the extracts that reached Headquarters was not at all 'extraordinary'. Quite the contrary: it was entirely consistent with a military communication. Why, other than to pass on sensitive intelligence, would a husband tell his nineteen-year-old wife nursing a baby that 'several Ships of the Line were to sail from Brest as soon as Transports could be procured' and that he is 'very apprehensive for the French fleet and Army'?[23]

Given its apparent gratuitousness, the explanatory note must have had some special purpose, which was as precursor to Odell's final cri de coeur: 'I wish it were possible to open a shorter road of correspondence.' Here, Odell was voicing more than irritation over the cumbersome inconvenience of the new arrangements. The strength of feeling signals that he no longer wanted to be associated with Arnold. How strongly Odell felt can best be judged in that, by dissociating himself, he would be relinquishing a lucrative commission with the British Army.

In Odell's opinion, he had good reason for wishing to withdraw. Arnold had become suspicious, volatile and jealous. Odell had already warned John about Arnold's recent manner. In a letter of 29 July, he had recalled opening two recent letters from Arnold 'brought yesterday by Mr Wallace, the person mentioned in the letters of the 15th and 18th and the agent to whom, as you will see, Mr Moore [Arnold] desires the 200 guineas may be paid.' Warming to his concerns, Odell had explained that 'these letters by Mr Wallace are of prior date to those brought by your messenger and contain nothing new, the bearer having been dispatched, as far as I can learn, chiefly with a view of ascertaining whether Mr Stevens or your humble Servant had faithfully conducted the correspondence.'

As far as Odell could make out, Arnold had got it into his head that the original 'channel' set up by Peggy and John using Stansbury and Odell was no longer to be trusted in the negotiations and had decided to rely instead on the 'other channel' of Mr Wallis [aka 'Wallace']. Puffing out his chest in professional indignation, Odell confidently predicted that 'Mr Moore will be convinced that his jealousy of "the persons employed" was utterly groundless,' in which case, 'when Mr Wallace returns' to Philadelphia, 'Mr Moore will probably leave "harping on my daughter" & think the terms contained in your last letter every way equal to what he can in reason expect.'[24] The warning signs were there: Arnold had become mistrustful, but of whom in the original 'channel'—Odell? Stansbury? Peggy?[25]—John must decide that for himself. For Odell's part, he no longer wished to be associated with Arnold.

So mistrustful had Arnold become that, despite the added risks, he began writing direct to John. In his letter of 30 August setting in motion plans for 'seeing you … in the course of ten days', Arnold abandoned the secure but elaborate procedure for enciphering via Philadelphia and instead adopted the simple device of a disguised hand and crafted the contents so the communication appeared to relate to a commercial transaction regarding a 'quantity of goods at Market.'[26] Adding to his risk, he enlisted his fellow-general Parsons as an unsuspecting intermediary. Posted at Nelsons Point on the Hudson, Parsons was well-placed to deliver the letter downriver to New York.

Still, these risks were worth it for Arnold: in return, he could insist—which he did in his letter of 7 September—that John also take equivalent risks by 'getting to our Lines by Stealth' so the meeting could take place at 'Colonel Sheldons quarters'.[27]

CHAPTER 29

'Armed Boats'

John had agreed to meet Arnold in person. It only remained, then, for John to agree that the meeting take place within American lines. So far, John had refused. No matter: Arnold would draw him in by stealth.

As matters stood, wherever the meeting took place—in the privacy of 'Sheldon's quarters', as Arnold wanted, or at an OutPost under 'Flag of Truce', as John wanted—all still depended on the unwitting acquiescence of Arnold's fellow officers: first General Parsons, now Colonel Sheldon who 'commanded the cavalry stationed on the outpost at Salem and North Castle,'[1] just north of New York and was positioned closest to the British lines. For Arnold and John to meet as Arnold planned, it would be on Sheldon's watch.

To allay suspicions, as cover Arnold cast John as one of his secret 'Confidants'. With so many American generals having their private sources operating within British lines, Sheldon had no reason to doubt Arnold's motives for wishing to meet this 'J. Anderson'.[2] That John would come dressed as for a commercial matter was equally plausible. That the meeting would take place at 'Colonel Sheldon's quarters'[3] in Lower Salem would, by its brazen openness, further allay any suspicions.

When, therefore, Sheldon received John's letter marked 'New York Sept. 7 1780',[4] he simply passed it on to Arnold. He did, however, query one point: 'enclosed I send you a letter which I received last evening from New York signed John Anderson, who mentions his name being made known to me. If this is the person you mentioned in your favour of yesterday, he must have had your information by letter, as I never heard his name mentioned before I received the letter.'[5] John and Arnold clearly needed to better synchronize their scripts.

Arnold could brush this discrepancy aside but not John's continued refusal to meet him within American lines at 'Colonel Sheldon's quarters'. Instead, so John explained in his letter to Sheldon, 'I am told my name is known to you and that I may hope your indulgence in permitting me to meet a friend near your Outpost. I will endeavour to go out with a flag which will be sent to Dobbs's Ferry on Monday next the 11th at 12 o'Clock when I should be happy to meet Mr G.' Worse still for Arnold's plan, John had also told Sheldon that 'should I not be allowed to go, the Officer who is to command the Escort ... can speak on the Affair.' At a glance, Arnold could see what John was contriving: he would come but would be dressed as a British officer in uniform, not disguised as a merchant. However, Arnold needed him within American lines <u>and</u> in disguise: only that way would he have John entirely within his power.

John had no reason to suspect Arnold's intentions. Still, he was on high alert. Stansbury had warned him; Odell also; Peggy maybe as well: Arnold had become volatile, unpredictable, jealous, possibly even vengeful. Addressing the last paragraph of the letter to Sheldon as if Arnold were the intended recipient, John set limits to the 'risk' he was prepared to take in pursuit of 'a Matter so interesting to the parties concern'd'. In coded language, he stated his position: 'I trust I shall not be detain'd but should any old grudge be a cause of it I shall rather risk that, than neglect the business in question or assume a mysterious Character to carry on an innocent affair as friends advise to come to your lines by stealth.'[6] Reading this, Sheldon was, surely, bemused by the reference to 'any old grudge'. For John, however, this 'old grudge' meant much more. John was warning Arnold to calm down: more was at stake than 'any old grudge', whatever Arnold's actual 'grudge' might be.

Arnold was beyond listening: on 10 September, he wrote an emphatic response, the impatient fury barely hidden as he made very clear to John that 'my Situation will not permit my meeting or having any private Intercourse with such an Officer'. The only option then was: 'you must therefore be Convinced that it will be necessary for you to Come or send some Person you can confide in to Colonel Sheldon's quarters.' Conceiving he had Clinton, if not John, in a vice-grip, he issued a barefaced dare: 'I do by all means advise you to follow the Plan you propose of getting to our Lines by Stealth. If you can do it without danger on your side, I will engage you shall be perfectly safe here.'[7]

That seemed clear enough: Arnold had no intention of keeping the meeting at Dobbs's Ferry on the terms John laid out in his letter to Sheldon. So why is it, then, that Arnold wrote to John on 15 September saying that 'On the 11th at Noon agreable to your Request, I attempted to go to Dobbs's Ferry'? It seems that Arnold had had a change of heart, or so he claimed, but, in the event, 'was prevented' from making the rendezvous 'by the Armed Boats of the Enemy who fired several times upon us, and Continued opposite the ferry until Night.'[8] This forced Arnold to take refuge at the northern end of the ferry crossing, with the result that he waited on one side of the crossing, John on the other. After a suitable interval both returned whence they had come, unaware that each had been at Dobb's Ferry.

All in all, a catalogue of mishap and misadventure, except there was only Arnold's word for what actually happened: that he ever came down the river that morning; that he was ever fired on by the British gunboats; and that he ever took refuge at the northern end of Dobb's Ferry. He certainly wrote to Sheldon on 9 September

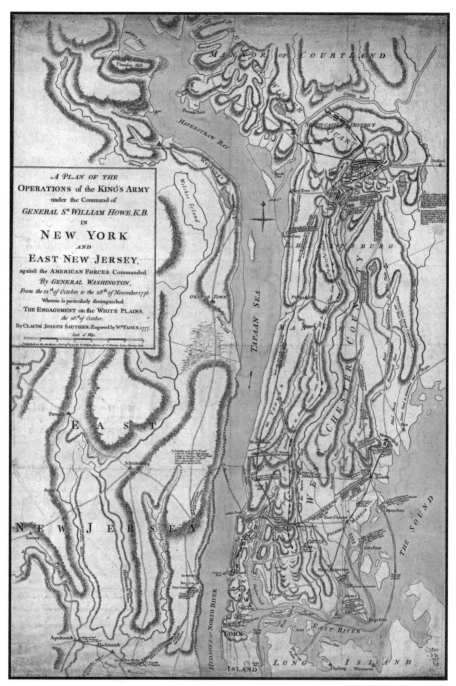

Map of Hudson River, Haverstraw Bay and Dobb's Ferry. (Library of Congress, Geography and Map Division)

saying he was 'determined to go as far as Dobb's Ferry and meet the flag'.[9] So it may be assumed that he intended to make the journey. He also wrote to Washington from 'Dobbs's Ferry'. Dating the letter 'September 11th', he explained that 'I am here this morning to establish signals to be observed in case the enemy come up the river'.[10] So it may also be assumed Arnold was at Dobb's Ferry that morning, albeit not at the southern end where John was.

As to the part played, or not played, by the 'Armed Boats', it is strange, indeed, that Arnold made no mention to Washington of having been fired on that morning. Surely this was the perfect opportunity to refer to the incident if only as proof-positive of the need to 'establish signals'. Given what Arnold had said in his letter of 10 September and in earlier correspondence, it seems very probable that he never had any intention of making the rendezvous at Dobb's Ferry once it was clear John was still insisting on the interview being conducted under 'Flag of Truce'. For what he planned next, it was crucial, however, that he claim to have 'attempted to go to Dobbs's Ferry' that morning. The 'Armed Boats'—if they were ever there that morning—became a plausible excuse for aborting the interview.

Arnold had—apparently—gone along with the British arrangements, but these had failed. Now it was his turn to set the terms for the interview. With the skill of a master military strategist, he moved to deploy the next stage of his 'Plan'. He must first neutralize Clinton. Seemingly, the British commander-in-chief was as desperate to turn Arnold as Arnold was to turn. Yet, every time Arnold had tried to set up an interview, his arrangements were vetoed. By whom? Clinton or John? Arnold did not know for certain, but if it were Clinton, Arnold now had a piece of intelligence to hand that he believed would ensure the British commander-in-chief's acquiescence this time.

Arnold included this crucial intelligence in his letter of 15 September, telling British Headquarters that 'General Washington will be at King's Ferry Sunday evening next on his way to Hartford, where he is to meet the French Admiral and General. He will lodge at Peak's Kill.'[11] Not only was Arnold giving sudden urgency to the 'cooperation' that he and British Headquarters had been chiselling away at for close on sixteen months, but he was presenting a heaven-sent opportunity for the British to end the war in one grand stroke. Fanciful it might have seemed but, with both sides increasingly desperate to end the conflict, kidnapping had become a major strategy of the war: the British had set their sights on Washington just as Clinton in May 1778[12] and, later, Prince William Henry, George III's third son, became targets for the Americans, in the Prince's case while he was serving in the Royal Navy on the American station.[13] How could Clinton possibly not take the bait?

Believing he had adequately neutralized Clinton, Arnold next turned his attention to John, intent on getting him within his power. For Arnold, the war was cover now for his man-on-man duel of wills with John. He believed he finally had the measure of John and knew how to snare him. Was it Peggy who let it slip? Did

Arnold work it out for himself from what he had learned about the Meschianza and its symbolism? Or, was it his instinctive military cunning? Somehow Arnold had discerned that John's guiding spirit was an abiding sense of honour. This was John's flaw, and Arnold was determined to use it to his advantage.

With this in mind, Arnold made his 'Plan' a chivalric challenge: refuse to make the interview on his terms, and John was a coward; accept it, and the laurels of war awaited John back in England So far, all 'the risques' had been on Arnold: he had passed innumerable secrets to the British; he had been 'deceived with False Friends'[14] ready to betray him; he had 'no Confidants'; and had 'made one too many already;' he had been shot at by 'Armed Boats'. His life hung by a thread. Now, it was John's turn to take 'risques'.

Arnold threw down the gauntlet: having blamed 'the Armed Boats' for his failure to make the meeting on 'the 11th at 12 o'Clock', significantly, he did not suggest making a fresh attempt to conduct the interview under flag at Dobb's Ferry. This, certainly from the British standpoint, would have been the logical next step. Instead, brooking no negotiation, Arnold gave John two options, both of which meant the meeting being conducted within American lines and John coming in disguise. John could 'pursue your Former Plan' for going to Sheldon's 'quarters' or 'those of Major Talmadge of his Regiment', either of whom 'will send an Escort with you to meet me'. Patently, this 'Former Plan' was Arnold's not John's, but that was a moot point. Matters had gone beyond negotiation. Arnold assured John he would be 'perfectly safe', but 'if you have any objections to this plan,' the alternative was that 'I will send a person in whom you may Confide, by Water to meet you at Dobbs's ferry on Wednesday 20th Inst between 11 & 12 oClock at Night, who will Conduct you to a place of Safety, where I will meet you.' Rolling the devil's dice, Arnold ploughed on regardless, describing how 'it will be necessary for you to be disguised' and 'you will be perfectly safe where I propose the meeting of which you shall be informed on Wednesday evening if you think proper to be at Dobbs's Ferry.'[15]

Arnold had thrown down the challenge, but would John accept it? A week earlier, he had refused to be drawn. Clearly, John was not that easily swayed. But John had a further weakness, Arnold was sure, and not just his sense of honour. Arnold knew how to tap into it. It had worked before. It would work again. Ruthlessly, he set his trap, the bait sure to be irresistible this time.

John was not to know it yet, but the 'person' who would be 'at Dobbs's ferry' on 'Wednesday 20th Inst' was Joshua Hett Smith. John had met Smith while escorting the Fusiliers' baggage train down the Hudson from Fort St. John's in the winter of 1775–6. Smith had opposed the Declaration of Independence, and his brother, William, was the current 'Chief Justice for New York and Canada.'[16] Smith's truest attachment was to his purse and, using the strategic location of his home, Belmont, overlooking Haverstraw Bay, he happily served both sides on the front line of this

216 THE LIFE OF JOHN ANDRÉ

civil war. His current attachment was to the rebel cause, having recently acted as go-between for Arnold's predecessor, Major General Robert Howe, in 'zealously … transmitting the reports of Howe's secret agents.'[17]

Since arriving at West Point, Arnold had been busily cultivating Smith, the proximity of Belmont to West Point important for the execution of his 'Plan'. Belmont was to be the 'place of Safety'. There, Arnold would set his trap. Peggy was due to join him from Philadelphia. She would be the bait, the timing of her arrival intended to coincide perfectly with the final crucial stages of his 'Plan'. The journey from Philadelphia was probably the longest Peggy had ever undertaken, so, to ensure her well-being, Arnold had sent Major David Franks, his aide-de-camp,[18] to accompany mother and baby son, Edward, on the journey north.

Arnold had drawn up a detailed itinerary for Peggy, including where she should stop each night. Warning her to 'bring her own sheets to sleep in on the road', he estimated that 'in seven days, if the weather is cool, you will perform the journey' which, by his calculations, meant that the seventh night should bring her, 'if not fatigued, to Joshua Smith, Esq … where you will be hospitably received and well accommodated.' Her journey that day he calculated to be '6 miles further' from her previous overnight stop at Kakiat, but she would be only '3 from King's Ferry'.[19] There, she would cross the Hudson, before travelling on to Arnolds' new family home across the Hudson at Robinson's House.[20] Set well back from the river in the lower reaches of the Highlands, this mansion had served as a Continental Army hospital during the early years of the war, but, now, doubled up as the West Point commander's home and headquarters. Major Franks and Arnold's secretary, Colonel Richard Varick, had already installed themselves there.

Due to leave Philadelphia at the end of August, in the event Peggy did not set off until 6 September and, with the journey taking longer than Arnold had anticipated, she did not reach Belmont until the 14th. Arnold was waiting fretfully. So impatient was he that, on the 5th, he had sent one of Sheldon's dragoons to join her en route. The orders to the dragoon were to continue on along the planned route until he met her carriage. Doubtless, the solicitousness of a husband and father entered into Arnold's emotions as he awaited Peggy's arrival, but knowing where she was and when she would arrive at Belmont was intrinsic to the success of what, in his letter to John of 15 September, he boldly termed 'my Plan'.[21] It was crucial she come to Belmont as agreed. She was there with her husband on the 15th when he composed the letter which set out this 'Plan'.

Yet, there was no point Arnold insisting on John meeting him at this 'place of Safety' 'on Wednesday 20th Inst' if John did not believe that Peggy would also be there. There is no direct evidence that John knew of her arrangements to leave Philadelphia and journey to Robinson's House. Nevertheless, it is implausible that John would have been unaware of them. Arnold had set them up well in advance.

Stansbury was no longer trusted by Arnold, but he would have heard that Peggy was leaving Philadelphia and would have passed the message to New York.

Still, that was not enough for Arnold if Peggy were to serve her purpose as the sweetener in his bait. He needed John to know Peggy's exact itinerary and timetable. Arnold could not inform him directly. That would have aroused suspicion. Instead, he had Peggy—wittingly or unwittingly—do it. Either way, he had to engineer it so John came by the information as if by accident. Once again, the 'Articles' of millinery became the dumb agents, Arnold setting up this part of his 'Plan' even before the earlier aborted trip to Dobb's Ferry on the 11th.

He had Peggy write to Major Giles about the 'Articles' before she left Philadelphia on the 6th. Giles was still held by the British in New York which required her letter to go, first, to Arnold, thence, to Sheldon who 'forwarded Mrs Arnold's letter for Major Giles to Colonel Delancey' at British Headquarters. According to Sheldon, Delancey, in turn, confirmed to him that 'if any articles are sent to me for Mrs Arnold he will take particular care of them and inform me immediately.'[22] Playing the dutiful husband, Arnold explained to his fellow general Parsons in a letter of 7 September that these were 'some trifling articles purchased for her in New York by Colonel Webb and Major Giles about eighteen months past, which they could not bring out. They have lain there ever since with Major Giles.' Why they had suddenly become important was that, 'by her desire, I have some little time since requested Colonel Sheldon to endeavour to get them out by one of his flags.'[23]

Peggy's letter arriving on Delancey's desk when it did could not have worked better for Arnold's plan. Delancey was a loyalist officer serving in the quartermaster general's office at British Headquarters, and he and John were old friends from their Philadelphia theatre days when they collaborated on the Meschianza. Delancey would have known of John's relationship with Peggy. Irrespective of this personal connection, Delancey had a duty to share with the adjutant general's office any correspondence arriving from the enemy.

It is inconceivable, then, that Peggy's letter to Major Giles was not opened and its contents not shared with John. Arnold was counting on this. What the letter said is unknown, but Peggy would surely have explained that her letter was prompted by her imminent move. It would have been a small step to sketch out her itinerary, including when she planned to leave Philadelphia and when she would arrive at first, Belmont, then Robinson's House. That was all John needed to know and all that Arnold needed him to know. The bait was set and sweetened. It only required John to take it.

CHAPTER 30

'A Personal Conference'

On 17 September, British Headquarters made one last attempt to arrange an 'interview' with Arnold on their terms. This time, Clinton decided to take charge personally. There was confusion, however: Clinton was unaware that John's previous attempt had been arranged ostensibly to settle commercial matters between Arnold and 'John Anderson'. Clinton thought the cover story for the meeting was so Arnold and Beverley Robinson could settle a dispute concerning the earlier confiscation of Robinson's House. This explains Clinton's letter to John on 11 September telling him that 'Col. Robinson will probably go with the Flag himself. As you are at the Fore Post you may as well be of the party.'[1]

There was nothing untoward in this: after sixteen months of stop-start negotiations with Arnold, John no longer troubled his commander-in-chief with their every twist and turn. When Arnold first made contact with British Headquarters back in 1779, Clinton stood at John's shoulder redrafting his every reply. Now he had total confidence in John, such that, on 31 August, he wrote to London recommending him for promotion to the rank of adjutant general.[2]

Clinton had tried to show interest in the outcome of the meeting planned for 11 September, letting John know: 'you will find me on your return at Gen. Kniphausen.'[3] Since returning from the south, however, the commander-in-chief had become increasingly paralysed with indecision. His confusion over John's ongoing arrangements for a grand stroke epitomized this creeping inertia. His sudden decision to take charge of plans to reset the meeting with Arnold in no way reflected on John's previous handling of negotiations. Rather, Clinton had been galvanized by the surprise appearance on 14 September of Admiral Rodney, bringing with him ten sail-of-the-line. His arrival in New York 'changed the whole prospect' of the war. At a stroke, the British had overwhelming naval superiority in American waters, and 'the French, according to a later report, "gave themselves up for lost on the arrival of Rodney"'.[4]

It was not just the arrival of ten capital ships that changed the balance of power. A popular hero after his defeat, the year before, of the Spaniards besieging Gibraltar,

Rodney also brought his acclaimed record for can-do dynamism. A much-needed antidote to the lethargy of the recent admirals—Gambier and Arbuthnot—assigned to the American station, his arrival shook Clinton out of his torpor. It also proved a tonic for John: the admiral's son, George, had been a contemporary of John's at Göttingen, and the admiral and the deputy adjutant general would surely have shared detailed discussions on the merits and practicability of the grand stroke which had been in the planning for so long. Rodney was all for the attack on West Point and so galvanized Clinton that troops, ships and transports were put on standby ready to move up the Hudson. Adding to the sense that here was a moment not to be missed, intelligence had come in that Washington's forces were on the move which meant they would be at their most vulnerable. It remained only for Arnold to deliver up West Point.

Clinton was a man transformed. Suddenly all was hustle and bustle, and, so he later claimed, 'it became necessary at this instant that the secret correspondence under feigned names, which had so long been carried on, should be rendered into certainty.'[5] Elbowing John aside, Clinton delivered a blizzard of decisions that could, once again, kill negotiations with Arnold stone dead. The first was to make Robinson, not 'John Anderson', the ostensible reason for requesting a meeting. This made no sense if the purpose was to dupe the Americans who must approve the meeting: Sheldon was expecting 'John Anderson' not Robinson. More to the point, Arnold had stipulated that he meet the 'John Anderson' with whom he had corresponded.

Ignoring these considerations, Clinton blundered on regardless, dispatching Robinson up the Hudson armed with a letter requesting a meeting with Arnold. Arriving at Haverstraw Bay on board the *Vulture* sloop-of-war, Robinson had Sutherland, the captain, transmit the letter to Arnold who, by then, was at Robinson's House. Opening the letter in front of his aide-de-camp and secretary, Arnold tossed it aside dismissively. The following day, having consulted Washington, Arnold dictated an official reply rejecting the request for a meeting and telling Robinson, still waiting in Haverstraw Bay, to put 'any other proposals' in writing.

Arnold also wrote Robinson a private letter. This, his secretary did not see. In it, Arnold again refused to meet Robinson, repeating substantially what he had said in his 15 September letter to John: 'I shall send a person to Dobbs Ferry, or on board the Vulture, Wednesday night the 20th instant, and furnish him with a boat and flag of truce. You may depend on his secrecy and honour, and that your business of whatever nature shall be kept a profound secret.'

Arnold's letters were passed down to Headquarters, reaching there on Tuesday 19 September. Reading them, surely Clinton could no longer doubt how this 'interview' was to be arranged. With the reference to 'a boat', Arnold was once again demanding that the 'interview' be in the form of what he had called 'a personal Conference' held in secret within American lines. Moreover, just so Headquarters understood who should come to this 'Conference', Arnold also explained that 'I have enclosed a letter for a gentleman in New York from one in the country on private business, which I beg of you to forward.' Was the reference to 'private business' coding only for the supposed 'Commercial Nature' of the 'Conference' or did Arnold have some personal matters to settle with John? If the latter, surely there was no misunderstanding the note of menace when the letter concluded: 'make no doubt he will be permitted to come at the time mentioned.'[6]

That the enclosed letter repeated the contents of the two earlier ones from 10 and 15 September, clearly Arnold intended John should come—alone—to the 'personal Conference'. Confident John would do just that, he even wrote a pass to this effect in advance. Post-dated to the 20th, it stated: 'permission is given to Joshua Smith, Esquire, a gentleman, Mr. John Anderson, who is with him, and his two servants to pass and repass the guards near King's Ferry at all times.'[7] It was John alone or no-one.

Alarm signals should have started sounding in British Headquarters, but, for Clinton, the arrival of Rodney with his mighty fleet was too good an opportunity to miss. He must strike now or not at all. Arnold was counting on this: he, too, had heard about Rodney's arrival, hence his two uncompromising letters to Robinson. Clinton knew he must relent, but doubtless comforted himself with Arnold's promise that the interview at the new location would be conducted under 'flag of truce'. He had also ordered John to remain in uniform. Surely nothing could go wrong.

With so much at stake, Clinton still hung back, doubtless gambling that Arnold was bluffing and, as happened the previous time, would protest loudly but, in the event, come to Dobb's Ferry. On the morning of the 20th, Clinton gave John a letter to be sent up river to Robinson waiting on the *Vulture*: the letter ordered the *Vulture* to return to Dobb's Ferry and, there, await the arrival of Arnold's 'person'. Yet, Arnold had written telling Robinson it was 'advisable for the *Vulture* to remain where she was till the time appointed,'[8] in which case removing the *Vulture* at this very moment risked signalling to Arnold that the British had called the interview off.

With each new order, Clinton seemed intent on killing off any chance of an 'interview' taking place. John had witnessed these sudden bursts of manic energy before, especially when Clinton was torn, as during the southern campaign.[9] Better to leave the *Vulture* in place and wait. Taking control, John 'determined'—as he later explained to Clinton—'to be myself the bearer of your Excellency's Letters as far as the Vulture,' his excuse being that 'the tide was favourable on my Arrival at the Sloop Yesterday'.[10] That way, he would be on the spot and could report events as they unfolded dynamically. Arnold had been counting on this move: by separating Clinton and his confidant, he could pick them off one by one: Clinton was at Headquarters fretting over his imminent moment of glory; John was about to play lone partizan. Both would be operating independently, answering increasingly to his commands. Arnold could start closing the trap.

Arriving 'on board the *Vulture* at about 7 o'clock' that evening, John learned that the barge bringing Arnold's 'person' had not made an appearance. Nor had Arnold's

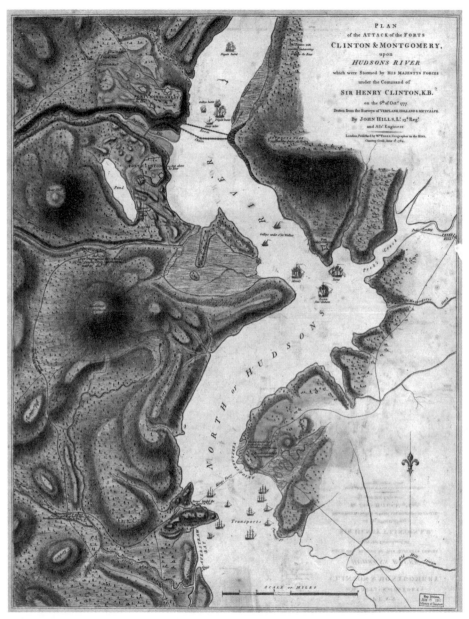

PLAN
of the ATTACK of the FORTS
CLINTON & MONTGOMERY,
upon
HUDSONS RIVER
which were Stormed by HIS MAJESTYS FORCES
under the Command of
SIR HENRY CLINTON, K.B.
on the 6th of Oct.r 1777
Drawn from the Surveys of VERPLANK, HOLLAND & METCALFE
By JOHN HILLS, L.t 23.d Reg.t
and Ass.t Engineer
London, Published by W.m Faden, Geographer to the KING,
Charing Cross, June 15, 1784.

Map of Haverstraw Bay on the Hudson River. (Library of Congress, Geography and Map Division)

barge been seen on John's twelve-mile journey up from Dobb's Ferry. Robinson, Sutherland and John decided to wait out the night. Still, no-one had come by the following morning, whereupon Robinson and Sutherland were all for dropping down the river to Dobb's Ferry. John took charge. There must be an explanation why Arnold's 'person' had not come. The *Vulture* must remain on station until Arnold's 'person' arrived. All that was needed was patience. To buy time, John feigned illness. The ploy worked. The *Vulture* stayed put.

It was time to update Clinton. John wrote to him the following morning, the 21st. In the letter, he stated succinctly how matters stood and what he was planning: 'Nobody has appeared. This is the second excursion I have made without an ostensible reason, and Colonel Robinson both times of the party. A third would infallibly fire suspicions. I have therefore thought it best to remain here on pretence of sickness, as my inclosed letter will feign'. As to the way forward, John planned to 'try further expedients'. Among these was that 'Captain Sutherland with great propriety means to send a flag to complain of this to General Arnold.'[11] This expedient was at John's behest: American guns had begun firing on the *Vulture*, which was the perfect excuse to have Sutherland contact Arnold again. The protest would surely bring Arnold's 'person' to the *Vulture*.

John was right: in the late hours of Thursday the 21st, a small boat pulled away from the jetty at King's Ferry and, rowed by two sturdy brothers, Samuel and Joseph Cahoon, took Smith—Arnold's 'person'—the six miles downriver to where the *Vulture* was waiting. According to Robinson in his report to Clinton three days later: 'Mr Smith came on board with two men and brought me the following letter from Arnold open. "This will be delivered to you by Mr Smith, who will conduct you to a place of safety. Neither Mr Smith nor any other person shall be made acquainted with your proposals. If they (which I doubt not) are of such a nature that I can officially take notice of them, I shall do it with pleasure. If not you shall be permitted to return immediately. I take it Colonel Robinson will not propose anything that is not for the interest of the United States as well as himself."' Accompanying this open letter, 'Mr Smith had a paper from Arnold in the nature of a flag for himself, one man, and two Servants to go down by water to Dobb's Ferry for ye purpose of forwarding some letters to N York on private business'. Smith also had 'a second paper as a pass to bring with him two servants and a Gent. Mr. John Anderson.' Together with this, 'he had a third small Scrap of paper on which was wrote nothing more than Gustavus to John Anderson.' As 'Gustavus' was the codename used by Arnold during the earlier 'secret correspondence', John could be sure Smith was who he said he was.

Arnold was offering two interviews: one with 'Colonel Robinson', another with 'John Anderson' but it was evident that only one of the interviews could, practically, take place. Moreover, by the wording of the passes, only Robinson could attend his, only John his. The British had to choose: Robinson or John. According to Robinson: 'upon considering all these matters Majr Andree thought it was best for him to go alone, as both our names was not mentioned in any one of the papers, and it appeared to him (as indeed it did to me) that Arnold wished to see him…

I therefore submitted to be left behind, and Majr Andree went off between twelve and one o'clock Thursday night.'

This was exactly how Arnold expected the British to reason, exactly how he had contrived events so John would come alone to the 'personal Conference' that night—the urgency of Clinton's plans with Rodney; the threat from Arnold's shore guns; the previous aborted meeting; the uncertainty over the latest rendezvous; the lateness of the hour; the imminence of daylight; the thought, maybe, that Peggy was staying nearby—all contributing to hurry the fateful decision, John herded like a lone Gadarene swine towards the lip of a precipice unseen in the darkness of Haverstraw Bay.

Nothing mattered for Arnold at this point other than for the 'Conference' to take place that night. When, according to Robinson, 'Smith told me Arnold would be about one o'clock at a place called the Old Trough or Road, a little above De Noyelles's with a spare horse to carry him to his house,'[12] this was Arnold hustling John along unseen. In the rush, John had no time to send a report to Clinton and when, in the flurry of last-minute arrangements, Sutherland suggested that John discard his regimental coat, he replied that he 'had Clinton's orders … to go in his uniform, and by no means to relinquish his character,' but still descended into the waiting boat, 'wearing a large blue watch-coat'[13] over his scarlet uniform.

John settled in for the journey across the bay to a rendezvous at 'the foot of a mountain called the Long Clove'[14] on the western shore some four miles from Smith's

Sketch by John André of his journey by barge to the rendezvous with Benedict Arnold. (New York Public Library)

residence, Belmont. He knew the area reasonably well, having doubtless surveyed it following the capture of Fort Fayette and Stony Point back in June 1779, but the darkness of the night would have obscured any landmarks. As the shoreline drew near, John could still convince himself that he was going under Arnold's official 'flag', that the 'blue watch-coat' he had borrowed from Sutherland was only so as to hide his identity from Smith's two oarsmen, and that he was safe in Arnold's hands for the brief time he would be ashore. His orders from Clinton were simple: 'to reduce to an absolute certainty whether the person I had so long corresponded with was actually Major General Arnold commanding at West Point.'[15] The interview could, accordingly, be very brief: as Arnold had said in his note, John could then 'return immediately' to the *Vulture*.

Coming ashore, Smith went in search of Arnold who was hidden nearby 'among the firs'. According to Smith's later account, 'I mentioned to him Colonel Robinson's reason for not accompanying me and the delegation of a young gentleman, Mr Anderson, whom I had brought with me', whereupon Arnold 'appeared much agitated and expressed chagrin at the disappointment of not seeing Colonel Robinson.'[16] Arnold's agitation was, by inference, because John's 'youth and gentleness had not argued the possession of a weighty trust'.[17] Certainly, Smith was of the opinion that John's 'youthful appearance and the softness of his manners did not seem to me to be qualified for a business of such moment; his nature seemed fraught with the milk of human kindness'.[18]

Some doubt should be cast on Smith's opinion: it was expressed many years later, when his *Authentic Narrative* was published in 1809 and his audience was the British public. It, quite naturally, differed from the one he gave at his trial in 1780 when he was fighting for his life. Certainly, his interpretation of Arnold's reactions is open to question. Arnold would already have heard from Peggy—if not from other Philadelphia belles—about John's 'youth and gentleness'. Indeed, one of the reasons that Arnold chose John as his preferred interlocutor was because of his 'youth', another being his 'gentleness'. Why Arnold 'appeared much agitated' was not from shock or surprise; instead it was from relief and excitement that his 'Plan' was falling into place. For Smith to admit this as a possibility was to make himself complicit—wittingly or unwittingly—in the execution of Arnold's plan.

Having located Arnold 'among the firs', Smith brought John to him and left the two to conduct their long-awaited 'personal Conference' in the darkness of the wood. So Smith's story goes, 'they continued in conference such a time' he felt compelled to 'inform them of the approaching dawn of day.'[19] What they discussed that the interview took so long remains hidden from history, but it is a reasonable certainty, given the prevailing darkness, that the subject was not the maps and other documents on West Point's defences which Arnold had been gathering over the previous week. John would have time enough to study these back at Headquarters: moreover, he well understood fortifications.

Most likely, given Arnold's consuming interest in money during the earlier 'secret correspondence', these dark hours were spent wrangling over the terms of the financial settlement. Thus far, the negotiations conducted through secret channels over the past sixteen months had foundered on Arnold's repeated demand that the British indemnify him, 'whether Services are performed or not' and the matching insistence by the British that this indemnity 'can never be made'.

For Arnold, it was time to break the deadlock: according to him certainly, the financial 'proposals' were the main reason for the 'Conference': his letter to Robinson had made it clear that, as presented at the interview, these 'proposals' should be 'of such a nature that I can officially take notice of them'. This impasse was not resolved at the 'Conference'. Neither side was going to back down, Arnold because he saw no need to, John because he did not have the authority to make the vital concession Arnold was demanding. Nor would John have made the concession on his own cognizance: to issue such an indemnity without proper authority would have cost him his career, this at a time when he was endeavouring to restore the family honour. Moreover, John had not been expecting the subject of financial 'proposals' to come up at the interview. His duty was to report back to Clinton that Arnold was who he said he was, following which negotiations on financial proposals could reopen but under 'secret correspondence'.

Instead, John found himself drawn into long haggling which proved fruitless but ate up vital time. This was what Arnold intended. After sixteen months of meandering negotiations, he had little confidence that a financial agreement would be reached, not least because West Point could not be the grand stroke Clinton yearned after. The British had captured the fort at Stony Point then lost it, the same again at Verplank's Point. Why would West Point be any different? Moreover, with the arrival of Rodney's fleet, Washington was already moving to seal off the Hudson, hence why Arnold had allowed the *Vulture* to be bombarded over the past few days and would allow it again the following day.

It was enough for Arnold's 'Plan' that he and John had had the interview. Smith—a lawyer—would be a perfect witness to that fact. However, Smith must not attend, as evidenced by his later protest that he was 'greatly mortified at not being present at the interview to which I conceived myself entitled from my rank in life'.[20] If he had been present, he could have revealed the truth about what transpired at 'the Conference with Major André' that night, which was that John never agreed to Arnold's demand for an indemnity.

Instead, with Smith excluded, but in close attendance, Arnold could claim—which he later did successfully—that John had, crucially, agreed to indemnify him "in Case a discovery of my Plan should oblige me to take refuge in New York before it could be fully carried into Execution".[21] Thereafter, it would be his word against John's: the British would have to stand by that (supposed) agreement made in the field, otherwise no other Rebels would turn. All this assumed that John would live.

Much better, much simpler, if John were to die. In those circumstances, the British would only have Arnold's word for what was agreed at the 'personal Conference'. For Arnold, it was first and foremost about the money: knowing how bitter had been the financial disputes between Arnold and Congress, the British should have known this. They certainly understood that they must buy Arnold's loyalty. Nevertheless, they still thought him a man of honour. For John, certainly, it was incomprehensible that an officer—friend or foe— could be anything other than honourable.

With Smith's warning of 'the approaching dawn of day', the 'Conference' came to an end. John must now hurry back to the *Vulture*.

CHAPTER 31

'My Great Mortification'

So the story went, a catalogue of mishaps and misadventures began to unfold immediately following the 'personal Conference', the result of which was that John could not return to the *Vulture* as planned. Having alerted Arnold and John to 'the approaching dawn of day', according to Smith 'shortly afterwards, both came down to the boat, and General Arnold with much earnestness solicited me to return with Mr Anderson to the Vulture; but I pointed out the impracticability of effecting his wish, from the great distance and the fatigue of the hands. He then applied to the men, who declared themselves unable to gratify his wish, through want of strength to accomplish it, and the ebb tide being against them.' Accordingly, Arnold 'relinquished his solicitations'.

Any prospect that 'Mr Anderson' might return to the *Vulture* in the near future further receded when, come daybreak, 'our attention was called to the cannonade from Gallows Point against the Vulture which was compelled to fall down the river and appeared to be set on fire.' Understandably, 'Mr Anderson …appeared vexed that the ship had been compelled to leave her position'.[1] There was no cause for alarm however. The *Vulture* would, surely, be back that night. Meantime, 'Mr Anderson' could hide out at nearby Belmont.

The short ride John now took to the relative safety of Belmont was a further, crucial step in Arnold's 'Plan' to entrap him: 'I got on horseback with him [Arnold] to proceed to … house,' so John explained in his later 'Statement' and, 'in the way passed a guard I did not expect to see, having Sir Henry Clinton's directions not to go within an enemy's post, or to quit my dress.' John had crossed into American-held territory, a key moment as he acknowledged in his later 'Statement' when also stating 'that, when I found myself within an enemy's post, I changed my dress.'[2]

Arriving at Belmont, Smith took to his bed 'to recover from the fatigues of the night' and 'General Arnold and John Anderson were left alone the far greater part of the day.' Arnold briefly went away, but, returning 'towards evening … proposed that I should convey Mr Anderson back to the Vulture which had nearly regained her former situation'. Again, the plan for John to return to the *Vulture* was thwarted,

Joshua Hett Smith's house overlooking Haverstraw Bay.

this time Smith the apparent cause, it not being 'possible from the state of sickness under which I now laboured.' Instead, Arnold 'proposed my accompanying John Anderson part of his way on his return to New-York, by land, as soon as my health would permit.'[3]

The seemingly accidental way these events unravelled does not stand up to scrutiny, nor does Smith's interpretation of Arnold's motivations: it was no surprise the length of the interview, no surprise the oarsmen being too tired to row back; no surprise the ebb tide; no surprise the cannonade by guns under Arnold's overall command. All these circumstances could have been foreseen and were ... by Arnold. But if they could be foreseen by Arnold, surely they could be by John also, certainly in the vital matter of his transport to and from the *Vulture*.

At issue was how John could have come to depend, at the outset, on two men, Samuel and Joseph Cahoon, and, latterly, on the sickly Smith for his safe return to the *Vulture*. According to Clinton's later 'Narrative' of events, John was leaving the *Vulture* to come ashore when, it being 'found that there were only two Men to row a very large Boat, it was proposed that one of the Vultures Boats go armed to tow them, but this was objected to strongly by Mr Smith and Major André as not consistent with the Character of a Flag of Truce.'[4] This followed on an earlier request from Smith for 'a loan of two oarsmen from the crew; which request was denied'.[5]

The account of this 'request' can be discounted, being that Smith was the only source. By contrast, the proposal to tow Smith's boat was entirely believable being based on what Sutherland and Robinson reported. That John rejected the proposal confirms what guided his thinking at this time, namely that he was protected by a flag of truce, that he should do nothing to violate its integrity, and that—last but not least—he had no reason to violate it being as it was issued by an American general. For him a flag of truce was the ultimate symbol of the honourable war he was fighting.

Of course, Arnold was no longer fighting an honourable war: for him, it was imperative that John not return to the *Vulture*. To what extent his hand guided the exact circumstances that led to John being dependent on two men—the Cahoons— for his safe return to the *Vulture* is difficult to assess accurately but judging that John was a man of honour acting under a chivalric challenge, it sufficed for Arnold to have first instructed Smith to refuse, as a violation of his flag, any changes proposed to John's mode of transport for the journeys to and from the *Vulture*.

Crucial as was ensuring that John not return to the *Vulture*, equally important was Arnold not letting on that this was his plan, hence the display of 'earnestness' that he put on for Smith's benefit. Not only must Arnold camouflage his true motives with Smith, who, as a lawyer, must be his independent witness, but, more immediately, he must pacify John who 'appeared vexed' and might take matters into his own hands. This was a small risk given that, by coming ashore, then passing through the enemy's post' in disguise, John had effectively made himself a hostage to Arnold. He just did not know it yet. In his ignorance, John could still insist that he return to New York via the *Vulture*. Whatever thoughts John was harbouring about Arnold and Smith at the time when, again, Arnold returned 'to his command at West Point, leaving Mr Anderson very disconsolate with me',[6] one certainty he could count on was that the *Vulture* would do all in its power to rescue him ... so long as he could make it down river. All he had to do was to wait. This reasoning John sought to articulate in his later 'Statement' when he claimed: 'before we parted, some mention had been made of my crossing the river, and going by another route; but I objected much against it, and thought it was settled that in the way I came, I was also to return.'

John was correct in this assertion: before departing—this time not to return— Arnold had written out two passes, one for the land route and a second for John to go by water directly to Dobb's Ferry. What John did not know was that Arnold had agreed privately with Smith that the only practicable option open to John must be the land route. Smith was planning to join his family across the river. John would have to accompany him. Arnold's alibi was intact, so he thought. The trap had closed shut. Now, John only had Smith to blame for his predicament.

It was as if on cue then, that, the next day, Smith's attack of 'ague' having abated, 'Mr [Smith] to my great mortification persisted in his determination of carrying me by the other route'[7] and, despite John's protests, refused 'to reconduct me back the next night as I had been brought.' Finally, it dawned on John that 'thus become a prisoner, I had to concert my escape.'[8]

So, why then, if Smith was not to be trusted, did now John agree to accompany him on the land route? Was it simply, as Arnold had reasoned, that John had no practicable option? By all measures of self-preservation, John had to know that he was increasing the danger to himself. The land route was long and hazardous as it would entail John adopting full disguise, passing further American posts, crossing the Hudson at King's Ferry, and descending to British-held White Plains through an area closely controlled by the Americans. The chances of capture were magnified.

Yet, safety was no longer John's primary consideration. Instead, speed was now uppermost in his thinking. After what he had found out at the 'personal Conference' with Arnold, it was imperative he return to New York post-haste. In these circumstances, he could no longer wait at Belmont and take his chances. He must trust Smith a little longer.

So it was that, changing his clothes again, John set off with Smith, and the two 'reached the ferry at Stony Point before it was dark.'[9] John's desperate bid to 'escape' had begun.

CHAPTER 32

'The Chance of Passing Undiscovered'

According to Smith, after crossing over the Hudson on the evening of 22 September, 'we rode up to the tent of Colonel Livingston, the commanding officer at Verplank's Point.'[1] Livingston recalled the encounter: 'I asked him where he was going. He said up towards General Arnold's, or that route; and I gave him one letter to be delivered to General Arnold... I then urged him to stay awhile and take supper or a drink of grog.' Smith declined, however, saying 'that there was a gentleman

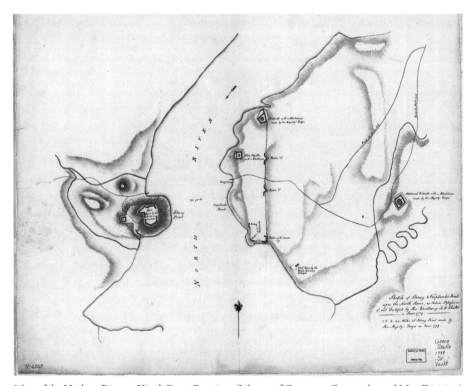

Map of the Hudson River at King's Ferry Crossing. (Library of Congress, Geography and Map Division)

waiting for him who had just rode on, and was in a hurry to get off.' Then, Smith 'rode off'. Luckily for John, Livingston 'did not see the person who was with him, it being dark and he having rode forward.'[2] If they had met, Livingston might have recognized John as the British quartermaster at the capitulation ceremony at Fort St. John's in 1775.

Now they were across the river, John and Smith should have turned immediately south, instead of which they headed north from Verplank's Point making for Peekskill. This would take them to Robinson's House, and for John, a meeting, maybe, with Peggy. Arriving at Peekskill, however, for some reason there was a change of plan. Instead of continuing north to Robinson's House, Smith had them turn east to Crompond. Whatever happened that Smith changed the route remains lost from view: Smith was brief in his version of events, John even briefer, his account of immediate events since leaving Belmont set down in his later 'Statement:' 'at the decline of the sun, I set out on horseback, passed King's Ferry and came to Crompond, where a party of militia stopped us and advised we should remain'.[3]

John may have met with Peggy in Peekskill. If so, it was the shortest of meetings. Equally, Arnold may have sent a note telling Smith not to bring John to Robinson's House. Arnold needed no pretext to do this, but, returning to Robinson's House, he had found Franks and Varick in simmering revolt over his cosy relationship with Smith. A more likely explanation for the decision to abandon a visit to Robinson's House was John's mounting haste to reach the British lines.

To do that, the two conspirators must first run a gauntlet of checkpoints and chance encounters, each one reinforcing the urgency of escape. 'Five or six miles' on from Verplank's Point, the two were 'challenged by a patrole party'. This was 'the party of militia' mentioned by John. After lengthy interrogation which, according to Smith, made John 'very uneasy', the two were allowed to continue on their way, having first 'presented the passports'. Nevertheless, with darkness upon them, Captain Boyd, the American officer commanding, urged them not to continue 'travelling in the night'.[4] Indeed, he 'intreated us not to proceed one inch farther in the night, as it was very dangerous, for the Cow Boys had been out the preceding night.'

'Cow Boys', as Smith would explain for his British readers in his 'Narrative' from 1809, 'was a name given to those with a British interest… Skinners was the appellation of their opponents.'[5] These two gangs of 'banditti' were operating freely in the no-man's land that the two travellers were about to enter between American and British lines. Despite these risks, John was all for continuing, but Smith insisted they return to where they could find lodgings 'several miles' back.

According to Smith, he and John 'slept in the same bed; and I was often disturbed with the restless motions, and uneasiness of mind exhibited by my bed-fellow, who on observing the first approach of day summoned my servant to prepare the horses for departure… He was at first much dejected but a pleasing change took place in his countenance when summoned to mount his horse.'[6]

Reaching 'Pine's Bridge' without mishap the following morning, they parted company, there 'being accounted the south boundary of the American lines'. Smith later portrayed the 'parting' as amicable, even though he had delayed mentioning his 'determination to go no further' until 'breakfast' that morning at 'a low house' run by an 'old matronly Dutch woman'. John was 'affected at parting, and offered me a valuable gold watch in remembrance, as a keep-sake, which I refused.'

Smith retraced his steps and headed north to Fishkill, stopping off first at 'Robinson's House' to report to Arnold. There, 'I mentioned to General Arnold the distance I accompanied Mr Anderson, which gave him apparently much satisfaction.'[7] No little wonder! Hearing this news, Arnold could, indeed, congratulate himself. Unwittingly—or was it wittingly?—Smith had done exactly what Arnold wanted of him. There had been an outside possibility Smith would be brave enough to take John all the way to the British lines, but returning he would have had awkward questions from the Americans to answer, and Arnold judged Smith was too fond of his current rebel loyalties to jeopardize these. Moreover, until the war kicked off again in earnest, the American lines were frozen where they were, and, unluckily for Smith, his family and all his worldly goods were trapped on the wrong side. All things considered, then, Smith had had no option but to jettison John well short of White Plains.

Still, Arnold would have been surprised that someone had not recognized John thus far. The area John and Smith had just passed through was teeming with American officers who had been recently exchanged. One of them would surely have seen John around New York in his redcoat uniform.[8] Arnold's best shot now was that John would be taken by the Skinners. He was counting on that: he had heard rumours that no lone traveller could make it through no-man's land without being stripped, then ransomed to the highest bidder. Arnold already knew this from his own enquiries, but Smith had confirmed the same, not in so many words but with the look of terror in his eyes when Arnold suggested he take John all the way to White Plains. To add to Arnold's chances of good fortune, the Americans were currently paying all-comers—Skinners and Cowboys alike—more for stolen military clothing and accoutrements than the British. This meant whoever caught John would bring him to an American outpost. Arnold had chosen well with Smith.

As for John, he had proved more of a problem than Arnold had anticipated. Those last few hours before they parted company at Belmont were touch-and-go, especially from the moment John donned the disguise. He became like a haunted prey and was within a whisker of refusing to go north, but the mention of Peggy had, doubtless, tamed him. It had certainly proved difficult persuading him to take the documents Arnold had collected describing West Point's fortifications. He had left this masterstroke to the last minute in the hope John would not look them over, but he had and protested when Arnold proposed he take them to show Clinton. He had argued there was no need. He had an excellent memory. Arnold had to insist. That was when he sensed John might not be fooled by their value. Still, John's opinion did not count. Clinton's did, and he was sure to be taken in by the maps, so desperate he was for his beloved 'grand stroke'.

Either way, it mattered little to Arnold what happened to John now. He had all eventualities covered. If John made it to New York, Arnold was still safe. The problems over John's escape route he could blame on Smith, and no-one at British headquarters could possibly suspect his double treachery so desperate were they to pull off their beloved 'grand stroke'. That it would fail was a certainty, but this was why it was so imperative he insist on the indemnity.

If, on the other hand, John did not make it—and, after what Smith had reported, this was the most likely outcome—again there was no proof of his double treachery, only his word against John's and if the documents hidden in John's boots did their work properly, John would not be alive long enough to tell his version. Whoever took charge of John if he was captured, the news was meant to come to Arnold first as the general in local command. If, perchance, that did not happen, Arnold had already thought through his contingency arrangements. Now that he knew where John was, he had better activate them quickly. The next twenty-four hours would be crucial. He must order his barge to be ready on standby, in case he had to make a run for it.

And he had nothing to fear from Peggy. Ever since the baby, she was mute as death. Still, at the right moment, he might have to remind her how much she was implicated.

CHAPTER 33

'I Was Betrayed'

As events turned out, it was not a moment too soon Arnold ordering up his barge. While he was busy congratulating himself, John's escape to the safety of White Plains had already come to a shuddering halt. In his later 'Statement', John recounted what transpired after he and Smith parted company: 'In the morning, I came with …[Smith][1] as far as within two miles and a half of Pine's Bridge, where he said he must part with me, as the Cow-boys infested the road thenceforward. I was now near thirty miles from Kingsbridge, and left to the chance of passing that space undiscovered. I got to the neighbourhood of Tarrytown, which was far beyond the points described as dangerous, when I was taken by three volunteers who, not satisfied with my pass, rifled me, and finding papers, made me a prisoner.'[2]

Finally, 'the run of good fortune'[3] that John had enjoyed since being liberated from captivity in December 1776 was over. He was back a prisoner for a second time. Worse, however, was to come. Seizing on a recent law which had legitimized such captures by offering as 'prize any property they might find on a captured enemy,'[4] the three 'volunteers' (alias 'Skinners')—John Paulding, Isaac van Wart and David Williams—hotfooted it with their booty to the nearest American post. This was at North Castle where, just recently, 'Lieut Colonel Jameson' had taken command 'in the room of Colo Sheldon'.[5]

Quite coincidentally, the arrival of this 'John Anderson, merchant' had long been expected at the post albeit in very different circumstances: ahead of the earlier meeting planned for 'the 11th', Arnold had written to Sheldon warning him to 'look out for John Anderson if he came there from New York.' There was even a letter on hand written by this 'Anderson' to Sheldon. Dated 7 September, it began 'I am told my name is made known to you.' Arnold had also left instructions 'to send him up to headquarters'[6] at Robinson's House, which was what Jameson now did even though the 'Skinners' had said the merchant, when captured, was heading towards, not away from, New York. Then again, who would take the word of three 'Skinners' whose notion of truth was questionable?

Not in doubt, however, were the maps and documents found on this 'merchant'. Realizing these were 'of a very dangerous tendency'[7] but suspecting only that they had been stolen, Jameson sent them, not to Arnold at Robinson's House, but rather to Washington who was then journeying from Hartford, in Connecticut, to West Point. On duty also at North Castle was Major Tallmadge. He had received a similar request from Arnold—this one on the 13th—requesting that 'if Mr James Anderson, a person I expect from New York, should come to your quarters, I have to request that you will give him an escort of two horsemen to bring him on his way to this place, and send an express that I may meet him.'[8] Tallmadge was a senior officer in Washington's secret service, and hearing from Jameson what had just transpired, he immediately suspected that this 'John Anderson' was a spy in cahoots with Arnold.

Seeing the prisoner for the first time and observing 'his manner of walking to and fro on the floor and turning on his heel to retrace his steps,' Tallmadge was further 'struck by his military deportment and convinced that he had been bred to arms.' He prevailed on Jameson to countermand his earlier orders, whereupon 'John Anderson' was brought back to North Castle. Still disbelieving, Jameson insisted, nevertheless, on sending word to Arnold at Robinson's House that this 'John Anderson' had been captured.

Overnight into 24 September, John was put to share 'an appartment' with 'Mr Bronson who was attached to Sheldon's regiment' where 'he relaxed into familiar conversation' and, indulging 'his favourite resource for amusement … sketched with his pencil a group of ludicrous figures representing himself and his escort under march.'[9] Also attending John was 'Lieut King of the Dragoons'. He later described the downbeat prisoner now in his custody: 'he looked somewhat like a reduced gentleman. His small-clothes were nankeen, with handsome white-top boots—in fact his undress military clothes. His coat purple, with gold-lace, worn somewhat threadbare, with a small-brimmed beaver on his head.' This was John dressed in clothes given to him by Smith. As to John's appearance, 'he wore his hair in a queue, with long black beard, his clothes somewhat dirty'.

According to King, 'while walking together' John suddenly 'observed he must make a confidant of somebody, and he knew not a more proper person than myself, as I had appeared to befriend a stranger in distress.' Abandoning his character of a merchant and formally declaring himself an army officer, he confided to King 'who he was and gave … a short account of himself from the time he was taken in St. Johns in 1775 to that time.'[10] Following this, John requested writing materials and promptly wrote a letter of confession to Washington.

This letter began by explaining why John had decided to write: 'What I have as yet said concerning myself was in the justifiable attempt to be extricated. I am too little accustomed to duplicity to have succeeded. I beg your Excellency will be persuaded, that no alteration in the temper of my mind, or apprehension for my safety, induces me to take the step of addressing you, but that it is to rescue myself from an imputation of having assumed a mean character for treacherous purposes or self-interest. It is to vindicate my fame that I speak and not to solicit security.'

As John wrote this, he was already addressing an audience beyond Washington whose opinions he valued most as judges of his actions. It was this audience—his commander-in-chief, fellow officers, mother, sisters, friends, even Anna Seward—who he believed must learn the truth of why he had acted as he did and why he was in his current predicament. At this point he announced that 'the person in your possession is Major John André, Adjutant General to the British Army'.

Continuing, he launched into the germs of the plot explaining that 'the influence of one commander in the army of his adversary is an advantage taken in war. A correspondence for this purpose I held as confidential (in the present instance) with his Excellency Sir Henry Clinton.' Next, John went into the narrative of his time once he came up from New York to the *Vulture*: 'To favor it, I agreed to meet upon ground not within the posts of either army, a person who was to give me intelligence; I came up in the Vulture man of war for this effect and was fetched by a boat from the ship to the beach. Being there I was told that the approach of day would prevent my return, and that I must be concealed until the next night. I was in my Regimentals, and had fairly risked my person.'

Now John came to the crux of his version of events, when, in his opinion, honour became dishonour, trust became betrayal: 'against my stipulation, my intention and without my knowledge beforehand, I was conducted within one of your posts. Your Excellency may conceive my sensation on this occasion and will imagine how much more must I have been affected by a refusal to reconduct me back the next night as I had been brought. Thus become a prisoner, I had to concert my escape. I quitted my uniform and was passed another way in the night, without the American posts to neutral ground and informed I was beyond all armed parties and left to press for New York. I was taken at Tarrytown by some volunteers. Thus as I have had the honour to relate was I betrayed (being Adjutant General of the B. Army) into the vile condition of an enemy in disguise within your posts.'

Of course, John could not name his betrayer. To do so would have been to make himself as dishonourable as him. John was well-versed in the art of interrogating captured soldiers. So, to pre-empt any attempts by the Americans to winkle out this information, John rounded off the confession part of his letter with the formal statement: 'having avowed myself a British Officer, I have nothing to reveal but what relates to myself which is true on the honour of an Officer and a Gentleman.'

Trusting that he was speaking one officer to another, John next came to the subject of his impending treatment as a prisoner and appealed: 'the request I have to make to your Excellency and I am conscious I address myself well, is that in any rigor policy may dictate, a decency of conduct towards me [may] mark that tho' unfortunate I am branded with nothing dishonourable as no motive could be mine but the service of my king and as I was involuntarily an impostor.'[11]

As recounted by King, the events portray John as gullible and naïve, even pathetic as he, seemingly, buckled under the slightest application of pressure, first confiding in King, then confessing to Washington. However, the truth of who John was at this critical moment could not be more different, as attested by his whole life so far, as a son, a brother, a friend, and, above all, 'an Officer and a Gentleman'. As always, John was impelled by honour.

What King did not—could not—understand were the motives that brought John to, first, confide, then, confess. Nor could Clinton or Rodney understand, especially when it emerged that John's urge to confide and confess was not limited to this one letter, but rather part of a sequence which had begun even as John was taken with such apparent ease by the 'three volunteers'. To explain away John's ready urge to confess, American commentators like King cast it as a quasi-religious unburdening of heavy guilt. This chimed with the moral rightness of the Revolution. Britons—especially Clinton and Rodney—saw it as more accidental, a temporary mental aberration brought on by the strain of the moment. According to Clinton, 'dejected by the Failure of a decisive Stroke, and the Sentence pronounced on Him, he has been I fear persuaded and so infatuated as to acknowledge Himself a Spy.' Fired by his own words, Clinton went so far as to claim that the subsequent Board of Enquiry set up by the Americans to pass judgment on John had 'contrary to Justice, Custom, and Humanity ... laid hold of, and upon this Confession, possibly extorted, condemned Him.'[12]

John's 'low spirits' became a mantra for Clinton, this explanation repeated three times in a letter he wrote to his sisters in the immediate aftermath of what he termed 'our late extraordinary Adventure'. He vociferated how, 'as there can be no prooffs of his being a spy, they took advantage of a letter of his written in low spirits...'[13] This became the currency of the British camp, repeated when mediators went to negotiate John's release and were shown 'a low spirited Letter of André's...'[14]

What none of the commentators—American and British alike—knew and what John could only hint at in his letter to Washington was the realization he had already come to that he had been betrayed. This awful reality had dawned on him when first 'conducted within one of your posts' and 'thus become a prisoner', as he and Arnold made their way to Belmont. Piecing the threads together even as John concerted his 'escape', everything that had transpired since Arnold and Peggy approached him in May 1779 acquired the horrible logic of dread predestination. Thenceforth, as John journeyed on with Smith, he expected capture at every turn and began preparing for it. How exactly it would eventuate and by whose hand, he did not know—and he certainly had no death wish to be captured—but by the time it did happen at the hands of the 'three volunteers', John was well-prepared for the inevitable consequences and determined to use it to advantage.

Hence his confidences to King were by way of a rehearsal for the confession he must next make. The confession itself was equally premeditated and calculated, its words carefully weighed, its commanding intention a necessary, pre-emptive step to ensure—ahead of the forensic scrutiny that must inevitably be applied to his every action thus far—that he gave his version of those actions, not to save his life—which he understood was very likely forfeit—but to protect the honour he held most dear.

To do so, he made a clear distinction between the honourable partizan—which he believed he was—and the 'mean', 'vile', dishonourable spy, which, 'against my stipulation, my intention and without my knowledge beforehand', he had become through another's treachery. This was not some subtle semantic distinction. It went to the heart of what it was to be 'an Officer and a Gentleman'. Nor was it made by John alone. Clinton understood the distinction, making the point in the letter to his sisters from 4 October when he still hoped for news that John had been released. In it, he complained that 'notwithstanding every argument has been used W [ashington] will consider M. André as a Spy, for my own part I have given the affair all the examination I can and I look upon it deserving no such appellation.'[15]

John had made his confession. As soon as he finished the letter, it was sealed and hurriedly sent to Washington who was then making his way from Hartford to Robinson's House and still unaware of the conspiracy. John must now wait for the verdict on his conduct. However, there was much more to his confession than a self-serving attempt to protect his honour for posterity. From the moment John realized that Arnold planned to betray him, he decided that the 'grand stroke' must not go ahead. Sight of the worthless 'papers' Arnold had foisted on him detailing the West Point fortifications only confirmed his judgment. The attack must not happen. That was why he held on to the 'papers', even at great risk to himself. Assuming that, against all the odds contrived by Arnold, John were to make it to New York, the documents in his boots were to be the proof John needed to convince Clinton that Arnold was not to be trusted and the 'grand stroke' a bloody trap. Otherwise, why would John have held on to the documents? This—apart from John's voluntary confession—was the one piece of direct evidence that incriminated him. Clinton, among others, could not understand why John 'even took charge of Papers (for which there was no necessity)'.[16] John did so because he must.

Now that he had, indeed, been captured and could no longer communicate directly with Clinton, John—ever the 'intelligent' officer—had already computed the military alternatives and concluded that the documents were still useful, in this instance, to have the Americans stop the attack, which was why he allowed the documents in his boots to be found and why he wrote his letter of confession at a point in time when, clearly, he did not need to. He must act quickly: even as he languished under close arrest, Clinton and Rodney might be advancing up the Hudson. If so, they were heading into a killing field. Waiting only to hear from King that the incriminating papers had gone, not to Arnold, but, as he hoped, to Washington, he immediately wrote his letter of confession. He was sure that the letter, together with the 'papers' already sent up, would have the desired effect.

Washington would immediately bolster the defences along the Hudson, an event that would not go unnoticed by British Headquarters. Clinton would abandon any plans to take West Point. This was John's intention.

In addition, Washington would start hunting down John's co-conspirators. At this stage, John did not know Arnold's whereabouts or what had happened to him, but calculated that, with the incriminating papers in American hands, it was a matter of time before he was taken too. John may have been tempted to name Arnold as co-conspirator in the letter, but, matters of honour aside, he risked Arnold taking further revenge on him by implicating Peggy. Under no circumstances must that happen. Powerless to do much else for the moment, John must await the turn of events. He did not have long to wait.

CHAPTER 34

'It will be but a Momentary Pang'

Events now moved to Robinson's House, where, together with Franks and Varick, Arnold was awaiting the imminent arrival of Washington en route from Hartford. In a later letter to his sister, Jane, Varick described what unfolded at 'Headquarters' beginning on 'Monday morning, 25th September about 10 o'clock'. According to Varick's testimony, 'I lay sick in my bed' when 'Arnold received advice by two letters that Major André, Adjutant-General of the British Army, was taken with sundry papers in Arnold's handwriting, and, without waiting to see General Washington, who was within one mile of us, I am informed he called for a horse, bid the officer who brought the letters to be silent, went upstairs and took leave (I suppose) of his more than amiable wife—left her in a swoon and rode off to the lands telling Major Franks to advise General Washington that he was gone on some business to West Point, and would return in an hour.'

Instead, so Varick soon discovered, Arnold 'rowed down the river with his barge crew and passed King's Ferry as a flagg and went on board the *Vulture* a British man-of-war.' Between times, Washington had arrived at Robinson's House and promptly gone off to West Point in search of Arnold. Varick next described at length how Peggy 'raving mad … fell on her knees with prayers and entreaties to spare her innocent babe.' Finally, the doctor came and, when Peggy 'seemed a little composed she burst again into pitiable tears and exclaimed to me alone on her bed with her that she had not a friend left here. I told her she had Franks and me and General Arnold would soon be home from West Point with General Washington. She exclaimed "No. General Arnold will never return, he is gone; he is gone for ever, there, there, there the spirits have carried up there."'

Still not knowing what had become of Arnold, Washington returned to Robinson's House, whereupon he was called to Peggy's bedchamber. She had become hysterical again, telling Varick that 'there was a hot iron on her forehead and no one but General Washington could take it off and wanted to see the General.' When Washington came to her, she wailed 'that is the man who was going to assist Colonel Varick in killing my child. She repeated the same sad story about General Arnold. Poor distressed, unhappy, frantic and miserable lady.'[1]

All pointed to Arnold's treason, but final proof only came when, about four o'clock that same day, a letter arrived from Arnold, confirming his actions, but asking Washington "'for your protection for Mrs Arnold [who] is as good and innocent as an angel, and is incapable of doing wrong'". Arnold made no mention of John, but assured Washington 'that Varick and Franks, "as well as Joshua Smith Esq. (who I know is suspected) are totally ignorant of any transactions of mine that they had reason to believe were injurious to the public."'[2]

Events moved quickly from there, the desperate search on for Arnold's co-conspirators. Soon anyone close to Arnold—including Varick and Franks—came under suspicion. Numerous arrests were made, everyone expected to account for their recent movements. Meantime, Smith, who had been named by Arnold as an innocent, was tracked down to Fishkill where he was with his family. Dragged out of his bed at 'about midnight on the 25th of September', he was brought to Robinson's House to be confronted by Washington who accused him of 'the blackest treason against the citizens of the United States.' Smith then heard—so he said—for the first time that the 'John Anderson whom you have piloted through our lines proves to be Major John Andre the Adjutant General of the British Army' [and] 'now our prisoner'.[3] Smith would now go on trial for his life.

Following hard on the heels of Smith came 'Major John André', brought under heavy escort by Major Tallmadge in the early hours of 26 September, his guard having 'marched all night.'[4] Of their arrival, Smith described 'hearing the tramp of a number of horses near the place where I was confined and soon after could distinguish the voice of the unfortunate André, and of General Washington and his suite who soothed him with all the blandishments that his education and rank demanded'.[5] Other sources have denied that Washington ever came face to face with John. Yet, it seems strange that Washington would have interrogated Smith but not John, when the urgent imperative at this precise moment was that both 'confess who were your accomplices'.[6] Be that as it may, Smith 'distinctly heard Colonel Hamilton say to a brother officer ... that Major André was really an accomplished young man, and he was sorry for him, for the general was determined to hang him.'[7]

What was revealed to John during this 'Examination' is hidden from view, but, for John, it was enough that he had been brought to Robinson's House, that Arnold was gone from there to the *Vulture*, and that Peggy was still at liberty. This told him what he needed to know: that she was still unsuspected. Now his priority became to ensure that she remained so. Her life now hung by a thread, at her husband's mercy. Whatever 'frantick' thoughts John might still have, he must remember that it was the two of them—he and Peggy—who, all the way back at the time of the Meschianza, had come together in common bond to stop the dread Revolution. His life was almost certainly forfeit now, but it was his duty—to his personal honour—to ensure that she survive. To do this, he must divert attention off Arnold onto himself. The Americans wanted blood. He would give them his own. Quite deliberately, then, he made a further confession, its timing guaranteed for maximum effect. Washington described how it came about in his letter to Clinton on 30 September: 'this Gentleman confessed with the greatest Candour in the Course of his Examination "that it was impossible for him to suppose he came on shore under the Sanction of a Flag."'[8]

Clinton would later argue that the Americans 'took advantage of a letter of his written in low spirits wherein he may imply that he did not go ashore under the sanction of flag and upon this and upon no other they pretend to condemn him … the only evidence they have is a low spirited letter of his own, seeming to imply that he went ashore not under the protection of a flag.'[9] But, of course, Clinton did not understand John's strategy: he had quite expressly gifted the Americans the final piece of proof they needed. His fate was sealed.

As hoped, his latest confession had the desired result: Washington might suspect Peggy of complicity—especially given her earlier histrionics—but with no evidence from John to link her to the conspiracy, 'having recovered somewhat, on the 27th she left us, escorted by Major Franks for Philadelphia, by leave of his Excellency.'[10] Washington was surely glad to be rid of her into the hands of the harpies of Philadelphia and politicians of Congress: let them do their worst. For him, to hang a woman was not part of the Revolution he was fighting to uphold.

John, meantime, could only hope and pray Peggy would remain safe. The next day, his 'Examination' over, he, too, was moved but to Mabie's tavern at Tappan there to await his trial. On the 29th, he was brought before a board of general officers composed of fourteen senior officers, and during the short proceedings, John called no witnesses and offered no new evidence. Adhering to the strict pattern of behaviour he had adopted since being captured by the 'three volunteers', John insisted on making the task of the board as easy as possible.

His answers to questions were intended to incriminate him further. On the matter of the flag, he was even more emphatic than before, stating that it was 'impossible for him to suppose he came on shore under a sanction, and added that if he came on shore under that sanction he certainly might have returned under it.' As to his accomplices, he stuck to his earlier line requesting that he not be 'interrogated concerning anything which did not immediately relate to himself and that he be excused from accusing any other.' This saved Smith's life—for which Smith was grateful—but, more importantly for John, it ensured Peggy remained safe too.

As a result of John's testimony, the board had no choice, and its unanimous verdict was that 'Major André, adjutant general of the British army ought to be considered as a spy from the enemy, and that agreeable to the law and usage of nations, it is their opinion he ought to suffer death.'[11] The next day, Washington approved the sentence, the time set for it to be carried out: the following afternoon, Sunday, 1 October at 5 o'clock.

Following this decision, John was permitted to write to Clinton. By now, as John explained, he was aware of 'the serious light in which my Conduct is Considered and the rigorous determination that is impending'. The ostensible purpose of the letter was a natural desire by John to absolve his commander-in-chief of any blame in his

Self-portrait by John the night before he was executed. (Yale University Art Gallery)

current predicament which he did when saying that 'the Events of coming within an Enemys posts and of Changing my dress which led me to my present Situation were contrary to my own Intentions as they were to your Orders: and the circuitous route which I took to return was imposed (perhaps unavoidably) without alternative upon me.'[12] John had mentioned all the circumstances which made him guilty, except being in possession of 'the Papers' and not coming under a flag. These were strange omissions to have made at a time when John knew this would be his last letter to Clinton. Yet, the omissions were deliberate, the intention being to communicate to Clinton in coded language what he had already told Washington: namely that he had been betrayed by Arnold and that the Papers and the Flag were the proof of Arnold's perfidy. John was not trying to exonerate himself, rather to warn Clinton not to trust Arnold.

John's warning had the desired effect. On 3 October, Clinton wrote a letter to Lord George Germain, Secretary of State for the American Colonies, issuing a damning indictment of Arnold's recent conduct: 'He [Arnold] desires a Conference with my Adjutant General thro' whom alone we had conversed. He names a Place in neutral ground, sends a Flag of Truce to receive the Adjutant General, orders him to change his name and Cloaths, and promises to return Him safe when his Conversation is finished. The Adjutant General in consequence of this goes ashore under the Flag sent for Him, does nothing on shore but by General Arnold's orders and Privacy, is dismissed by that General with a Passport from Him behind their Lines and is taken up three miles on this Side in neutral ground by three militia men, carried back and delivered up to the Enemy: the Report of the Capture is made to General Arnold. He is taken on the Saturday and Arnold does not receive the Report 'till Monday when He flys—In short all this past where and when Arnold commanded.'[13]

Washington, of course, had read John's letter to Clinton before allowing it to be sent on. He quickly grasped that John was accusing Arnold of betrayal. A window of opportunity had opened to make all right, if only Arnold could be exchanged for John. On 30 September, a strange letter arrived at British Headquarters. The letter was unsigned, although its author would subsequently be identified as Alexander Hamilton, Washington's aide-de-camp.[14] Clinton had no way of knowing this. However, it was clear from the contents that it was from an officer close to Washington who had seen the letter John had just sent to Clinton.

The letter proposed that 'perhaps he [John] might be released for General Arnold, delivered up without restriction or condition, which is the prevailing wish. Major André's character and situation seem to demand this of your justice and friendship. Arnold appears to have been the guilty author of the mischief; and ought properly to be the victim, as there is good reason to believe he meditated a double treachery, and had arranged the interview in such a manner, that if discovered in the first instance, he might have it in his power to sacrifice Major André to his own safety.'[15] Whatever private feelings Clinton had, as commander-in-chief he had no option but to reject the suggestion as a trade dishonourable to the British Army. Nevertheless, while waiting on Clinton's response, Washington delayed John's execution.

Meantime, to make sure the Americans did not go back on their decision to have John executed, Arnold wrote a bloodthirsty letter to Washington threatening that if the sentence were carried out, 'I shall think myself bound by every tie and honour to retaliate on such unhappy persons of your army as may fall within my power... But if this warning should be disregarded, and he should suffer, I call heaven and earth to witness that your Excellency will be justly answerable for the torrent of blood that may be spilt in consequence.'[16]

Any threats less likely to secure John's release could not have been conceived. Unsurprisingly, Washington dismissed them, his judgment on Arnold being: 'He wants feeling! From some traits of his character which have lately come to my knowledge, he seems to have been hackneyed in villainy, and so lost to all sense of honour and shame that while his faculties will enable him to continue his sordid pursuits there will be no time for remorse.'[17] Good luck to the British that they were stuck with him.

While waiting for the sentence to be carried out, John wrote one last letter to Washington. 'I trust that the request I make of your Excellency at this serious period, and which is to soften my last moments, will not be rejected. Sympathy towards a soldier will surely induce your Excellency, and a military tribunal to adapt the mode

The last letter written to George Washington by John André prior to his execution. (By kind permission of Major J. E. A. André)

of my death to the feelings of a man of honour. Let me hope, Sir, that if aught in my character impresses you with esteem towards me, if aught in my misfortune marks me as the victim of policy and not resentment, I shall experience the operation of these feelings in your breast by being informed that I am not to die on a Gibbet.'[18]

His request was denied. Reflecting on this, Hamilton wrote to his fiancée, Elizabeth Schuyler, shortly after, telling that 'I urged a compliance with André's request to be shot, and I do not think it would have had an ill effect. But some people are only sensitive to motives of policy, and sometimes from a narrow disposition mistake it. When André's tale comes to be told, and present resentment is over, the refusing him the privilege of choosing [the manner] of death will be branded with too much obduracy.'[19]

After a short delay to allow the British to make representations, John was executed by hanging on Tuesday 2 October 1780. Seeing the gibbet only as he approached the place of execution, Major John André addressed the assembled witnesses: 'All I request of you, gentlemen, is that you will bear witness to the world that I died like a brave man.' His last words were 'It will be but a momentary pang.'

Epilogue

'WESTMINSTER ABBEY'

John was dead, his body buried near where he had been hanged in Tappan. The war carried on, many Americans ambivalent, like Alexander Hamilton, that the wrong man had been hanged and that, even if in justice John deserved to die, it was sad that he had to. The sadness was genuine: not far from the truth was 'the well-known fact' reaching London shortly after the execution that Washington, 'as well as the whole board of officers that sat on his trial were all the time dissolved in tears. His [John's] noble conduct filled them with admiration and pity.'[1] The Marquis de Lafayette, a senior commander of French forces fighting alongside Washington, confided to his wife back home in France how John 'behaved with so much frankness, courage and delicacy' that he 'could not help lamenting his unhappy fate'.[2] This was soon after participating at the board of enquiry which condemned John to death. Likewise, Washington described John as 'an Accomplished Man and Gallant Officer', this just days after signing the order for his execution.

These sentiments from the American camp were confirmed by Mary, wife of an 'officer in the Revolutionary Army', who recorded that John 'is spoken of by the officers as the soul of honor.' Trapped in British-occupied Long Island, she also confided to her journal 'how my heart bleeds' on hearing of John's 'sad end'. Launching into a long panegyric on an enemy she had never met, Mary agonized how ''Tis true he was a spy and dies the death of a spy, but his many noble traits and accomplishments, ardent temperament, integrity and gentleness win admiration and excite compassion and regret.'

Echoing the thoughts of many, Mary lamented 'I cannot think of his bitter fate. General Washington, it is thought would have granted his last affecting request (to die by the musket) but others sternly just, refused the boon and he died ignominiously.' Struggling to understand her confused emotions as she grieved 'at his bitter end', she asked 'is it on account of his fascinating qualities, the blandishment which rank, beauty and chivalrous bearing cast around him? Or is it simply as a man that I pity and deplore him?'[3] Many Americans like Mary would debate long and hard over the rightness of their actions, but would still come to the same ambivalent conclusion, war the ultimate arbiter why so much that felt wrong must happen nevertheless.

No such flickers of doubt ever entered Arnold's mind. He had achieved what he set out to do. No-one—not even his wife—suspected the truth. Nor would they: he had the perfect alibi. Having sealed John's death warrant with his letter to Washington promising eternal retribution, he quickly moved on to securing the 'large amount of money'[4] that he considered his just reward. His heart not missing a beat, he wrote to Clinton on 18 October and, taking John's name in vain, he called in the 'promise'[5] made at 'the interview'. As Arnold anticipated, the British duly paid up, if not the full £10,000 he was demanding, certainly not far short of this amount when the pension for life was added to the immediate cash award of some £6300. A rich reward, indeed, for a grand stroke that he never believed could happen. Hearing of this settlement, Americans would liken Arnold to Judas as they imagined him counting his thirty pieces of silver.

Still, Arnold had one more prize to make his own, and his alone. Fleeing down the Hudson, he had asked of Washington that Peggy 'may be permitted to return to her friends in Philadelphia, or come to me, as she may choose...'[6] Washing his hands of any suspicions he may have had that Peggy's bedside hysterics were convenient histrionics and that she was somehow complicit in Arnold's treachery, Washington left the decision on her fate to the Revolution's politicians. Returned unceremoniously to Philadelphia, Peggy quickly found herself ostracised, and it would have been with mixed feelings that she surrendered to the decision of the supreme executive council of Pennsylvania that she leave the safety of her family and join her husband in New York.

According to the 18 November 1780 edition of New York's Royal Gazette, 'on Tuesday last [the 14th of November] arrived in town the lady and son of Brigadier General Arnold.'[7] There, she found Arnold already fully immersed in Britain's dying attempts to save the thirteen colonies. With the West Point expedition abandoned, Rodney had upped and left for the West Indies, taking substantially all his grand fleet with him. Alone again, Clinton could only mourn John's fate and await in deepening depression the slow demise of his own career, wedded as it now was to the fruitless quest for victory, even, honourable defeat.

Whatever thoughts Clinton nursed about Arnold's 'double treachery', policy dictated not only that he reward the turncoat but that he make use of him militarily. Arnold was appointed a brigadier general and, after being assigned to lead a raid into Virginia, was given command of a major expedition into Connecticut that culminated in the notoriously wanton devastation of the port town of New London. Praise was muted, criticism implied in the official 'General Orders' report submitted by Clinton who lamented that 'the Destruction of the Town ... is a Misfortune that gives him much Concern.'[8]

Arnold's days in North America were numbered. Moreover, no-one truly trusts a traitor.[9] Whatever jealousies John's meteoric rise may have excited during his lifetime, whatever misgivings there may have been regarding the foolhardiness of his decision to go ashore at Haverstraw Bay, John's fellow officers closed ranks round one of their own and against Arnold. Certainly John's 'Death is very severely felt by ye Commr in Chief, as it consequently will be the Army'.[10]

Like the Americans, John's fellow officers instinctively felt that the wrong man had been hanged. According to a report in June 1781 from *Freeman's Journal*, an American newspaper, 'it is said lord Cornwallis refused to see him and that the officers in his lordship's army (who are chiefly gentlemen) refused to serve with him.'[11] It was not long before this animosity burst out into the open, a report in London from October 1781 telling how 'General Arnold has lost all his credit among the British troops, and the English shun to associate with him.'[12]

Arnold's continued presence among them became untenable and, after barely a year serving the loyalist cause, Arnold left New York for London, his ship departing on 15 December. Arriving there, Arnold enjoyed, at best a mixed reception, more often open hostility from a British public smarting from their lingering suspicions of his treachery towards John and resenting that the turncoat had brought no miraculous change to Britain's fortunes in America. By November 1781 he was already being referred to as a 'wretched miscreant'.[13]

Unlike her husband, New York society had quickly taken to Peggy, full, as it was, of like-minded refugees escaping Congress and its puritan strictures. That said, she was evidently carrying a weight in her mind for, according to one who knew her at this time, although 'all allow she has great sweetness in her countenance' it seemed that she 'wants animation, sprightliness, and that fire in her eyes'.[14] This was not the same Peggy who had posed for John ahead of the Meschianza. She left New York for London at the same time as her husband, but travelled in a private ship, where, according to a fellow traveller, she enjoyed chiefly 'military company.'[15]

Once in London, Peggy recovered some of her spirit and soon became a favourite of the Bon Ton, adopted especially by Lady Amherst. Known as the 'Fair American',[16] she was even presented at court.[17] She and Arnold had four more children, her past bond to John seemingly forgotten. Still, marriage was often a prison for loveless women in eighteenth-century Britain and as time passed husband and wife eventually went their separate ways, Arnold initially to Canada in 1785, Peggy left behind to clear up his mounting debts.

How Peggy fitted into John's story, none beyond those in the Philadelphia–New York 'channel' knew for many years, the 'secret correspondence' that she and John had planned from the time of the Meschianza long kept hidden by Clinton in his private papers. None—that is apart from Arnold—suspected the closeness of their bond. None realized that the 'Delia' in the final poem written by John, as 'the fatal hour' drew near during his captivity at Tappan, could be Peggy and that it was she being addressed in his sad refrain: 'Ah! Who can tell if thou my dear will e'er remember me.' Who, reading the poem, understood the significance of John's decision to cast himself as 'Damon' in it? Yet, this said it all: 'Damon' was immortalized as a hero of Greek history for agreeing to take the place of his lifelong friend, Pythias, who was to be executed on the orders of Dionysius.

What John's mother, sisters and brother knew of Peggy and this 'channel' as John planned for the 'grand stroke' remains a mystery, but it is a reasonable certainty—given how silent he had been all these years about his secret war activities—that he said nothing. Nor did John say anything as he faced death. In this respect, it is strange that, writing to Clinton to say farewell, John did not also write to his mother. Maybe a letter was written and given secretly to his servant who was charged with bringing his personal effects—including his tea urn—back to the family. If so, it remains to be found. What is known for sure is that, in his letter to Clinton, John requested that the value of his commission be assigned to his mother and sisters.

It is not known whether Clinton managed to get word to John's mother before she read the shattering news as it hit the headlines of British newspapers on 14 November announcing that John had been captured, 'hung up as a Spy' and 'his body buryed beneath the Gallows on which he was executed'. For days thereafter, the newspapers were full of conflicting reports and swirling rumours how he came to be captured. On one point, all seemed agreed: that John 'met his Death with the Heroick Firmness of a British Chief.'[18]

The *London Evening Post* was especially quick to remind readers that John's death was also a very personal tragedy. All while lamenting that 'the death of the gallant Major André must pain the heart of every well-wisher to this Country', it prompted readers that it 'must be doubly afflicting to those who were particularly acquainted with the amiableness of his character and the accomplishments of his mind.'[19] On this same note, another newspaper told readers that 'Major André, who lately fell a Sacrifice to his own Intrepidity, left a lady and four children in this city bemoaning his loss.'[20]

All through these immediate lamentations, John's family and friends remained stoical, keeping their pain hidden silently. Others spoke up, however, determined to seize on John's tragic fate and endow him with the enlarged stature of a national hero deserving pride of place in a nascent pantheon of 'Great Britons' whose epic heroism was marked out as uniquely British by virtue of the tragedy, pathos and self-sacrifice of their deaths. Gone were the smugness, arrogance and tyranny of Britain, the all-conquering, which had prevailed in the immediate aftermath of the Seven Years' War. John epitomized in his short life and the manner of his death a new patriot-nation: wounded, humbled and reclothed in what came to be known as the 'sentimental sublime,'[21] the emerging Great Britain was now 'the home of a modern and Christian hero,' a young everyman figure replete with 'benevolent sentiments whose actions merit heaven'.[22]

The artist, Benjamin West, had launched this new patriotic iconography with his painting depicting General Wolfe's apotheosis. Next came Anna Seward, first, with her poem, *Elegy on Captain Cook*, published in 1780, then, a year later, with her

Monody on Major André. Little known on the national stage thus far, Anna's career was launched by these two poems.[23] Fortified by their success, she took ownership of John's legacy. Her *Monody* caught the sullen mood of a frustrated nation facing defeat as she inveighed heatedly 'against war, against American treachery and most pointedly against General Washington'.[24] Little versed in the rules of war, she understood this one fundamental principle of eighteenth-century warfare: that civilized combatants do not hang an 'officer and a gentleman'. That 'Remorseless W******'[25] refused John's last request to be shot damned him in her eyes and, even when, stung by the lingering vitriol unleashed by her poem, Washington sent an emissary many years later to plead the necessities of war, Anna 'absolved the general of responsibility for André's execution' but quite stubbornly 'never forgave his refusal to spare André from hanging.'[26]

She was equally forceful in her claim to ownership of John's personal identity. Her avowed bond with John 'thro' Friendship's soft'ning medium on her soul' gave the *Monody* the power of personal tragedy which ensured the elevated status of this 'lovely youth' as that most cherished of literary characters in the eighteenth century, the sentimental man of feeling. For her, John was the 'young genius' whose 'talents for poetry, music and painting' were cruelly cut short at the 'hands of the insatiate dogs of war', as he sought to 'win bright glory from my country's foes.'

To underwrite the authorial validity of the sections in the *Monody* where she claimed personal knowledge of John, she published, as an addendum, three letters which he had written to her 'as Julia' in 1769. Thus licensed, Anna—again as 'Julia'—felt empowered to rewrite the history of John's relationship with Honora Sneyd recasting his decision to enrol in the army as the sentimental product of 'inauspicious love', and his time in America as a testimony to 'constant love'.[27] These fictions brought protests from the André family, but in vain.

By then the public had joined with Anna in taking full ownership of John's legacy, one newspaper stating that 'it will not be too much to assert that he was one of the most promising young men this nation ever produced. The whole army in America will bear witness to the truth of this assertion.'[28] Others were more outspoken, the *Morning Herald* inveighing against 'the wanton murder of the loyal ANDRÉ.' Impelled by 'the common-place feelings of common men' who wished to acknowledge 'the gallant Major André, our beloved countryman',[29] clamours rose for his memory to be immortalized. Hence, it was in this mood of national mourning that, having first granted John's mother a thousand guineas from the privy purse and an annual pension of £300 for life (with reversion to her children), 'His Gracious Sovereign George III caused … a Monument' to be 'erected in Westminster Abbey for Major John André'.

Press coverage was extensive, the *London Chronicle* reporting in its 9 November 1782 edition that 'this monument is composed of a sarcophagus elevated on a pedestal upon the panel of which is engraved the following inscription:

The monument to John André In Westminster Abbey. (Library of Congress)

Sacred to the Memory of Major JOHN ANDRÉ Who raised by his merit at an early period of his life to the rank of Adjutant General of the British forces in America, and employed in an important but hazardous enterprise, fell sacrifice to his zeal for his King and Country on the 2d October 1780, aged 29, universally beloved and esteemed by the army in which he served, and lamented even by his foes.'

In a final comment, the newspaper recorded that 'on the top of the sarcophagus, a figure of Britannia reclined, laments the premature fate of so gallant an Officer. The British Lion too seems instinctively to mourn his untimely death.'[30]

Endnotes

Prologue

1   John Adams Diary 22 in Adams Family Archives, electronic archive, 4 September–9 November 1774 p.2.
2   J. R. Williams (ed.), *Philip Vickers Fithian Journal and Letters 1767–1774* (Princeton, N.J.: Princeton Historical Association, 1900), p.301.
3   Ibid., pp.242–3.
4   *Dunlap's Pennsylvania Packet* (20 June 1774).
5   Williams (ed.), *Philip Vickers*, p.182.
6   John Adams Diary 21, p.43.
7   Williams (ed.), *Philip Vickers*, p.181.
8   Ibid., p.230.
9   *Lady's Magazine* (January 1774), V, p.7.
10 *Lady's Magazine* (July 1774), V, p.342.
11 *WEP* (6 April 1769).
12 Williams (ed.), *Philip Vickers*, p.260. See footnote citing resolution adopted by the Virginia Assembly on 26 May 1774.
13 Ibid., pp.171–2.
14 *LEP* (1 February 1774).
15 *Lady's Magazine* (January 1774), V, p.54.
16 Williams (ed.), *Philip Vickers*, p.105.
17 *GEP* (21 January 1774) citing *Boston (New England) Gazette*, 20 December 1773).
18 *Lady's Magazine* (March 1774), V, p.166.
19 *PA* (4 June 1774).
20 *Daily Advertiser* (7 June 1774).
21 *PA* (4 June 1774).
22 See 'The Papers of General Samuel Smith' in *Historical Magazine* (February 1870), VII, p.82.
23 'Ship Registers for the Port of Philadelphia 1726–1775' in *The Pennsylvania Magazine of History and Biography* 28 No. 3 (1904), pp.346–374 and No.4 (1904), pp.470–507.
24 See B. Paullo, 'Pennsylvania Archives, Second Series Volume II' in the 'USGenWeb Archives'.
25 See 'Ship Registers for the Port of Philadelphia 1726–1775' in *Pennsylvania Magazine of History and Biography* Vol. 28 No.4 (1904), pp.470–507 and for a biographical sketch of John Inglis see G. B. Keen, 'The Descendants of Joran Kyn, the founder of Upland' in *Pennsylvania Magazine of History and Biography* 5 No.3 (1881), p.339. See also P. Force (ed.), *American Archives, Fourth Series, containing a Documentary History of the English Colonies in North America...* (6 vols., Washington: St. Clair Clarke and Force, 1840), V, p.54 where 'Captain Inglis' was made a prisoner following a naval skirmish near Savannah, Georgia with revolutionary forces in March 1776.
26 W. Duane (ed.), *Extracts from the Diary of Christopher Marshall kept in Philadelphia and Lancaster during the American Revolution 1774–1781* (Albany, New York: J. Munsell, 1877), p.6.

27 *PA* (29 March 1777).
28 *Dunlap's Pennsylvania Packet* (20 June 1774).
29 Williams (ed.), *Philip Vickers*, p.148.
30 Letter from James Tilghman Jr. to George Washington dated 7 April 1774 in S. M. Hamilton (ed.), *Letters to George Washington and Accompanying Papers* (Society of the Colonial Dames of North America, Library of Congress).
31 Williams (ed.), *Philip Vickers*, p.148.
32 'Mechanicks' was a term in common usage at the time denoting tradesmen. See 'Letter from the Committee of Mechanicks of Boston' dated 24 September 1774 in 'American Archives', an online resource from Northern Illinois University.
33 John Adams Diary 21, p.43.
34 Williams (ed.), *Philip Vickers*, p.xiv.
35 Ibid., p.181.
36 *MC* (18 July 1774).
37 André letter dated 17 December 1776 from John André to his mother, Mary-Louisa, in the family records held by Major J. E. A. André, which referred to 'a Mr Smith who had been a fellow passenger on board the St. George.'
38 See 'The Papers of General Samuel Smith' in *Historical Magazine* (February 1870), VII, pp.81–2.
39 Anon., *Emigrants from England 1773–1776* (Boston, Massachusetts: New England Historic Genealogical Society, 1913), p.88.
40 See 'Extracts from the Journal of Miss Sarah Eve' in *Pennsylvania Magazine of History and Biography* Vol. 5 No.1 (Historical Society of Pennsylvania, 1881), pp.29–30 which writes of 'King Tammany as he used to be called, but now I think they have got him canonized, for he is now celebrated as St. Tammany.'
41 See P. M'Robert, *A Tour Through Part of the North Provinces of America 1774–1775* (Edinburgh: 1776), pp.29–31 for a detailed description of the city and its layout in 1775.
42 J. Wilkinson, *Memoirs of my Own Times* (3 vols., Philadelphia, Pennsylvania: A. Small, 1816), I, p.12.
43 A. L. George, *Old Philadelphia. Cradle of American Democracy* (Charleston, South Carolina: Arcadia Publishing, 2003), p.62.
44 Anon., *Journals of the House of Commons...* (London: by order of the House of Commons, 1803) XXXVI, p.339.
45 *St. James's Chronicle* (14 April 1769). 'Yesterday, at his House, at Clapton, Anthony Andre, Esq.'
46 André letter dated 19 October 1769 from John André to Anna Seward. See *Morning Herald* (17 July 1781).

Chapter 1 – Refugees

1 *PA* (16 August 1753).
2 'Moneyed men': S. R. Cope, 'The Stock Exchange Revisited. A New Look at the Market in Securities in London in the Eighteenth Century' in *Economica* New Series 45 No.177 (February 1978), p.12 citing I. de Pinto, *An Essay on Circulation and Credit* (T. Ridley, London, 1774), p.39; 'Change-Alley Broker': ibid., p.9 citing A Winter Evening's Conversation...at a Noted coffee-house in Change-Alley (London: G. Smith, 1748), np; 'jobbing-brokers': ibid., p.4 citing 'Philanthropos' (T. Mortimer) *The Nefarious Practice of Stock-Jobbing Unveiled* (London, 1756), np; 'Mercuries': *PA* (19 April 1765); 'the chicaneries of Bubble': *PA* (16 August 1753); 'Nefarious Practice of Stock-Jobbing': Cope, p.4 citing 'Philanthropos' (T. Mortimer) *The Nefarious Practice of Stock-Jobbing Unveiled* (London, 1756), np.
3 Known also as the Levant Company.

4 *Penny London Post* (15 May 1747) (os).

5 The French forename was anglicized for the official naturalization. See Anon. *Journal of House of Lords* 27 March 1748 1–10 pp.176–183 in Journal of the House of Lords 27 1746–1752 (London 1767–1830), BHO: 'Andre Nat. Bill. A Message was brought from the House of Commons, by Mr Wilson and others. With a Bill intituled "An Act for naturalizing Anthony André and David André," to which they desire the Concurrence of this House.'

6 So-called 'Huguenots' were the first 'refugees', their experience bringing this word from French into the English language.

7 *General Advertiser* (17 November 1752) (os).

8 Sherratt & Hughes (printer), *Letters of Denization and Acts of Naturalization for Aliens in England & Ireland 1701–1800* (London: Publications of the Huguenot Society, 1923), Vol. XXVII, p.149.

9 See Register of Baptism for John André on 16 May 1750 per Ancestry.com.

10 D. Garrioch, *The Huguenots of Paris and the Coming of Religious Freedom 1685–1789* (Cambridge: Cambridge University Press, 2014), p.122.

11 D. C. A. Agnew, *Protestant Exiles from France in the Reign of Louis XIV* (3 vols., London: Reeves and Turner, 1871), II, p.vi.

12 Ibid., II, p.54.

13 Sherratt & Hughes, *Letters of Denization* XXVII, p.44. This same Andrew left unclaimed dividends in 1749 per *The Names and Descriptions of the Proprietors of Unclaimed Dividends on the Publick Funds*, published by the South Sea Company and printed by J. Tipp, London, 1791, p.131, as did James Girardot.

14 *Penny London Post* (15 May 1747) (os). (30,000l = PV £6.2 million)

15 Sherratt & Hughes, *Letters of Denization* XXVII, p.44.

16 Garrioch, *The Huguenots of Paris*, p.135.

17 Sherratt & Hughes, *Letters of Denization* XXVII, p.127.

18 See J. B. Burke, *A Genealogical and Heraldic History of the Landed Gentry in Great Britain and Ireland* (2 vols., Harrison, London, 1871), I. p.145 which described Anne's father, Paul Foissin, as an 'East India merchant in Paris'.

19 *WEP* (31 October 1751) (os).

20 Sir F. Pollock (ed.), *The Revised Reports being A Republication Of Such Cases in the English Courts of Common Law and Equity from the year 1785* (London, Sweet and Maxwell Ltd, 1891), Vol. II (1790–4), pp.235–7.

21 *Remembrancer (1747)* (28 July 1750) (os). See also L. Sutherland, *Politics and Finance in the Eighteenth Century* (London: Hambledon Press, 1984), pp.41–2.

22 *Daily Journal* (7 February 1730) (os).

23 *GEP* (24 January 1751) (os).

24 Pollock (ed.), *The Revised Reports*, pp.235–7.

25 *Daily Journal* (7 February 1730) (os).

26 *Daily Post* (2 February 1733) (os).

27 See *PA* (12 April 1762).

28 *Daily Journal* (7 February 1730) (os).

29 Burke, *A Genealogical and Heraldic History... I*, p.146.

30 A. D. Francis, *Portugal 1717–1808. Joanine, Pombaline and Rococo Portugal as seen by British Diplomats and Traders* (London: Tamesis Books, 1985), p.35.

31 Ibid., pp.106–8.

32 T. Vanneste, *Global Trade and Commercial Networks. Eighteenth Century Diamond Merchants* (London: Pickering and Chatto, 2011), p.41.

33 See Vanneste, *Global Trade and Commercial Networks*, pp.54, 155, 172.

34 Francis, pp.107–8.

35 L. Namier & J. Brooke (eds.), *The History of Parliament. The House of Commons 1754–90* (3 vols., London: Secker and Warburg, 1985) II, pp.118–9.

36 *LEP* (26 September 1745) (os).

37 *PA* (12 April 1754).

38 *Read's Weekly Journal* (18 January 1752) (os).

39 Namier & Brooke (eds.), *The History of Parliament. The House of Commons 1754–90* II, pp.118–9.

40 Sherratt & Hughes, *Letters of Denization* XXVII, p.139.

41 Ibid., p.145.

42 G. Bannerman, *Merchants and the Military in Eighteenth Century Britain* (Abingdon: Routledge, 2015), p.126.

43 Namier & Brooke (eds.), *The History of Parliament. The House of Commons 1754–90*, II, pp.118–9. These contracts were: '1740–56 for remitting money for the forces at Gibraltar and Minorca (generally about £200,000 per year); and 1741–56 for provisioning the troops in Minorca'.

44 See Anon., *Journals of the House of Commons…* (London: by order of the House of Commons, 1803) XXXII, p.936 which referred to a cargo of '1065 Quarters of Wheat' to be delivered in December 1743 to 'Messrs André and Co of Genoa' (p.394) who, as 'Proprietors of the Cargo of Corn … was by them sent over into England, and there paid by the Victualling Board.'

45 John-Lewis settled in Britain and was naturalized in March 1753. See *Journals of the House of Lords*, XXVIII, p.54.

46 W. Betham, *The Baronetage of England* (London: E. Lloyd, 1804), Vol. IV, p.295.

47 *PA* (2 December 1755). Charles Dodd was a partner in the firm of 'Perochon, Dodd, Firth and Company' See Vanneste, *Global Trade and Commercial Networks*, p.93. Charles Dodd traded in 'barley and Indian corn' according to H. E. S. Fisher, *The Portugal Trade. A Study of Anglo-Portuguese Commerce 1700–1770* (Abingdon: Routledge, 1971), p.67. For the 'Bonifas Brothers', see Vanneste, *Global Trade and Commercial Networks*, p.148.

48 For the Girardots see Garrioch, *The Huguenots of Paris*, p.138. For the Girardots and Andrés, see C. Le Fort, G. Revilliod, E. Frick (eds.), *Le Livre du Recteur, Catalogue des Etudiants de l'Academie de Geneve de 1559 a 1859* (Geneva, Switzerland 1860), pp.232. 234, 243.

49 See Register of Births in Ancestry.com.

50 *LEP* (24 March 1768).

51 *GEP* (15 October 1751) (os).

52 See Register of Baptisms in Ancestry.com. 'Jean' was another of John André's uncles, according to J. L. Chester, 'Some Particulars respecting the Family of Major John André' in *Proceedings of the Massachusetts Historical Society* 14 (1875–6), p.219.

53 See Register of Baptisms in Ancestry.com.

Chapter 2 – 'A Heap of Rubble'

1 *PA* (2 December 1755). This 'Andrew' was the 'Girardot-Buissieres' naturalized in 1742 and should not be confused with another Andrew Girardot de Chancourt, born in August 1743, baptised in the 'parish of St. James's, Westminster' and also in the process of making Britain his new home. The maternal uncle of John André, this second 'Andrew' was naturalized in 1752. To avoid confusion with the earlier generation of the dynasty, he was referred to in the press as 'And. Girardot jun. Esq'.

2 T. Vanneste, *Global Trade and Commercial Networks. Eighteenth Century Diamond Merchants* (London: Pickering and Chatto, 2011), p.142.

3 *PA* (2 December 1755).

4 L. Namier & J. Brooke (eds.), *The History of Parliament. The House of Commons 1754–90* (3

vols., London: Secker and Warburg, 1985), II, pp.118–9. Bristow had first made his name in England as 'a considerable Underwriter of Government loans' and, in 1744, had 'subscribed £150,000 in an English government loan' (see Vanneste, p.54.) He subsequently branched out into the notoriously fickle area of international finance. His reach extended even into the Baltic, where, in 1753, 'Messrs John Bristow, Edmund Boehm and Samson Gideon' lent the sum of 'ninety thousand pounds' to 'the City of Dantzick'. See *Read's Weekly Journal* (17 March 1753).

5   Having secured the election of John Girardot de Tillieux to the board of the South Sea Company in 1733, Bristow arranged for John's maternal uncle, 'And. Girardot jun.' to be elected in 1760 (See *Read's Weekly Journal* (2 February 1760).

6   X. Caron, 'Images d'une Elite au XVIIIe Siècle, Quarante Négociants Anoblis face à la Question Sociale.' in *Histoire, Economie et Societé* 3 No.3 (3eme trimester, 1984), p.395.

7   Letter dated 28 November 1760 from L. Darell to John-Lewis André in family records held by Major J. E. A. André.

8   H. Chamberlain, *A New and Compleat History of the Cities of London and Westminster* (London: J. Cooke, 1770), p.478.

9   Ann Marguerite was the Andrés' second daughter, Mary Hannah, the first being born in 1752. A further daughter, Louisa Catherine, was born in December 1755, and a second son, William Lewis, in 1760. See Ancestry.com. So far in this text, John's mother has been called 'Marie-Louise'. Henceforth she is addressed as 'Mary-Louisa', being that Ann's baptism was when her name is first seen to be anglicized.

10   P. Gauci, *The Politics of Trade. The Overseas Merchant in State and Society 1660–1720* (Oxford: Oxford University Press, 2003), p.41.

11   See J. F. Bosher, 'Huguenot Merchants and the Protestant International in the Seventeenth Century' in *The William and Mary Quarterly* 52 No.1 (January 1995), pp.77–102 and D. J. Ormrod, 'The Atlantic Economy and the Protestant Capitalist International 1651–1775' *Historical Research* 66 (1993), pp.197–208. Among these were the Thellusson, Naville, Gaussen, Amyand, Fonnereau and Clarmont families.

12   *PA* (16 August 1753).

13   *Remembrancer (1747)* (28 July 1750) (os). See also L. Sutherland, *Politics and Finance in the Eighteenth Century* (London: Hambledon Press, 1984), pp.41–2.

14   Sutherland, *Politics and Finance*, p.42. fn.2 citing Samson Gideon, the most successful government financier of the first half of the eighteenth century.

15   See P. L R. Higonnet, D. S. Landes, H. Rosovsky (eds.), *Favorites of Fortune. Technology, Growth and Economic Development Since the Industrial Revolution* (Cambridge, Massachusetts: Harvard University Press, 1991), p.257.

16   *Universal Magazine of Knowledge and Pleasure*, VII, 1750, p.44.

17   *Universal Chronicle* (7 July 1759), p.219.

18   *St. James's Chronicle* (7 July 1768).

19   *A Society of Merchants and Tradesmen, The Compleat Compting-House Companion or Young Merchant and Trader's Sure Guide* (London: W. Johnston, 1763), p.201.

20   *St. James's Chronicle* (21 May 1763).

21   *LG* (23 May 1763).

Chapter 3 – 'The Three Mile Stone'

1   *Gazetteer and New Daily Advertiser* (15 July 1766).

2   *LEP* (21 April 1767).

3   *A Society of Merchants and Tradesmen*, p.183.

4   Ibid., p.433. Another source asserted that the Andrés had been living for some five years in 'a red-brick house on the north side of Capworth Street, with grounds stretching back to Lea Bridge Road' in the neighbouring village of Leyton. 'The house which was square in front with bow-windows at the back, may have been built by Anthony André to replace an older one in 1758'. See W. R. Powell (ed.), *A History of the County of Essex* (London: Victoria County History, 1973), VI, pp.184–197.

5   Anon., *The Edinburgh Gazetteer* (6 vols., Archibald, Constable and Co, Edinburgh, 1822), VI, p.563.

6   See *PA* (20 March 1755). Peter Lefebure (also spelt Lefevre) was 'Secretary to the Foreign Office in the General Post-Office'. See also *LEP* (2 January 1752) (os).

7   See Powell (ed.), *A History of the County of Essex*, VI, pp.184–197.

8   *A Society of Merchants and Tradesmen*, p.257.

9   *PA* (26 March 1763).

10 *Gazetteer and New Daily Advertiser* (23 September 1768). It has been suggested by one source that the property in Clapton chosen as their home was Beecholme House, located opposite Brooke House, the most substantial property in the area and formerly 'a royal seat called King's Place,' built in 1532 'on the later border between Upper and Lower Clapton' (See T. F. T. Baker (ed.), *A History of the County of Middlesex* (London: Victoria County History, 1995), Vol. X (Hackney), pp.44–51.

11 G. & J. Cary, *Cary's New Itinerary* (London: G. & J. Cary, 1826), p.515.

12 *A Society of Merchants and Tradesmen*, p.355.

13 D. C. A. Agnew, *Protestant Exiles from France in the Reign of Louis XIV* (3 vols., London: Reeves and Turner, 1871), II, p.100. Both 'Jullerand Mourgue' and 'Michael Reau' chose to be buried, the latter in 1742, in what became the family vault at Clapton's St. Augustine's Church. Mary Girardot Reau was naturalized in 1709 per Sherratt & Hughes (printer), *Letters of Denization and Acts of Naturalization for Aliens in England & Ireland 1701–1800* (London: Publications of the Huguenot Society, 1923), Vol. XXVII, p.89.

14 See D. Lysons, *The Environs of London: the County of Middlesex* (London: T. Cadell jun. and W. Davies, 1795), II, pp.450–516. Mary Girardot was the wife of Andrew Girardot-Buissiers who was naturalized in 1742 (see Sherratt & Hughes, *Letters of Denization*, XXVII, p.145). She was also the 'Mary Girardot Buissiers' by whose will the London Hospital received a donation of £20 in 1768. (See Anon., *A General State of the London Hospital for the Relief of Sick and Wounded Seamen, Manufacturers and labouring Poor, their Wives and Families* (London, 1787), p.xxi. Following her death in 1767, Mary also chose to be buried at St. Augustine's, Clapton.

15 See R. B. Gardner, *The Admission Registers of St. Paul's School from 1748 to 1876* (London: George Bell and Sons, 1884), p.142 where at the end of the list of 'scholars' taught under the delightfully named 'Mr Thicknesse' during his term of office as 'High Master' between 1748 and 1769, the school's alumni book simply states that 'John André … must be included among Thicknesse's pupils, though his name is not found in the Registers'. There is a suggestion from an unnamed source—possibly a school contemporary of John's—that he initially attended Westminster School. The 23 November 1780 edition of the *Public Advertiser* carried a report that 'Major Andre discovered when a Boy those easy Manners and that associating Temper which afterwards made him live with such general Acceptance… He was bred at Westminster during the latter End of Dr Markham's time.'

16 *Lloyd's Evening Post* (19 March 1766).

17 Gardner, *The Admission Registers of St. Paul's School*, p.130.

18 B. Wriston, 'The Howard Van Doren Shaw Memorial Collection' in *Art Institute of Chicago Museum Studies* (4, 1969), p.90.

19 *PA* (7 May 1761).

Chapter 4 – 'Young Gentlemen'

1 G. Wilson, *The Life of the Hon. Henry Cavendish* (London: Harrison and Son, 1851), p.16.

2 L. Namier & J. Brooke (eds.), *The History of Parliament. The House of Commons 1754–90* (3 vols., London: Secker and Warburg, 1985), II, p.110.

3 *Lloyd's Evening Post* (5 May 1766), 'Hackney School' being a further variation on the title attributed to the establishment.

4 Namier & Brooke (eds.), *The History of Parliament. The House of Commons 1754–90*, II, p.110.

5 N. Hans, *New Trends in Education in the Eighteenth Century* (Abingdon: Routledge, 1998), p.72.

6 *St. James's Chronicle* (31 January 1768).

7 *LEP* (6 March 1770).

8 S. L. Barczewski, 'Yorke, Philip, second Earl of Hardwicke' in ODNB.

9 R. Blanchard, 'A Prologue and Epilogue for Nicholas Rowe's Tamerlane by Richard Steele' in Modern Language Association's PMLA, 47 No.3 (September 1932), pp.772–6. The 'Hon. Henry Cavendish' was also eleven 'when he became a pupil at Dr. Newcome's School in Hackney' in 1742 (See Wilson, *The Life of the Hon. Henry Cavendish*, p.16).

10 R. Simpson, *Memorials of St. John at Hackney* (Guildford: J. Billing and Sons, 1882), p.182. The only evidence that might contradict this dating is from the 1767 edition of the *Universal Pocket Companion*, another Vade Mecum, which still listed Anthony André at Walthamstow. Internal dating within this source hinted, however, that the information in this third edition had not been updated beyond 'August 1 1760'. See L. Hawks and Co, G. Keith, J. Rivington, R. Baldwin, *The Universal Pocket Companion* (London, 1767), 'Contents' np. It seems John's father wished to be enrolled as an official member of his local congregation but without having to undertake any of the associated duties.

11 J. L. Chester, 'Some Particulars respecting the Family of Major John André' in *Proceedings of the Massachusetts Historical Society* 14 (1875–6), p.218.

12 Anthony could count on being richer still when his aging mother, Mary, died, and he inherited the remaining two-thirds of the David André estate.

13 *LC* (6 March 1764). Born in 1753, Harrington followed his father and grandfather into the army, becoming an ensign in the Coldstream Guards in 1769. (See S. M. Farrell, 'Stanhope, Charles' in ODNB.) He later served in America, using his other title, 'Lord Petersham'.

14 Ibid., (6 March 1764).

15 M. Durban, 'Cavendish, William, fifth duke of Devonshire' in ODNB.

16 See K. W. Schweizer, 'Cavendish, William, fourth duke of Devonshire' in ODNB and Hans, *New Trends in Education in the Eighteenth* Century p.244.

17 According to one source, William 'attended a school before becoming duke, but it is unknown which one. (See M. Durban, 'Cavendish, William, fifth duke of Devonshire' in ODNB.) Yet, it is a matter of record that Lord John Cavendish, one of the 'three bachelor uncles' responsible for William's education, approached Dr Newcome for advice at this time. Edmund Pyle explained why in his *Memoirs of a Royal Chaplain*: Newcome 'kept a school at Hackney where a number of the sons of the nobility were educated, among whom were William, Marquis of Hartington who succeeded as [4th] Duke of Devonshire in 1755.' (See E. Pyle, *Memoirs of a Royal Chaplain, 1729–1763* (London: John Lane, Bodley Head, 1905), p.281).

18 Hans, *New Trends in Education in the Eighteenth Century*, p.244.

19 Namier & Brooke (eds.), *The History of Parliament. The House of Commons 1754–90*, II, p.110.

20 Ibid., III, p.147 citing letter from C. Molineux to J. Fabie dated 18 May 1771 in Molineux letter book.

21 L. Hawks and Co, G. Keith, J. Rivington, R. Baldwin, *The Universal Pocket Companion* (London, 1767), pp.39–40.

22 *Bingley's Journal* (13 July 1771).

23 *Gazetteer and New Daily Advertiser* (22 March 1764).

24 'Miscellaneous Letters', in *Pennsylvania Magazine of History and Biography* 43, No.3 (1919), p.262.

25 A. Matthews (ed.), *Letters of Dennys De Berdt 1757–77* (Cambridge, Mass: John Wilson and Son, 1911), pp.294–5.

26 *Lloyds Evening Post* (31 December 1762).

27 *LC* (1 March 1763). See also Baker (ed.) in 'Hackney Education' X, pp.148–165 per BHO.

28 J. Nichols, *A Select Collection of Poems* (London: J. Nichols, 1784), Vol. VIII, pp.152–3.

29 J. André, *The Frantick Lover* (New York, New York: Blue Ox Press, 1941), np.

30 Letter from C. Molineux to Rev B. Cary dated 5 January 1771 from Molineux letter book cited in Namier & Brooke (eds.), *The History of Parliament. The House of Commons 1754–90*, III, p.146.

31 Namier & Brooke (eds.), *The History of Parliament. The House of Commons 1754–90*, III, p.147.

32 See 'Member Biographies: Vaughan, Benjamin' in R. Thorne (ed.), *The History of Parliament. The House of Commons 1790–1820* (available from Boydell and Brewer, 1986).

33 L. C. Judson, *A Biography of the Signers of the Declaration of Independence and of Washington and Patrick Henry* (Philadelphia, Pennsylvania, J. Dobson and Thomas, Cowperthwait & Co., 1839), p.253.

34 Ibid., p.122.

35 Rising sixteen when he acted in the school's April 1751 production, the earl of Euston was nearing the end of his time at the school. Later that same year, he was hurried off to Cambridge, which he attended from 1751 to 1753, before embarking on a two-year Grand Tour, which 'completed his education in the manner appropriate to an eighteenth century gentleman'. See P. Durrant, 'FitzRoy, Augustus Henry, third duke of Grafton' in ODNB.

36 S. M. Farrell, 'Cavendish, Lord John' in ODNB.

37 Wilson, *The Life of the Hon. Henry Cavendish,* p.16.

38 André letter dated 19 October 1769.

39 C. Le Fort, G. Revilliod, E. Frick (eds.), *Le Livre du Recteur, Catalogue des Etudiants de l'Academie de Geneve de 1559 a 1859* (Geneva, Switzerland 1860), p.232.

40 Letter from André to A. Seward dated 1 November 1769. See *Morning Herald* (17 July 1781).

41 See P. L. R. Higonnet, D. S. Landes, H. Rosovsky (eds.), *Favorites of Fortune. Technology, Growth and Economic Development Since the Industrial Revolution* (Cambridge, Massachusetts: Harvard University Press, 1991), pp.254–5.

42 *LEP* (17 September 1763). See also D. C. A. Agnew, *Protestant Exiles from France in the Reign of Louis XIV* (3 vols., London: Reeves and Turner, 1871), II, p.447.

43 *LEP* (17 March 1763).

Chapter 5 – 'Claptonians'

1 D. Defoe, *A Tour Thro' the whole Island of Great Britain Divided into Circuits or Journies…* (2 vols., London: G. Strahan, 1725), II, p.2.

2 E. Walford, *Old and New London* (London: Cassell & Company, 1892), V, p.524.

3 *Gazetteer and New Daily Advertiser* (1 August 1767).

4 *Lloyd's Evening Post* (2 June 1767).

5 Ibid., (24 February 1769).

6 André letter dated 19 October 1769.

7 According to D. Lysons, *The Environs of London: the County of Middlesex* (London: T. Cadell jun. and W. Davies, 1795), II, pp.481–2, the annual average number of baptisms registered rose from 99 in the years 1746–55, to 114 in the years 1756–1765, then leapt to 142 in the years 1766–1775 and the number of households increased commensurately: from 983 in 1756 to 1,212 in 1779.

8 *Gazetteer and New Daily Advertiser* (31 October 1767).

9 Lysons, *The Environs of London: the County of Middlesex*, II, p.472.

10 *Gazetteer and New Daily Advertiser* (25 June 1768).

11 Lysons, *The Environs of London: the County of Middlesex*, II, p.472.

12 *LEP* (17 March 1764).

13 *Lloyd's Evening Post* (5 July 1765).

14 Ibid., (18 July 1768).

15 *LEP* (12 November 1767).

16 *PA* (6 December 1766).

17 *St. James's Chronicle* (7 July 1768).

18 *Gazetteer and New Daily Advertiser* (20 September 1766).

19 *Gazetteer and New Daily Advertiser* (15 August 1770).

20 *PA* (14 October 1766). The higher you were on these lists the higher the amount you subscribed.

21 T. H. Croker, T. Williams, S. Clark, *The Complete Dictionary of Arts and Sciences* (3 vols., London, 1766), I, np. This list was set alphabetically, which meant that any relative generosity by Anthony went unnoticed.

22 Anon., *Proceedings of the Committee for Relieving the Poor Germans...* (London: J. Haberkorn, 1765), title page. Maybe as a gauge of their relative wealth at this time, both David and John-Lewis subscribed '10s 6d', whereas Samuel Bosanquet, the André family's patron, put up 20*l*, one of the largest donations.

23 Lysons, *The Environs of London: the County of Middlesex*, II, p.516.

24 See J. L. Chester, 'Some Particulars respecting the Family of Major John André' in *Proceedings of the Massachusetts Historical Society* 14 (1875–6), p.220.

25 See *Read's Weekly Journal* (2 February 1760).

26 *PA* (20 August 1765).

27 *St. James's Chronicle* (12 July 1766).

28 G. E. Bannerman, *Merchants and the Military in Eighteenth Century Britain* (Abingdon: Routledge, 2015), ebook np.

29 *LEP* (1 August 1761).

30 Ibid., (14 February 1761).

31 André letter dated 19 October 1769.

32 See *GEP* (16 November 1780).

33 See *MJ* (6 May 1769).

34 Letter from André to A. Seward dated 3 October 1769. See *Morning Herald* (17 July 1781).

35 W. Sargent, *The Life and Career of Major John André* (Boston, Massachusetts: Ticknor and Fields, 1861), pp.402–3.

36 F. Fleming, *Killing Dragons. The Conquest of the Alps* (London: Granta Books, 2001), np.

37 L. Namier & J. Brooke (eds.), *The History of Parliament. The House of Commons 1754–90* (1964), 'The Members' III, np via BHO available from Boydell and Brewer.

38 A. Blackstock & E. Magennis (eds.), *Politics and Political Culture in Britain and Ireland 1750–1850* (Belfast: Ulster Historical Foundation, 2007), p.108. 'how long he [Conolly] stayed there and whether he graduated, are unclear'.

39 See H. H. Milman, *The Life of Edward Gibbon* (Paris: Baudry's European Library 1840), p.66.

40 See letter from James Boswell to William Temple dated 17 April 1764 in B. De Zuylen, *Boswell in Holland 1763–1764* (New York, New York: McGraw-Hill, 1928), pp.224–8. According to one source, 'it has been calculated that some 150 Englishmen visited Voltaire during the 1760s, though the host himself guessed at well over twice that number'. See R. Pearson. *Voltaire Almighty. A Life in Pursuit of Freedom* (London: Bloomsbury, 2010), np.

41 See J. Rae, *The Life of Adam Smith* (New York, New York: Cosimo Classics, 2006), pp.188–194.

42 C. Le Fort, G. Revilliod, E. Frick (eds.), *Le Livre du Recteur, Catalogue des Etudiants de l'Academie de Geneve de 1559 a 1859* (Geneva, Switzerland 1860), pp.260–1.

43 Her will was proved in Geneva in November 1767. See Chester, 'Some Particulars respecting the Family of Major John André' p.219.

44 *LEP* (16 January 1766). This was a reference to Jean-Jacques Rousseau, the French philosopher.

45 Ibid., (13 February 1766).

46 *WEP* (24 July 1766).

47 *St. James's Chronicle* (30 December 1766).

48 *LC* (3 January 1767).

49 S. G. Tallentyre, *The Life of Voltaire* (New York, New York: Knickerbocker Press, 1910), p.468.

50 *LEP* (8 January 1767).

51 *PA* (13 February 1767).

52 André letter dated 19 October 1769.

Chapter 6 – 'Change Alley

1   André letter dated 19 October 1769.

2   D. Noy, *Dr Johnson's Friend and Robert Adam's Client Topham Beauclerk* (Newcastle-upon-Tyne: Cambridge Scholars Publishing, 2016), p.48.

3   André letter dated 19 October 1769.

4   Anon., *Universal Pocket Dictionary* (London: L. Hawes & Co, 1767), p.108.

5   W. Maitland, *The History and Survey of London...* (2 vols., London: T. Osborne, J. Shipton, J. Hodges, 1756), I, p.840.

6   See *A Society of Merchants and Tradesmen*, pp.182–237.

7   Maitland, *The History and Survey of London...*, I, p.840.

8   These were the Duvals, Nouialles, Rigails, Rondeaus and Fonnereaus. See Anon., *Universal Pocket Dictionary* (London: L. Hawes & Co, 1767), pp.128–162.

9   André letter dated 19 October 1769.

10 F. A. de Voltaire, *Candide* (English version: New York, New York: Boni & Liveright, 1918), p.122.

11 André letter dated 19 October 1769. See also *PA* (19 April 1765) for disparaging reference to these 'Mercuries'.

12 *The Universal Magazine of Knowledge and Pleasure*, XXXIV (1764), p.86.

13 See C. H. Wilson, *Anglo-Dutch Commerce and Finance in the Eighteenth Century* (Cambridge: The University Press, 1941), pp.164–5.

14 Letter dated 15 January 1763 from Chamier to the Earl of Bute in 'Musgrave Collection of Autographs in British Museum vol. iii' cited in D. C. A. Agnew, *Protestant Exiles from France, chiefly in the reign of Louis XIV* (3 vols., Private Circulation, 1886), II, p.465.

15 Sir John Hawkins, *The Works of Samuel Johnson* L.L.D. (1787), I, pp.422–3 cited in G. B. Hill (ed.), *Boswell's Life Of Johnson* (6 vols., New York, New York: Harper & Brothers, 1799), I, p.553 fn. Among his gentlemanly pursuits, Chamier enjoyed the sybaritic company of the political writer, Edmund Burke, the dramatist, Oliver Goldsmith, and the court painter, Sir Joshua Reynolds, who, with him, were founder members of Dr Johnson's famous 'Literary Club'.

16 S. Seymour and S. Haggerty, 'Slavery Connections of Brodsworth Hall 1600–c1830' (Final Report for English Heritage, 2010), p.26.

17 J. L. Chester, 'Some Particulars respecting the Family of Major John André' in *Proceedings of the Massachusetts Historical Society* 14 (1875–6), p.220.

18 Noy, *Dr Johnson's Friend and Robert Adam's Client Topham Beauclerk*, p.48.

19 F. M. Smith, 'An Eighteenth-Century Gentleman, The Honourable Topham Beauclerk' in *The Sewanee Review* 34 No.2 (April 1926), p.206.

20   = PV £836,000.

21   The loan was called in on 29 December 1764 shortly after Beauclerk's return to England, and 'payment to them', according to his biographer, 'must be connected to his gambling loss in Venice'. But 'the Andrés do not appear to have operated at Venice themselves,' which had his biographer, Noy, surmising that 'perhaps a debt was sold on to them' or that Beauclerk 'already had a connection which enabled him to call on them in an emergency.' See Noy, *Dr Johnson's Friend and Robert Adam's Client Topham Beauclerk*, p.48.

22   Smith, 'An Eighteenth-Century Gentleman…' p.205.

23   Noy, *Dr Johnson's Friend and Robert Adam's Client Topham Beauclerk*, p.48.

24   *PA* (3 May 1766).

25   A. Burke, 'The English Merchants in Canada 1759–1766' (Montreal, Canada: University of Ottawa MA thesis, 1968), pp.3–4.

26   *Lloyd's Evening Post* (28 May 1766).

27   *PA* (3 May 1766).

28   Burke, 'The English Merchants', pp.40–2 and p.66.

29   *Gazetteer and New Daily Advertiser* (13 August 1764).

30   See Burke, 'The English Merchants' p.71 fn. 20 referring to Proclamation by General Murray, Quebec, 23 November 1759 p.11.

31   J. Almon, *A Collection of all the Treaties of Peace, Alliance and Commerce between Great Britain and other Powers from the Revolution in 1688 to the present time* (2 vols., London, 1772), II, p.298.

32   *Gazetteer and New Daily Advertiser* (2 January 1766).

33   *Lloyd's Evening Post* (28 May 1766).

34   *Gazetteer and New Daily Advertiser* (10 October 1765). Among these 'military gentlemen' was Alexander Johnstone, colonel in charge of fortifications on the island, who bought Baccaye, a sugar plantation, in 1766.

35   *Gazetteer and New Daily Advertiser* (17 December 1766).

36   See T. Pearce, 'The Amyand Correspondence from 1764–1766' in *BWI Study Circle Bulletin* 204 (March 2005), pp.27–8.

37   See 'Public Notary and Land Records' at sos.ri.gov. online archive re: Protested bill of exchange De Monchy on Bosanquet & Fatio for John and Henry Peschier, 3 endorsements, Grenada, 27 February 1770 pp.71–2.

38   M. Dresser & A. Hann (eds.), *Slavery and the British Country House* (Swindon: English Heritage, 2013), pp.84–6.

39   See 'Public Notary and Land Records' at sos.ri.gov. online archive re: (Protested bill of exchange Fournillier on Ant & Jn Ls Andre for Thomas and James Lucas 5 endorsements, Grenada, 18 November 1763), p.25.

40   See Seymour and Haggerty, *Slavery Connections of Brodsworth Hall 1600–c1830* (Final Report for English Heritage, 2010), p.46 footnote 162 which refers to a record in the London Family History Centre: 'LFHC Grenada Register of [Land] Records, Index 1764–1871 (Vols. AZ1-A-E6) Film 1563217, H1 139ff, Indenture between Peter and Marie Fournillier and Andre Antoine, 1767.'

41   See 'Public Notary and Land Records' at sos.ri.gov. online archive re: Protested bill of exchange Fournillier on Ant & Fr. Ls Andre for John Hasler, 3 endorsements, Grenada, 22 February 1769 p.68.

42   See Grenada Land Registry: Grenada Register of [Land] Records 2nd Series cited as source in S. Seymour and S. Haggerty, *Slavery Connections of Brodsworth Hall 1600–c1830*.

43   M. Quintanilla, 'The World of Alexander Campbell: An Eighteenth-Century Grenadian Planter' in *Albion, A Quarterly Journal concerned with British Studies* 35 No. 2 (Summer 2003), p.236.

44   André letter dated 19 July 1772 from John André to John Lewis André in Wichita State University Libraries Special Collections and University Archives MS 90–04 Box 1 FF8 André Family Papers Letter 2.

45 See N. Hunt, 'EAP148 Inventory of Archival Holdings in Jamaica': MS 1212 'Indenture between J.L. André of London and A. Campbell regarding the reconveyance of Tivoli Plantation'. (British Library: The Endangered Archives Programme, 2007) np.

46 See N. Hunt, 'EAP148 Inventory of Archival Holdings in Jamaica': MS 1300 'Indenture between A. Campbell et al and H. Hope et al regarding Agreement of the Mortgage on Tivoli Plantation in Grenada'. (British Library: The Endangered Archives Programme, 2007), np.

47 Quintanilla, 'The World of Alexander Campbell', p.237 fn.34.

48 See 'Public Notary and Land Records' at sos.ri.gov. online archive re: 'Protested bill of exchange Samolict Blamarque on Pierre Chellusson [sic] for John Hasler, endorsed to Barrow & Rowe, Peleg Clark, Grenada, 9 March 1769', p.8.

Chapter 7 – 'The Great Scheme'

1 *Gazetteer and New Daily Advertiser* (18 September 1766).

2 T. Evans and W. Davis (eds.), *Seventh Report from the Committee of Secrecy Appointed by the House of Commons ... to enquire into the State of the East India Company* (London, 1773), Appendix No 9: 'Extract of Letter from Lord Clive, President at Bengal, to the Court, 30 September 1765' np. See also H. V. Bowen, 'Lord Clive and Speculation in East India Company Stock, 1766' in *The Historical Journal* 30 No.4 (December 1987), p.909.

3 L. Sutherland, *Politics and Finance in the Eighteenth Century* (London: Hambledon Press, 1984), pp.177–8.

4 Bowen, 'Lord Clive', p.908 citing Clive to Walsh 17 April 1765.

5 *Lloyd's Evening Post* (1 January 1767).

6 See Bowen, 'Lord Clive', p.909 fn. 29.

7 *St. James's Chronicle* (17 April 1766). See also Bowen, 'Lord Clive', p.913.

8 Bowen, 'Lord Clive', p.908 citing Clive to Walsh 17 April 1765.

9 Ibid., p.911 fn. 48 citing Walsh to Clive 31 March 1766.

10 Ibid., p.911.

11 J. L. Chester, 'Some Particulars respecting the Family of Major John André' in *Proceedings of the Massachusetts Historical Society* 14 (1875–6), p.220.

12 Bowen, 'Lord Clive', p.912.

13 *Lloyd's Evening Post* (1 January 1767).

14 *Public Ledger* (12 July 1766).

15 Sutherland, *Politics and Finance*, p.334 citing letter dated 1 July 1766 from Orme to I. Panchaud.

16 Ibid., p.333.

17 H. V. Bowen, 'Investment and Empire in the later Eighteenth Century: East India Stockholding 1756–1791' in *The Economic History Review* 2 No. 2 (May 1989), see table p.199.

18 G. K. McGilvary, *Guardian of the East India Company: The Life of Laurence Sulivan* (London: Tauris Academic Studies, 2006), p.150.

19 S. R. Cope, 'The Stock Exchange Revisited. A New Look at the Market in Securities in London in the Eighteenth Century' in *Economica* New Series 45 No.177 (February 1978), p.2 citing J. Houghton, *A Collection for the Improvement of Husbandry and Trade* (London, 1692), np.

20 Sutherland, *Politics and Finance*, p.340.

21 See McGilvary, *Guardian of the East India Company*, p.150.

22 See BL online reference: GB 59 Mss Eur G27/51/2 ff 209–210.

23 J. Keay, *The Honourable East India Company. A History of the English East India Company* (London: HarperCollins, 1993, paperback edition), p.365.

24 J. G. Parker, 'The Directors of the East India Company 1754–1790' (Edinburgh: PhD thesis,

University of Edinburgh, 1977), p.80. Lionel went on to become a director and chairman of the company. (See J. B. Burke, *A Genealogical and Heraldic History of the Landed Gentry in Great Britain and Ireland* (2 vols., Harrison, London, 1871), p.258.)

25   T. Evans and W. Davis (eds.), *Seventh Report from the Committee of Secrecy Appointed by the House of Commons…to enquire into the State of the East India Company*, Appendix No.17.

26   T. Davies, 'New Perspectives on European Private Trade in the Eighteenth Century. British Merchant Networks and the Western Indian Ocean' (University of Warwick), np: fn. 26 referring to BL, IOR E/1/14 ff. 336–337v and E/1/23 ff. 127–128v. See also M. Woolf, 'Joseph Salvador 1716–1786' in *Transactions*. (Jewish Historical Society of England) 21, 1962–1967 pp.104–137.

27   Evans and Davis (eds.), *Seventh Report from the Committee of Secrecy*, Appendix No.17. This partnership appears in the Company's 1770 register.

28   See Woolff, 'Joseph Salvador 1716–1786', pp.104–137 and F. Trivelatto, *The Familiarity of Strangers: The Sephardic Diaspora, Livorno and Cross-Cultural Trade in the Early Modern Period* (New Haven, Connecticut: Yale University Press, 2009), pp.222–4.

29   Evans and Davis (eds.), *Seventh Report from the Committee of Secrecy*, Appendix No.17.

30   André letter dated 19 October 1769.

31   *LM* (February 1771), XXXX, p.74.

32   See Bowen, 'Lord Clive', pp.917–8.

33   See Sutherland, *Politics and Finance*, pp.348–9.

34   See Parker, 'The Directors of the East India Company 1754–1790', pp.38–9 and Sutherland, *Politics and Finance*, p.200.

35   Sutherland, *Politics and Finance*, p.341.

36   Ibid., p.205.

37   A. Wood Renton (ed.), *The English Reports, House of Lords* Case 46 'John Lewis André Appellant, Alexander Crauford Respondent' [22 March 1771] (Edinburgh: William Green & Sons, 1900) I, p.625.

38   See *LC* (3 May 1766).

39   See Sutherland, *Politics and Finance*, pp.341–2.

40   Wood Renton (ed.), *The English Reports*, p.625.

41   See *St. James's Chronicle* (7 July 1768).

Chapter 8 – 'Lame Ducks'

1   *St. James's Chronicle* (4 April 1769).
2   *PA* (4 April 1769).
3   *WEP* (6 April 1769).
4   *St. James's Chronicle* (8 April 1769).
5   Ibid., (15 April 1769).
6   *WEP* (6 April 1769).
7   *St. James's Chronicle* (8 April 1769).
8   *St. James's Chronicle* (15 April 1769).
9   *LC* (25 May 1769).
10   *St. James's Chronicle* (25 May 1769).
11   *LC* (25 May 1769).
12   *St. James's Chronicle* (25 May 1769).
13   *Independent Chronicle* (27 October 1769).
14   L. Sutherland, *Politics and Finance in the Eighteenth Century* (London: Hambledon Press, 1984), pp.341–3.

15 *St. James's Chronicle* (17 July 1769).
16 *LC* (18 July 1769).
17 *St. James's Chronicle* (20 July 1769).
18 *Lloyd's Evening Post* (5 December 1770).
19 A. Wood Renton (ed.), *The English Reports, House of Lords* Case 46 'John Lewis André Appellant, Alexander Crauford Respondent' [22 March 1771] (Edinburgh: William Green & Sons, 1900), I, p.626.
20 *St. James's Chronicle* (15 April 1769).
21 *Lloyd's Evening Post* (15 April 1769).

Chapter 9 – Shakespeare's Jubilee

1   See 'Church of England Baptisms, Marriages, Burials, 1538–1812, Hackney, St. John at Hackney' as recorded by Ancestry.com.
2   André letter dated 19 October 1769.
3   André letter dated 1 November 1769.
4   André letter dated 19 October 1769. See also B. Rizzo (ed.), *Early Journals and Letters of Fanny Burney Vol.4 The Streatham Years 1780–1781* (Oxford: Oxford University Press, 2003), p.128 for a lively description of Peter Boissier in later life.
5   See G. W. Marshall (ed.), *The Genealogist* (London: George Bell & Sons, 1882), VI, pp.168–172.
6   W. Sargent, *The Life and Career of Major John André* (Boston, Massachusetts: Ticknor and Fields, 1861), p.402.
7   André letter dated 3 October 1769.
8   *St. James's Chronicle* (19 September 1769).
9   *GM* (July 1769), XXXIX, p.364.
10 *GM* (September 1769), XXXIX, p.422.
11 *St. James's Chronicle* (5 August 1769).
12 E. C. Everard, *Memoirs of an Unfortunate Son of Thespis* (Edinburgh: James Ballantyne & Co, 1818), p.13.
13 *GM* (September 1769), XXXIX, pp.422–3.
14 *St. James's Chronicle* (19 September 1769).
15 *GM* (September 1769), XXXIX, pp.422–3.
16 J. Boswell, *The Life of Samuel Johnson L. L. D.* (5 vols., London: John Murray, 1831), II, p.71.
17 Brighthelmstone is now known as Brighton.
18 Boswell, *The Life of Samuel Johnson*, II, p.71.
19 André letter dated 19 October 1769.
20 Everard, *Memoirs of an Unfortunate Son of Thespis*, p.117.
21 *GM* (September 1769), XXXIX, pp.422–3.
22 *LM* (September 1769), XXXVIII, p.455.
23 André letter dated 19 October 1769. When, elsewhere in this same letter to Anna, John alluded to 'Signora Cynthia' lighting his way home to Clapton, he was inviting Anna into another coded message, this of the many references to 'Cynthia' in Shakespeare, not least in *Romeo and Juliet*. (See A. Findlay, *Women in Shakespeare. A Dictionary* (London: Continuum, 2010), p.91.
24 André letter dated 3 October 1769.
25 A. Seward, 'Eyam', in W. Wood, *The History and Antiquities of Eyam* (London: Thomas Miller, 1842), p.142. See also *European Magazine* (1792), XXII, p.308.
26 W. Scott (ed.), *The Poetical Works of Anna Seward* (3 vols., Edinburgh: James Ballantyne & Co, 1810), I, p.cliv.

27 *WEP* (21 September 1769).

28 T. Pennant, *A Tour in Scotland* (London: B. White, 1776), p.5.

29 P. H. Hembry, *The English Spa 1560–1815. A Social History* (Madison, NJ: Fairleigh Dickinson University Press, 1990), p.306.

30 *PA* (22 July 1766).

31 *LEP* (25 August 1767).

32 Ibid., (27 August 1767).

33 *Lloyd's Evening Post* (30 June 1769).

34 F. N. C. Mundy, *Poems* (Oxford: W. Jackson, 1768), p.28.

35 Ibid., p.24.

36 Ibid., p.77.

37 A. Seward, *Letters of Anna Seward* (6 vols., Edinburgh: Archibald Constable & Company, 1811), V, p.222. Anna also mentioned that 'Dr Falconer of Bath was of our party'.

38 Mundy, *Poems*, p.7.

39 André letter dated 3 October 1769.

40 Mundy, *Poems*, p.81.

41 André letter dated 3 October 1769.

42 André letter dated 1 November 1769.

43 *PA* (29 September 1769).

44 A. Seward, 'Sonnet III' in *Original Sonnets on various subjects and Odes paraphrased from Horace* (London: G. Sael, 1799), p.5.

45 Pennant, *A Tour in Scotland*, p.5.

46 Seward, 'Sonnet III', p.5.

47 André letter dated 19 October 1769.

48 It is worth noting that Eclipse, the horse which had won all its races since its first outing in May, was set to run again at 'Lichfield Races' beginning on 'Tuesday the 19th Day of September'. As Anna's father also held an important position in the local ecclesiastical hierarchy being 'collated to the prebend of Pipa Parva at Lichfield Cathedral', the Sewards needed to be back home for the races, as well as to attend the 'balls, ordinaries and concerts as usual' and to host the 'public Breakfast at the Vicar's Hall on Wednesday, Thursday and Friday Mornings' which were all part of the 'Races' calendar. (See *St. James's Chronicle* (7 September 1769). Unsurprisingly, the 'King's 100 guineas' event was 'won easy', by Eclipse, further ensuring its reputation as the wonder horse of all times. See *WEP* (23 September 1769).

49 See BHO: 'Lichfield from the Reformation to c.1800' in M. W. Greenslade (ed.), *A History of the County of Stafford Vol.14. Lichfield* (London, 1990), pp.14–24.

50 Everard, *Memoirs of an Unfortunate Son of Thespis*, p.118.

51 Darwin's so-called Lunaticks are supposed to have 'provided the dominant intellectual behind the Industrial Revolution in England' (D. King-Hele, 'Erasmus Darwin, the Lunaticks and Evolution' in *Notes and Records of the Royal Society of London* 52 No.1 (January 1998), p.155.) Dr. Darwin alone counted numerous inventions as his own, including a copying-machine and speaking-contraption.

52 R. L. Edgeworth, *Memoirs of Richard Lovell Edgeworth Esq.* (London: Richard Bentley, 1844), p.150.

53 André letter dated 3 October 1769.

54 See H. Mackenzie, *The Man of Feeling* (London: Cassell, 1886), a novel first published in 1771.

55 See margin note to the André letter dated 3 October 1769.

56 André letter dated 19 October 1769.

57 André letter dated 3 October 1769.

58 André letter dated 19 October 1769.

59 André letter dated 1 November 1769.
60 André letter dated 19 October 1769.
61 André letter dated 1 November 1769.
62 André letter dated 3 October 1769.
63 André letter dated 19 October 1769.
64 André letter dated 3 October 1769.
65 André letter dated 19 October 1769.
66 André letter dated 3 October 1769.
67 André letter dated 19 October 1769.
68 André letter dated 1 November 1769.
69 *MJ* (12 September 1769) reporting from the 31 July 1769 edition of the *Philadelphia Gazette*.
70 *WEP* (7 December 1769).

Chapter 10 – 'A Gloomy Compting House'

1   André letter dated 3 October 1769.
2   André letter dated 1 November 1769.
3   André letter dated 3 October 1769. See also *Daily Advertiser* (4 February 1772) which described a 'Farm-house, opposite Brook House, at Clapton' being sold by auction together with 'Live and Dead Stock in the Farming Way' including 'Geldings, a fine young Bull, Cows, Hogs'.
4   André letter dated 3 October 1769.
5   André letter dated 19 October 1769.
6   André letter dated 3 October 1769.
7   André letter dated 19 October 1769.
8   André letter dated 3 October 1769.
9   See W. Musgrave, *Obituary prior to 1800* (London: Harleian Society, 1900), XLVI, p.34. and *GEP* (28 April 1770).
10 André letter dated 3 October 1769.
11 André letter dated 1 November 1769.
12 André letter dated 3 October 1769.
13 André letter dated 1 November 1769.
14 When listing this among his items of 'news' in his letter dated 19 October 1769, John doubtless had in mind newspaper accounts in, among others, the *Middlesex Journal* for 3 October 1769 which reported that 'several of the magistrates in the neighbourhood of Spitalfields went to several public-houses about there to preserve peace and good order.'
15 *MJ* (3 October 1769).
16 See G. W. Marshall (ed.), *The Genealogist* (London: George Bell & Sons, 1882), VI, pp.168–172.
17 *PA* (4 April 1769).
18 *MJ* (3 October 1769).
19 Anon., *The Military Register … for the year 1770* (London: J. Almon, 1771), p.30.
20 *LG* (19 November 1774).
21 *MJ* (3 October 1769).
22 J. Brown, *Reports of Cases upon Appeals and Writs of Error in the High Court of Parliament* (Dublin: E. Lynch, 1784), VI, pp.444–7.
23 A. Wood Renton (ed.), *The English Reports, House of Lords* Case 46 'John Lewis André Appellant, Alexander Crauford Respondent' [22 March 1771] (Edinburgh: William Green & Sons, 1900), I, p.625.
24 Brown, *Reports of Cases upon Appeals and Writs of Error in the High Court of Parliament*, VI, pp.444–7.

25 *PA* (16 August 1753) (os).

26 *MJ* (22 April 1769). This 'Black List' was a macabre play on its normal namesake, 'that black list, called *The Annual Bill of Mortality*' (*LEP* 18 December 1766).

27 André letter dated 19 October 1769.

28 André letter dated 1 November 1769.

29 E.V. Lucas, *A Swan and her Friends* (London: Methuen & Co, 1907), p.45.

30 See *Morning Herald* (17 July 1781).

31 D. Heiland, 'Swan Songs. The Correspondence of Anna Seward and James Boswell' in *Modern Philology* 90, No.3 (February 1993), pp.382–3.

32 Lucas, *A Swan and her Friends*, p.38.

33 Ibid., p.41.

34 Ibid., p.43.

35 R. L. Edgeworth, *Memoirs of Richard Lovell Edgeworth Esq.* (London: Richard Bentley, 1844), pp.152–5.

36 Anon., *Journals of the House of Lords* XXXIII, p.63. See also Brown, VI, pp.444–7.

37 Edgeworth, *Memoirs of Richard Lovell Edgeworth Esq.*, pp.154–5.

38 Lucas, *A Swan and her Friends*, p.45.

Chapter 11 – 'House of Lords'

1 See Anon., *The English Reports House of Lords* (Edinburgh: William Green & Sons, 1900), I, Appendix A, pp.625–8.

2 *LC* (29 December 1759).

3 S. R. Cope, 'The Stock Exchange Revisited. A New Look at the Market in Securities in London in the Eighteenth Century' in *Economica* New Series 45 No.177 (February 1978), p.13.

4 *Lloyd's Evening Post* (12 October 1770). The attacks on 'Change Alley continued remorselessly throughout 1770, the newspapers lashing out at 'that base Alchymic bubble of the nation' (*LEP* (16 October 1770)), where 'Change Alley Lyes' (*Lloyd's Evening Post* 25 April 1770) are all 'trumped up to assist some Change Alley business.' (*MJ* 31 March 1770).

5 See J. Brown, *Reports of Cases upon Appeals and Writs of Error in the High Court of Parliament* (Dublin: E. Lynch, 1784), VI, pp.444–7.

6 See Anon., *English Reports* I, pp.625–8.

7 See Brown, *Reports of Cases*, VI, pp.444–7.

8 Cope, 'The Stock Exchange Revisited', p.13.

9 See Anon., *English Reports* I, pp.625–8.

10 *LG* (9 April 1771).

11 F. S. Vivian, 'John André as a Young Officer' in *Journal of the Society for Army Historical Research* XL, No.162 (June 1962), p.62.

12 The Crauford family-seat was at Newark Castle in Kilbirnie, Lanarkshire and a first baronetcy conferred on it in 1628. Alexander's father, Quintin, was 'one of the Justiciary Baillies of the West Seas of Scotland' (J. Paterson, *History of the Counties of Ayr and Wigton* (Edinburgh; James Stillie, 1864), Vol. II, p.445).

13 *MJ* (11 April 1771).

14 See G. A. Cranfield, *The Press and Society from Caxton to Northcliffe* (Abingdon: Routledge, 2016), p.59.

15 See A. H. Craufurd, *General Craufurd and his Light Division* (Pickle Partners Publishing, ebook edition, 2011), np.

16 See *Lloyd's Evening Post* (2 May 1768).

17 *MJ* (11 April 1771). The transaction cited to prove this complaint was the recent appointment

within the company of 'a relation of Sir Gilbert Eliott's, a Scotchman' and one of the many MPs who had a specific interest in the Company. See the career of Andrew Stuart in L. Namier & J. Brooke (eds.), *The History of Parliament. The House of Commons 1754–90* (3 vols., London: Secker and Warburg, 1985), I, pp.495–8.

18 See C. H. and D. Philips, 'Alphabetical List of Directors of the East India Company from 1758 to 1858', *The Journal of the Royal Asiatic Society of Great Britain and Ireland* No.4 (October 1941), p.329.

19 William Murray was created Lord Mansfield in 1756. See J. Oldham, 'Murray, William' in ODNB.

20 *House of Lords Journal*, XXXIII (March 1771), p.131.

21 See D. C. A. Agnew, *Protestant Exiles from France in the Reign of Louis XIV* (3 vols., London: Reeves and Turner, 1871), II, p.251.

22 See Agnew, *Protestant Exiles from France*, II, p.283.

23 See R. Burnham and R. McGuigan, *The British Army Against Napoleon, Facts, Lists, Trivia 1805–1815* (Barnsley: Frontline Books, 2010), p.140 and p.152. See also H. C. B. Rogers, *The British Army of the Eighteenth Century* (London: George Allen & Unwin, 1977), pp.54–5.

24 In 1770, the annual pay for a lieutenant in the Seventh Regiment of Foot was £85 3s 4d (PV = c.£15,000). See Anon., *The Military Register … for the year 1770* (London: J. Almon, 1771), p.188. the annual pay of a lieutenant in the Foot Guards was £143 (PV = c.£26,000)

25 *LM* (January 1763), XXXII, p.50.

26 Ibid., (July 1763), XXXII, p.390.

27 *MJ* (9 September 1770).

28 *Bingley's Journal* (15 September 1770). By 30 November, 'policies were opened at Old and New Lloyds and several coffee-houses…to give nine guineas to receive 100 if war is declared in seven days' (*Lloyd's Evening Post* 30 November 1770).

29 Rogers, *The British Army of the Eighteenth Century*, p.54. See also *MC* (29 April 1774) for the cost of various regimental uniforms and accoutrements.

30 *Penny London Post* (15 May 1747) (os).

31 André letter dated 3 October 1769.

32 *LM* (February 1771), XL, p.106.

33 *GEP* (27 June 1771). See also *MJ* (26 September 1769) and *Independent Chronicle* (29 January 1770).

34 D. Wahrman, *The Making of the Modern Self. Identity and Culture in Eighteenth Century England* (New Haven, Connecticut: Yale University Press, 2004), p.63.

35 *MJ* (7 February 1771).

36 André letter dated 3 October 1769.

37 P. Groves, *Historical Records of the 7th or Royal Regiment of Fusiliers* (Guernsey: F. B. Guerin, 1903), p.286.

38 R. L. Edgeworth, *Memoirs of Richard Lovell Edgeworth Esq.* (London: Richard Bentley, 1844), p.155.

39 C. L. Kairoff, *Anna Seward and the End of the Eighteenth Century* (Baltimore, Maryland: John Hopkins University Press, 2011), p.84.

40 Edgeworth, *Memoirs of Richard Lovell Edgeworth Esq.*, p.155.

41 See Burnham and McGuigan, *The British Army Against Napoleon*, p.151.

42 Ibid., p.140.

43 See Agnew, *Protestant Exiles from France* II, p.501.

44 Anon., *The Military Register … for the year 1770* (London: J. Almon, 1771), p.36.

45 See F. S. Vivian, Letter dated 4 April 1955 heading 'Nine Chapters from an unpublished biography of Major John André' in National Army Museum Archives ref. 2004—09–199.

46 *LG* (13 April 1773).

47 See Will Registers. England and Wales: Prerogative Court of Canterbury Wills, 1384–1858 per www.Ancestry.com.

48 See Agnew, *Protestant Exiles from France* II, p.199.
49 See Burnham and McGuigan, *The British Army Against Napoleon*, pp.140 and 152.
50 Vivian, 'John André as a Young Officer', p.62.

Chapter 12 – 'The Drill Book'

1   See F. S. Vivian, 'John André as a Young Officer' in *Journal of the Society for Army Historical Research* XL, No.162 (June 1962), p.66.
2   See W. C. Ford, *British Officers serving the American Revolution 1774–1783* (Brooklyn, New York: Historical Printing Club, 1897), p.61 when Robert Donkin was promoted to captain on 25 December 1770.
3   R. Donkin, *Military Collections and Remarks* (New York, New York: H. Gaine, 1777), p.133 fn.
4   Vivian, 'John André as a Young Officer', p.68 citing Royal Warrant of 11 February 1767.
5   B. Cuthbertson, *B. Cuthbertson's System for the Complete Interior Management and Economy of a Battalion of Infantry* (Bristol: Routh's and Nelson, 1776 edition), p.2.
6   J. Love, *Geodaesia. The Art of Surveying and Measuring Land made Easy* (London: J. Rivington, 1771), see title page.
7   T. Simpson, *Select Exercises for Young Proficients in the Mathematicks* (London: J. Nourse, 1752), see title page.
8   Love, *Geodaesia*, see title page.
9   See Vivian, 'John André as a Young Officer', p.71.
10 Cuthbertson, *B. Cuthbertson's System*, p.33.
11 *LEP* (29 August 1771).
12 Cuthbertson, *B. Cuthbertson's System*, p.35.
13 Ibid., p.38.
14 Ibid., p.107.
15 Ibid., p.vi.
16 Ibid., p.37.
17 Ibid., p.132.
18 Ibid., p.37.
19 *PA* (11 May 1768).
20 See W. S. Dunn, *Choosing Sides on the Frontier in the American Revolution* (Westport Connecticut: Praeger, 2007), p.101.
21 Anon., *Critical Memoirs of the Times* (London: G. Kearsley, 1769), p.25.
22 *PA* (11 May 1768).
23 *LEP* (13 July 1771).
24 *PA* (11 May 1768).
25 See C. A. Whatley, *Scottish Society 1707–1830* (Manchester: Manchester University Press, 2000), p.162.
26 *MJ* (12 March 1771).
27 *Craftsman* (30 March 1771).
28 *GEP* (2 April 1771).
29 *Craftsman* (30 March 1771).
30 *London Packet* (8 April 1771).
31 *MJ* (13 April 1771).
32 *GEP* (4 May 1771).
33 *MJ* (13 April 1771).
34 See D. Paterson, *A Travelling Dictionary* (London: T. Carnan, 1781). Calculations based on the same ultimate destination being Chatham barracks.

35 André letter dated 19 October 1769.

36 Anon., *The Journals of the House of Commons…* (London: by order of the House of Commons, 1804), XXXIII, p.33 See also Vivian, 'John André as a Young Officer', p.62.

37 The higher figure would be after the recent augmentation. See Vivian, 'John André as a Young Officer', p.62.

38 See Vivian, 'John André as a Young Officer', p.73 fn.

39 *Gazetteer and New Daily Advertiser* (10 August 1771).

40 Vivian, 'John André as a Young Officer', pp.71–2.

41 *LEP* (18 June 1771).

42 *MJ* (20 June 1771).

43 *LEP* (11 July 1771).

44 Ibid., (16 July 1771)

45 Ibid., (15 August 1771).

46 Vivian, 'John André as a Young Officer', p.74.

47 *PA* (5 August 1771).

48 *MJ* (8 August 1771).

49 *GEP* (8 August 1771). The public nature of these reviews contrasts with the secretiveness of Prussian military reviews, a point made by George Hanger while the guest of Prussian officers in 1773. See G. Hanger, *The Life, Adventures and Opinions of Col. George Hanger* (2 vols., London: J. Debrett, 1801), I, pp.37–8.

50 Vivian, 'John André as a Young Officer', p.74.

51 *Gazetteer and New Daily Advertiser* (10 August 1771).

52 André letter dated 3 October 1769.

53 Cuthbertson, *B. Cuthbertson's System*, p.2.

54 Vivian, 'John André as a Young Officer', p.63.

55 Ibid., p.75.

56 It may only be a coincidence that, soon after the judgment was handed down in the Crauford case, on 5 April 1771 the *Gazetteer and New Daily Advertiser* carried a notice for the 'sale by auction' of a 'Leasehold Estate' at 'Upper Clapton', consisting of 'ten bed-chambers, three parlours, a large dining-hall … and a good coach house.' What, apart from the size, stature and location of the property, suggests that the Andrés may have been the occupants was the length of the unexpired lease, which at 93 years would suggest that departure was brought on by an unexpected change in circumstances.

57 *GEP* (19 September 1771).

58 Ibid., (8 August 1771).

59 *Bingley's Journal* (17 August 1771).

60 *GEP* (8 August 1771).

61 *LEP* (17 August 1771).

62 Vivian, 'John André as a Young Officer', p.77.

63 D. E. Parker, 'The Little War Meets British Military Discipline in America 1755–1781' (University of New Hampshire Master of Arts Dissertation, 1788), p.vii.

64 *LEP* (24 August 1771).

65 André letter dated 3 October 1769.

66 André letter dated 1 November 1769.

Chapter 13 – 'Petite Guerre'

1 See W. C. Ford, *British Officers serving in the American Revolution 1774–1783* (Brooklyn, New York: Historical Printing Club, 1897), p.17: Under 'List of officers.' André, John. 7th reg. Date of Commission: 24th September 1771.'

2   P. Groves, *Historical Records of the 7th or Royal Regiment of Fusiliers* (Guernsey: F.B. Guerin, 1903), p.286.

3   *Gazetteer and New Daily Advertiser* (28 January 1772).

4   *LEP* (10 September 1771).

5   *Westminster Journal* (21 September 1771).

6   *LEP* (3 October 1771).

7   See Anon., *The Military Register…for the year 1770* (London: J. Almon, 1771), pp.41–2 and p.51.

8   D. C. A. Agnew, *Protestant Exiles from France in the Reign of Louis XIV* (3 vols., London: Reeves and Turner, 1871), II, p.180.

9   See *St. James's Chronicle* (29 October 1767) which announced: '7th Reg Foot: Francis Le Maistre Gent. to be Adjutant, vice Humphrey Owen, by purchase'.

10   See *PA* (8 September 1768) which announced: '7th Regiment of Foot: Lieutenant John Despard from Half-Pay, vice Samuel Strode, who exchanges.'

11   See *LC* (31 December 1768).

12   See Agnew, *Protestant Exiles from France* II, pp.204–6.

13   *LC* (31 December 1768).

14   See J. Philippart, *The Royal Military Calendar* (2 vols., London: A. J. Valpy, 1815), I, p.256 and *LG* (28 April 1772).

15   See Anon., *Fielding's New Peerage of England, Scotland & Ireland* (London: John Murray, undated), p.62.

16   See A. E. Fyler, *The History of the 50th or (The Queen's Own) Regiment* (London: Chapman and Hall, 1895), pp.20–29.

17   F. S. Vivian, 'John André as a Young Officer' in *Journal of the Society for Army Historical Research* XL, No.162 (June 1962), p.73.

18   *MJ* (7 April 1771).

19   *Bingley's Journal* (13 April 1771).

20   Vivian, 'John André as a Young Officer', p.73.

21   See B. Cuthbertson, *B. Cuthbertson's System for the Complete Interior Management and Economy of a Battalion of Infantry* (Bristol: Routh's and Nelson, 1776 edition), pp.67–8, pp.116–9 and sundry other sections where the duties of Quarter-Master are described in detail, among which providing lodging while an army was on the move and ensuring proper clothing and accoutrements.

22   J. Lacroix-Leclair and E. Ouellet, 'The Petite Guerre in New France, 1660–1759. An Institutional Analysis' in *Canadian Military Journal* Valour 11. No.4 np. These quotations have been translated from the original French text.

23   See Philippart, *The Royal Military Calendar* I, p.76.

24   R. Donkin, *Military Collections and Remarks* (New York, New York: H. Gaine, 1777), p.222.

25   Ibid., p.240. See also G. Hanger, *The Life, Adventures and Opinions of Col. George Hanger* (2 vols., London: J. Debrett, 1801), I, pp.33–4 for the role of 'partizans' in the Seven Years' War and showing that irregular operations had become a usual mode of warfare.

26   Ibid., p.239.

27   Ibid., p.230.

28   A. L. Poulet, *Jean-Antoine Houdon. Sculptor of the Enlightenment* (Chicago, Illinois: University of Chicago Press, 2005), p.41.

Chapter 14 – 'A Terrible Conflagration'

1   *PA* (20 May 1772).

2   *Gazetteer and New Daily Advertiser* (23 May 1772).

3   *Scots Magazine* (May 1772), XXXIV, p.261.

4   *Gazetteer and New Daily Advertiser* (23 May 1772).
5   André letter dated 14 May 1772 from John André to John Lewis André. See Wichita State University Libraries Special Collections and University Archives MS 90-04 Box 1 FF8 André Family Papers Letter 1.
6   De Maandelyske Nederlandsche Mercurius (May 1772), p.201.
7   *Gazetteer and New Daily Advertiser* (23 May 1772).
8   André letter dated 14 May 1772.
9   André letter dated 14 May 1772.
10 *LM* (January 1781), L, p.7.
11 André letter dated 19 July 1772 from John André to John Lewis André. See Wichita State University Libraries Special Collections and University Archives MS 90–04 Box 1 FF8 André Family Papers Letter 2.
12 Letter from William Short to Thomas Jefferson with enclosure 23 August 1785'. See Jefferson Papers, *Founders Online* National Archives (last modified 29 June 2017).
13 See T. West, *The Curious Mr Howard. Legendary Prison Reformer* (Hook: Waterside Press, 2011), pp.323–4.
14 M. Starke, *Travels in Europe for the use of Travellers on the Continent* (London: John Murray, 1833 edition), pp.654–5.
15 André letter dated 14 May 1772.
16 See A. Moore, 'The evidence for artistic contact between Norfolk and The Netherlands 1500–1800' in J. Roding and L. H. van Voss (eds.), *The North Sea and Culture 1550–1800* (Hilversum: Verloren Publishers, 1996), p.370.
17 E. Robson (ed.), *Letters from America 1773–1780* (Manchester: Manchester University Press, 1951), pp.xiii–xiv.
18 Ibid., pp.3–9.
19 G. Hanger, *The Life, Adventures and Opinions of Col. George Hanger* (2 vols., London: J. Debrett, 1801), I, pp.34–5. See also letters from R. Anderson, *The Works of John Moore, M.D. with Memoirs of his Life and Writings* (7 vols., Edinburgh: Stirling & Slade, 1820), I, pp.59–62 which describe Moore's journey through the German states (including Göttingen) in company with the Duke of Hamilton and expressly becoming 'acquainted' with many German military officers (pp.200–211).
20 *St. James's Chronicle* (31 October 1769).
21 *MJ* (23 May 1773).
22 See 'the king of Prussia's great convoy destined for the siege of Olmutz' in R. Donkin, *Military Collections and Remarks* (New York, New York: H. Gaine, 1777), p.239.
23 Donkin, *Military Collections and Remarks*, p.224.
24 See *MC* (29 April 1774) for details (including 'livr 3000 annual pension') for attending 'a Military School' in Strasburg.
25 *St. James's Chronicle* (1 April 1769).
26 *MJ* (27 April 1769).
27 G. M. Stewart, 'British Students at the University of Göttingen in the Eighteenth Century' in *German Life and Letters* 33. No.1 (October 1979), pp.25–6.
28 *Gazetteer and New Daily Advertiser* (12 April 1769).
29 *PA* (8 February 1770).
30 *Gazetteer and New Daily Advertiser* (8 February 1766).
31 *LEP* (26 October 1771).
32 Ibid., (28 May 1771). Professor Pepin was English, possibly of Huguenot descent, his only known publications being a translation of 'La Véritable Politique des Personnes de Qualité', its English title being 'The Man of Fortune's Faithful Monitor', which served as a work for the easy learning of French, and a series of handbooks for learning German and English.

33 Stewart, 'British Students at the University of Göttingen', pp.32–3.
34 Hanger, *The Life, Adventures and Opinions of Col. George Hanger*, I, pp.27–8.
35 Stewart, 'British Students at the University of Göttingen', p.33.
36 See W. Promies (ed.), *G. C. Lichtenberg, Schriften und Briefe* Sudelbucher, Band II (Munich: Carl Hanser Verlag, 1971), p.905.
37 See *Bingley's London Journal* (24 October 1772) for casual use of this term.
38 Hanger, *The Life, Adventures and Opinions of Col. George Hanger*, I, pp.29–31.
39 *LG* (1 April 1771).
40 C. C. Orr, 'Charlotte and the Northern Republic of Letters' in C. C. Orr (ed.), *Queenship in Europe 1660–1815* (Cambridge: Cambridge University Press, 2004), p.387.
41 *MJ* (1 May 1773).
42 Stewart, 'British Students at the University of Göttingen', p.32.
43 See editorial notes to letter from Philip Dormer Stanhope to Philip Stanhope dated 17 September 1757 per *Electronic Enlightenment* and *PA* (7 December 1770).
44 Aware that, in return for the introduction, his uncle would expect any useful market intelligence, John set out in detail the current politics of the VOC, explaining that Oudermeulen had the ear of the 'Prince d'Orange' and would shortly be sent to the East Indies to reform the VOC. (See A. Singh, 'Fort Cochin in Kerala (1750–1830). The Social Condition of a Dutch Community in an Indian milieu' (University of Leyden, 2007 dissertation), p.57 fn.17.)
45 André letter dated 14 May 1772.
46 E. Gibbon, *The Auto-Biography of Edward Gibbon Esq* (New York, New York: Buckland & Sumner, 1846 edition), p.150.
47 André letter dated 14 May 1772.
48 *LEP* (5 May 1772).
49 *Gazetteer and New Daily Advertiser* (5 May 1772).
50 *LEP* (5 May 1772).

Chapter 15 – 'A Man of Nearly Womanlike Modesty and Gentleness'

1 G. M. Stewart, 'British Students at the University of Göttingen in the Eighteenth Century' in *German Life and Letters* 33. No.1 (October 1979), p.33.
2 André letter dated 19 July 1772 from John André to John Lewis André. See Wichita State University Libraries Special Collections and University Archives MS 90–04 Box 1 FF8 André Family Papers Letter 2. This crisis was triggered by the shenanigans of the 'Macaroni Gambler' (See Anon., 'The Macaroni Gambler', 1772 (British Museum Image BM 5016), Alexander Fordyce, when the firm of 'Mess. Neale, James, Fordyce and Down, bankers in London, stopped payment' on 'the 10th of June'. Their actions led to the collapse of the 'Douglas Heron and Company Bank' of Ayr and, in turn, ruined many Scottish families who were its investors. (See *Scots Magazine* (June 1772), XXXIV, pp.310–311.)
3 J. A. Home (ed.), *The Letters and Journals of Lady Mary Coke* (4 vols., Bath: Kingsmead Reprints, 1970), IV, p.89. Lady Mary, the daughter of the 2nd Duke of Argyll and wife of the reviled Edward, Viscount Coke, was a copious letter-writer and diarist. Spanning the years 1756 to 1774, her letters and journals recorded what seem like her every thought – however mundane or trivial - as she travelled extensively in Europe. Although Lady Mary and John visited the same courts and towns, there is no record that they met.
4 André letter dated 19 July 1772.
5 *Scots Magazine* (June 1772), XXXIV, p.311.

6   André letter dated 19 July 1772. See also Anon., *Akademische Nachrichten auf das Jahr 1773–4* (Erlangen, undated) which gave a list of all academic staff at the university for 1773–4 (pp.60–9)

7   R. Loewenberg, 'A Letter on Major André from Germany' in *American Historical Review* 49 No.2 (January 1944), p.261. See German original in 'the second volume of [Lichtenberg's] letters (Göttingen, 1846), p.258, which is the eighth volume of his collected works.'

8   André letter dated 19 July 1772.

9   See K. Weinhold, *Heinrich Christian Boie* (Halle: Waissenhausse, 1868), p.37.

10   André letter dated 19 July 1772.

11   *Lady's Magazine* (June 1772), III, p.283.

12   *LEP* (23 June 1772).

13   P. Groves, *Historical Records of the 7th or Royal Regiment of Fusiliers* (Guernsey: F. B. Guerin, 1903), p.405.

14   André letter dated 19 July 1772.

15   The 'bad Climate' referred to was in the West Indies, where more soldiers died from tropical diseases than in combat.

16   *Lady's Magazine* (June 1772), III, p.283.

17   Pensacola was Britain's military headquarters for south Florida and the naval base from which it defended the southern flanks of its American colonies against Spanish America. See *MJ* (24 June 1773) which refers to 'the station of Pensacola…where it is intended to have always a cruizing squadron for the protection of our trade in the Gulph of Mexico.'

18   See J. Bohstedt, *The Politics of Provisions: Food Riots, Moral Economy and Market Transition in England c.1550–1850* (Abingdon: Routledge, 2016), p.105 which counted some thirty-seven food riots in the years 1772–3.

19   See W. Wheater, *Historical Record of the Seventh or Royal Regiment of Fusiliers* (Leeds: Private Circulation, 1875), p.66.

20   W. S. Dunn Jr., *Choosing Sides on the Frontier in the American Revolution* (Westport, Connecticut: Praeger, 2007), p.101.

21   Home (ed.), *The Letters and Journals of Lady Mary Coke* IV, p.138.

22   R. Donkin, *Military Collections and Remarks* (New York, New York: H. Gaine, 1777), p.238.

23   André letter dated 19 July 1772.

24   M. Batt, *The Treatment of Nature in German Literature from Gunther to the Appearance of Goethe's Werther* (Chicago, Illinois: University of Chicago Press, 1902), p.53.

25   Letter from Johann Heinrich Voss to Ernst Theodor Johann Bruckner dated 20 September 1772 in A. Voss (ed.), *Briefe von Johann Heinrich Voss* (Halberstadt: C. Bruggemann, 1829), p.91.

26   See R. Kramer, *Cherubino's Leap: In Search of the Enlightenment Moment* (Chicago, Illinois: University of Chicago Press, 2016), pp.85–6.

27   Weinhold, *Heinrich Christian Boie*, p.50.

28   See H-J. Heerde, *Das Publikum der Physik, Lichtenberg's Horer* (Göttingen: Wallenstein, 2006), pp.296–7.

29   G. C. Lichtenberg, *Schriften und Briefe* Sudelbucher, Band II (Munich. Carl Hanser, 1971), p.609.

30   Loewenberg, 'A Letter on Major André from Germany', p.261.

31   See J. Lichtenberg, *Vermischte Schriften* (Göttingen: Dieterich, 1844), IV, p.308.

32   See list of militia regiments garrisoned in Göttingen in T. S. McMillin, *Guide to Hanover Military Records 1514–1866 on Microfilm at the Family History Library* translated by A. L. and O. K. Ladenburger (Inverness, Illinois: Lind Street Research, 2014), pp.160–188.

33   W. Promies (ed.), *G. C. Lichtenberg, Schriften und Briefe* Sudelbucher, Band II (Munich: Carl Hanser Verlag, 1971), p.911.

34   J. Gorton, *A General Biographical Dictionary* (3 vols., London: Whitaker & Co., 1838), III, np.

35   See C. Diederich, *Musenalmanach* (Göttingen) 'MDCCLXXII' frontispiece.
36   Weinhold, *Heinrich Christian Boie*, p.36.
37   André letter dated 19 July 1772.
38   Weinhold, *Heinrich Christian Boie*, p.75.
39   See Weinhold, *Heinrich Christian Boie*, p.75 fn.1.
40   The *Stammbuch* was a popular form of personal literature kept by, among others, young army officers.
41   J. H. Voss, *Sammtliche Poetische Werke* (Leipzig: I. Muller, 1850), IV, p.8.
42   W. Herbst, *Johann Heinrich Voss* (Leipzig, B.G. Teubner, 1872), I, p.80.
43   Voss, *Sammtliche Poetische Werke*, IV, p.9.
44   Letter from Voss to Ernst Theodor Johann Bruckner dated 20 September 1772 in Voss (ed.), *Briefe von Johann Heinrich Voss*, pp.94–5.

Chapter 16 – 'Parting'

1   *Lady's Magazine* (September 1772), III, p.437.
2   *PA* (14 October 1772).
3   *LC* (6 October 1772).
4   *PA* (23 October 1772).
5   *LC* (6 October 1772).
6   G. A. Billias (ed.), Letter from Governor William L. Leyborne to the Earl of Hillsborough dated 30 July 1772 in 'Manuscripts of the Earl of Dartmouth' in *The American Revolutionary Series* (Boston, Massachusetts: Gregg Press, 1972), II, p.530.
7   *PA* (23 October 1772).
8   *LC* (6 October 1772).
9   Report dated 25 January 1773 (Scotland v.47 No.60) from Lord Justice Clerk (Miller) to the Earl of Suffolk in BHO: George III, January 1773 in R. A. Roberts (ed.), *Calendar of Home Office Papers (George III) 1773–5* (London, 1899), pp.2–10.
10   *LEP* (5 January 1773).
11   J. Sherratt to the Earl of Rochford 'transmitting an extract of a letter dated 24 January from a gentleman at Bodmin.' 28 January 1773 (Dom. Geo. III, pcl 86. No.2 a, b) in BHO: George III, January 1773 in R. A. Roberts (ed.), pp.2–10.
12   *GEP* (6 February 1773).
13   *Lloyd's Evening Post* (10 February 1773).
14   Report dated 12 February 1773 from Mr Chamier to Sir Stanley Porten (War Office v.26 No. 3 a to f in BHO: George III, February 1773 in R. A. Roberts (ed.), pp.10–23.
15   Ibid., pp.23–34.
16   W. S. Dunn Jr., *Choosing Sides on the Frontier in the American Revolution* (Westport, Connecticut: Praeger, 2007), p.101.
17   Undated Memorandum from c.8 October 1772 in Billias (ed.), Letter from Governor William L. Leyborne to the Earl of Hillsborough dated 30 July 1772 in 'Manuscripts of the Earl of Dartmouth' in *The American Revolutionary Series* II, p.532.
18   *LEP* (22 April 1773).
19   *MC* (29 April 1773).
20   A. French (ed.), *A British Fusilier in Revolutionary Boston* (Cambridge, Massachusetts: Harvard University Press, 1926), p.3.
21   *LEP* (18 April 1773).
22   French (ed.), *A British Fusilier in Revolutionary Boston*, p.22.
23   Dunn Jr., *Choosing Sides on the Frontier in the American Revolution*, p.101.

24 French (ed.), *A British Fusilier in Revolutionary Boston*, p.22.

25 Ibid., p.6.

26 Ibid., p.16.

27 Ibid., p.4.

28 These included the veteran, Lieutenant John Despard, and the newly promoted Major Stopford, Captain Hesketh and Lieutenant Hamer: See *St. James's Chronicle* (24 November 1772).

29 See M. Roberts, 'Great Britain and the Swedish Revolution 1772–3' in *Historical Journal*, VII No.1 (1964), pp.1–46.

30 Letter from Voss to Bruckner dated 24 February 1773 in A. Voss (ed.), *Briefe von Johann Heinrich Voss* (Halberstadt: C. Bruggemann, 1829), p.125.

31 See *Critical Review* (London, 1773), p.394 which reviews a novel entitled *The Sentimental Spy or the Adventures of a Footman* panning it with the pithy comment that 'if such books answer the ends of publication, to the author and to the bookseller there's still encouragement for those who write.'

32 See J. M. Black, *Plotting Power. Strategy in the Eighteenth Century* (Bloomington, Indiana: Indiana University Press, 2017), p.131.

33 See F. Spencer, 'An Eighteenth-Century Account of German Emigration to the American Colonies' in *Journal of Modern History* 28 No.1 (March 1956), p.55 citing a contemporary *Court and City Register*.

34 Anon., *Journals of the House of Commons* (London: 1803) XXXVI, p.337.

35 Ibid., XXXVI, p.334.

36 Letter from Voss to Bruckner dated 20 September 1772 in Voss (ed.), *Briefe von Johann Heinrich Voss*, p.95.

37 K. Weinhold, *Heinrich Christian Boie* (Halle: Waissenhausse, 1868), pp.75–6.

38 *GEP* (21 March 1771).

39 Ibid., (13 June 1771). See J. I. Israel, *Democratic Enlightenment. Philosophy, Revolution and Human Rights 1750–1790* (Oxford: Oxford University Press, 2011), p.279.

40 See Anon., *A Short Tour Made in the Year One Thousand Seven Hundred and Seventy One* (London: 1775), pp.33–70 for Yorke's efforts in 1771 to court the heir-apparent.

41 A. L. Poulet, *Jean-Antoine Houdon. Sculptor of the Enlightenment* (Chicago, Illinois: University of Chicago Press, 2005), p.52.

42 Ibid., p.43.

43 *MC* (16 June 1772).

44 See 'Regiment Saxe-Gotha' in T. S. McMillin, *Guide to Hanover Military Records 1514–1866 on Microfilm at the Family History Library* translated by A. L. and O. K. Ladenburger (Inverness, Illinois: Lind Street Research, 2014), p.141.

45 J. A. Home (ed.), *The Letters and Journals of Lady Mary Coke* (4 vols., Bath: Kingsmead Reprints, 1970), IV, p.89.

46 O. Deneke, *Lichtenbergs Leben* (Heimeran, 1944), p.198.

47 R. Loewenberg, 'A Letter on Major André from Germany' in *American Historical Review* 49 No.2 (January 1944), p.261.

48 *MJ* (23 October 1773).

49 J. Black, *European International Relations 1648–1815* (Basingstoke: Palgrave, 2002), np.

50 *MC* (14 September 1773).

51 *Philobiblion, A Monthly Bibliographical Journal* (1862), p.134. See *German Museum, or Monthly Repository Museum of the Literature of Germany* (3 vols., London, 1800–1) II, p.18.

52 See G. Hanger, *The Life, Adventures and Opinions of Col. George Hanger* (2 vols., London: J. Debrett, 1801), I, pp.38–43.

53 See J. G. Rosengarten, 'A Defence of the Hessians' in *Pennsylvania Magazine of History and Biography* 23 No.2 (July 1899), p.159.

54 R. Anderson, *The Works of John Moore M.D. with Memoirs of his Life and Writings* (7 vols., Edinburgh: Stirling & Slade, 1820), I, p.174.

55 Letter from Voss to Bruckner dated 24 February 1773 in Voss (ed.), *Briefe von Johann Heinrich Voss*, p.125.

56 W. Herbst, *Johann Heinrich Voss* (Leipzig: B.G. Teubner, 1872), I, p.80. See also P. Kahl, 'Neue Quellen und Kleinere Beitrage' (Lichtenberg Gesellschaft, 1987–2006), p.156.

57 'Philes', *Philobiblion, A Monthly Bibliographical Journal* (1862), p.134. See also German Museum, or Monthly Repository Museum of the Literature of Germany (3 vols., London, 1800–1), II, p.18.

58 W. White, *Notes and Queries* (London: George Bell, 1854), IX, p.111.

59 See *PA* (23 June 1762).

60 *Lloyd's Evening Post* (11 October 1773).

61 Anon., Anmerkungen … des gedachten Magistrats (Hanau, 1773), np.

62 *LEP* (1 February 1774).

63 *Boston Gazette* (20 December 1773) as reported in *GEP* (21 January 1774).

Chapter 17 – 'America is in a Flame'

1 *GEP* (21 January 1774).

2 W. Eddis, *Letters from America, Historical and Descriptive* (London, 1792), p.159: letter dated 28 May 1774.

3 *LEP* (14 April 1774).

4 See F. S. Vivian, letter dated 4 April 1955 heading 'Nine Chapters from an unpublished biography of Major John André' in National Army Museum Archives ref. 2004-09-199' p.10c fn.16 citing Barrington to colonels of 4th, 43rd, 47th, 18th, 23rd, 64th, 65th Foot War Office 2d April 1774. P.R.O. W.O.4.92 in National Army Museum Archives ref. 2004-09-199.

5 *LEP* (14 April 1774).

6 See Vivian, 'Nine Chapters…' p.10c fn.17 citing 'Barrington to O.C. at Portsmouth War office 3d May 1774. P.R.O. W.O.4.92' in National Army Museum Archives ref. 2004-09-199.

7 *LEP* (30 April 1774).

8 *PA* (16 April 1774).

9 M. Chamberlain, *Memorial of Captain Charles Cochrane. A British Officer in the Revolutionary War 1774–1781* (Cambridge, Massachusetts: John Wilson and Son, 1891), p.4. The purchase brought with it the promotion to captain he had been seeking, as confirmed by the 'War-Office' on 16 May when 'Lieut Charles Cochrane of the 7th regiment of foot to be captain vice James Ogilvie by purchase.' (See *Scots Magazine* (May 1774), XXXVI, p.280.)

10 C. K. Bolton (ed.), *Letters of Hugh Earl Percy from Boston and New York 1774–1776* (Boston, Massachusetts: C. E. Goodspeed, 1902), p.25.

11 See S. Conway, 'Percy, Hugh, Second Duke of Northumberland' in ODNB.

12 S. Reid, *British Redcoat 1740–1783* (Oxford: Osprey Publishing, 2012), np. See also M. H. Spring, *With Zeal and with Bayonets Only: The British Army on Campaign in North America 1775–1783* (Norman, Oklahoma: University of Oklahoma Press, 2008), pp.246–8.

13 Ibid., np.

14 R. Cusick, *Wellington's Rifles The Origins, Development and Battles of the Rifles Regiments in the Peninsular War and at Waterloo* (Barnsley: Pen & Sword, 2013), p.60.

15 See letter dated 15 October 1778 from Captain Ferguson to Sir Henry Clinton in *St. James's Chronicle* (3 December 1778).

16 Reid, *British Redcoat 1740–1783*, np.

17 *MC* (3 October 1774).

18 J. A. Home (ed.), *The Letters and Journals of Lady Mary Coke* (4 vols., Bath: Kingsmead Reprints, 1970), IV, p.408.

19 *MC* (3 October 1774).

20 See Vivian, 'Nine Chapters…' p.10c fn.16 citing Barrington to colonels of 4th, 43rd, 47th, 18th, 23rd, 64th, 65th Foot War Office 2d April 1774. P.R.O. W.O.4.92 in National Army Museum Archives ref. 2004-09-199.

21 *MC* (18 July 1774).

22 *MJ* (19 July 1774).

23 *GEP* (30 June 1774). Also the *Canadian* was set to depart 'for Quebec' (*MJ* (14 July 1774)) from Deal on 14 July, and, according to a report on 23 July, 'upwards of 100 sail of ship' had arrived in Quebec 'within about two months time' (*St. James's Chronicle* (23 July 1774).

24 *PA* (4 June 1774).

25 *Gazetteer and New Daily Advertiser* (11 June 1774).

26 *LEP* (28 June 1774).

27 *LC* (2 July 1774).

28 *GEP* (16 July 1774).

29 S. M. Baule, *Protecting the Empire's Frontier* (Athens, Ohio: Ohio University Press, 2014), p.22.

30 Earl of Dartmouth to Gov. Thomas Gage 17 October 1774 in C. E. Carter (ed.), *The Correspondence of General Thomas Gage* (Ann Arbor, 1931), Vol. II, p.175 cited in J. K. Rowland, 'General Thomas Gage, the Eighteenth Century Literature of Military Intelligence, and the Transition from Peace to Revolutionary War, 1774–1775' in *Historical Reflections* Vol. 32 No.3 'Crossing the Border-Expanding the Enlightenment' (Fall 2006), p.504.

31 J. Adams to A. Adams, letter of 28 August 1774 in Adams Family Papers, electronic archive, 4 September–9 November 1774.

32 Eddis, *Letters from America, Historical and Descriptive*, p.189. See also Bolton (ed.), *Letters of Hugh Earl Percy from Boston and New York*, p.37 where Lord Percy wrote to his father that 'letters sent by the Post are opened and often stopt.'

33 W. Duane (ed.), *Extracts from the Diary of Christopher Marshall kept in Philadelphia and Lancaster during the American Revolution 1774–1781* (Albany, New York: J. Munsell, 1877), p.10.

34 *Virginia Gazette* (4 August 1774).

35 See diary entry, 31 August 1774, in Washington Papers, August 1774, *Founders Online*, National Archives. Original source: *The Diaries of George Washington, 1 January 1771–75*, Vol. 3 (November 1781, Donald Jackson, Charlottesville, University Press of Virginia, 1978), pp.266–272.

36 J. Jackson, 'Washington in Philadelphia' (a paper read before the Historical Society of Pennsylvania in 1932, pp.110–154), p.119 (online resource).

37 See John Adams Diary in Adams Family Papers.

38 J. Adams to A. Adams. Letter of 28 August 1774 in Adams Family Papers.

39 A. Adams to J. Adams. Letter of 15 August 1774 in Adams Family Papers.

40 A. Adams to J. Adams. Letter of 19 August 1774 in Adams Family Papers.

41 *GEP* (10 November 1774).

42 Duane (ed.), *Extracts from the Diary of Christopher Marshall*, p.9.

43 J. R. Williams (ed.), *Philip Vickers Fithian Journal and Letters 1767–1774* (Princeton, New Jersey: Princeton Historical Association, 1900), p.235. Fithian was tutor to the children of Colonel Carter, a militia officer and important figure in provincial politics, who numbered the Lees, Washingtons, Turbervilles and Tayloes among his friends.

44 Duane (ed.), *Extracts from the Diary of Christopher Marshall*, p.5. See also *Pennsylvania Journal* (26 October 1774), which recorded 'Ship Concord, Volans' arrived 'from London'.

45 *Pennsylvania Journal* (20 July 1774).

46 Duane (ed.), *Extracts from the Diary of Christopher Marshall*, p.5.

47 *LEP* (23 April 1774). See also *GEP* (12 July 1774) which recorded statistics for the number of emigrants leaving Irish ports for America.

48 *PA* (1 June 1774).

49 See Duane (ed.), *Extracts from the Diary of Christopher Marshall*, pp.8–9.

50 *Pennsylvania Journal* (26 October 1774).

51 See *PA* (11 July 1774).

52 *MC* (12 October 1774), according to 'Port News' for 10 October 1774.

53 Duane (ed.), *Extracts from the Diary of Christopher Marshall*, p.10.

Chapter 18 – 'Five Feet of Snow'

1 Letter from Lord Percy to General Harvey dated Boston, 28 July 1775 in C. K. Bolton (ed.), *Letters of Hugh Earl Percy from Boston and New York 1774–1776* (Boston, Massachusetts: C. E. Goodspeed, 1902), p.58.

2 Letter dated 'Camp at Boston Oct. 31 1774' from Captain W. G. Evelyn to the Hon.ble Mrs Leveson Gower which notes the arrival of 'my old friend Colonel Prescott' in G. D. Scull (ed.), *Memoir and Letters of Captain W. Glanville Evelyn* (Oxford: James Parker, 1879), p.34.

3 *Gazetteer and New Daily Advertiser* (13 January 1775).

4 Ibid., (17 January 1775). While in London, Prescott planned very considerately to visit Mrs Boscawen. As Captain Evelyn explained to his cousin, the Honourable Mrs Leveson Gower: 'If you should be in town, this letter will be delivered to you by Colonel Prescott, who has obtained leave to go home, and has most obligingly desired to be charged with these letters, that he may have an opportunity of seeing your Mama and giving her pleasing and satisfactory accounts of her son.' (See letter dated 'Boston Dec.6 1774' from Captain W. G. Evelyn to the Hon.ble Mrs Leveson Gower which notes the arrival of 'my old friend Colonel Prescott' (See Scull (ed.), *Memoir* p.42). Given Prescott's solicitude for Mrs Boscawen, a widow, it is possible he also called on Mary-Louisa during this trip.

5 A. French (ed.), *A British Fusilier in Revolutionary Boston* (Cambridge, Massachusetts: Harvard University Press, 1926), p.45.

6 K. Weinhold, *Heinrich Christian Boie* (Halle: Waissenhausse, 1868), p.75 fn.1.

7 See E. E. Dana (ed.), *The British in Boston, being the diary of Lieutenant John Barker of the King's Own Regiment from November 15 1774 to May 31 1776* (Cambridge, Massachusetts: Harvard University Press, 1924), np.

8 See *LEP* (25 July 1774).

9 André letter dated 'Sunday 5th March 1775' written to his sister Mary. Transcript in family records held by Major J. E. A. André.

10 French (ed.), *A British Fusilier in Revolutionary Boston*, pp.27–8.

11 The Native American tribes were divided in their loyalties, some siding with the British, some with the emergent Continental Army. On 13 July 1775, a now famous speech was made on behalf of the Continental Congress. Addressing the Iroquois Six Nations Confederacy - the Mohawks, Oneidas, Tuscaroras, Onondagas, Cayugas and Senekas - the appeal for support had limited success, only the Tuscaroras and Oneidas actively supporting the rebellion. The other tribes nominally decided to stay neutral in what was deemed a 'family quarrel', but the British had success in courting the Mohawk and Huron tribes. Which of these tribes John was referring to as 'the Indians' is difficult to judge, but most likely they were Mohawks who, by June 1775, were actively negotiating with the British.

12 André letter dated 'Sunday 5th March 1775'.

13 Thus far, bush-fighting was considered an ancillary form of warfare, but increasingly it was moving into the mainstream of British military thinking. When a review of the Royal Artillery was being planned on Blackheath, London in July 1775, the set-piece would be a 'grand bush-fight, and several grand attitudes of war' according to the *Gazetteer and New Daily Advertiser* for 5 July. See also E. W. Andrews (ed.), *Journal of a Lady of Quality* (New Haven, Connecticut: Yale University Press, 1923) which on pages 189–190 described a 'bush-fighting' review by British troops in Wilmington, North Carolina in the spring of 1775.

14 André letter dated 'Sunday 5th March 1775'.

15 See *Lloyd's Evening Post* (14 November 1775) citing the *Quebec Gazette* (29 September 1775).

16 See A. F. Lefkowitz, *Benedict Arnold's Army, The 1775 American Invasion of Canada During the Revolutionary War* (El Dorado Hills, California: Savas Beatie, 2008), p.80. 'Shettican' was also known variously as 'Sartigan', 'Sertigan' and in the British newspapers as 'St Igan'.

17 See Lefkowitz, *Benedict Arnold's Army*, p.326.

18 Anon., (W. Burke), *An Impartial History of the War in America...* (London: R. Faulder, 1780), p.231. See *PA* (26 December 1775) for a description of the fort as it was in 1748.

19 See handwritten original 'Narrative of the Seige of St. John's' in Charles Preston Fonds R7098-O-2-E, MG 23 B10 Preston, Charles St. John's Siege' in Library and Archives, Ottawa, Canada and 'Narrative of the Siege of St. John's' in A. G. Doughty, *Report of the Work of the Public Archives for the Years 1914 and 1915* (Ottawa: J. de L. Tache, 1916), Appendix B, p.25.

20 André letter dated 'Sunday 5th March 1775'.

21 See 'Letter from Ticonderoga dated May 23 1775' in *New England Chronicle* (1 June 1775) reprinted in *Craftsman* (17 July 1775).

22 See *New York Gazette* (16 September 1775) as reported in *LC* (16 November 1775).

23 *LC* (16 November 1775).

24 *London Packet* (18 December 1775).

25 See Lefkowitz, *Benedict Arnold's Army*, p.326.

26 See letter from 'General Howe to the Earl of Dartmouth', dated 'Boston, November 27, 1775' in P. Force (ed.), *American Archives, Fourth Series, containing a Documentary History of the English Colonies in North America...* (6 vols., Washington: St. Clair Clarke and Force, 1840) III, p.1680.

27 *LG* (23 December 1775) in Force (ed.), *American Archives, Fourth Series,* IV, p.439.

28 *LC* (19 December 1775).

29 *Chester Chronicle* (22 January 1776).

30 If so, she was like so many parents, British and American alike, who must quickly accustom themselves to the realities of this increasingly ugly war. Even the American general, Alexander McDougall, could barely disguise his anguish as he sought information from General Gates about his son's whereabouts at this time: 'the Northern Expedition has I fear cost me my two sons; the Eldest died of the Fatigue attending the Seige of St. John's; the Youngest was taken a prisoner on the river of St. Lawrence on the late retreat; and on my account I fear he may be ill treated... If there may be an exchange of prisoners I must beg your attention to the boy.' See letter dated New York, 24 June 1776 from General Alexander MacDougall to General Horatio Gates in 'Miscellaneous Letters' in *Pennsylvania Magazine of History and Biography* Vol.43, No.3 (1919), p.263

31 Entry for 14 October in 'Narrative of the Siege of St. John's' in Doughty, *Report of the Work of the Public Archives for the Years 1914 and* 1915, Appendix B p.22.

32 André letter dated 'New York the 17 Dec 1776'. Transcript in family records held by Major J. E. A. André.

33 C. Stedman, *The History of the Origin, Progress and Termination of the American War* (2 vols., Dublin: P. Wogan et al., 1794), I, p.149.

34 Letter from Brigadier-General Prescott to Major Preston dated 31 August 1775 in Doughty, *Report of the Work of the Public Archives for the Years 1914 and* 1915, Appendix B, pp.5–6. Given that Prescott became a bogeyman for Americans, ending his orders on the note—'I will send you directions how he is to be disposed of'- could have been a gift to American propaganda—if found—except that this was the customary language applied to disposition of prisoners.

35 See *PA* (9 January 1776).

36 Undated letter from Prescott to Preston in Doughty, *Report of the Work of the Public Archives for the Years 1914 and* 1915, Appendix B, p.7. It has been suggested that the date of this letter was 'probably first week of September 1775', but a close reading indicates that the date was in mid-September by which time the siege was well underway but not closed tight.

37 'Journal of Colonel Guy Johnson from May to November 1775' in E. B. O'Callaghan (ed.), *Documents relative to the Colonial History of New York…* (Albany, New York: Weed, Parsons, 1857), Vol. VIII, pp.661–2. This journal gives a detailed account of negotiations between Prescott and Johnson relative to the participation of the Indians in the defence of St. John's and Montreal.

38 See handwritten original 'Narrative of the Siege of St. John's' in Charles Preston Fonds R7098-O-2-E, MG 23 B10 Preston, Charles St. John's Siege' in Library and Archives, Ottawa, Canada and 'Narrative of the Siege of St. John's' in Doughty, *Report of the Work of the Public Archives for the Years 1914 and* 1915, Appendix B, p.25.

39 Entry for 3 November in 'Narrative of the Siege of St. John's' in Doughty, *Report of the Work of the Public Archives for the Years 1914 and* 1915, Appendix B, p.25.

40 Entry for 17 September in 'Narrative of the Siege of St. John's' in Doughty, *Report of the Work of the Public Archives for the Years 1914 and* 1915, Appendix B, p.13.

41 B. Cuthbertson, *B. Cuthbertson's System for the Complete Interior Management and Economy of a Battalion of Infantry* (Bristol: Routh's and Nelson, 1776 edition), p.147.

42 Entry for 17 September in 'Narrative of the Siege of St. John's' in Doughty, *Report of the Work of the Public Archives for the Years 1914 and* 1915, Appendix B, p.13.

43 Ibid., Appendix B, p.25.

44 J. M. Hadden, *Hadden's Journal and Orderly Books* (Albany, New York: Joel Munsell's Sons, 1884), p.3.

45 Entry for 3 November 1775 in 'Narrative of the Siege of St. John's' in Doughty, *Report of the Work of the Public Archives for the Years 1914 and* 1915, Appendix B, p.25.

46 See Philip J. Schuyler to Governour Trumbull, Ticonderoga 10 November 1775, 'Officers of the Royal Fusiliers taken at St. John's November 3 1775' in Force (ed.), *American Archives, Fourth Series* III, p.1427.

47 *LC* (19 December 1775).

48 I. Q. Leake, *Memoir of the Life and Times of General John Lamb* (Albany, New York: Joel Munsell, 1857), p.118. Lamb, then a captain, served under General Montgomery and led the siege of Fort St. John's, disagreeing with the—in his opinion—favourable terms granted by Montgomery to the British and the subsequent decision that 'many of the prisoners taken at Montreal, among whom were some of the officers of rank, should remain on parole within the city'. See pp.116–122.

49 According to sundry 'American Intercepted Letters' which were 'probably opened at the Post Office', letters dated 4 to 6 November 1775 and written by citizens of Montreal did make it out of the city before its capitulation on 12 November. See 'George III, November 1775' in R. A. Roberts (ed.), *Calendar of Home Office Papers 1773–75* (London, 1899), pp.456–492 via BHO.

50 Leake, p.118. See also Lefkowitz, p.326.

51 Anon., (Burke), *An Impartial History*, p.235.

52 *PA* (27 December 1775).

53 W. Wheater, *Historical Record of the Seventh or Royal Regiment of Fusiliers* (Leeds: Private Circulation,

1875), p.68. See also *LEP* (10 February 1776). Among these 'Regulars' were the contingent of 'sixty soldiers' from the 7th regiment who had remained in Montreal when Colonel Maclean beat an earlier retreat to Quebec City after failing in his mission to relieve Fort St. John's. (See Lefkowitz, p.326 and *PA* 9 January 1776.)

54 *Craftsman* (4 November 1775).
55 Ibid., (11 November 1775).
56 Anon., (Burke), *An Impartial History*, p.230.
57 *Chester Chronicle* (22 January 1776), citing the *St. James's Chronicle* in respect to 'uncertain' and misleading 'Advices from America' concerning events in Canada at this time.
58 See E. Duling, 'Ethan Allen and *The Fall of British Tyranny*: A Question of what Came First.' (Online resource), np.
59 I. Senter, *The Journal of Isaac Senter* (Philadelphia, Pennsylvania: Historical Society of Pennsylvania, 1846), pp.32–3. Per the title of this work, Senter was 'a physician and surgeon detached from the American Army encamped at Cambridge Mass. on a secret expedition against Quebec under the command of Col. Benedict Arnold'.

Chapter 19 – 'Adverse Winds and Hard Frosts'

1 André letter dated 'New York the 17 Dec 1776'. Transcript in family records held by Major J. E. A. André.
2 *Lady's Monthly Museum* (October 1811), XI, p.182.
3 The main provincial newspapers at the time were the *New York Gazette and the Weekly Mercury*, *Massachusetts Gazette*, *Dunlap's Pennsylvania Packet*, *Pennsylvania Journal* and *Rivington's New York Gazetteer*. Further afield was the *Virginia Gazette*.
4 André letter dated 'New York the 17 Dec 1776'.
5 Lancaster was chosen by Congress as one of the destination for British prisoners in part because it was far enough away from the coast to limit the risk of rescue. A fellow Briton, Nicholas Cresswell, visited this town in August 1776 and had this to say of it: 'dined at Lancaster, *The Sign of the Two Highlandmen*. Landlord's name Ross. This a large town, but the situation is disagreeable between two hills, several good buildings and some manufactories of Guns and Woollen, but no navigation.' Cresswell also noted 'four hundred English prisoners here' See L. McVeagh (ed.), *The Journal of Nicholas Cresswell 1774–1777* (New York, New York: Dial Press, 1924), p.152.
6 See account by Ethan Allen of his capture in September 1775 by General Prescott who called him 'many hard names, among which he frequently used the word rebel...' in P. Force (ed.), *American Archives, Fourth Series, containing a Documentary History of the English Colonies in North America...* (6 vols., Washington: St. Clair Clarke and Force, 1840) III, p.801.
7 Letter from General Schuyler to Captain Hulbert dated 'Ticonderoga November 1 1775' in Force (ed.), *American Archives, Fourth Series,* IV, p.816 advising the proper conduct for escorting the British officers as prisoners.
8 See 'Articles of Capitulation' in A. G. Doughty, *Report of the Work of the Public Archives for the Years 1914 and 1915* (Ottawa: J. de L. Tache, 1916), Appendix B, p.17.
9 'Letter from Walter Livingston to the Continental Congress' dated 'Albany, November 24 1775' in Force (ed.), *American Archives, Fourth Series,* III, p.1663.
10 See negotiations for Articles of Capitulation in Force (ed.), *American Archives, Fourth Series,* III, p.1394.
11 'Articles of Capitulation' in Doughty, *Report of the Work of the Public Archives for the Years 1914 and* 1915, Appendix B, p.17.
12 When Ethan Allen captured 'a Major, a captain and two lieutenants in the Regular Establishment of George the Third at Fort Ticonderoga in May 1775 he wrote to 'Governour Trumbull' of

Connecticut saying that 'I make you a present of' these officers, their value being that 'they may serve as ransoms for our friends at Boston, and particularly for Captain Brown of Rhode Island.' (See 'Letter from Col. Ethan Allen to Gov Trumbull,' dated 'Ticonderoga, 12th May 1775' in Papers relating to the Expedition to Ticonderoga April and May 1775 (online archive), p.178.)

13 The same happened in December 1776 with 'a multitude of people going to see the Hessian prisoners march to the barracks' after the Battle of Trenton. See N. B. Wainwright and S. L. Fisher, "A Diary of Trifling Occurrences" Philadelphia 1776–78 in *Pennsylvania Magazine of History and Biography* Vol.82, No. IV (October 1958), p.419.

14 See Letter from General Schuyler to Captain Hulbert dated 'Ticonderoga November 1 1775' advising the proper conduct—including 'the utmost attention and politeness'—for escorting the British officers as prisoners. (Force (ed.), *American Archives, Fourth Series,* IV, p.816.)

15 'Letter from 'General Schuyler to the President of Congress' dated 'Ticonderoga November 11, 1775' in Force (ed.), *American Archives, Fourth Series,* III, pp.1520–1.

16 *Chester Chronicle* (22 January 1776).

17 Minutes of the Continental Congress dated 'Friday, November 17, 1775' in Force (ed.), *American Archives, Fourth Series,* III, p.1921.

18 Letter from Governour Trumbull to General Schuyler dated 'Lebanon, January 1, 1776' in Force (ed.), *American Archives, Fourth Series,* IV, p.532.

19 'Letter from 'John Hancock, President' dated 'Philadelphia, November 17, 1775' in Force (ed.), *American Archives, Fourth Series,* III, p.1588.

20 Letter from Colonel Timothy Bedel dated 'Nov.2 eight o'clock at night' in Force (ed.), *American Archives, Fourth Series,* III, p.1208.

21 Minutes of 'Continental Congress, December 8, 1775' in Force (ed.), *American Archives, Fourth Series,* III, p.1945.

22 Letter from General Schuyler to Governour Trumbull 'dated Ticonderoga November 10, 1775' in Force (ed.), *American Archives, Fourth Series,* III, p.1427.

23 Minutes of the Continental Congress dated 'Friday, November 17, 1775' in Force (ed.), *American Archives, Fourth Series,* III, p.1921.

24 'Letter from Edward Mott to Governour Trumbull' dated 'Kingston, November 26 1775' in Force (ed.), *American Archives, Fourth Series,* III, p.1676.

25 See C. L. Landis, *Major John André's German Letter* (Lancaster, Pennsylvania: New Era Printing, 1914), p.11.

26 J. W. Jordan, 'Bethlehem during the Revolution: Extracts from the diaries in the Moravian Archives at Bethlehem, Pennsylvania' in *Pennsylvania Magazine of History and Biography* Vol. XII, No.4, 1888, pp.387–8.

27 See K. Miller, *Dangerous Guests. Enemy Captives and Revolutionary Communities during the War for Independence* (Ithaca, New York: Cornell University Press, 2014), np.

28 'Minutes of Continental Congress on Thursday, December 7, 1775' in Force (ed.), *American Archives, Fourth Series,* III, p.1945.

29 There were 30 women and 51 children taken prisoner at Chambly alone. See letter from General Schuyler to Governour Trumbull 'dated Ticonderoga November 10, 1775' in Force (ed.), *American Archives, Fourth Series,* III, p.1427.

30 'Letter from 'John Hancock, President' to the Deputy Commissary dated 'Philadelphia, November 17, 1775' in Force (ed.), *American Archives, Fourth Series,* III, p.1588.

31 'Letter from Walter Livingston to the Continental Congress' dated 'Albany, November 24 1775' in Force (ed.), *American Archives, Fourth Series,* III, p.1663.

32 Letter from Lancaster (Pennsylvania) Committee to President of Congress, dated 'January 3, 1776' in Force (ed.), *American Archives, Fourth Series,* IV, p.561. Connolly was reimbursed 'the sum of

250 dollars ... for expenses in conducting Captain John Livingston and Lieutenant Anstruther from Kingston to Lancaster' per Minutes of Continental Congress, dated 'January 10, 1776' in Force (ed.), *American Archives, Fourth Series,* IV, p.1637.

33 Minutes of Continental Congress, dated 'December 5, 1775' in Force (ed.), *American Archives, Fourth Series,* III, p.1941.

34 Anon., *Journals of the American Congress from 1774 to 1788* (4 vols., Washington: Way and Gideon, 1823), I, p.207.

35 Minutes of Continental Congress, dated 'Saturday, December 16, 1775' in Force (ed.), *American Archives, Fourth Series,* III, p.1953. To show that Mott had acted properly, Congress approved at the same time that 'a sum not exceeding eighty dollars be paid to Captain Motte, being so much advanced and paid by him for necessaries to his men in conducting the Prisoners'. It later approved his further 'expenses etc in conducting the prisoners taken at St. John's from Kingston in the colony of New-York to Lancaster, Pennsylvania a balance of 367.7 dollars. (See Anon., *Journals of the American Congress* I, p.224 relating to transactions approved on 3 January 1776).

36 Minutes of Continental Congress, dated 'Saturday, December 16, 1775' in Force (ed.), *American Archives, Fourth Series,* III, p.1953.

37 See 'Returns of Officers of Several New-York Regiments' dated 20 October 1775 in Force (ed.), *American Archives, Fourth Series,* III, p.1118.

38 Minutes of New York Provincial Congress, dated 'February 17, 1776' in Force (ed.), *American Archives, Fourth Series,* V, p.298.

39 Minutes of New York Provincial Congress, dated 'March 1, 1776' in Force (ed.), *American Archives, Fourth Series,* V, p.321. See also the report of Commissioners of Fortifications to New York Congress dated 'December 7 1775' in Force (ed.), *American Archives, Fourth Series,* IV, pp.254–5.

40 See list in 'Mr. Walker's Statement' dated February 1776 in Force (ed.), *American Archives, Fourth Series,* IV, p.1178. Curiously, Captain Brice was on this list, despite also being on his parole after being wounded at Fort Chambly and sent to Montreal to recover.

41 'A List of His Majesty's Troops on board the Vessels near Montreal November 21, 1775' in Force (ed.), *American Archives, Fourth Series,* III, p.1694.

42 Postscript to letter from General Schuyler to the President of Congress dated 'Ticonderoga, November 27 1775' in Force (ed.), *American Archives, Fourth Series,* III, p.1682.

43 Letter from General Schuyler to President of Congress dated 'Albany December 21 1775' in Force (ed.), *American Archives, Fourth Series,* IV, p.375.

44 Letter from General Schuyler to President of Congress dated 'Albany December 26 1775' in Force (ed.), *American Archives, Fourth Series,* IV, p.468.

45 Letter from the New-Jersey Committee of Safety to President of Congress dated 'Trenton, January 23 1776' in Force (ed.), *American Archives, Fourth Series,* IV, p.815.

46 Minutes of Continental Congress dated 'January 22, 1776' in Force (ed.), *American Archives, Fourth Series,* IV, p.1650.

47 Letter from General Schuyler to President of Congress dated 'Albany December 21 1775' in Force (ed.), *American Archives, Fourth Series,* IV, p.375.

48 Anon., *Journals of the American Congress* I, p.248.

49 Jordan, 'Bethlehem during the Revolution' in *Pennsylvania Magazine of History and Biography* Vol. XII, No.4 (1888), pp.387–8.

50 Minutes of Continental Congress dated 'February 29, 1776' in Force (ed.), *American Archives, Fourth Series,* IV, p.1672.

51 André letter dated 'New York the 17 Dec 1776'.

52 See *Lloyd's Evening Post* (19 August 1776).

53 André letter dated 'New York the 17 Dec 1776'.

Chapter 20 – 'No Political Correspondence'

1   See letter to the president of Congress dated 'Lancaster, January 20 1776' in P. Force (ed.), *American Archives, Fourth Series, containing a Documentary History of the English Colonies in North America...* (6 vols., Washington: St. Clair Clarke and Force, 1840), IV, p.801.

2   Letter from Lancaster (Pennsylvania) Committee to President of Congress, dated 'January 3, 1776' to President of Congress in Force (ed.), *American Archives, Fourth Series,* IV, p.561.

3   Letter from Pennsylvania Committee of Safety to President of Congress, dated 'February 20, 1776' to President of Congress in Force (ed.), *American Archives, Fourth Series,* IV, pp.1213–1214.

4   Minutes of Lancaster (Pennsylvania) Committee, dated 'December 21, 1775' to President of Congress in Force (ed.), *American Archives, Fourth Series,* IV, p.371.

5   Letter from President of Congress to the Committee of Lancaster, Pennsylvania, dated 'January 18, 1776' in Force (ed.), *American Archives, Fourth Series,* IV, pp.762–3.

6   In addition to Kinnear, there were 'Tim Newmarch, Jas Wm Baillis, John Despard, Wm C. Hughes, P. Anstruther, William Duff, Jos Campbell, Geo Peacocke from the 'Royal Fusileers'. See Letter to the President of Congress dated 'Lancaster, January 20 1776' in Force (ed.), *American Archives, Fourth Series,* IV, p.802.

7   See Letter to the President of Congress dated 'Lancaster, January 20 1776' in Force (ed.), *American Archives, Fourth Series,* IV, pp.801–2.

8   These paroles were forwarded to Congress in a letter from 'the Committee of Inspection of the Town of Lancaster, dated 21st December 1775.' See Minutes of Continental Congress dated 'December 21 1775' in Force (ed.), *American Archives, Fourth Series,* III, p.1961.

9   Minutes of Continental Congress, dated 'November 17, 1775' in Force (ed.), *American Archives, Fourth Series,* III, p.1844.

10 Letter from Committee of Trenton (New Jersey) to President of Congress dated 'December 9, 1775' in Force (ed.), *American Archives, Fourth Series,* IV, p.225. The collective parole was worded 'We, the subscribers, acquiesce in the above resolve. Witness our hands' and was signed by 'J. Stopford, Major, Rigausill, Major, J. Hamton, Lieutenant, J. Shuttleworth, Lieutenant, Richard Huddleston, Surgeon Royal Fusiliers, Ibbetson Hamer, Lieutenant, David Allgee.'

11 Letter from Samuel Tucker dated 'Trenton, April 2, 1776' to President of Congress in Force (ed.), *American Archives, Fourth Series,* V, p.748.

12 Letter from Committee of Trenton (New Jersey) to President of Congress dated 'December 9, 1775' in Force (ed.), *American Archives, Fourth Series,* IV, p.817.

13 See letter to President of Congress dated 'Lancaster, January 20 1776' in Force (ed.), *American Archives, Fourth Series,* IV, p.802.

14 Minutes of Lancaster (Pennsylvania) Committee, dated 'December 21, 1775' to President of Congress in Force (ed.), *American Archives, Fourth Series,* IV, p.371.

15 Yeates wrote that 'from the returns given to us, we find that there are twenty-four women and twenty-five children belonging to the Soldiers of the Seventh Regiment and six women and eight children belonging to the Twenty-Sixth Regiment.' See Minutes of Lancaster (Pennsylvania) Committee, dated 'January 10, 1776' to President of Congress in Force (ed.), *American Archives, Fourth Series,* IV, p.619.

16 Minutes of Lancaster (Pennsylvania) Committee, dated 'January 10, 1776' to President of Congress in Force (ed.), *American Archives, Fourth Series,* IV, p.619. See also M. A. Stern, *David Franks, Colonial Merchant* (University Park, Pennsylvania: Pennsylvania State University Press, 2010), p.117.

17 Cited in W. U. Hensel, *Major André as a Prisoner of War at Lancaster PA, 1775–6* (Lancaster, Pennsylvania: New Era Printing, 1904), p.26.

18 'Major André's Parole' in *Pennsylvania Magazine of History and Biography* Vol. I, No.1 (1877), p.54.

19 J. Allen, 'Diary of James Allen, Esq., of Philadelphia Counsellor-at-Law' in *Pennsylvania Magazine of History and Biography* Vol. IX, No.2 (July 1885), p.196.

20 I. D. Rupp, *History of Lancaster County* (Lancaster, Pennsylvania: Gilbert Hills, 1844), p.75.

21 André letter dated 10 April 1776 from John André to Eberhart Michael dated 10 April 1776 in C. L. Landis, *Major John André's German Letter* (Lancaster, Pennsylvania: New Era Printing, 1914), p.7.

22 See letter from late 1775 cited in T. E. Schmauk, *A History of the Lutheran Church in Pennsylvania (1638–1820)* (Philadelphia, Pennsylvania: General Council Publication House, 1930), Vol. I, pp.335–6.

23 Because the two regiments left Lancaster in such a hurry, the officers departed 'without having it their power to discharge the moneys due for their lodgings and diet.' These accounts were submitted to Congress for payment. Among them was one for 'the trifling sum of six pounds ten shillings' in respect of 'Michael Bartgis's demand for a room, fire, candles etc for Lieutenants Despard of the Seventh and—André of the Seventh'. See letter from Lancaster (Pennsylvania) Committee, dated 'April 11, 1776' to the President of Congress in Force (ed.), *American Archives, Fourth Series*, V, p.850.

24 See E. Wolf, II, *Germantown and the Germans* (Philadelphia, Pennsylvania: The Library Company of Philadelphia, 1983), p.116. See also F. R. Diffenderffer, 'Early German Printers of Lancaster' in *Journal of the Lancaster County Historical Society*, 1903–4.

25 See Landis, *Major John André's German Letter*, pp.14–29 for biographical sketches of many of these people John knew in Lancaster.

26 Letter from Eberhart Michael to John André dated 26 April 1776 in Landis, *Major John André's German Letter*, p.9. Hillegas went on to become the first Treasurer to the new United States.

27 See Letter from Lancaster (Pennsylvania) Committee, dated 'April 11, 1776' to the President of Congress in Force (ed.), *American Archives, Fourth Series*, V, p.850.

28 André letter dated 10 April 1776 in Landis, *Major John André's German Letter*, p.7.

29 Letter from Eberhart Michael to John André dated 26 April 1776 in Landis, *Major John André's German Letter*, p.9.

30 Anon., *Journals of the American Congress from 1774 to 1788* (4 vols., Washington: Way and Gideon, 1823), I, p.532.

31 Rupp, *History of Lancaster County*, p.374.

32 Ibid., p.394.

33 Ibid., p.403.

34 Minutes of Pennsylvania Assembly dated 'April 6, 1776' in Force (ed.), *American Archives, Fourth Series*, V, p.714.

35 Anon., *Journals of the American Congress*, I, p.310. See also p.294.

36 Minutes of Pennsylvania Assembly dated 'November 25 1775' in Force (ed.), *American Archives, Fourth Series*, III, p.1800.

37 Letter from Lancaster (Pennsylvania) Committee, dated 'April 11, 1776' to the President of Congress in Force (ed.), *American Archives, Fourth Series*, V, p.848.

38 Letter from Pennsylvania of Safety to President of Congress, dated 'February 20, 1776' to President of Congress in Force (ed.), *American Archives, Fourth Series*, IV, pp.1213–1214.

39 See J. Hadden, *Hadden's Journal and Orderly Book* (Albany, New York: Joel Munsell's Sons, 1884), p.41, fn which cites an article from the *Connecticut Courant* and *Hartford Weekly Intelligencer* (27 May 1776).

40 Letter from Lancaster (Pennsylvania) Committee, dated 'April 11, 1776' to the President of Congress in Force (ed.), *American Archives, Fourth Series*, V, p.849.

41 Minutes of Pennsylvania Committee of Safety for March 1776 in Force (ed.), *American Archives, Fourth Series*, V, p.718.

42 Minutes of Continental Congress dated 'December 5, 1775' in Force (ed.), *American Archives, Fourth Series*, III, p.1941.

43 Minutes of Pennsylvania Committee of Safety dated 'March 14, 1776' in Force (ed.), *American Archives, Fourth Series,* V, p.725.

44 Letter from Lancaster (Pennsylvania) Committee, dated 'April 11, 1776', to President of Congress in Force (ed.), *American Archives, Fourth Series,* V, p.848.

45 André letter dated 10 April 1776 in Landis, *Major John André's German Letter,* p.7.

46 W. B. Sprague, *Annals of the American Episcopal Pulpit* (New York, New York: Robert Carter and Brothers, 1859), p.247.

47 Letter from Lancaster (Pennsylvania) Committee, dated 'April 11, 1776' to the President of Congress in Force (ed.), *American Archives, Fourth Series,* V, p.849.

48 Hensel, *Major André as a Prisoner of War,* p.15.

49 Letter from Lancaster (Pennsylvania) Committee, dated 'April 11, 1776' to the President of Congress in Force (ed.), *American Archives, Fourth Series,* V, p.849.

50 Hensel, *Major André as a Prisoner of War,* p.18. See also J. D. Speidel, 'The Artistic Spy: A Note on the Talents of Major André' in *New York History* Vol. 68 No. 4 (Oct. 1987), p.396 citing Thomas Cope, 1851 Gratz Collection in The History Society of Pennsylvania, Philadelphia.

51 Sprague, *Annals of the American Episcopal Pulpit,* p.169.

52 Hensel, *Major André as a Prisoner of War,* p.18. See also Speidel, 'The Artistic Spy', p.396 citing Thomas Cope, 1851 Gratz Collection in The History Society of Pennsylvania, Philadelphia.

53 Speidel, 'The Artistic Spy', p.396 citing Thomas Cope, 1851 Gratz Collection in The History Society of Pennsylvania, Philadelphia.

54 André letter dated 'New York the 17 Dec 1776'. Transcript in family records held by Major J. E. A. André.

55 Proceedings of Continental Congress dated 'Philadelphia, Tuesday September 3 1776' in P. Force (ed.), *American Archives, Fifth Series, containing a Documentary History of the English Colonies in North America…* (3 vols., Washington: St. Clair Clarke and Force, 1840), II, p.1329.

56 André letter dated 'New York the 17 Dec 1776'.

57 André letter dated 10 April 1776 in Landis, *Major John André's German Letter,* p.7.

58 André letter dated 'New York the 17 Dec 1776'.

59 *Lady's Magazine* (May 1776), VII, p.278.

60 André letter dated 'New York the 17 Dec 1776'.

61 See Landis, *Major John André's German Letter,* p.13.

62 See S. Conway, '"The Great Mischief Complain'd of." Reflections on the Misconduct of British Soldiers during the Revolutionary War' in *The William and Mary Quarterly* Vol.47 No.3, pp.370–390 for discussion of the effect on the civilian population.

63 Letter from Major French and others (Prisoners) to the Continental Congress dated 'Hartford, Connecticut March 21 1776' in Force (ed.), *American Archives, Fourth Series,* V, p.453. See also Hadden, *Hadden's Journal and Orderly Books,* pp.40–1, fn.

64 Proceedings of Continental Congress dated 'Philadelphia, Tuesday September 3 1776' in Force (ed.), *American Archives, Fifth Series,* II, p.1329.

65 André letter dated 'New York the 17 Dec 1776'.

66 Anon., *Journals of the House of Commons…* (London: by order of the House of Commons, 1803), XXXV, p.564.

67 F. Kapp, *Der Soldatenhandel deutscher Fürsten nach Amerika* (Berlin: Julius Springer, 1874), p.34.

68 R. Atwood, *The Hessians. Mercenaries from Hessen-Kassel in the American Revolution* (Cambridge: Cambridge University Press, 1980), p.24.

69 Anon., *Journals of the House of Commons,* XXXV, p.564.

70 André letter dated 'New York the 17 Dec 1776'.

71 See W. L. Stone (Editor and translator) *Letters and Journals relating to the War of the American Revolution…by Mrs General Riedesel* (Albany, New York: Joel Munsell, 1867).

72 Anon., *Journals of the House of Commons*, XXXV, p.564.

73 See *MJ* (2 March 1776) when the terms of the Treaty with 'the Landgrave of Hesse Cassel' were published and named 'Sieur William Faucitt' as 'Minister Plenipotentiary'.

74 See G. M. Stewart, 'British Students at the University of Göttingen in the Eighteenth Century' in *German Life and Letters* 33. No.1 (October 1979), pp.32–3.

75 See Hadden, *Hadden's Journal and Orderly Books*, p.145, fn which refers to Carr Clerke as aide-de-camp to General Burgoyne. Another alumnus of Göttingen, George Hanger, also served in America, albeit for a Hessian corps of Jagers. See G. Hanger, *The Life, Adventures and Opinions of Col. George Hanger*... (2 vols., London: J. Debrett, 1801), II. pp.67–9.

76 André letter dated 'New York the 17 Dec 1776'.

77 S. Day, *Historical Collections of the State of Pennsylvania* (Philadelphia, Pennsylvania: George W. Gorton, 1843), p.268.

Chapter 21 – 'The Crooked Hill Tavern'

1   André letter dated 'New York the 17 Dec 1776'. Transcript in family records held by Major J. E. A. André.

2   *PA* (20 August 1765).

3   Letter from Richard Peters to Jasper Yeates dated 'Philadelphia September 27 1776' in P. Force (ed.), *American Archives, Fifth Series, containing a Documentary History of the English Colonies in North America*... (3 vols., Washington: St. Clair Clarke and Force, 1840), II, p.562.

4   Letter from General Washington to the Board of War dated 'Brunswick November 30 1776' in Force (ed.), *American Archives, Fifth Series,* III, p.920.

5   Letter from General Washington to General Howe dated 'Brunswick December 1 1776' in Force (ed.), *American Archives, Fifth Series,* III, p.1028.

6   Anon. (A. Graydon), *Memoirs of a Life chiefly passed in Pennsylvania*... (Edinburgh: William Blackwood, 1822), pp.235–7. See also W.T.R. Saffell, *Records of the Revolutionary War* (New York, New York: Pudney & Russell, 1858) p.315.

7   S. Kemble, 'Kemble's Journal' in *Collections of the New York Historical Society for the Year 1883* (New York, New York: 1884), p.103.

8   W. Howe, *The Narrative of Lieut. Sir Gen. William Howe in a Committee of the House of Commons* (London: H. Baldwin, 1781), p.6.

9   L. McVeagh (ed.), *The Journal of Nicholas Cresswell 1774–1777* (New York, New York: Dial Press,1924), pp.152–5.

10 Ibid., p.220. Cresswell was not the only loyalist to be interviewed at this time. Joseph Galloway, a Pennsylvania politician and early delegate to Congress, swam across the Delaware with his horse following Washington's surprise attack at Trenton. Arriving in New York in December 1776, Galloway was introduced to Ambrose Serle, Howe's secretary, and it was 'information principally from Mr. Galloway' which convinced Howe that the expedition to Pennsylvania would be well-received there. See J. M. Coleman, 'Joseph Galloway and the British Occupation pf Philadelphia' in *Pennsylvania History, A Journal of Mid-Atlantic Studies* Vol. 30 No. 3 (July 1963), pp.278–280.

11 Ibid., p.220.

12 André letter dated 'New York the 17 Dec 1776'.

13 McVeagh (ed.), *The Journal of Nicholas Cresswell*, p.220.

14 André letter dated 'New York the 17 Dec 1776'.

15 W. B. Sprague, *Annals of the American Episcopal Pulpit* (New York, New York: Robert Carter and Brothers, 1859), p.247.

16 See Sprague, *Annals of the American Episcopal Pulpit*, p.169. and E. L. Pennington, 'The Anglican

Clergy of Pennsylvania in the American Revolution' in *Pennsylvania Magazine of History and Biography* Vol. 63 No.4 (Oct.1939), pp.401–431.

17 See Minutes of Continental Congress for 'December 2 1775' in Force (ed.), *American Archives, Fourth Series,* III, p.1939 and Minutes of Continental Congress for 'February 6, 1776' in Force (ed.), *American Archives, Fourth Series,* IV, p.1664.

18 N. B. Wainwright and S. L. Fisher, '"A Diary of Trifling Occurrences" Philadelphia 1776–78' in *Pennsylvania Magazine of History and Biography* Vol. 82 No.4 (October 1958), p.418 fn.28.

19 André letter dated 10 April 1776 in Landis, *Major John André's German Letter,* p.7.

20 See André letter dated 'Reading the 2nd Decr 1776' addressed to Caleb Cope, cited in W. Sargent, *The Life and Career of Major John André* (Boston, Massachusetts: Ticknor and Fields, 1861), pp.95–6.

21 André letter dated 10 April 1776 in Landis, *Major John André's German Letter,* p.7.

22 See letter from Eberhart Michael to John André dated 26 April 1776 in Landis, *Major John André's German Letter,* p.9.

23 See Sargent, *The Life and Career of Major John André,* p.96 fn.

24 André letter dated 'New York the 17 Dec 1776'.

25 André letter dated 'Reading the 2nd Decr 1776' addressed to Caleb Cope, cited in Sargent, *The Life and Career of Major John André,* pp.95–6.

26 Cited in W. U. Hensel, *Major André as a Prisoner of War at Lancaster PA (1775–6* (Lancaster, Pennsylvania: New Era Printing, 1904), pp.25–6.

27 See F. R. Diffenderffer, *The Loyalists in the Revolution* (Lancaster, Pennsylvania: 1919), np.

28 See Anon., *A List of the General and Field Officers...* (London: J. Millan, 1778), p.80.

29 Ibid., p.61.

30 See *MP* (27 March 1777).

31 Kemble, 'Kemble's Journal', p.107.

32 See Anon., *A List of the General and Field Officers...,* p.61, and *LEP* (12 November 1776).

33 See letter dated 'New York Island September 24th 1776' from Captain W. G. Evelyn to the Honourable Mrs Boscawen which notes 'the imminent exchange ... for General Prescott' in G. D. Scull (ed.), *Memoir and Letters of Captain W. Glanville Evelyn* (Oxford: James Parker, 1879), p.86.

34 Kemble, 'Kemble's Journal', p.93.

35 Ibid., p.103.

36 Howe, *The Narrative of Lieut. Sir Gen. William Howe,* p.8.

37 See M. C. Harris, *Brandywine: A Military History of the Battle that Lost Philadelphia* (El Dorado Hills, California: Savas Beatie, 2013), p.189.

38 See *MC* (27 March 1777).

39 H. C. Lodge (ed.), *André's Journal An Authentic Record of the Movements and Engagements of the British Army in America from June 1777 to November 1778 as recorded from day to day by Major John André* (2 vols., Boston, Massachusetts: Bibliophile Society, 1903), I, pp.35–6.

40 Letter dated 'Piscataway May 30th 1777' from Murray to Mrs Smyth in E. Robson (ed.), *Letters from America 1773–1780* (Manchester: Manchester University Press, 1951), p.45.

Chapter 22 – 'No Firelock'

1 H. C. Lodge (ed.), *André's Journal An Authentic Record of the Movements and Engagements of the British Army in America from June 1777 to November 1778 as recorded from day to day by Major John André* (2 vols., Boston, Massachusetts: Bibliophile Society, 1903), I, p.50.

2 G. D. Scull (ed.), 'Journal of Captain John Montrésor, July 1 1777 to July 1 1778, Chief Engineer of the British Army' in *Pennsylvania Magazine of History and Biography* Vol. 5 No.4 (1881), p.396 fn.

3   W. Howe, *The Narrative of Lieut. Sir Gen. William Howe in a Committee of the House of Commons* (London: H. Baldwin, 1781), p.23.

4   Ibid., p.27.

5   Lodge (ed.), *André's Journal*, I, p.88.

6   Ibid., I, pp.68–9.

7   André letter dated 'German Town near Philadelphia, the 28th Sept. 1777' from John André to his mother. Transcript in family records held by Major J. E. A. André.

8   Scull (ed.), 'Journal' in *Pennsylvania Magazine of History and Biography* Vol. 5 No.4 (1881), p.393.

9   Ibid., p.399.

10 Ibid., p.396.

11 Ibid., p.401.

12 Ibid., pp.396–7.

13 Ibid., p.393.

14 Lodge (ed.), *André's Journal*, I, pp.67–8.

15 Letter dated 'Head of Elke, Maryland Sept 1st 1777' from Murray to Mrs Smyth in E. Robson (ed.), *Letters from America 1773–1780* (Manchester: Manchester University Press, 1951), p.47.

16 Lodge (ed.), *André's Journal*, I, p.78.

17 Ibid., I, p.76.

18 Scull (ed.), 'Journal' in *Pennsylvania Magazine of History and Biography* Vol. 5 No.4 (1881), p.408.

19 Lodge (ed.), *André's Journal*, I, p.68.

20 Scull (ed.), 'Journal' in *Pennsylvania Magazine of History and Biography* Vol. 6 No.1 (1882), p.43.

21 Lodge (ed.), *André's Journal*, I, p.68.

22 Ibid., I, p.42.

23 Ibid., I, p.68.

24 Ibid., I, p.74.

25 See J. M. Coleman, 'Joseph Galloway and the British Occupation of Philadelphia' in *Pennsylvania History: A Journal of Mid-Atlantic Studies* Vol. 30 No.3 (July 1963), p.288.

26 Lodge (ed.), *André's Journal*, I, p.74. For Erskine's importance to the acquisition of secret intelligence by Howe during this campaign, see Coleman, 'Joseph Galloway and the British Occupation of Philadelphia', p.288.

27 For the pilots procured for the campaign by Joseph Galloway, see Coleman, 'Joseph Galloway and the British Occupation of Philadelphia', p.285.

28 See W. H. Siebert, 'The Loyalists of Pennsylvania' in *Ohio State University Bulletin* Vol. XXIV No.23 (Apr. 1920), pp.39–44.

29 Letter dated 'Head of Elke, Maryland Sept 1st 1777' from Murray to Mrs Smyth in Robson (ed.), *Letters from America 1773–1780*, p.47.

30 André letter dated 'German Town near Philadelphia, the 28th Sept. 1777'.

31 Lodge (ed.), *André's Journal*, I, pp.79–80.

32 Ibid., I, p.85.

33 See Anon., *A List of the General and Field Officers...* (London: J. Millan, 1778), p.111.

34 Letter dated 'Philadelphia Novr 29, 1777' from Murray to Mrs Smyth in Robson (ed.), *Letters from America 1773–1780*, pp.50–1.

35 Letter dated 'Newton Kilns, Long Island August 31st 1776' from Murray to Mrs Smyth in Robson (ed.), *Letters from America 1773–1780*, p.36, the reference to 'Metheen' being the family seat at 'Methven Castle, Perth, N. Britain' in Scotland.

36 Letter dated 'Head of Elke, Maryland Sept 1st 1777' from Murray to Mrs Smyth in Robson (ed.), *Letters from America 1773–1780*, p.48.

37 Lodge (ed.), *André's Journal*, I, p.109.

38 Ibid., I, p.115.

39 André letter dated 'German Town near Philadelphia, the 28th Sept. 1777'.

40 André letter dated 'German Town near Philadelphia, the 28th Sept. 1777'.

41 Letter dated 'Philadelphia, Novr 29, 1777' from Murray to Mrs Smyth in Robson (ed.), *Letters from America 1773–1780*, p.50.

42 André letter dated 'German Town near Philadelphia, the 28th Sept. 1777'

43 J. F. Watson, *Annals of Philadelphia and Pennsylvania…* (3 vols., Philadelphia, Pennsylvania: E. S. Stuart, 1884), II, p.554.

44 André letter dated 'German Town near Philadelphia, the 28th Sept. 1777'.

45 Lodge (ed.), *André's Journal*, I, p.88.

46 André letter dated 'German Town near Philadelphia, the 28th Sept. 1777'

47 Scull (ed.), 'Journal' in *Pennsylvania Magazine of History and Biography* Vol. 5 No.4 (1881), p.417.

48 André letter dated 'German Town near Philadelphia, the 28th Sept. 1777'.

49 Lodge (ed.), *André's Journal*, I, p.92.

50 André letter dated 'German Town near Philadelphia, the 28th Sept. 1777'.

51 Lodge (ed.), *André's Journal*, I, p.92.

52 Ibid., I, p.94.

53 *LGE* (2 December 1777) published in *MP* (3 December 1777).

54 André letter dated 'German Town near Philadelphia, the 28th Sept. 1777'. Compare this account to the one by Montrésor who wrote of having 'put between 4 and 500 to the bayonet.' See Scull (ed.), 'Journal' in *Pennsylvania Magazine of History and Biography* Vol. 6 No.1 (1882), p.39.

55 André letter dated 'German Town near Philadelphia, the 28th Sept. 1777'.

56 Lodge (ed.), *André's Journal*, I, p.100.

57 *LGE* (2 December 1777) published in *MP* (3 December 1777).

Chapter 23 – 'The Fair Quakers'

1   André letter dated 'German Town near Philadelphia, the 28th Sept. 1777'. Transcript in family records held by Major J. E. A. André.

2   J. Allen, 'Diary of James Allen, Esq., of Philadelphia Counsellor-at-Law' in *Pennsylvania Magazine of History and Biography* Vol. IX, No.4 (Jan. 1886), p.426.

3   Letter dated 16 December 1777 from Major Carl Baurmeister to von Jungkenn in C. Baurmeister, B. A. Uhlendorf, E. Vosper, 'Letters of Major Carl Baurmeister during the Philadelphia Campaign 1777–1778' in *Pennsylvania Magazine of History and Biography* Vol. 60 No.1 (Jan. 1936), p.41.

4   J. G. Simcoe, *Simcoe's Military Journal* (New York, New York: Bartlett & Welford, 1844), p.32.

5   H. C. Lodge (ed.), *André's Journal An Authentic Record of the Movements and Engagements of the British Army in America from June 1777 to November 1778 as recorded from day to day by Major John André* (2 vols., Boston, Massachusetts: Bibliophile Society, 1903), I, p.126.

6   Ibid., I, pp.128–9.

7   G. D. Scull (ed.), 'Journal of Captain John Montrésor, July 1 1777 to July 1 1778, Chief Engineer of the British Army' in *Pennsylvania Magazine of History and Biography* Vol. 6 No.2 (1882), p.192.fn

8   Letter dated 'Philadelphia, March 5, 1778' from Murray to Mrs Smyth in E. Robson (ed.), *Letters from America 1773–1780* (Manchester: Manchester University Press, 1951), p.52.

9   Letter dated 'Philadelphia, March 5, 1778' from Murray to Mrs Smyth in Robson (ed.), *Letters from America 1773–1780*, pp.52–3.

10 André letter dated 'German Town near Philadelphia, the 28th Sept. 1777'.

11 Letter dated 'Philadelphia, Novr 29, 1777' from Murray to Mrs Smyth in Robson (ed.), *Letters from America 1773–1780*, p.50.

12 J. M. Coleman, 'Joseph Galloway and the British Occupation of Philadelphia' in *Pennsylvania History: A Journal of Mid-Atlantic Studies* Vol. 30 No.3 (July 1963), p.274.

13 Ibid., p.288 citing 'Galloway's testimony on Feb, 12 1784' in *Loyalist Transcripts*, Vol. XL, p.79.

14 See S. B. Shenstone, *So Obstinately Loyal; James Moody 1744–1809* (Montreal, Canada: McGill-Queen's University Press, 2002), pp.105–6 citing a report by John Vonderhovan dated 24 October 1780.

15 Coleman, 'Joseph Galloway and the British Occupation of Philadelphia', p.294. Major Balfour was one of six aides-de-camp serving Howe. See M. C. Harris, *Brandywine: A Military History of the Battle that Lost Philadelphia* (El Dorado Hills, California: Savas Beatie, 2013), p.189.

16 E. Boudinot, *Journal of Historical Recollections of American Events during the Revolutionary War* (Philadelphia, Pennsylvania: F. Bourquin, 1894), p.53.

17 Letter dated 16 December 1777 from Major Carl Baurmeister to von Jungkenn in Baurmeister, Uhlendorf, Vosper, *Pennsylvania Magazine of History and Biography*, Vol. 60 No.1 (Jan. 1936), p.41.

18 T. W. Bean (ed.), *History of Montgomery County, Pennsylvania* (Philadelphia, Pennsylvania: Everts & Peck, 1884), p.167 fn.1. See J. Bakeless, *Turncoats, Traitors and Heroes* (Philadelphia, Pennsylvania: J.B. Lippincott Company, 1959), pp.211–8 for the full story of Lydia's heroics.

19 Boudinot, *Journal of Historical Recollections*, p.iv.

20 Bean (ed.), *History of Montgomery County*, p.167 fn.1.

21 See Harris, *Brandywine*, pp.189–190 fn.20.

22 Scull (ed.), 'Journal' in *Pennsylvania Magazine of History and Biography* Vol. 6 No.1 (1882), p.41.

23 S. Kemble, 'Kemble's Journal' in *Collections of the New York Historical Society for the Year 1883* (New York, New York: 1884), p.150.

24 Howe, *Brandywine*, p.41.

25 Allen, 'Diary of James Allen, Esq., of Philadelphia Counsellor-at-Law' in *Pennsylvania Magazine of History and Biography* Vol. IX, No.4 (January 1886), p.427. Allen, a loyalist, made this comment in his 2 December 1777 entry.

26 J. L. Boyle & S. Armstrong, 'Notes and Documents from Saratoga to Valley Forge: Diary of Lt S. Armstrong' in *Pennsylvania Magazine of History and Biography* Vol. 121 No.3 (July 1997), p.263. According to this diary, the order was issued on 4 February, the Americans fearing that 'as it is supposed that they are sent out to insinuate those that have deserted the British Army & Inlisted into ours, that they will receive a Pardon & Bounty to return which women come out under a pretence of bringing out many necessaries & also of carr[y]ing Provision in for their own support.'

27 Boudinot, *Journal of Historical Recollections*, p.50.

28 Coleman, 'Joseph Galloway and the British Occupation of Philadelphia', p.294, citing 'Galloway's testimony on Feb, 12 1784' in *Loyalist Transcripts*, Vol. XXV, p.250.

29 See Shenstone, *So Obstinately Loyal; James Moody 1744–1809*, p.105 citing a report by John Vonderhovan dated 24 October 1780.

30 See W. Duane (ed.), *Extracts from the Diary of Christopher Marshall kept in Philadelphia and Lancaster during the American Revolution 1774–1781* (Albany, New York: J. Munsell, 1877). Christopher Marshall is an important source about French officers and spies in action in and around Philadelphia at this time. His *Journal* referred to the following: 'the French Engineer' in Philadelphia on 8 July 1776 (p.83); 'Gen Farmoah, French Officer' who 'came to town some days past' on 22 February 1777 (p.116), 'the French Engineer, Baraset de Kermorvan' who came to visit Marshall 'from camp' on 16 December 1777 (p.150), and an unnamed 'French spy from Philadelphia' who was 'brought under a file of musqueteers by Capt Lang to be examined by Paul Fooks' on 9 March 1778 (p.171).

31 Lodge (ed.), *André's Journal*, I, p.187.

32 André letter dated 'N. York, 12th Sept 1778' from John André to his 'Uncle'. Transcript in family records held by Major J. E. A. André.

33 Lodge (ed.), *André's Journal*, I, p.135.

34 Scull (ed.), 'Journal' in *Pennsylvania Magazine of History and Biography* Vol. 6 No.2 (1882), p.196.

35 Ibid., Vol. 6 No.2 (1882), p.201.

36 See letter dated 20 January 1778 from Major Carl Baurmeister to von Jungkenn in Baurmeister, Uhlendorf, Vosper, *Pennsylvania Magazine of History and Biography* Vol. 60 No.1 (January 1936), pp.34–52 and letters dated 24 March and 18 April 1778 from Major Carl Baurmeister to von Jungkenn in Baurmeister, Uhlendorf, Vosper, *Pennsylvania Magazine of History and Biography* Vol. 60 No.2 (Apr. 1936), pp.161–183.

37 Duane (ed.), *Extracts from the Diary of Christopher Marshall*, p.156.

38 See Lodge (ed.), *André's Journal*, I, pp.xvii–xviii.

39 See Simcoe, *Simcoe's Military Journal*, pp.38–60.

40 Duane (ed.), *Extracts from the Diary of Christopher Marshall*, pp.161–2. Among these 'friends' was, close by, 'our brave Gen. Washington, as he and his army are now obliged to encounter all the inclemency of this cold weather, as they with him are living out in the woods with slender covering.'

41 Ibid., p.165.

42 Ibid., p.168.

43 K. Haulman, 'Fashion and the Culture Wars of Revolutionary Philadelphia' in *The William and Mary Quarterly* Third Series Vol.62 No.4 (Oct. 2005), pp.647–8.

44 According to E. F. Ellet, *The Women of the American Revolution* (2 vols., New York, New York: Baker & Scribner, 1850), I, p.182 a 'meschianza' or 'mischianza' was 'an Italian word signifying a medley or mixture'.

45 Haulman, 'Fashion and the Culture Wars of Revolutionary Philadelphia', p.651.

46 *LEP* (2 July 1778).

47 Scull (ed.), 'Journal' in *Pennsylvania Magazine of History and Biography* Vol. 6 No.3 (1882), p.285.

48 D. E. Fisher, 'Social Life in Philadelphia during the British Occupation' in *Pennsylvania History: a Journal of Mid-Atlantic Studies* Vol. 37 No.3 (July, 1970), p.251 citing J. T. Scharf and T. Westcott, *History of Philadelphia 1606–1884* (Philadelphia, Pennsylvania: 1884) II, p.378. Among the officers to contribute but not participate was James Murray who 'had the honour of beeng a subscriber to the value and amount of 160 guineas.' See letter dated 'New York, Octbr 22d 1778' from Murray to David Smyth in Robson (ed.), *Letters from America 1773–1780*, p.59.

49 Watson, *Annals of Philadelphia and Pennsylvania…*, II, p.292.

50 *St. James's Chronicle* (7 July 1778).

51 Watson, *Annals of Philadelphia and Pennsylvania…*, II, p.292. See T. C. Pollock, 'Notes on Professor Pattee's "The British Theater in Philadelphia in 1778"' in *American Literature* Vol.7 No.3 (Nov. 1935), pp.310–314.

52 G. O. Seilhamer, *History of the American Theatre during the Revolution and after* (Philadelphia, Pennsylvania: Globe Printing House, 1889), p.26 fn.1 citing 'Gaine's Critique'.

53 Pollock, 'Notes on Professor Pattee's "The British Theater in Philadelphia in 1778"', pp.311–2.

54 Haulman, 'Fashion and the Culture Wars of Revolutionary Philadelphia', p.653.

55 H. D. Biddle (ed.), *Extracts from the Journal of Elizabeth Drinker…* (Philadelphia, Pennsylvania: J.B. Lippincott Company, 1889), p.103.

56 Scull (ed.), 'Journal' in *Pennsylvania Magazine of History and Biography* Vol. 6 No.1 (1882), p.41.

57 Ibid., p.56. This was the figure given to the Quarter Master General on 6 November 1777 when ordered to 'fix our Quarters near this city.'

58 N. B. Wainwright and S. L. Fisher, '"A Diary of Trifling Occurrences" Philadelphia 1777–1778' in *Pennsylvania Magazine of History and Biography* Vol. 82 No.4 (Oct., 1958), p.462. See also Fisher, 'Social Life in Philadelphia during the British Occupation', p.246.

59 Letter dated 'Philadelphia, March 5, 1778' from Murray to Mrs Smyth in Robson (ed.), *Letters from America 1773–1780*, pp.52–4.

60 S. Kemble, 'Gen. Sir William Howe's Orders' in *Collections of the New York Historical Society for the Year 1883* (New York, New York: 1884), p.553.

61 Fisher, 'Social Life in Philadelphia during the British Occupation', p.252.

62 Biddle (ed.), *Extracts from the Journal of Elizabeth Drinker...*, p.103.

63 Watson, *Annals of Philadelphia and Pennsylvania...*, II, p.293.

64 Fisher, 'Social Life in Philadelphia during the British Occupation', p.251.

65 *St. James's Chronicle* (7 July 1778).

66 See Haulman, 'Fashion and the Culture Wars of Revolutionary Philadelphia', pp.651–3 regarding the Meschianza and, more generally, pp.641–2 which told of 'colony-wide non-importation and non-consumption regulations' passed by 'the Continental Association "to encourage frugality, economy and industry" and "discountenance and discourage every species of extravagance and dissipation" including "exhibitions of shews, plays and other expensive diversions and entertainments."'

67 Fisher, 'Social Life in Philadelphia during the British Occupation', p.251.

68 Haulman, 'Fashion and the Culture Wars of Revolutionary Philadelphia', p.651.

69 Ibid., p.653.

70 Watson, *Annals of Philadelphia and Pennsylvania...*, II, p.292.

71 See OBJ 060 in 'Arts and Artifacts' Collection of the Library Company of Philadelphia, Philadelphia, Pennsylvania and J. J. Smith & J. F. Watson (eds.), *American Historical and Literary Curiosities* (Philadelphia, Pennsylvania: T. K & P. G. Collins, 1847), No.26, under Contents of No.1 np.

72 Inscription on Object No Z.2355 in the Collection of the New-York Historical Society

73 See OBJ 061 and OBJ 062 in 'Arts and Artifacts' Collection of the Library Company of Philadelphia, Philadelphia, Pennsylvania.

74 *St. James's Chronicle* (7 July 1778).

75 Haulman, 'Fashion and the Culture Wars of Revolutionary Philadelphia', p.653.

76 *St. James's Chronicle* (7 July 1778).

77 See *LC* (9 September 1777).

78 See *MC* (19 February 1778) with news from New York dated 3 January 1778 announcing the arrival there of 'Lieutenant André, of the Royal Fusileers'.

79 Scull (ed.), 'Journal' in *Pennsylvania Magazine of History and Biography* Vol. 6 No.3 (1882), p.285.

80 See C. Stedman, *The History of the Origin, Progress and Termination of the American War* (2 vols., Dublin: P. Wogan et al., 1794), I, p.335.

81 G. Wrottesley, *History of the Family of Wrottesley of Wrottesley...* (Exeter: William Pollard & Co, 1903), pp.357–8 citing 'Carlisle Correspondence printed by the Historical MS Commission'.

82 See 'Wrottesley, John' in L. Namier & J. Brooke (eds.), *The History of Parliament; House of Commons 1754–1790* (3 vols., London: Secker & Warburg, 1985), III, pp.665–6.

83 Wrottesley, *History of the Family of Wrottesley of Wrottesley...*, pp.357–8 citing 'Carlisle Correspondence printed by the Historical MS Commission'.

84 *LEP* (2 July 1778).

85 *MP* (13 July 1778).

86 Ibid., (31 March 1778).

87 Ibid., (13 July 1778).

88 *St. James's Chronicle* (7 July 1778).

89 Ellet, *The Women of the American Revolution*, I, p.182.

90 Smith & Watson (eds.), *American Historical and Literary Curiosities*, No.27 under Contents of No.1 np.

91 See *Lady's Magazine* (1778) IX, p.332 and p.389. According to W. Sargent, *The Life and Career of Major John André* (Boston, Massachusetts: Ticknor and Fields, 1861), p.177 fn, the article in question appeared in the 1793 edition of the *Lady's Magazine*, being a reprint of the 'larger' version which appeared in the *Gentleman's Magazine* in August 1778.

92 *MC* (8 April 1779).
93 Anon., *Strictures on the Philadelphia Mischianza…* (London: J. Bew, 1779), title page.
94 See Smith & Watson (eds.), *American Historical and Literary Curiosities*, No.25 under Contents of No.1 np.
95 See 'Wrottesley, John' in Namier & Brooke (eds.), *The History of Parliament. The House of Commons 1754–90*, III, pp.665–6 citing Almon, *A Collection of all the Treaties*, XI, 14. pp.186–8, xvi pp.102–3 for accounts of Sir John Wrottesley's later speeches in Parliament attacking government policy in America.
96 *St. James's Chronicle* (7 July 1778).

Chapter 24 – 'Implicit Confidence'

1   H. C. Lodge (ed.), *André's Journal An Authentic Record of the Movements and Engagements of the British Army in America from June 1777 to November 1778 as recorded from day to day by Major John André* (2 vols., Boston, Massachusetts: Bibliophile Society, 1903), II, p.21.
2   Ibid., II, pp.16–7.
3   Ibid., I, p.xviii.
4   *LG* (24 October 1778).
5   Lodge (ed.), *André's Journal*, pp.16–7.
6   S. Kemble, 'Kemble's Journal' in *Collections of the New York Historical Society for the Year 1883*: (New York, New York: 1884), p.162.
7   Lodge (ed.), *André's Journal*, II, p.16.
8   Scull (ed.), 'Journal' in *Pennsylvania Magazine of History and Biography* Vol. 6 No.3 (1882), p.284.
9   See J. Bakeless, *Turncoats, Traitors and Heroes* (Philadelphia, Pennsylvania: J.B. Lippincott Company, 1959), pp. 223–6.
10 Lodge (ed.), *André's Journal*, II, pp.16–7.
11 André letter dated 'N. York, 12th Sept 1778'. Transcript in family records held by Major J. E. A. André.
12 Kemble, 'Kemble's Journal' p.188. 'Old' in these circumstances referred more to Kemble's length of service—twenty-one years—than his age—thirty-eight.
13 Ibid., p.188.
14 Ibid., p.150.
15 Ibid., p.297.
16 S. Kemble, 'Gen. Sir Henry Clinton's Orders' in *Collections of the New York Historical Society for the Year 1883* (New York, New York: 1884) p), pp.586–7.
17 Kemble, 'Kemble's Journal', p.153.
18 Ibid., p.171.
19 Ibid., pp.168–9.
20 R. Clayton, 'Extracts from the Orderly Book of Major Robert Clayton of the Seventeenth Regiment 1778' in *Pennsylvania Magazine of History and Biography* Vol. 25 No.1 1901 p.103.
21 Kemble, 'Kemble's Journal' pp.165–6.
22 Ibid., pp.183–4.
23 C. Van Doren, *Secret History of the American Revolution* (New York, New York: Viking Press, 1951), p.233 citing Rawdon to Clinton.
24 See W. B. Willcox, *Portrait of a General Sir Henry Clinton in the War of Independence* (New York, New York: Alfred A. Knopf, 1964), pp.285–7.
25 Ibid., p.278.
26 See Ibid., pp.278–289.
27 Kemble, 'Kemble's Journal', p.176. See also a letter from Washington to Clinton dated 4 April

1779 setting up the meeting where Washington wrote: 'I am under the necessity of requesting that it may be deferred 'till Monday the 12th instant when Col Davies and Lt. Col Harrison will meet Colo. Hyde and Captn André at Amboy in the forenoon.' See J. C. Fitzpatrick (ed.), *The Writings of George Washington from the Original Manuscript Sources 1745–1799* (Washington DC: United States Government Printing Office, 1936), Vol. 14, p.334.

28 W. Sargent, *The Life and Career of Major John André* (Boston, Massachusetts: Ticknor and Fields, 1861) pp.218–9.

29 F. Moore, *Diary of the American Revolution* (New York, New York: Charles Scribner, 1860) Vol. II pp.120–4. John was growing in confidence as a propagandist, going on to compose a satirical piece, 'The Cow-Chase, an Heroick Poem, in Three Cantos' also published in the *Royal Gazette*. Appearing in three instalments between 16 August and 23 September 1780, it mocked the latest exploits of the Continental Army, singling out a failed expedition in July that year by General Wayne to dislodge a 'Refugees' Block-House on Hudson's River'. See Sargent, *The Life and Career of Major John André*, pp.234–249.

30 Sargent, *The Life and Career of Major John André*, p.219.

31 Kemble, 'Kemble's Journal' p.180. John's rapid rise excited many jealousies among officers close to or in British Headquarters. He was mocked as Clinton's 'first friend' and 'bosom confidant' and described as a 'cringing, insidious sycophant.' Cited in W. S. Randall, *Benedict Arnold. Patriot and Traitor* (London: Bodley Head, 1991), p.472.

32 Kemble, 'Kemble's Journal', pp.183–5.

33 Ibid., pp.187–8.

34 Ibid., p.188, fn.

35 Lodge (ed.), *André's Journal*, II, pp.47–8.

36 See *Gazetteer and New Daily Advertiser* (2 December 1778).

37 See C. I. A. Ritchie (ed.), 'A New York Diary of the Revolutionary War' in *New York Historical Society Quarterly* Vol. I. No 3 (July 1966), pp.279–280.

38 Kemble, 'Kemble's Journal', p.163.

39 Cited in R. M. Hatch, *Major John André. A Gallant in Spy's Clothing* (Boston, Massachusetts: Houghton Mifflin, 1986), p.121.

40 See Van Doren, *Secret History of the American Revolution*, p.112.

41 C. Berger, *Broadside and Bayonets. The Propaganda War of the American Revolution* (Philadelphia. Pennsylvania: University of Pennsylvania Press, 1961), p.150.

42 André letter dated 'N. York, 12th Sept 1778'. James Murray also wrote of his activity 'burning and destroying' on this expedition, expressing the hope furthermore that 'the fashion may take root' and thereby 'might prove as speedy a means of finishing the rebellion as what has been hitherto adopted.' See Letter dated 'New York Octbr 24th 1778' from Murray to Mrs Smyth in Robson (ed.), *Letters from America 1773–1780*, p.61.

43 Lodge (ed.), *André's Journal*, II, p.30.

44 André letter dated 'Philadelphia Camp, the 20th November 1777'.

45 See *St. James's Chronicle* (23 January 1779).

46 P. R. Misencik, *Sally Townsend. George Washington's Teenage Spy* (Jefferson, North Carolina: McFarland & Company, 2016), p.121.

47 J. G. Simcoe, *Simcoe's Military Journal* (New York, New York: Bartlett & Welford, 1844), p.93.

48 Lodge (ed.), *André's Journal*, II, p.50.

49 André letter (undated)—part of which is missing—from John André to an unknown recipient in England. Transcript in family records held by Major J. E. A. André.

50 Van Doren, *Secret History of the American Revolution*, p.233 citing letter from William Eden, a Peace Commissioner, to Clinton dated 27 May 1779.

Chapter 25 – 'These Double Faces'

1   C. Van Doren, *Secret History of the American Revolution* (New York, New York: Viking Press, 1951), p.192 citing letter dated 5 May 1779 from Arnold to Washington in Washington Papers, J. Sparks (ed.), *The Writings of George Washington* (12 vols., Boston, Massachusetts: Russell, Odiorne and Metcalf, 1835) VII, p.523.

2   Ibid., p.170.

3   Ibid., p.184.

4   L. B. Walker, 'The Life of Margaret Shippen, Wife of Benedict Arnold' in *Pennsylvania Magazine of History and Biography* Vol. 24 No.4 (1900), p.414, citing 'Mrs Gibson'.

5   G. G. Galloway and R. C. Werner, 'Diary of Grace Growden Galloway, Kept at Philadelphia July 1, to September 30, 1779' in *Pennsylvania Magazine of History and Biography* Vol. 58 No.2 (1934), p.160.

6   Van Doren, *Secret History of the American Revolution*, p.185.

7   Walker, in *Pennsylvania Magazine of History and Biography* Vol. 24 No.4 (1900), p.428, citing *Century Magazine* (March 1894).

8   W. Duane (ed.), *Extracts from the Diary of Christopher Marshall kept in Philadelphia and Lancaster during the American Revolution 1774–1781* (Albany, New York: J. Munsell, 1877), pp.211–2.

9   Van Doren, *Secret History of the American Revolution*, p.193.

10   Walker, in *Pennsylvania Magazine of History and Biography* Vol. 25 No.1 (1901), p.40 citing letter from Miss Tilghman dated 14 April 1779.

11   Van Doren, *Secret History of the American Revolution*, p.192.

12   Letter to 'George Washington from Major general Benedict Arnold, 5 May 1779' in *Founders Online*, National Archives. Original source: *The Papers of George Washington, Revolutionary War Series* Vol. 20 8 April-31 May 1779, (ed. Edward G. Lengel, Charlottesville, University Press of Virginia, 2010), pp.327–329.

13   Ibid., p.196 citing J. G. Taylor, *Some New Light on the Later Life and Last Resting Place of Benedict Arnold and of his Wife Margaret Shippen* (1931).

14   E. F. Crane (ed.), *The Diary of Elizabeth Drinker* (Philadelphia, Pennsylvania: University of Pennsylvania Press, 1994), np. See entry for 4 November 1778.

15   Van Doren, *Secret History of the American Revolution*, p.196 citing Taylor.

16   André letter dated 10 May 1779 from André to Stansbury cited in Van Doren, *Secret History of the American Revolution*, Appendix, p.440.

17   André letter dated '—1779' from André to Margaret Chew cited in Van Doren, *Secret History of the American Revolution*, Appendix, p.440.

18   André letter dated 10 May 1779 from André to Stansbury cited in Van Doren, *Secret History of the American Revolution*, Appendix, p.440.

19   Van Doren, *Secret History of the American Revolution*, pp.217–8.

20   Letter from Stansbury to André dated 11 July 1779 cited in Van Doren, *Secret History of the American Revolution*, Appendix, p.449.

21   André letter dated 10 May 1779 from André to Stansbury cited in Van Doren, *Secret History of the American Revolution*, Appendix, p.440.

22   André letter dated '—1779' from André to Margaret Chew cited in Van Doren, *Secret History of the American Revolution*, Appendix, p.440.

23   André letter dated 10 May 1779 from André to Stansbury cited in Van Doren, *Secret History of the American Revolution*, Appendix, p.440.

24   André letter dated '—1779' from André to Margaret Chew cited in Van Doren, *Secret History of the American Revolution*, Appendix, p.440.

25   According to H.C.B. Rogers, *The British Army of the Eighteenth Century* (London: Routledge,

1977) the office of Adjutant General 'dealt with all matters relating to discipline, the policy of arming and clothing the troops and the Regulations and Orders for the Army which were issued from time to time under the king's authority.' (online resource, np). These functions expanded when the adjutant general was located at the war front and included, in some instances, the collection of intelligence.

26 André letter dated 10 May 1779 from André to Stansbury cited in Van Doren, *Secret History of the American Revolution*, Appendix, p.440.

27 André letter dated 10 May 1779 from André to Clinton cited in Van Doren, *Secret History of the American Revolution*, Appendix, p.440.

28 Letter from André to Clinton dated 10 May 1779 cited in Van Doren, *Secret History of the American Revolution*, Appendix, p.440.

29 Letter from William Eden, a Peace Commissioner, to Clinton dated 27 May 1779 cited in Van Doren, *Secret History of the American Revolution*, p.233.

Chapter 26 – 'Mutual Confidence'

1 Letter dated 10 May 1779 from André to Stansbury cited in C. Van Doren, *Secret History of the American Revolution* (New York, New York: Viking Press, 1951), Appendix, p.439.

2 Unsent draft of letter from André to Arnold for letter sent in mid-June 1779 cited in Van Doren, *Secret History of the American Revolution*, Appendix, p.446.

3 Letter dated mid-June 1779 from André to Arnold cited in Van Doren, *Secret History of the American Revolution*, Appendix, p.448.

4 Letter from Arnold to André dated 23 May 1779 in Van Doren, *Secret History of the American Revolution*, Appendix, p.442.

5 See 'Revolutionary Journal of Margaret Morris of Burlington N.J. December 6 1776 to June 11 1778' in *Bulletin of Friends' Historical Society of Philadelphia* Vol. 9 No. 1 (May, 1919), pp. 2–14.

6 Van Doren, *Secret History of the American Revolution*, p.204.

7 Letter from Odell to André dated 18 July 1779 cited in Van Doren, *Secret History of the American Revolution*, Appendix, p.450.

8 Letter from Arnold to André dated 23 May 1779 cited in Van Doren, *Secret History of the American Revolution*, Appendix, p.442.

9 Van Doren, *Secret History of the American Revolution*, p.198 citing P. W. Phipps, *The Life of Colonel Pownoll Phipps* (1894), p.88.

10 *GM* (August 1778), XLVIII, p.354.

11 Letter from Arnold to André dated 23 May 1779 cited in Van Doren, *Secret History of the American Revolution*, Appendix, p.442.

12 Unsent draft of letter from André to Arnold for letter sent in mid-June 1779 cited in Van Doren, *Secret History of the American Revolution*, Appendix, p.446.

13 Letter from Arnold to André dated 23 May 1779 cited in Van Doren, *Secret History of the American Revolution*, Appendix, p.442.

14 Letter from André to Arnold sent in mid-June 1779 cited in Van Doren, *Secret History of the American Revolution*, Appendix, p.448.

15 Unsent draft of letter from André to Arnold for letter sent in mid-June 1779 cited in Van Doren, *Secret History of the American Revolution*, Appendix, p.446.

16 Letter from André to Arnold sent in mid-June 1779 cited in Van Doren, *Secret History of the American Revolution*, Appendix, p.448.

17 Letter from Stansbury to André dated 11 July 1779 cited in Van Doren, *Secret History of the American Revolution*, Appendix, p.449.

18 Letter from Odell to André dated 18 July 1779 cited in Van Doren, *Secret History of the American Revolution*, Appendix, pp.450–1.

19 Letter from Peggy Arnold to André dated 13 October 1779 cited in Van Doren, *Secret History of the American Revolution*, Appendix, p.455.

20 See 'Shopping List' in Van Doren, Appendix, pp.451–2 and, for 'clouting diaper', see K. A. Staples and M. Shaw, *Clothing through American History* (Santa Barbara, California: Greenwood, 2013), 'Children's Fashions' p.405.

21 Van Doren, *Secret History of the American Revolution*, p.192 citing letter dated 5 May 1779 from Arnold to Washington in Washington Papers, J. Sparks (ed.), *The Writings of George Washington* (12 vols., Boston, Massachusetts: Russell, Odiorne and Metcalf, 1835), VII, p.523.

22 Letter from Odell to André dated 18 July 1779 cited in Van Doren, *Secret History of the American Revolution*, Appendix, p.450.

23 Letter from André to Arnold sent in end-July 1779 cited in Van Doren, *Secret History of the American Revolution*, Appendix, p.453.

24 Letter from André to Peggy Arnold dated 16 August 1779 cited in Van Doren, *Secret History of the American Revolution*, Appendix, p.454.

25 Letter from Peggy Arnold to André dated 13 October 1779 cited in Van Doren, *Secret History of the American Revolution*, Appendix, p.455.

26 Letter from André to Peggy Arnold dated 16 August 1779 cited in Van Doren, *Secret History of the American Revolution*, Appendix, p.454.

27 Letter from Odell to André dated 21 December 1779 cited in Van Doren, *Secret History of the American Revolution*, Appendix, p.458.

28 P. R. Misencik, *Sally Townsend. George Washington's Teenage Spy* (Jefferson, North Carolina: McFarland & Company, 2016), pp.111–2.

29 W. Irving, *The Life of George Washington* (New York, New York: Cosimo Classics, 2005), III, p.255.

30 *Southern and Western Magazine and Review* (Charleston, South Carolina: 1845), II. p.40.

31 W. S. Randall, *Benedict Arnold, Patriot and Traitor* (London: Bodley Head, 1991), online edition np.

32 W. Sargent, *The Life and Career of Major John André* (Boston, Massachusetts: Ticknor and Fields, 1861), pp.151–2.

33 Sally was a poetic figure who symbolized unfaithfulness in women. See Anon., *The Muse in Good Humour* (London: F. & J. Noble: 1757), 'The Foolish Inquiry' pp.120–4 and Anon., *The Poetical Tell-Tale* (London: J. Fletcher, 1764), pp.14–16 where the theme was jealousy and 'frantick' the suspicions of the cuckolded husband. See also I. Bickerstaff, *Thomas and Sally or The Sailor's Return* (Belfast: J. Magee, 1767 edition), a play first staged in 1760 where Sally successfully resists the advances of the squire but only because of the 'Sailor's Return' in the nick of time.

34 J. André, *The Frantick Lover* (New York, New York: Blue Ox Press, 1941), np.

Chapter 27 – Southern Interlude

1 C. Van Doren, *Secret History of the American Revolution* (New York, New York: Viking Press, 1951), p.131.

2 Ibid., p.221 citing Christopher Sower's abstract of his representations to Clinton, lodged in the Clinton papers.

3 Ibid., p.132.

4 Ibid., p.221.

5 Ibid., p.223.

6 W. B. Willcox, *Portrait of a General Sir Henry Clinton in the War of Independence* (New York, New York: Alfred A. Knopf, 1964), p.297.

7   Ibid., p.301.

8   André letter (undated)—part of which is missing—from John André to an unknown recipient in England. Transcript in family records held by Major J. E. A. André.

9   Some of the 'functions' and 'duties' of an adjutant general were, indeed, well within John's capabilities, being as they were, in many instances, a continuation of those he had undertaken while Clinton's aide-de-camp. Samples of the more mundane functions were as recorded in His Majesty's Stationery Office, *Command Papers, Great Britain Parliament, Great Britain*. Historical Manuscripts Commission: 'Report of American Manuscripts in the Royal Institution of Great Britain' Vol. II' (Dublin: John Falconer, 1906): in May 1779, 'The Commander-in-Chief's Answer' was given 'by Capt. J. André' in a dispute touching a claim for flour alleged to have been provided for the use of the British army.' (p.445); on 9 September 1779, 'Captain John André' wrote from 'Headquarters' saying that 'His Excellency wishing that the innocent wife and children of John Taswell may not be the victims if his ill-behaviour desires him to relieve their distress by giving a guinea to the woman…' (p.27); on 8 May, 1780, 'money' was 'advanced Maj Patrick Ferguson, on account of the detachment under his command' (p.318); on 18 July 1780, Cornwallis wrote to Clinton from 'Charlestown' regarding 'an alarming deficiency of medicines, of medical assistance and stores for the hospital. Dr Hayes directed…to write to André relative to the things being sent.' (p.158); on 18 August 1780, John wrote to 'David Mathews, Mayor of New York', regarding 'the pretensions of certain claimants of rent for houses' (p.174).

10 André letter (undated). News of the capture of Grenada reached England in September (see *LEP* (7 September 1779)), but John had the news in early August, Marshall receiving it in Lancaster, Pennsylvania on 6 August according to his diary entry for that day. See W. Duane (ed.), *Extracts from the Diary of Christopher Marshall kept in Philadelphia and Lancaster during the American Revolution 1774–1781* (Albany, New York: J. Munsell, 1877), pp.227–8.

11 André letter (undated).

12 *LGE* (15 June 1780).

13 See F. Bevc, *Puritans, Patriots and Pioneers. An Elwell Family History* (Private publication, 2016), p.198.

14 'New Jersey Journal ii. No. lxxi June 21 1780' in 'Original Papers relating to the Siege of Charleston' (Charleston, South Carolina: Walker, Evans & Cogswell,1898), p.55.

15 Letter dated 17 April 1780 cited in W. Sargent, *The Life and Career of Major John André* (Boston, Massachusetts: Ticknor and Fields, 1861), pp.225–6.

16 Letter of 8 May 1780 cited in His Majesty's Stationery Office, p.318.

17 Letter of 18 July 1780 cited in His Majesty's Stationery Office, p.158.

18 See R. M. Hatch, *Major John André. A Gallant in Spy's Clothing* (Boston, Massachusetts: Houghton Mifflin, 1986), pp.192–3.

19 S. Day, *Historical Collections of the State of Pennsylvania* (Philadelphia, Pennsylvania: George W. Gorton, 1843), p.268.

20 Sargent, *The Life and Career of Major John André*, pp.228–9.

21 Letter dated 17 April 1780 cited in Sargent, *The Life and Career of Major John André*, pp.225–6.

22 W. B. Willcox (ed.), *The American Rebellion: Sir Henry Clinton's Narrative of His Campaigns 1775–1782 with an Appendix of Original Documents* (New Haven, Connecticut: Yale historical publications, manuscripts and edited texts, XXI, 1954), p.184.

23 Willcox, *Portrait of a General Sir Henry Clinton* p.315 citing letter dated 3 April 1780 from André to Clinton.

24 Ibid., p.317.

25 Ibid., p.317 citing letter dated 3 April 1780 from André to Clinton.

26 Ibid., p.323 citing letter dated 5 July 1780 from André to [Richard] Symes in Huntingdon MS. HM 22,426.

Chapter 28 – 'False Friends'

1. Knyphausen's notes regarding Arnold dated May 1780 cited in C. Van Doren, *Secret History of the American Revolution* (New York, New York: Viking Press, 1951), Appendix, p.458.
2. Letter from Arnold to Beckwith or André dated 15 June 1780 cited in Van Doren, *Secret History of the American Revolution*, Appendix, p.460.
3. Letter from Arnold to Beckwith or André dated 16 June 1780 cited in Van Doren, *Secret History of the American Revolution*, Appendix, p.461.
4. Knyphausen's memo regarding Arnold dated May 1780 cited in Van Doren, *Secret History of the American Revolution*, Appendix, p.459.
5. Letter from Beckwith to André dated 20 June 1780 cited in Van Doren, *Secret History of the American Revolution*, p.271.
6. Letter from Joseph Chew to André dated 20 June 1780 cited in Van Doren, *Secret History of the American Revolution*, p.271.
7. Knyphausen's memo regarding Arnold dated May 1780 cited in Van Doren, *Secret History of the American Revolution*, Appendix, p.459.
8. Letter from Arnold to André dated 11 July 1780 cited in Van Doren, *Secret History of the American Revolution*, Appendix, pp.462–3.
9. André letter dated mid-June 1779 from André to Arnold cited in Van Doren, *Secret History of the American Revolution*, Appendix, p.448.
10. Letter from André to Arnold sent in end-July 1779 cited in Van Doren, *Secret History of the American Revolution*, Appendix, p.453.
11. Letter from Arnold to André dated 12 July 1780 cited in Van Doren, *Secret History of the American Revolution*, Appendix, p.463.
12. Letter from André to Arnold dated mid-June 1779 cited in Van Doren, *Secret History of the American Revolution*, Appendix, p.448.
13. Letter from André to Arnold dated 13 July 1780 cited in Van Doren, *Secret History of the American Revolution*, Appendix, p.464. The letter of 24 July was from Odell to Stansbury, which went to Arnold as a cover letter for one from John to Arnold dated 24 July. See Van Doren, *Secret History of the American Revolution*, Appendix, pp.465–6.
14. Letter from André to Arnold dated 24 July 1780 cited in Van Doren, *Secret History of the American Revolution*, Appendix, p.466.
15. Letter from Beckwith to André dated 30 July 1780 cited in Van Doren, *Secret History of the American Revolution*, p.467.
16. Letter from Beckwith to André dated 27 August 1780 cited in Van Doren, *Secret History of the American Revolution*, p.469.
17. Letter from Stansbury to André dated 7 July 1780 cited in Van Doren, *Secret History of the American Revolution*, Appendix, p.462.
18. Letter from Arnold to André dated 15 July 1780 cited in Van Doren, *Secret History of the American Revolution*, Appendix, p.465.
19. Letter from Odell to Stansbury dated 24 July 1780 cited in Van Doren, *Secret History of the American Revolution*, Appendix, p.465.
20. Letter from Arnold to André dated 15 July 1780 cited in Van Doren, *Secret History of the American Revolution*, Appendix, p.465.
21. Letter from Stansbury to Odell dated 24 August 1780 cited in Van Doren, *Secret History of the American Revolution*, Appendix, p.468.
22. Letter from Odell to André dated 24 August 1780 cited in Van Doren, *Secret History of the American Revolution*, Appendix, p.469.

23 Letter from Arnold to Peggy Arnold dated 30 July 1780 cited in Van Doren, *Secret History of the American Revolution*, Appendix, p.468.

24 Letter from Odell to André dated 29 July 1780 cited in Van Doren, *Secret History of the American Revolution*, Appendix, p.466.

25 About this time, Arnold's sister, Hannah, started whispering in his ear with insinuations about Peggy's loose behaviour, saying how she had a reputation for attracting to herself 'a dangerous companion for a particular lady in the absence of her husband'. In her letter to Arnold on 4 September 1780, Hannah wrote: 'I could tell you of frequent private assignations and of numberless billets doux, if I had an inclination to make mischief' cited in Van Doren, *Secret History of the American Revolution*, p.304.

26 Letter from Arnold to André dated 30 August 1780 cited in Van Doren, *Secret History of the American Revolution*, Appendix, p.470.

27 Letter from Arnold to André dated 10 September 1780 cited in Van Doren, *Secret History of the American Revolution*, Appendix, p.471. This letter quotes from Arnold's letter of 7 September 1780 which has been lost.

Chapter 29 – 'Armed Boats'

1 J. Sparks (ed.), *The Writings of George Washington* (12 vols., Boston, Massachusetts: Russell, Odiorne and Metcalf, 1835), VII, p.522.

2 Letter from André to Sheldon dated 7 September 1780 cited in C. Van Doren, *Secret History of the American Revolution* (New York, New York: Viking Press, 1951), Appendix, p.471.

3 Letter from Arnold to André dated 10 September 1780 cited in Van Doren, *Secret History of the American Revolution*, Appendix, p.471.

4 Letter from André to Sheldon dated 7 September 1780 cited in G. Robinson, *New Annual Register … for the Year 1780* (London, 1784), p.150.

5 Letter from Sheldon to Arnold dated 9 September 1780 cited in Sparks (ed.), *The Writings…* VII, p.523.

6 Letter from André to Sheldon dated 7 September 1780 cited in Robinson, *New Annual Register …*, p.150.

7 Letter from Arnold to André dated 10 September 1780 cited in Van Doren, *Secret History of the American Revolution*, Appendix, p.471.

8 Letter from Arnold to André dated 15 September 1780 cited in Van Doren, *Secret History of the American Revolution*, Appendix, p.472.

9 Letter from Arnold to Sheldon dated 9 September 1780 cited in Sparks (ed.), *The Writings…* VII, p.523.

10 Letter from Arnold to Washington dated 11 September 1780 cited in Sparks (ed.), *The Writings…* VII, p.524.

11 Letter from Arnold to André dated 15 September 1780 cited in Van Doren, *Secret History of the American Revolution*, Appendix, pp.472–3.

12 See S. Brumwell, *Turncoat. Benedict Arnold and the Crisis of American Liberty* (New Haven, Connecticut: Yale University Press, 2018) p.200.

13 See D. A. B. Ronald, *Young Nelsons* (Oxford: Osprey Publishing, 2009), pp.44–5.

14 Letter from Arnold to André dated 11 July 1780 cited in Van Doren, *Secret History of the American Revolution*, Appendix, p.463.

15 Letter from Arnold to André dated 15 September 1780 cited in Van Doren, Appendix, p.472.

16 See M. L. Delafield, 'William Smith—The Historian. Chief Justice of New York and Canada' in *Magazine of American History* (April & June 1881), np.

17   Van Doren, *Secret History of the American Revolution*, p.289.

18   This David Franks should not be confused with his uncle, also David Franks, who was the agent for provisions, first, to the British army, then, to the Continental Army.

19   Van Doren, *Secret History of the American Revolution*, p.305 citing Arnold's copy of a letter to Peggy in Washington Papers at Library of Congress.

20   So named because it had been confiscated from Beverley Robinson, a diehard loyalist and colonel in the Loyal American Regiment.

21   Letter from Arnold to André dated 15 September 1780 cited in Van Doren, *Secret History of the American Revolution*, Appendix, p.472.

22   Letter from Sheldon to Arnold dated 6 September 1780 in Washington Papers at Library of Congress cited in Van Doren, *Secret History of the American Revolution*, pp.301–2.

23   Letter from Arnold to Parsons dated 8 September 1780 cited in A. Bushnell (ed.), *Varick Court of Enquiry...* (Boston, Massachusetts: Bibliophile Society, 1907), pp.197–8.

Chapter 30 – 'A Personal Conference'

1   Letter from Clinton to André dated 11 September 1780 cited in C. Van Doren, *Secret History of the American Revolution* (New York, New York: Viking Press, 1951), Appendix, p.472.

2   See Van Doren, *Secret History of the American Revolution*, pp.320–1.

3   Letter from Clinton to André dated 11 September 1780 cited in Van Doren, *Secret History of the American Revolution*, Appendix, p.472.

4   W. B. Willcox (ed.), *The American Rebellion: Sir Henry Clinton's Narrative of His Campaigns 1775–1782 with an Appendix of Original Documents* (New Haven, Connecticut: Yale historical publications, manuscripts and edited texts, XXI, 1954), p.337.

5   Letter from Clinton to Lord George Germain (undated from this period) cited in J. Sparks, *The Library of American Biography* (Boston, Massachusetts: Hilliard Gray & Co, 1835) Vol. III p.168 and W. Sargent, *The Life and Career of Major John André* (Boston, Massachusetts: Ticknor and Fields, 1861), p.261.

6   J. Sparks (ed.), *The Writings of George Washington* (12 vols., Boston, Massachusetts: Russell, Odiorne and Metcalf, 1835), VII, pp.526–7.

7   Pass dated 20 September 1780. See Sargent, *The Life and Career of Major John André*, p.283.

8   Sparks (ed.), *The Writings...*, VII, p.528.

9   In Clinton's later 'Narrative', he inferred that, from this moment onwards, John was operating outside his Commander in Chief's control. Careful in his words, he stated that 'the Commander in Chief agreed to Major André's going to Dobb's Ferry with a Flag of Truce... Thus far the Transaction was carried on with the Knowledge of the Commander in Chief, who before Major André's Departure gave him every Caution that Prudence suggested, not to change his Dress as proposed by General Arnold, but to wear his Uniform and on no Account to take Papers.' See Van Doren, *Secret History of the American Revolution*, Appendix, p.484.

10   André letter to Clinton dated 21 September 1780 cited in Van Doren, *Secret History of the American Revolution*, Appendix, p.484.

11   Letter from André to Clinton dated 21 September 1780 cited from Clinton's 'Narrative' in Van Doren, *Secret History of the American Revolution*, Appendix, p.485.

12   Letter from Robinson to Clinton dated 24 September 1780 cited in Van Doren, *Secret History of the American Revolution*, Appendix, p.474.

13   Sargent, *The Life and Career of Major John André*, p.287.

14   J. H. Smith, *An Authentic Narrative of the Causes which Led to the Death of Major André...* (New York, New York: Evert Duyckinck, 1809), p.20.

15 Sargent, *The Life and Career of Major John André*, p.416 citing Clinton's unpublished two-volume *History of his American Campaigns* Vol. II p.43.

16 Smith, *An Authentic Narrative*, p.21.

17 Sargent, *The Life and Career of Major John André*, p.289.

18 Smith, *An Authentic Narrative*, p.20.

19 Smith, *An Authentic Narrative*, p.21.

20 Smith, *An Authentic Narrative*, p.21.

21 See letter from Arnold to Clinton dated 18 October 1780 wherein he claimed: 'In the Conference with Major André, He was so fully Convinced of the reasonableness of my proposal of being allowed Ten thousand pounds Sterling for my Services, Risque, and the loss which I should sustain in Case a discovery of my Plan should oblige me to take refuge in New York before it could be fully carried into Execution, that he assured me "tho he was commissioned to promise me Only Six thousand pounds Sterling, He would use his influence and recommend it to your Excellency to allow the sum I proposed, and from his State of the matter He informed he had no doubt your Excellency would accede to the proposal..."' (cited in Van Doren, *Secret History of the American Revolution*, Appendix, pp.480–1).

Chapter 31 – 'My Great Mortification'

1 J. H. Smith, *An Authentic Narrative of the Causes which Led to the Death of Major André...* (New York, New York: Evert Duyckinck, 1809), pp.21–3.

2 André's 'Statement' cited in W. Sargent, *The Life and Career of Major John André* (Boston, Massachusetts: Ticknor and Fields, 1861), pp.349–350.

3 Smith, *An Authentic Narrative*, pp.21–3.

4 Clinton's 'Narrative' cited in C. Van Doren, *Secret History of the American Revolution* (New York, New York: Viking Press, 1951), Appendix, p.485.

5 Sargent, *The Life and Career of Major John André*, p.288.

6 Smith, *An Authentic Narrative*, p.23.

7 André's 'Statement' cited in Sargent, *The Life and Career of Major John André*, pp.349–350.

8 Letter from André to Washington dated 24 September 1780 cited in J. Sparks (ed.), *The Writings of George Washington* (12 vols., Boston, Massachusetts: Russell, Odiorne and Metcalf, 1835), VII, p.531.

9 Smith, *An Authentic Narrative*, p.24.

Chapter 32 – 'The Chance of Passing Undiscovered'

1 J. H. Smith, *An Authentic Narrative of the Causes which Led to the Death of Major André...* (New York, New York: Evert Duyckinck, 1809), p.25.

2 C. Van Doren, *Secret History of the American Revolution* (New York, New York: Viking Press, 1951), p.338 citing H. B. Dawson (ed.), *Record of the Trial of Joshua Hett Smith Esq., for alleged Complicity in the Treason of Benedict Arnold* (1866), pp.17–18.

3 André's 'Statement' cited in Sargent, *The Life and Career of Major John André*, pp.349–350.

4 Smith, *An Authentic Narrative*, p.25.

5 Ibid., p.26.

6 Ibid., p.27.

7 Ibid., p.30.

8 Numerous accounts would emerge subsequently from those claiming to have run across John on his journey south to the British lines. Among these, John remembered 'Colonel Samuel

Blachley Webb, a former prisoner of war whom he had known in New York.' R. M. Hatch, *Major John André. A Gallant in Spy's Clothing* (Boston, Massachusetts: Houghton Mifflin, 1986), p.240.

Chapter 33 – 'I Was Betrayed'

1 John left this blank: not knowing how far the conspiracy had unravelled, he kept Smith's name out of this and all his future accounts.

2 André's 'Statement' cited in W. Sargent, *The Life and Career of Major John André* (Boston, Massachusetts: Ticknor and Fields, 1861), pp.349–350. Contemporary commentators lingered at length on the supposed circumstances of John's capture, including the negotiations between John and his captors, his naivety in admitting that he was British, and the motives of the captors, all of which is a diversion from the essential narrative of John's whole life-telling, not least because there are so many versions of the events, all of which became muddled in the alternate heroism and pathos of the iconic moment.

3 André letter (undated)—part of which is missing—from John André to an unknown recipient in England. Transcript in family records held by Major J. E. A. André.

4 C. Van Doren, *Secret History of the American Revolution* (New York, New York: Viking Press, 1951), p.340.

5 Letter from Arnold to André dated 'Sepr 15 1780' cited in Van Doren, *Secret History of the American Revolution*, Appendix, p.472.

6 Van Doren, *Secret History of the American Revolution*, p.341.

7 Letter from 'Lieutenant-colonel Jameson' to Arnold dated 'North Castle, 23 September 1780' cited in J. Sparks (ed.), *The Writings of George Washington* (12 vols., Boston, Massachusetts: Russell, Odiorne and Metcalf, 1835), VII, p.530.

8 Letter from Arnold to Major Tallmadge dated 13 September 1780 cited in A. Bushnell (ed.), *Varick Court of Enquiry...* (Boston, Massachusetts: Bibliophile Society, 1907), p.113.

9 J. Sparks, *The Library of American Biography* (Boston, Massachusetts: Hilliard Gray & Co, 1835), III, pp.233–5.

10 Cited in Sargent, *The Life and Career of Major John André*, pp.323–4.

11 Letter from André to Washington dated 'Salem, 24 September 1780' cited in Sparks (ed.), *The Writings of George Washington*) VII, pp.531–2.

12 Clinton letter dated October 1780 in Van Doren, *Secret History of the American Revolution*, Appendix, p.477.

13 Letter from Clinton to his sisters dated 4 to 9 October 1780 cited in Van Doren, *Secret History of the American Revolution*, Appendix, p.478.

14 Clinton 'Narrative' cited in Van Doren, *Secret History of the American Revolution*, Appendix, p.489.

15 Letter from Clinton to his sisters dated 4 to 9 October 1780 cited in Van Doren, *Secret History of the American Revolution*, Appendix, p.478.

16 Clinton letter dated October 1780 cited in Van Doren, *Secret History of the American Revolution*, Appendix, p.477.

Chapter 34 – 'It will be but a Momentary Pang.'

1 Letter from Varick to his sister 'Jane' dated 1 October 1780 in A. Bushnell (ed.), *Varick Court of Enquiry...* (Boston, Massachusetts: Bibliophile Society, 1907), pp.190–1.

2 Cited in C. Van Doren, *Secret History of the American Revolution* (New York, New York: Viking Press, 1951), p.349 and in J. H. Smith, *An Authentic Narrative of the Causes which Led to the Death of Major André...* (New York, New York: Evert Duyckinck, 1809), p.104.

3 Smith, *An Authentic Narrative*, p.32.

4   J. Sparks (ed.), *The Writings of George Washington* (12 vols., Boston, Massachusetts: Russell, Odiorne and Metcalf, 1835), III, p.254.

5   Smith, *An Authentic Narrative*, p.37.

6   Ibid., p.32.

7   Ibid., p.37.

8   Letter from Washington to Clinton dated 30 September 1780 cited in Van Doren, *Secret History of the American Revolution*, Appendix, pp.487–8.

9   Letter from Clinton to his sisters dated 4 to 9 October 1780 cited in Van Doren, *Secret History of the American Revolution*, Appendix, p.478.

10   Letter from Varick to his sister 'Jane' dated 1 October 1780 cited in Bushnell (ed.), *Varick Court of Enquiry...*, p.191.

11   Van Doren, *Secret History of the American Revolution*, pp.356–8 citing John Laurance, Advocate General, his the only formal record of proceedings and reprinted in Sargent, *The Life and Career of Major John André*, pp.346–356.

12   André letter to Clinton dated 'Tapaan 29th Sept 1780' in family records held by Major J. E. A. André.

13   Report from Clinton to Germain dated 3 October 1780 cited in Van Doren, *Secret History of the American Revolution*, Appendix, pp.476–7.

14   See Van Doren, *Secret History of the American Revolution*, p.366.

15   Letter from Hamilton (in a disguised hand) to Clinton dated 30 September 1780 cited in Van Doren, *Secret History of the American Revolution*, Appendix, p.476.

16   Letter from Arnold to Washington dated 1 October 1780 cited in Van Doren, *Secret History of the American Revolution*, Appendix, p.491.

17   Van Doren, *Secret History of the American Revolution*, p.371 citing J. C. Fitzpatrick (ed.), *Writings* (26 vols., 1931–8), XX, p.173.

18   André letter to Washington dated 'Tappan Oct 1st 1780' in family records held by Major J. E. A. André.

19   Letter from Hamilton to Elizabeth Schuyler cited in W. Sargent, *The Life and Career of Major John André* (Boston, Massachusetts: Ticknor and Fields, 1871), p.370.

Epilogue

1   *LEP* (14 November 1780).

2   Letter from the Marquis de Lafayette to his wife dated 8 October 1780 in Lafayette family, *Memoirs, Correspondence and Manuscripts of General Lafayette* (New York, New York: Saunders and Otley, 1837), Vol. I. p.357.

3   S. Barclay (ed.), *Personal Recollections of the American Revolution* (New York, New York: Rudd & Carleton, 1869), pp.137–9.

4   Ibid., p.145.

5   Letter from Arnold to Clinton dated 18 October 1780 cited in C. Van Doren, *Secret History of the American Revolution* (New York, New York: Viking Press, 1951), Appendix, p.481

6   Letter from Arnold to Washington dated 25 September 1780 cited in Van Doren, *Secret History of the American Revolution*, p.349.

7   Cited in *LC* (25 January 1781).

8   *LC* (6 November 1781).

9   What one newspaper termed 'a Want of Confidence in General Arnold'. See *PA* (4 December 1781).

10   A. R. Newsome, 'A British Orderly Book 1780–1781' in *North Carolina Historical Review* Vol.9 No.1 (Jan. 1932), p.76. See also J. G. Simcoe, *Simcoe's Military Journal* (New York, New York:

Bartlett & Welford, 1844), p.152 where Simcoe had 'given directions that the regiment should immediately be provided with black and white feathers as mourning, for the late Major André'.

11 *Freeman's Journal* (20 June 1781).

12 *London Courant* (18 October 1781).

13 Ibid., (14 November 1781).

14 Cited in Van Doren, *Secret History of the American Revolution*, p.384.

15 Cited in Van Doren, *Secret History of the American Revolution*, p.422.

16 *London Courant* (13 February 1782).

17 See *PA* (15 February 1782) and *PA* (4 February 1782).

18 *St. James's Chronicle* (14 November 1780).

19 *LEP* (14 November 1780).

20 *Adam's Weekly Courant* (21 November 1780).

21 C. T. Kairoff, *Anna Seward and the End of the Eighteenth Century* (Baltimore, Maryland: Johns Hopkins University Press, 2012), p.77. See J. Keith, *Poetry and the Feminine from Behn to Cowper* (Newark, Delaware: University of Delaware Press, 2005), p.143 for an understanding of the sentimental sublime as an ethos of moral and heroic conduct in the late eighteenth century.

22 Ibid., p.82.

23 See *LM* (February 1782), LI, p.139.

24 Kairoff, *Anna Seward and the End of the Eighteenth Century*, p.83.

25 *Morning Herald* (17 July 1781).

26 Kairoff, *Anna Seward and the End of the Eighteenth Century*, p.88.

27 *Morning Herald* (17 July 1781).

28 *LEP* (14 November 1780).

29 *Morning Herald* (4 February 1782).

30 *LC* (9 November 1782). See also *LM* (December 1782), LI, p.609.

Bibliography

John André Letters

Letter dated 14 May 1772 from John André to John Lewis André in Wichita State University Libraries Special Collections and University Archives MS 90-04 Box 1 FF8 André Family Papers Letter 1.

Letter dated 19 July 1772 from John André to John Lewis André in Wichita State University Libraries Special Collections and University Archives MS 90-04 Box 1 FF8 André Family Papers Letter 2.

Transcript of a letter from John André written to his sister, Mary, dated 'Sunday 5th March 1775' in family records held by Major J. E. A. André

Transcript of a letter from John André written to his mother, 'dated New York the 17 Dec 1776' in family records held by Major J. E. A. André

Transcript of a letter from John André to his mother, dated 'Philadelphia Camp, the 20th November 1777' in family records held by Major J. E. A. André

Transcript of a letter from John André to his 'Uncle', dated 'N. York, 12th Sept 1778' in family records held by Major J. E. A. André

Transcript of an undated letter (part of which is missing) from John André to an unknown recipient in England, in family records held by Major J. E. A. André

Transcript of a letter from John André to his 'Uncle', dated 'N. York, 12th Sept 1778' in family records held by Major J. E. A. André

Transcript of a letter from John André to his mother, dated 'German Town near Philadelphia, the 28th Sept. 1777' in family records held by Major J. E. A. André.

Archive Sources

Charles Preston Fonds R7098-O-2-E, MG 23 B10 Preston, Charles St. John's Siege' in Library and Archives, Ottawa, Canada

Newspapers and Periodicals

(Some have been abbreviated by their initials in endnotes, the abbreviation signified by the initials in brackets next to the full title.)

Adam's Weekly Courant
Bingley's Journal
Bingley's London Journal
Chester Chronicle
Craftsman
Critical Review
Daily Advertiser
Daily Journal

Daily Post
De Maandelyske Nederlandsche Mercurius
Dunlap's Pennsylvania Packet
European Magazine
Evening Advertiser
Freeman's Journal
Gazetteer and New Daily Advertiser
General Advertiser
Gentleman's Magazine (GM)
General Evening Post (GEP)
Independent Chronicle
Lady's Magazine
London Courant
London Gazette (LG)
London Gazette Extraordinary (LGE)
London Magazine (LM)
London Packet
Lloyd's Evening Post
London Evening Post (LEP)
London Chronicle (LC)
Morning Herald
Morning Chronicle (MC)
Middlesex Journal (MJ)
Morning Post (MP)
Parker's General Advertiser
Public Advertiser (PA)
Pennsylvania Journal
Penny London Post
Public Ledger
Read's Weekly Journal
Remembrancer (1747)
St. James's Chronicle
Scots Magazine
Southern and Western Magazine and Review
Universal Chronicle
Universal Magazine of Knowledge and Pleasure
Virginia Gazette
Westminster Journal
Whitehall Evening Post (WEP)

Books

D. C. A. Agnew, *Protestant Exiles from France in the Reign of Louis XIV* (3 vols., London: Reeves and Turner, 1871)

J. Almon, *A Collection of all the Treaties of Peace, Alliance and Commerce between Great Britain and other Powers from the Revolution in 1688 to the present time* (2 vols., London, 1772)

R. Anderson, *The Works of John Moore M.D. with Memoirs of his Life and Writings* (7 vols., Edinburgh: Stirling & Slade, 1820)

E. W. Andrews (ed.), *Journal of a Lady of Quality* (New Haven, Connecticut: Yale University Press, 1923)

Anon., *Anmerkungen…des gedachten Magistrats* (Hanau, 1773)

Anon., *Critical Memoirs of the Times* (London: G. Kearsley, 1769)

Anon., *The Edinburgh Gazetteer* (6 vols., Edinburgh: Archibald, Constable and Co, 1822)

Anon., *Emigrants from England 1773–1776* (Boston, Massachusetts: New England Historic Genealogical Society, 1913)

Anon., *The English Reports House of Lords* (Edinburgh: William Green & Sons, 1900)

Anon., *Fielding's New Peerage of England, Scotland & Ireland* (London: John Murray, undated)

Anon., *A General State of the London Hospital for the Relief of Sick and Wounded Seamen, Manufacturers and labouring Poor, their Wives and Families* (London, 1787)

Anon., *German Museum, or Monthly Repository Museum of the Literature of Germany* (3 vols., London, 1800–1)

Anon. (A. Graydon), *Memoirs of a Life chiefly passed in Pennsylvania…* (Edinburgh: William Blackwood, 1822)

Anon. (W. Burke) *An Impartial History of the War in America…* (London: R. Faulder, 1780)

Anon., *Journals of the American Congress from 1774 to 1788* (4 vols., Washington: Way and Gideon, 1823)

Anon., *Journals of the House of Commons…* (London: by order of the House of Commons, 1803)

Anon., *Journals of the House of Lords*

Anon., *A List of the General and Field Officers…* (London: J. Millan, 1778)

Anon., *Military Register…for the year 1770* (London: J. Almon, 1771)

Anon., *Proceedings of the Committee for Relieving the Poor Germans…* (London: J. Haberkorn, 1765)

Anon., *A Short Tour Made in the Year One Thousand Seven Hundred and Seventy One* (London: 1775)

Anon., *Strictures on the Philadelphia Mischianza…* (London: J. Bew, 1779)

Anon., *Universal Pocket Dictionary* (London: L. Hawes & Co, 1767)

F. Asbury, *Journal of Rev. Francis Asbury* (3 vols., New York, New York: Lane & Scott, 1852)

R. Atwood, *The Hessians. Mercenaries from Hessen-Kassel in the American Revolution* (Cambridge: Cambridge University Press, 1980)

C. B. Bailey, *Patriotic Taste. Collecting Modern Art in Pre-Revolutionary Paris* (New Haven, Connecticut: Yale University Press, 2002)

J. Bakeless, *Turncoats, Traitors and Heroes* (Philadelphia, Pennsylvania: J.B. Lippincott Company, 1959)

T. F. T. Baker (ed.), *A History of the County of Middlesex* (London: Victoria County History, 1995)

G. E. Bannerman, *Merchants and the Military in Eighteenth Century Britain* (Abingdon: Routledge, 2015)

A. L. Barbauld, *Poems of Anna Laetitia Barbauld* (London: J. Johnson, 1792)

S. Barclay (ed.), *Personal Recollections of the American Revolution* (New York, New York: Rudd & Carleton, 1869)

M. Batt, *The Treatment of Nature in German Literature from Gunther to the Appearance of Goethe's Werther* (Chicago, Illinois: University of Chicago Press, 1902)

S. M. Baule, *Protecting the Empire's Frontier Officers of the 18th (Royal Irish) Regiment of Foot during its North American Service 1767–1776* (Athens, Ohio: Ohio University Press, 2014)

T. W. Bean (ed.), *History of Montgomery County, Pennsylvania* (Philadelphia, Pennsylvania: Everts & Peck, 1884)

C. Berger, *Broadside and Bayonets. The Propaganda War of the American Revolution* (Philadelphia, Pennsylvania: University of Pennsylvania Press, 1961)

W. Betham, *The Baronetage of England* (London: E. Lloyd, 1804)

F. Bevc, *Puritans, Patriots and Pioneers An Elwell Family History* (Private publication, 2016)

H. D. Biddle (ed.), *Extracts from the Journal of Elizabeth Drinker…* (Philadelphia, Pennsylvania: J.B. Lippincott Company, 1889)

G. A Billias (ed.), *The American Revolutionary Series* (Boston, Massachusetts: Gregg Press, 1972)

J. M. Black, *European International Relations 1648–1815* (Basingstoke: Palgrave, 2002)

J. M. Black, *Plotting Power. Strategy in the Eighteenth Century* (Bloomington, Indiana: Indiana University Press, 2017)

A. Blackstock & E. Magennis (eds.), *Politics and Political Culture in Britain and Ireland 1750–1850* (Belfast: Ulster Historical Foundation, 2007)

J. Bohstedt, *The Politics of Provisions: Food Riots, Moral Economy and Market Transition in England c.1550–1850* (Abingdon: Routledge, 2016)

C. K. Bolton (ed.), *Letters of Hugh Earl Percy from Boston and New York 1774–1776* (Boston, Massachusetts: C. E. Goodspeed, 1902)

J. Boswell, *The Life of Samuel Johnson L.L.D.* (5 vols., London: John Murray, 1831)

E. Boudinot, *Journal of Historical Recollections of American Events during the Revolutionary War* (Philadelphia, Pennsylvania: F. Bourquin, 1894)

J. Brown, *Reports of Cases upon Appeals and Writs of Error in the High Court of Parliament* (Dublin: E. Lynch, 1784)

S. Brumwell, *Turncoat. Benedict Arnold and the Crisis of American Liberty* (New Haven, Connecticut: Yale University Press, 2018)

H. Bryan, *Martha Washington, First Lady of Liberty* (New York, New York: John Wiley & Sons, 2002)

J. B. Burke, *History of the Landed Gentry of Great Britain and Ireland* (2 vols., London: Harrison, 1871)

R. Burnham and R. McGuigan, *The British Army Against Napoleon, Facts, Lists, Trivia 1805–1815* (Barnsley: Frontline Books, 2010)

J. Burrows, *Report of Cases Argued and Adjudg'd in the Court of King's Bench* (5 vols., London: E and R. Brooke, 1790)

A. Bushnell (ed.), *Varick Court of Enquiry…* (Boston, Massachusetts: Bibliophile Society, 1907)

G. & J. Cary, *Cary's New Itinerary* (London: G. & J. Cary, 1826)

H. Chamberlain, *A New and Compleat History of the Cities of London and Westminster* (London: J. Cooke, 1770)

M. Chamberlain, *Memorial of Captain Charles Cochrane. A British Officer in the Revolutionary War 1774–1781* (Cambridge, Massachusetts: John Wilson and Son, 1891)

E. F. Crane (ed.), *The Diary of Elizabeth Drinker* (Philadelphia, Pennsylvania: University of Pennsylvania Press, 1994)

G. A. Cranfield, *The Press and Society from Caxton to Northcliffe* (Abingdon: Routledge, 2016)

A. H. Craufurd, *General Craufurd and his Light Division* (Pickle Partners Publishing, ebook edition, 2011)

T. H. Croker, T. Williams, S. Clark, *The Complete Dictionary of Arts and Sciences* (London, 1766)

R. Cusick, *Wellington's Rifles The Origins, Development and Battles of the Rifles Regiments in the Pensinsular War and at Waterloo* (Barnsley: Pen & Sword, 2013)

B. Cuthbertson, *B. Cuthbertson's System for the Complete Interior Management and Economy of a Battalion of Infantry* (Bristol: Routh's and Nelson, 1776 edition).

E. E. Dana (ed.), *The British in Boston, being the diary of Lieutenant John Barker of the King's Own Regiment from November 15 1774 to May 31 1776* (Cambridge, Massachusetts: Harvard University Press, 1924)

S. Day, *Historical Collections of the State of Pennsylvania* (Philadelphia, Pennsylvania: George W. Gorton, 1843)

D. Defoe, *A Tour Thro' the whole Island of Great Britain Divided into Circuits or Journies…* (2 vols., London: G. Strahan, 1725)

O. Deneke, *Lichtenbergs Leben* (Munich, Germany: Heimeran, 1944).

C. Diederich, *Musenalmanach* (Göttingen, Germany) 'MDCCLXXII'

B. De Zuylen, *Boswell in Holland 1763–1764* (New York, New York: McGraw-Hill, 1928)

F. R. Diffenderffer, *The Loyalists in the Revolution* (Lancaster, Pennsylvania, 1919)

R. Donkin, *Military Collections and Remarks* (New York, New York: H. Gaine, 1777)

A. G. Doughty, *Report of the Work of the Public Archives for the Years 1914 and 1915* (Ottawa, Canada: J. de L. Tache, 1916) Appendix B

M. Dresser & A. Hann (eds.), *Slavery and the British Country House* (Swindon: English Heritage, 2013)

W. Duane (ed.), *Extracts from the Diary of Christopher Marshall kept in Philadelphia and Lancaster during the American Revolution 1774–1781* (Albany, New York: J. Munsell, 1877)

W.S. Dunn Jr., *Choosing Sides on the Frontier in the American Revolution* (Westport, Connecticut: Praeger, 2007)

W. Eddis, *Letters from America, Historical and Descriptive* (London, 1792)

R. L. Edgeworth, *Memoirs of Richard Lovell Edgeworth Esq.* (London: Richard Bentley, 1844)

E. F. Ellet, *The Women of the American Revolution* (2 vols., New York, New York: Baker & Scribner, 1850)

I. T. Evans and W. Davis (eds.), *Seventh Report from the Committee of Secrecy Appointed by the House of Commons...to enquire into the State of the East India Company* (London, 1773)

E. C. Everard, *Memoirs of an Unfortunate Son of Thespis* (Edinburgh: James Ballantyne & Co, 1818)

A. Findlay, *Women in Shakespeare. A Dictionary* (London: Continuum, 2010)

J. C. Fitzpatrick (ed.), *The Writings of George Washington from the Original Manuscript Sources 1745–1799* (Washington DC: United States Government Printing Office, 1936)

F. Fleming, *Killing Dragons. The Conquest of the Alps* (London: Granta Books, 2001)

P. Force (ed.), *American Archives, Fourth Series, containing a Documentary History of the English Colonies in North America...* (6 vols., Washington: St. Clair Clarke and Force, 1840)

P. Force (ed.), *American Archives, Fifth Series, containing a Documentary History of the English Colonies in North America...* (3 vols., Washington: St. Clair Clarke and Force, 1840)

W. C. Ford, *British Officers serving in the American Revolution 1774–1783* (Brooklyn, New York: Historical Printing Club, 1897)

A. D. Francis, *Portugal 1717–1808. Joanine, Pombaline and Rococo Portugal as seen by British Diplomats and Traders* (London: Tamesis Books, 1985)

A. French (ed.), *A British Fusilier in Revolutionary Boston* (Cambridge, Massachusetts: Harvard University Press, 1926)

A. E. Fyler, *The History of the 50th or (The Queen's Own) Regiment* (London: Chapman and Hall, 1895).

R. B. Gardner, *The Admission Registers of St. Paul's School from 1748 to 1876* (London: George Bell and Sons, 1884)

D. Garrioch *The Huguenots of Paris and the Coming of Religious Freedom 1685–1789* (Cambridge: Cambridge University Press, 2014)

P. Gauci, *The Politics of Trade. The Overseas Merchant in State and Society 1660–1720* (Oxford: Oxford University Press, 2003)

A. L. George, *Old Philadelphia. Cradle of American Democracy* (Charleston, South Carolina: Arcadia Publishing, 2003)

E. Gibbon, *The Auto-Biography of Edward Gibbon Esq.* (New York, New York: Buckland & Sumner, 1846 edition)

J. Gorton, *A General Biographical Dictionary* (3 vols., London: Whitaker & Co., 1838)

W. Griffiths, *Historical Notes of the American Colonies and Revolution from 1754 to 1775* (Burlington, New Jersey: J. L. Powell, 1843)

P. Groves, *Historical Records of the 7th or Royal Regiment of Fusiliers* (Guernsey: F.B. Guerin, 1903)

J. Hadden, *Hadden's Journal and Orderly Book* (Albany, New York: Joel Munsell's Sons, 1884)

S. M. Hamilton (ed.), *Letters to George Washington and Accompanying Papers* (Society of the Colonial Dames of North America, Library of Congress)

G. Hanger, *The Life, Adventures and Opinions of Col. George Hanger...* (2 vols., London: J. Debrett, 1801)

N. Hans, *New Trends in Education in the Eighteenth Century* (Abingdon: Routledge, 1998)

M. C. Harris, *Brandywine: A Military History of the Battle that Lost Philadelphia* (El Dorado Hills, California: Savas Beatie, 2013)

R. M. Hatch, *Major John André. A Gallant in Spy's Clothing* (Boston, Massachusetts: Houghton Mifflin, 1986)

L. Hawks and Co, G. Keith, J. Rivington, R. Baldwin, *The Universal Pocket Companion* (London, 1767)

P. H. Hembry, *The English Spa 1560–1815. A Social History* (Madison, New Jersey: Fairleigh Dickinson University Press, 1990)

W. U. Hensel, *Major André as a Prisoner of War at Lancaster PA, 1775–6* (Lancaster, Pennsylvania: New Era Printing, 1904)

H-J. Heerde, *Das Publikum der Physik, Lichtenberg's Horer* (Göttingen, Germany: Wallenstein, 2006)

W. Herbst, *Johann Heinrich Voss* (Leipzig, Germany : B.G. Teubner, 1872)

P. L. R. Higonnet, D. S. Landes, H. Rosovsky (eds.), *Favorites of Fortune. Technology, Growth and Economic Development since the Industrial Revolution* (Cambridge, Massachusetts: Harvard University Press, 1991)

G. B. Hill (ed.), *Boswell's Life Of Johnson* (6 vols., New York, New York: Harper & Brothers, 1799)

His Majesty's Stationery Office, *Command Papers, Great Britain Parliament, Great Britain*. Historical Manuscripts Commission: 'Report of American Manuscripts in the Royal Institution of Great Britain' Vol. II' (Dublin: John Falconer, 1906)

J. A. Home (ed.), *The Letters and Journals of Lady Mary Coke* (4 vols., Bath: Kingsmead Reprints, 1970)

W. Howe, *The Narrative of Lieut. Sir Gen. William Howe in a Committee of the House of Commons* (London: H. Baldwin, 1781)

W. Irving, *The Life of George Washington* (New York, New York: Cosimo Classics, 2005)

J. I. Israel, *Democratic Enlightenment. Philosophy, Revolution and Human Rights 1750–1790* (Oxford: Oxford University Press, 2011)

L. C. Judson, *A Biography of the Signers of the Declaration of Independence and of Washington and Patrick Henry* (Philadelphia, Pennsylvania: A., J. Dobson and Thomas, Cowperthwait & Co., 1839)

C. L. Kairoff, *Anna Seward and the End of the Eighteenth Century* (Baltimore, Maryland: John Hopkins University Press, 2011)

F. Kapp, *Der Soldatenhandel deutscher Fursten nach Amerika* (Berlin, Germany: Julius Springer, 1874)

J. Keay, *The Honourable East India Company. A History of the English East India Company* (London: HarperCollins, 1993)

J. Keith, *Poetry and the Feminine from Behn to Cowper* (Newark, Delaware: University of Delaware Press, 2005)

S. Kemble, 'Kemble's Journal' in *Collections of the New York Historical Society for the Year 1883*: New York: 1884)

R. Kramer, *Cherubino's Leap: In Search of the Enlightenment Moment* (Chicago, Illinois: University of Chicago Press, 2016)

Lafayette family, *Memoirs, Correspondence and Manuscripts of General Lafayette* (New York, New York: Saunders and Otley, 1837)

C. L. Landis, *Major John André's German Letter* (Lancaster, Pennsylvania: New Era Printing, 1914)

C. Le Fort, G. Revilliod, E. Frick (eds.), *Le Livre du Recteur, Catalogue des Etudiants de l'Academie de Geneve de 1559 a 1859* (Geneva, Switzerland: 1860)

I. Q. Leake, *Memoir of the Life and Times of General John Lamb* (Albany, New York: Joel Munsell, 1857)

A. F. Lefkowitz, *Benedict Arnold's Army, The 1775 American Invasion of Canada During the Revolutionary War* (El Dorado Hills, California: Savas Beatie, 2008)

G. C. Lichtenberg, *Schriften und Briefe* Sudelbucher, Band II (Munich, Germany: Carl Hanser, 1971)

H. C. Lodge (ed.), *André's Journal An Authentic Record of the Movements and Engagements of the British Army in America from June 1777 to November 1778 as recorded from day to day by Major John André* (2 vols., Boston, Massachusetts: Bibliophile Society, 1903)

J. Love, *Geodaesia. The Art of Surveying and Measuring Land made Easy* (London: J. Rivington, 1771)

E. V. Lucas, *A Swan and her Friends* (London: Methuen & Co, 1907)

D. Lysons, *The Environs of London: the County of Middlesex* (2 vols., London: T. Cadell jun. and W. Davies, 1795)

H. Mackenzie, *The Man of Feeling* (London: Cassell, 1886)

W. Maitland, *The History and Survey of London...* (2 vols., London: T. Osborne, J. Shipton, J. Hodges, 1756)

G. W. Marshall (ed.), *The Genealogist* (London: George Bell & Sons, 1882)

A. Matthews (ed.), *Letters of Dennys De Berdt 1757– 77* (Cambridge, Massachusetts: John Wilson and Son, 1911)

G. K. McGilvary, *Guardian of the East India Company: The Life of Laurence Sulivan* (London: Tauris Academic Studies, 2006)

P. M'Robert, *A Tour Through Part of the North Provinces of America 1774–1775* (Edinburgh: 1776)

L. McVeagh (ed.), *The Journal of Nicholas Cresswell 1774–1777* (New York, New York: Dial Press, 1924)

K. Miller, *Dangerous Guests. Enemy Captives and Revolutionary Communities during the War for Independence* (Ithaca, New York: Cornell University Press, 2014)

H. H. Milman, *The Life of Edward Gibbon* (Paris, France: Baudry's European Library, 1840)

P. R. Misencik, *Sally Townsend. George Washington's Teenage Spy* (Jefferson, North Carolina: McFarland & Company, 2016)

F. Moore, *Diary of the American Revolution* (New York, New York: Charles Scribner, 1860)

R. Moore (ed.), *The History and the Life of Thomas Ellwood* (Walnut Creek, CA: AltaMira Press, 2004)

F. N. C. Mundy, *Poems* (Oxford: W. Jackson, 1768)

W. Musgrave, *Obituary prior to 1800* (London: Harleian Society, 1900)

L. Namier & J. Brooke (eds.), *The History of Parliament; House of Commons 1754–1790* (3 vols., London: Secker & Warburg, 1985)

J. Nichols, *A Select Collection of Poems* (J. Nichols, London, 1784)

D. Noy, *Dr Johnson's Friend and Robert Adam's Client Topham Beauclerk* (Newcastle-upon- Tyne: Cambridge Scholars Publishing, 2016)

E. B. O'Callaghan (ed.), *Documents relative to the Colonial History of New York...* (Albany, New York: Weed, Parsons, 1857)

C. C. Orr (ed.), *Queenship in Europe 1660–1815* (Cambridge: Cambridge University Press, 2004)

D. Paterson, *A Travelling Dictionary* (London: T. Carnan, 1781)

J. Paterson, *History of the Counties of Ayr and Wigton* (5 vols., Edinburgh; James Stillie, 1864)

R. Pearson. *Voltaire Almighty. A Life in Pursuit of Freedom* (London: Bloomsbury, 2010)

T. Pennant, *A Tour in Scotland* (London: B. White, 1776)

J. Philippart, *The Royal Military Calendar* (2 vols., London: A.J. Valpy, 1815)

Sir F. Pollock (ed.), *The Revised Reports being A Republication Of Such Cases in the English Courts of Common Law and Equity from the year 1785* (London: Sweet and Maxwell Ltd, 1891)

A. L. Poulet, *Jean-Antoine Houdon. Sculptor of the Enlightenment* (Chicago, Illinois: University of Chicago Press, 2005)

W. R. Powell (ed.), *A History of the County of Essex* (London: Victoria County History, 1973)

W. Promies (ed.), *G.C. Lichtenberg, Schriften und Briefe* Sudelbucher, Band II (Munich, Germany: Carl Hanser, 1971).

E. Pyle, *Memoirs of a Royal Chaplain, 1729–1763* (London: John Lane, Bodley Head, 1905)

J. Rae, *The Life of Adam Smith* (New York, New York: Cosimo Classics, 2006)

W. S. Randall, *Benedict Arnold. Patriot and Traitor* (London: Bodley Head, 1991)

S. Reid, *British Redcoat 1740–1783* (Oxford: Osprey Publishing, 2012)

J. Richardson, *The Annals of London. A Year-by-Year of a Thousand Years of History* (Berkeley, California: University of California Press, 2000)

B. Rizzo (ed.), *Early Journals and Letters of Fanny Burney* Vol.4 *The Streatham Years 1780–1781* (Oxford: Oxford University Press, 2003)

G. Robinson, *New Annual Register…for the Year 1780* (London, 1784)

E. Robson (ed.), *Letters from America 1773–1780* (Manchester: Manchester University Press, 1951).

J. Roding and L.H. van Voss (eds.), *The North Sea and Culture 1550–1800* (Hilversum: Verloren Publishers, 1996).

H. C. B. Rogers, *The British Army of the Eighteenth Century* (London: George Allen & Unwin, 1977)

D. A. B. Ronald, *Young Nelsons* (Oxford: Osprey Publishing, 2009)

I. D. Rupp, *History of Lancaster County* (Lancaster, Pennsylvania: Gilbert Hills, 1844)

W. T. R. Saffell, *Records of the Revolutionary War* (New York, New York: Pudney & Russell, 1858)

W. Sargent, *The Life and Career of Major John André* (Boston, Massachusetts: Ticknor and Fields, 1861)

T. E. Schmauk, *A History of the Lutheran Church in Pennsylvania (1638–1820)* (Philadelphia, Pennsylvania: General Council Publication House, 1930)

G. D. Scull (ed.), *Memoir and Letters of Captain W. Glanville Evelyn* (Oxford: James Parker, 1879)

I. Senter, *The Journal of Isaac Senter* (Philadelphia, Pennsylvania: Historical Society of Pennsylvania, 1846)

A. Seward, 'Sonnet III' in *Original Sonnets on various subjects and Odes paraphrased from Horace* (London: G. Sael, 1799)

A. Seward, *Letters of Anna Seward* (6 vols., Edinburgh: Archibald Constable & Company, 1811)

S. B. Shenstone, *So Obstinately Loyal; James Moody 1744–1809* (Montreal, Canada: McGill-Queen's University Press, 2002)

G.O. Seilhamer, *History of the American Theatre during the Revolution and after* (Philadelphia, Pennsylvania: Globe Printing House, 1889)

A. Seward, *Eyam* in W. Wood, *The History and Antiquities of Eyam* (London: Thomas Miller, 1842)

Sherratt & Hughes (printer), *Letters of Denization and Acts of Naturalization for Aliens in England & Ireland 1701–1800* (London: Publications of the Huguenot Society, 1923)

J. G. Simcoe, *Simcoe's Military Journal* (New York, New York: Bartlett & Welford, 1844)

R. Simpson, *Memorials of St. John at Hackney* (Guildford: J. Billing and Sons, 1882)

T. Simpson, *Select Exercises for Young Proficients in the Mathematicks* (London: J. Nourse, 1752)

J. H. Smith, *An Authentic Narrative of the Causes which Led to the Death of Major André…* (New York, New York: Evert Duyckinck, 1809)

J. J. Smith & J. F. Watson (eds.), *American Historical and Literary Curiosities* (Philadelphia: T. K. & P. G. Collins, 1847)

A Society of Merchants and Tradesmen, *The Compleat Compting-House Companion or Young Merchant and Trader's Sure Guide* (London: W. Johnston, 1763)

J. Sparks, *The Library of American Biography* (Boston, Massachusetts: Hilliard Gray & Co, 1835)

J. Sparks, *The Writings of George Washington* (Boston, Massachusetts: Russell, Odiorne and Metcalf, 1835)

W. B. Sprague, *Annals of the American Episcopal Pulpit* (New York, New York: Robert Carter and Brothers, 1859)

M. H. Spring, *With Zeal and with Bayonets Only: The British Army on Campaign in North America 1775–1783* (Norman, Oklahoma: University of Oklahoma Press, 2008)

K. A. Staples and M. Shaw, *Clothing through American History* (Santa Barbara, California: Greenwood, 2013)

M. Starke, *Travels in Europe for the use of Travellers on the Continent* (London: John Murray, 1833 edition)

C. Stedman, *The History of the Origin, Progress and Termination of the American War* (2 vols., Dublin: P. Wogan et al., 1794)

W. L. Stone (Editor and translator), *Letters and Journals relating to the War of the American Revolution… by Mrs General Riedesel* (Albany, New York: Joel Munsell, 1867)

L. Sutherland, *Politics and Finance in the Eighteenth Century* (London: Hambledon Press, 1984)

S. G. Tallentyre, *The Life of Voltaire* (New York, New York: Knickerbocker Press, 1910)

F. Trivelatto, *The Familiarity of Strangers: The Sephardic Diaspora, Livorno and Cross-Cultural Trade in the Early Modern Period* (New Haven, Connecticut: Yale University Press, 2009)

C. Van Doren, *Secret History of the American Revolution* (New York, New York: Viking Press, 1951)

T. Vanneste, *Global Trade and Commercial Networks. Eighteenth Century Diamond Merchants* (London: Pickering and Chatto, 2011)

F. A. de Voltaire, *Candide* (English version: New York, New York: Boni & Liveright, 1918)

A. Voss (ed.), *Briefe von Johann Heinrich Voss* (Halberstadt, Germany: C. Bruggemann, 1829)

J. H. Voss, *Sammtliche Poetische Werke* (Leipzig, Germany: I. Muller, 1850)

D. Wahrman, *The Making of the Modern Self. Identity and Culture in Eighteenth Century England* (New Haven, Connecticut: Yale University Press, 2004)

E. Walford, *Old and New London* (6 vols., London: Cassell & Company, 1892)

H. Walpole, *The Letters of Horace Walpole, Earl of Orford* (6 vols., London: R. Bentley, 1840)

J. F. Watson, *Annals of Philadelphia and Pennsylvania...* (3 vols., Philadelphia, Pennsylvania: E.S. Stuart, 1884)

K. Weinhold, *Heinrich Christian Boie* (Halle, Germany: Weissenhausse, 1868).

T. West, *The Curious Mr Howard. Legendary Prison Reformer* (Hook: Waterside Press, 2011)

C. A. Whatley, *Scottish Society 1707–1830* (Manchester: Manchester University Press, 2000)

W. Wheater, *Historical Record of the Seventh or Royal Regiment of Fusiliers* (Leeds: Private Circulation, 1875)

W. White, *Notes and Queries* (London: George Bell, 1854)

J. Wilkinson, *Memoirs of my Own Times* (3 vols., Philadelphia, Pennsylvania: A. Small, 1816)

J. R. Williams (ed.), *Philip Vickers Fithian Journal and Letters 1767–1774* (Princeton, New Jersey: Princeton Historical Association, 1900)

W. B. Willcox (ed.), *The American Rebellion: Sir Henry Clinton's Narrative of His Campaigns 1775–1782 with an Appendix of Original Documents* (New Haven, Connecticut: Yale historical publications, manuscripts and edited texts, XXI, 1954)

W. B. Willcox, *Portrait of a General Sir Henry Clinton in the War of Independence* (New York, New York: Alfred A Knopf, 1964)

C. H. Wilson, *Anglo–Dutch Commerce and Finance in the Eighteenth Century* (Cambridge: The University Press, 1941)

G. Wilson, *The Life of the Hon. Henry Cavendish* (London: Harrison and Son, 1851).

E. Wolf, II, *Germantown and the Germans* (Philadelphia, Pennsylvania: the Library Company of Philadelphia, 1983)

A. Wood Renton (ed.), *The English Reports, House of Lords* (Edinburgh: William Green & Sons, 1900)

G. Wrottesley, *History of the Family of Wrottesley of Wrottesley...* (Exeter: William Pollard & Co, 1903).

Published Articles and Reports

J. Allen, 'Diary of James Allen, Esq., of Philadelphia Counsellor-at-Law' in *Pennsylvania Magazine of History and Biography* Vol. IX, No.2 (July 1885)

J. Allen, 'Diary of James Allen, Esq., of Philadelphia Counsellor-at-Law' in *Pennsylvania Magazine of History and Biography* Vol. IX, No.4 (Jan. 1886)

C. Baurmeister, B. A Uhlendorf, E. Vosper, 'Letters of Major Carl Baurmeister during the Philadelphia Campaign 1777–1778' in *Pennsylvania Magazine of History and Biography* Vol. 60 No.1 (Jan. 1936)

C. Baurmeister, B.A. Uhlendorf, E. Vosper, 'Letters of Major Carl Baurmeister during the Philadelphia Campaign 1777–1778' in *Pennsylvania Magazine of History and Biography* Vol.60 No.2 (Apr. 1936)

R. Blanchard, 'A Prologue and Epilogue for Nicholas Rowe's Tamerlane by Richard Steele' in Modern Language Association's PMLA, Vol. 47 No.3 (September, 1932)

J. F. Bosher, 'Huguenot Merchants and the Protestant International in the Seventeenth Century' in *The William and Mary Quarterly* Vol. 52 No.1 (January, 1995)

H. V. Bowen, 'Lord Clive and Speculation in East India Company Stock, 1766' in *The Historical Journal* Vol. 30 No.4 (December 1987).

H. V. Bowen, 'Investment and Empire in the later Eighteenth Century: East India Stockholding 1756–1791' in *The Economic History Review* Vol. 2 No. 2 (May 1989)

J. L. Boyle & S. Armstrong, 'Notes and Documents from Saratoga to Valley Forge: Diary of Lt S. Armstrong' in *Pennsylvania Magazine of History and Biography* Vol.121 No. 3 (July 1997)

M. Brown, 'The Jews of Hackney before 1840' in *Jewish Historical Studies* 30 (1987–8)

X. Caron, 'Images d'une Elite au XVIIIe Siecle, Quarante Negociants Anoblis face á la Question Sociale.' in *Histoire, Economie et Societé* Vol. 3 No.3 (3eme trimester, 1984)

J. L. Chester, 'Account of the Family of Major John André' in *Proceedings of the Massachusetts Historical Society* Vol. 14 (1875–1876)

R. Clayton, 'Extracts from the Orderly Book of Major Robert Clayton of the Seventeenth Regiment 1778' in *Pennsylvania Magazine of History and Biography* Vol. 25 No.1 1901)

J. M. Coleman, 'Joseph Galloway and the British Occupation of Philadelphia' in *Pennsylvania History: A Journal of Mid-Atlantic Studies* Vol. 30 no.3 (July 1963)

S. Conway, '"The Great Mischief Complain'd of." Reflections on the Misconduct of British Soldiers during the Revolutionary War' in *The William and Mary Quarterly* Vol. 47 No.3

S. R. Cope, 'The Stock Exchange Revisited. A New Look at the Market in Securities in London in the Eighteenth Century' in *Economica* New Series Vol. 45, No.177 (February 1978)

M. L. Delafield, 'William Smith – The Historian. Chief Justice of New York and Canada' in *Magazine of American History* (April & June 1881)

F. R. Diffenderffer, 'Early German Printers of Lancaster' in *Journal of the Lancaster County Historical Society*, 1903–4

E. Duling, 'Ethan Allen and *The Fall of British Tyranny*: A Question of what Came First.' (Online resource)

S. Eve, 'Extracts from the Journal of Miss Sarah Eve' in *Pennsylvania Magazine of History and Biography* Vol. 5 No.1 (Historical Society of Pennsylvania, 1881)

D. E. Fisher, 'Social Life in Philadelphia during the British Occupation' in *Pennsylvania History: a Journal of Mid-Atlantic Studies* Vol. 37 No.3 (July, 1970)

G. G. Galloway and R. C. Werner, 'Diary of Grace Growden Galloway, Kept at Philadelphia July 1, to September 30, 1779' in *Pennsylvania Magazine of History and Biography* Vol. 58 No.2 (1934)

K. Haulman, 'Fashion and the Culture Wars of Revolutionary Philadelphia' in *The William and Mary Quarterly* Third Series Vol. 62 No.4 (Oct. 2005)

D. Heiland, 'Swan Songs. The Correspondence of Anna Seward and James Boswell' in *Modern Philology* Vol. 90, No.3 (February 1993)

J. Jackson, 'Washington in Philadelphia' (a paper read before the Historical Society of Pennsylvania in 1932) online resource

J. W. Jordan, 'Bethlehem during the Revolution: Extracts from the diaries in the Moravian Archives at Bethlehem, Pennsylvania' in *Pennsylvania Magazine of History and Biography* Vol. XII, No.4, 1888

D. King-Hele, 'Erasmus Darwin, the Lunaticks and Evolution' in *Notes and Records of the Royal Society of London* Vol. 52 No.1 (January 1998)

J. Lacroix-Leclair and E. Ouellet, 'The Petite Guerre in New France, 1660–1759. An Institutional Analysis' in *Canadian Military Journal* Valour Vol. 11, No.4

R. Loewenberg, 'A Letter on Major André from Germany' in *American Historical Review* Vol. 49 No.2 (January 1944)

'Major André's Parole' in *Pennsylvania Magazine of History and Biography* Vol. 1, No.1 (1877)

T. S. McMillin, *Guide to Hanover Military Records 1514–1866 on Microfilm at the Family History Library* translated by A.L and O.K. Ladenburger (Inverness, Illinois: Lind Street Research, 2014)

A. R. Newsome, 'A British Orderly Book 1780–1781' in *North Carolina Historical Review* Vol.9 No.1 (Jan. 1932)

D. J. Ormrod, 'The Atlantic Economy and the Protestant Capitalist International 1651–1775' *Historical Research* Vol. 66 (1993)

M. Morris, 'Revolutionary Journal of Margaret Morris of Burlington N.J. December 6 1776 to June 11 1778' in Bulletin of Friends' Historical Society of Philadelphia Vol 9 No. 1 (May, 1919)

A. R. Newsome, 'A British Orderly Book 1780–1781' in *North Carolina Historical Review* Vol.9 No.1 (Jan. 1932)

T. Pearce, 'The Amyand Correspondence from 1764–1766' in 'BWI Study Circle Bulletin' No. 204 (March, 2005)

C. H. and D. Philips, 'Alphabetical List of Directors of the East India Company from 1758 to 1858' in *The Journal of the Royal Asiatic Society of Great Britain and Ireland* No.4 (October 1941)

T. C. Pollock, Notes on Professor Pattee's "The British Theater in Philadelphia in 1778" in *American Literature* Vol. 7 No.3 (Nov. 1935)

M. Quintanilla, 'The World of Alexander Campbell: An Eighteenth-Century Grenadian Planter' in *Albion, A Quarterly Journal concerned with British Studies* Vol. 35 No. 2 (Summer, 2003)

H. F. Rankin, 'The Colonial Theater. Its History and Operations' (Williamsburg, VA, 1955) Colonial Williamsburg Foundation Library Research Report Series 0057 (Williamsburg, Virginia, 1990)

C. I. A. Ritchie (ed.), 'A New York Diary of the Revolutionary War' in *New York Historical Society Quarterly* Vol. I. No 3 (July 1966)

M. Roberts, 'Great Britain and the Swedish Revolution 1772–3' in *Historical Journal*, Vol. VII No.1 (1964)

J. G. Rosengarten, 'A Defence of the Hessians' in *Pennsylvania Magazine of History and Biography* Vol. 23 No.2 (July 1899)

J. K. Rowland, 'General Thomas Gage, the Eighteenth Century Literature of Military Intelligence, and the Transition from Peace to Revolutionary War, 1774–1775' in *Historical Reflections* Vol. 32 No.3 Crossing the Border-Expanding the Enlightenment (Fall, 2006)

G. D. Scull (ed.), 'Journal of Captain John Montrésor, July 1 1777 to July 1 1778, Chief Engineer of the British Army' in *Pennsylvania Magazine of History and Biography* Vol. 6 No.1 (1882)

G. D. Scull (ed.), 'Journal of Captain John Montrésor, July 1 1777 to July 1 1778, Chief Engineer of the British Army' in *Pennsylvania Magazine of History and Biography* Vol. 6 No.2 (1882)

G. D. Scull (ed.), 'Journal of Captain John Montrésor, July 1 1777 to July 1 1778, Chief Engineer of the British Army' in *Pennsylvania Magazine of History and Biography* Vol. 6 No.3 (1882)

W. H. Siebert, 'The Loyalists of Pennsylvania' in *Ohio State University Bulletin* Vol. XXIV No.23 (Apr. 1920)

F. M. Smith, 'An Eighteenth-Century Gentleman, The Honourable Topham Beauclerk' in *The Sewanee Review* Vol. 34 No.2 (April, 1926)

F. Spencer, 'An Eighteenth-Century Account of German Emigration to the American Colonies' in *Journal of Modern History* Vol. 28 No.1 (March 1956)

J. D. Speidel, 'The Artistic Spy: A Note on the Talents of Major André' in *New York History* Vol. 68 No. 4 (Oct. 1987)

G. M. Stewart, 'British Students at the University of Göttingen in the Eighteenth Century' in *German Life and Letters* Vol. 33, No.1 (October 1979)

F. S. Vivian, 'John André as a Young Officer' in *Journal of the Society for Army Historical Research* Vol. XL, No.162 (June, 1962)

N. B. Wainwright and S. L. Fisher, '"A Diary of Trifling Occurrences" Philadelphia 1777–1778' in *Pennsylvania Magazine of History and Biography* Vol. 82 No.4 (Oct., 1958)

L. B. Walker, 'The Life of Margaret Shippen, Wife of Benedict Arnold' in *Pennsylvania Magazine of History and Biography* Vol. 24 No.4 (1900)

L. B. Walker, 'The Life of Margaret Shippen, Wife of Benedict Arnold' in *Pennsylvania Magazine of History and Biography* Vol. 25 No.1 (1901)

M. Woolff, 'Joseph Salvador 1716–1786' in *Transactions (Jewish Historical Society of England)* Vol. 21 (1962–1967)

B. Wriston, 'The Howard Van Doren Shaw Memorial Collection' in *Art Institute of Chicago Museum Studies* Vol. IV, 1969.

Online Resources

Adams Family Papers, an electronic archive provided by Massachusetts Historical Society.

Ancestry.com:

Will Registers, England and Wales: Prerogative Court of Canterbury Wills, 1384–1858

'Church of England Baptisms, Marriages, Burials, 1538–1812, Hackney, St. John at Hackney' Register of Baptisms

Register of Births

British History Online ('BHO')

'Lichfield from the Reformation to c.1800' in M. W. Greenslade (ed.), *A History of the County of Stafford Vol.14. Lichfield* (London, 1990)

George III, January 1773 in R. A. Roberts (ed.), *Calendar of Home Office Papers (George III) 1773–5* (London, 1899)

R. Thorne (ed.), *The History of Parliament. The House of Commons 1790–1820* (1986) available from Boydell and Brewer

Electronic Enlightenment

Jefferson Papers, *Founders Online* National Archives (last modified 29 June 2017)

Oxford Dictionary of National Biography ('ODNB')

S. L. Barczewski, 'Yorke, Philip, second Earl of Hardwicke'

S. Conway, 'Percy, Hugh, Second Duke of Northumberland'

T. Cooper, rev. P. Bancroft, 'Seward, Thomas'

W. P. Courtney (rev. S. J. Skedd) 'Chamier, Anthony'

M. Durban, 'Cavendish, William, fifth duke of Devonshire'

P. Durrant, 'FitzRoy, Augustus Henry, third duke of Grafton'

S. M. Farrell, 'Stanhope, Charles'

K. W. Schweizer, 'Cavendish, William, fourth duke of Devonshire'

Sundry online resources

'Public Notary and Land Records' at sos.ri.gov. online archive re: Protested bill of exchange De Monchy on Bosanquet & Fatio for John and Henry Peschier, 3 endorsements, Grenada, 27 February 1770

Washington Papers, *Founders Online*, National Archives. Original source: *The Diaries of George Washington, 1 January 1771–75*, Vol. 3 (November 1781, ed. Donald Jackson, Charlottesville, University Press of Virginia, 1978)

Washington Papers, *Founders Online*, National Archives. Original source: *The Papers of George Washington, Revolutionary War Series* Vol. 20 8 April–31 May 1779 (ed. Edward G. Lengel, Charlottesville, University Press of Virginia, 2010),

Unpublished Dissertations and Reports

A. Burke, 'The English Merchants in Canada 1759–1766' (Montreal, Canada: University of Ottawa MA thesis, 1968)

T. Davies, 'New Perspectives on European Private Trade in the Eighteenth Century. British Merchant Networks and the Western Indian Ocean' (University of Warwick)

D. E. Parker, 'The Little War Meets British Military Discipline in America 1755–1781' (University of New Hampshire Master of Arts Dissertation, 1988)

J. G. Parker, 'The Directors of the East India Company 1754–1790' (Edinburgh: PhD thesis, University of Edinburgh, 1977)

S. Seymour and S. Haggerty, 'Slavery Connections of Brodsworth Hall 1600–c1830' (Final Report for English Heritage, 2010)

R. Sier, 'A Study of Water Powered Industries in Essex' (Certificate in Local History, University of Essex, 2015)

A. Singh, 'Fort Cochin in Kerala (1750–1830). The Social Condition of a Dutch Community in an Indian milieu' (University of Leyden, 2007 dissertation).

F. S. Vivian, 'Nine Chapters from an unpublished biography of Major John André' in National Army Museum Archives ref. 2004-09-199.

Index

New Broad Street, 6, 9
port, xx, 100
Spitalfield, 103, 50, 65–6
Warnford Court, Throgmorton Street, 18, 21–2, 27, 33, 44, 49–50, 66, 77, 86
London Assurance, 8–9
Long Island, New York, 182, 247
Louise Dorothea, Duchess, 93
loyalists, *see* identity

Mabie's Tavern, 243
macaroni, (aka macharoni), *see* identity
Mackenzie, Lieut. Frederick, 64, 72, 91, 108
Macleane, Lauchlin, 30, 32–3
Manchester, England, 63, 65–6
manliness, *see* identity
Mante, Thomas, 93
maps, *see* secret war
Marshall, Christopher, 103–4, 165–6, 168, 187
Mathias, Emanuel, 93
Mendes da Costa family, 31
mercenaries, *see* Hessians
Meschianza, 166–172, 174, 184–6, 189, 192, 194, 196, 215, 217, 242, 249
  Knights of the Blended Rose, 168–9
  Knights of the Burning Mountain, 168, 171
  Ladies, 168–170, 172, 184
Michael, Eberhart, 134, 137, 146
Michaelis, Professor, *see* Göttingen University
Middleton, Arthur, *see* Dr Newcome's School
military manuals, *see* literature
military reviews, *see* Army
militia, 116, 138, 163, 181, 232, 245
Molineux, Crisp, MP, 14–15
"Monk", *see* secret war
Monmouth Court house, Battle of, *see* battles
Monody on Major André, *see* literature
Montgomery, Gen. Richard, 111, 115, 122–4, 129
Montreal, *see* Canada
Montrésor, Capt. John, 150–2, 154, 156, 161, 164–7, 174, 192
Moore, John, 95
'Moore, Mr J.', *see* secret war
'Mrs Moore', *see* secret war
Morris, Robert, xviii, 104
Mott, Capt. Edward, 122–4, 127, 129, 134
Motteux, John, 31

Mourgue family, 38, 48
Mud Island, Pennsylvania, 162
Muenchhausen, Capt. Friedrich von, 148
Munchhausen, George de, *see* Göttingen University
Mundy, Francis, 42
Murray, Lieut. Sir James, 78–9, 151, 154–6, 160–2, 168
Musenalmanach, *see* literature

Nancy and Molly, *see* ships
Nancy, *see* Tea-ships
'National Character', *see* identity
Nazareth, New Jersey, 123
Necker, Louis, 24
Nelson, Thomas (jun), *see* Dr Newcome's School
Newark, England, 66
Newburgh, Scotland, 90
New Bedford, 173–4, 181
New Jersey, 14, 102, 112, 117, 122, 127, 131–2, 139, 141, 144, 146, 179, 182, 191, 203, 207
New London, 181, 248
New Windsor, 123, 194
newspapers, *see* 'Public Prints'
Nimes, 3
non-importation, 47, 101
North Castle, New York, 211, 235–6
novels, *see* literature

Odell, Rev. Jonathan, 191–5, 209–210, 212
Offenbach, Germany, 95–6
O'Hara, Col., 167, 177
Orme, Robert, 30
'Osborn, James', *see* secret war
Oudermeulen, Cornelis van der, 82
Oyster Bay, New York, 182, 196

Paine, Robert, xix
Palatines, *see* emigrants
pamphlets, *see* literature
Panchaud, Isaac, 30, 34–5
Paoli, Battle of, *see* battles
Parsons, Gen., 210–211, 217
partizan, (aka partisan), *see* secret war
'Patriots', *see* identity
patronage, 2, 5, 8–9, 23, 32, 62, 72, 81, 147, 179, 202